MW00768516

The Cognitive Neuroscience of Development

The Cognitive Neuroscience of Development

Michelle de Haan
Developmental Cognitive Neuroscience Unit,
University College London

Mark H. Johnson
Centre for Birkbeck and Cognitive Development,
Birkbeck College, University of London

HOVE AND NEW YORK

First published 2003 by Psychology Press
27 Church Road, Hove, East Sussex, BN3 2FA

Simultaneously published in the USA and Canada
by Psychology Press
29 West 35th Street, New York, NY 10001

Psychology Press is part of the Taylor & Francis Group

British Library Cataloguing in Publication Data
A catalogue record for this book is available from the British Library

Library of Congress Cataloging in Publication Data

De Haan, Michelle, 1969–
The cognitive neurosciece of development / Michelle de Haan & Mark H. Johnson.
p. cm. – (Studies in developmental psychology)
Includes bibliographical references and index.
ISBN 1–84169–214–X
1. Cognitive neuroscience. 2. Developmental psychology. I. Johnson, Mark H. (Mark Henry), 1960– II. Title. III. Series.

QP360.5 .D423 2002
153–dc21 2002073939

ISBN 1-84169-214-X

Cover design by Code 5 Design Associates Limited
Typeset in Times by Newgen Imaging Systems (P) Ltd, Chennai, India.
Printed and bound in Great Britain by TJ International Ltd, Padstow, Cornwall

Contents

List of Contributors

Janette Atkinson, Visual Development Unit, Psychology Department, University College London, Gower Street, London WC1E 6BT, UK
E-mail: j.atkinson@ucl.ac.uk

Sheri A. Berenbaum, Department of Psychology, Penn State University, 519 Moore Building, University Park, PA 16802, USA
E-mail: sab31@psu.edu

Oliver Braddick, Visual Development Unit, Psychology Department, University College London, Gower Street, London WC1E 6BT, UK
E-mail: o.braddick@ucl.ac.uk

B.J. Casey, Sackler Institute for Developmental Psychobiology, Weill Medical College of Cornell University, 1300 York Avenue, Box 140, New York, NY 10021, USA
E-mail: bjc2002@med.cornell.edu

Elysia P. Davis, Institute of Child Development, University of Minnesota, 51 East River Road, Minneapolis, Minnesota 55455, USA
E-mail: davi0500@tc.umn.edu

Michelle de Haan, Developmental Cognitive Neuroscience Unit, Institute of Child Health, University College London, The Wolfson Centre, Mecklenburgh Square, London WC1N 2AP, UK
E-mail: m.de-haan@ich.ucl.ac.uk

Megan R. Gunnar, Institute of Child Development, University of Minnesota, 51 East River Road, Minneapolis, Minnesota 55455, USA
E-mail: gunnar@umn.edu

Mark H. Johnson, Centre for Brain & Cognitive Development, School of Psychology, Birkbeck College, 32 Torrington Square, London WC1E 7JL, UK
E-mail: mark.johnson@psychology.bbk.ac.uk

Christiana M. Leonard, PO Box 100244, Department of Neuroscience, McKnight Brain Institute, 100 Newell Drive, University of Florida, Gainesville, Florida 32611, USA
E-mail: leonard@mbi.ufl.edu

Monica Luciana, Department of Psychology, 75 East River Road, University of Minnesota, Minneapolis, Minnesota 55455, USA
E-mail: lucia003@tc.umn.edu

Scott Moffat, National Institute on Aging, 5600 Nathan Shock Dr, Baltimore, MD 21224, USA
E-mail: moffat@mvx.grc.nia.nih.gov

Charles A. Nelson, Institute of Child Development, University of Minnesota, 51 East River Road, Minneapolis, Minnesota 55455, USA
E-mail: canelson@tc.umn.edu

Susan W. Parker, Institute of Child Development, University of Minnesota, 51 East River Road, Minneapolis, Minnesota 55455, USA
E-mail: park0351@tc.umn.edu

John Richards, Department of Psychology, University of South Carolina, Columbia, SC 29208, USA
E-mail: richards-john@sc.edu

Susan Resnick, Laboratory of Personality and Cognition/Box 03, National Institute on Aging, 5600 Nathan Shock Drive, Baltimore, MD 21224-6825, USA
E-mail: susan.resnick@nih.gov

Helen Tager-Flusberg, Lab of Developmental Cognitive Neuroscience, Department of Anatomy & Neurobiology, Boston University School of Medicine, 715 Albany Street, L-814, Boston, MA 02118-2526, USA
E-mail: htagerf@bu.edu

Kathleen M. Thomas, Institute of Child Development, University of Minnesota, 51 East River Road, Minneapolis, MN 55455-0345, USA
E-mail: thoma114@umn.edu

Nim Tottenham, Sackler Institute for Developmental Psychobiology, Weill Medical College of Cornell University, 1300 York Avenue, Box 140, New York, NY 10021, USA
E-mail: tott0006@tc.umn.edu

Sara J. Webb, Institute of Child Development, University of Minnesota, 51 East River Road, Minneapolis, Minnesota 55455, USA
E-mail: sjwebb@u.washington.edu

Amy Wisniewski, Department of Pediatrics, Division of Pediatric Endocrinology, Johns Hopkins School of Medicine, 600 N. Wolfe Street/Park 211, Baltimore, MD 21287, USA
E-mail: amy@ionesco.psy.jhu.edu

Acknowledgements

The past years have seen rapid growth of the exciting new field of developmental cognitive neuroscience, and a growing collection of textbooks, readers, and handbooks on the topic. We believe this book makes a unique contribution to this literature through its coverage of a wide range of topics in a manner that is both accessible to those new to the field but that also provides enough detail to appeal to those with more knowledge in the area. The chapters are written by top international experts and provide an up-to-date review of each topic as well as presenting new theories and directions for the future. A special feature of the book, which we hope will make it useful for newcomers to the field and to instructors, is a glossary of vocabulary that is frequently used in the field but that might not be familiar to all readers.

This book was dependent upon the work of many people. Anne-Marie Fish was very helpful in co-ordinating and organising the volume. Many people at Psychology Press, including Caroline Osborne, Lucy Farr and Imogen Burch, have helped from conception to production. Sincere thanks are also due to the authors who made such excellent contributions.

Finally, we wish to thank our partners Haralambos Hatzakis and Annette Karmiloff-Smith, and our friends and families for their patience during the preparation of the book. Without their support it would simply not have been possible.

Studies in Developmental Psychology Published Titles

Series Editor
Charles Hulme, University of York, UK

The Development of Intelligence
Mike Anderson (Ed.)
The Development of Language
Martyn Barrett (Ed.)
The Social Child
Anne Campbell & Steven Muncer (Eds)
The Development of Memory in Childhood
Nelson Cowan (Ed.)
The Development of Mathematical Skills
Chris Donland (Ed.)
The Development of Social Cognition
Suzanne Hala (Ed.)
Perceptual Development: Visual, Auditory, and Speech Perception in Infancy
Alan Slater (Ed.)

Introduction

Michelle de Haan and Mark H. Johnson

As distinct from most other areas of psychology, a complete account of developmental change requires an interdisciplinary approach. It is thus surprising that over the past few decades the study of cognitive and behavioural development has often been conducted separately from the study of the brain. The aim of this book is to provide an overview of recent research that applies an integration of neurobiological and psychological perspectives to the study of typical and atypical cognitive development.

HISTORICAL PERSPECTIVE

The origins of developmental psychology can be traced to biologists such as Charles Darwin (1872/1965), who was one of the first to take a scientific approach to human behavioural development; and to Jean Piaget, who was originally trained as a biologist and imported theories of embryological development into his accounts of human cognitive development. Early developmental psychologists in America, such as McGraw and Gesell, tried to integrate brain development with what was known of behavioural development, focusing on motor development but also extending their conclusions to mental and social development (e.g. Gesell, 1929; McGraw, 1943). Although both McGraw and Gesell developed sophisticated informal theories about the non-linear and dynamic nature of development, their efforts to relate brain development to behavioural change remained largely speculative. At around the same time, in Europe, Lorenz and Tinbergen originated the field of ethology, and were particularly concerned with causal factors in the development of the natural behaviour of animals. Because of the more direct manipulations possible with animals, they addressed issues about the relative contribution of "innate" as opposed to "experiential" contributions to behaviour. The results of early experiments in which environmental conditions were manipulated during development led to the realization that the dissociation of behaviour into innate and acquired components was inadequate to account for some of the complexities of behavioural development. The notion that theories of behavioural development should take into account both the whole organism and the natural environment (social and physical) within which it develops, is currently regaining popularity (Gottlieb, 1992; Hinde, 1974; Johnson & Morton, 1991; Thelen & Smith, 1994).

From the mid-1960s up to the 1990s, biological approaches to human behavioural development fell out of favour for a variety of reasons, including the widely held belief among cognitive psychologists in the 1970s and 1980s that the "software" of the mind is best studied without reference to the "hardware" of the brain.

RENEWED INTEREST IN BRAIN DEVELOPMENT

The recent explosion of knowledge on brain development makes the task of relating it to behavioural changes considerably more viable than previously. In parallel, new molecular and cellular methods, along with theories of self-organizing dynamic networks, have led to great advances in our understanding of how vertebrate brains are constructed during ontogeny. These advances, along with those in functional neuroimaging (see Chapter 2), have led to the recent emergence of the interdisciplinary science of developmental cognitive neuroscience (see Johnson, 1997).

One reason for the lack of interest in the neural basis of cognitive development is that, until recently, many psychologists assumed that brain development, including postnatal development, involved only the unfolding of a genetic plan. Thus, brain development was viewed as a genetic- and molecular-level process, best left to neuroscientists to unravel. However, during the 1990s, developmental neuroscience studies have revealed that brain development is not merely the unfolding of a genetic "map" of brain structure. From very early in life, the activity of brain circuits plays an important part in subsequent development. For example, even during prenatal development spontaneous firing of cells within the retina shapes development of certain structures in the visual cortex (Shatz, 1992). Thus, some parts of the brain and nervous system appear to generate an internal "virtual environment" to aid the specialization of other regions. Postnatally, the relatively protracted period of postnatal development also provides the opportunity for inputs from the external environment to shape brain development (see Chapters 1 and 7).

Another reason for the recently renewed interest in relating brain development to cognitive change comes from advances in methodology that allow measurement of "functional" maps of brain activity based on either changes in cerebral metabolism, blood flow, or electrical activity (see Chapter 2). These methods allow hypotheses about the relations between cognitive and brain development to be generated and tested more readily than previously (see also Nelson & Bloom, 1997). Although there are special challenges involved in applying these methods to developing populations (see Chapter 2), event-related potential (ERP; see Chapters 3, 4, and 5), and magnetic resonance imaging (MRI; see Chapters 5, 9, and 10), have been applied to questions of typical and atypical development.

Advances in techniques in behavioural and molecular genetics have also opened up new possibilities. For example, it is now possible to "knock out" specific genes from the genome of an animal, and study effects on subsequent development. An example of this approach is the creation of a mouse model of Fragile X syndrome by disruption of the FMR1 gene that encodes fragile X mental retardation protein (Dutch–Belgian Fragile X Consortium, 1994). These mice show physical and behavioural characteristics similar to humans with Fragile X syndrome (Chapter 10) and have provided an important model for studying the physiological function of the fragile X gene and investigating the hypothesis that it plays a role in synaptic development (Irwin, Galvez, & Greenough, 2000). This method could open new vistas in the analysis of genetic contributions to cognitive and perceptual change in animals. For example, this approach might assist in understanding the role of the recently identified FOXP2 gene in development of speech and language (Lai et al., 2001). However, at present such studies tend to be restricted to a few strains of mice because of the availability of mouse embryonic stem cells. It should be noted that lesion of a single gene during development is likely to have a cascade of effects caused by the abnormal, or absent, interactions with other genes, and thus might be more complex to interpret than it initially appears.

Another useful approach for linking brain development to behaviour is the "marker task". This method involves the use of specific behavioural tasks that have been linked to a brain region or pathway in adult primates and humans by neurophysioloical, neuropsychological, or brain imaging studies. By testing infants or children with versions of such a task at different ages, the researcher can use the success or otherwise of individuals as indicating the functional development of the relevant regions of the brain. Examples include the use of the visual paired comparison test of visual recognition as a marker of hippocampal development (Chapter 6), the use of Piaget's A-not-B task as a marker of dorsolateral prefrontal cortex development (Chapter 7), and the use of the spatial cueing procedure as a marker of development of the posterior cortical attention network (Chapter 4). There are some caveats to the use of behavioural marker tasks—for example, that there might be developmental changes in the neural structures that underlie the same observable behaviour (see Chapter 4). The combined use of such tasks with direct measures of brain activity might provide an even more powerful approach.

Finally, the recent emergence of connectionist neural network models offers the possibility of assessing the information-processing consequences of developmental changes in the neuroanatomy and neurochemistry of the brain (see Chapter 6). For example, O'Reilly and Johnson (1994) demonstrated how the microcircuitry of a region of vertebrate forebrain could lead to certain self-terminating sensitive period effects. Such models promise to provide a bridge between our observations of development at the neural level and behavioural change in childhood.

ORGANIZATION OF THE BOOK

The opening two chapters of this book provide basic background on theories and methods for studying brain development that are discussed in more detail in later chapters. In Chapter 1 we outline the basic processes involved in prenatal and postnatal human brain development and how they relate to psychological development. A striking characteristic of the development of the human brain is that it continues for a long period after birth, thereby providing the opportunity for the external environment and the child's interactions in it to influence later phases of brain development. Several theories regarding the physiological basis of this developmental plasticity and their implication for understanding the effects of early brain injury are discussed. In Chapter 2, Thomas and Casey describe the basic principles, strengths, and weaknesses of three techniques used to study functional brain development in children: electrophysiology, structural magnetic resonance imaging, and functional magnetic resonance imaging. They emphasize that optimal use of these methods involves: (1) using them in combination to obtain strong temporal and spatial measures of brain activation; and (2) using high-quality behavioural paradigms that allow clear interpretations of the accompanying neuroimaging data.

Chapters 3 to 7 each focus on particular domains of cognitive development. In Chapter 3, Atkinson and Braddick outline the neural basis of visual and visuomotor development. In their model, subcortical processes initially dominate the young infant's processing, but these are increasingly controlled by developing cortical systems. Electrophysiolgoical measures and study of atypical populations are two important methods for providing evidence for this view. The importance of an integrated approach, incorporating visual, cognitive and motor abilities for full understanding of visual development is emphasized. In Chapter 4, Richards focuses in more detail on the development of visual attention, including sustained attention and orienting. He describes neurodevelopment models that relate changes in the brain areas involved in vision to developmental changes in these abilities and shows how research using psychophysiological measures provides important tests of these models. In Chapter 5, Nelson and Webb outline development of the neural substrates of memory. They argue that the multiple memory systems observed in the adult have their precursors in the infancy period. They also argue that "pre-explicit" and implicit forms of memory are present in early infancy, and that both forms of memory undergo developmental change due to cortical development. The explicit and implicit systems might differ, however, in that the former shows more plasticity than the latter following early damage.

In Chapter 6, Leonard outlines the neural substrates of speech and language development. Like Atkinson and Braddick, Leonard argues that a full understanding of development involves an integration of the traditionally distinct domains of perception, cognition and action. She reviews evidence from developmental psychology and neuroscience in support of her conclusion that perceptual and motor skills play a critical role in language development. In Chapter 7, Luciana gives an overview of neural and functional development of the frontal lobes. Whereas behavioural signs of prefrontal function are observable from the first years of life, she describes how both the physiological and functional development of prefrontal areas continues well into adolescence.

Chapters 8 and 9 focus on the interface of social development with brain and cognitive development. In Chapter 8, Davis, Parker, Tottenham, and Gunnar describe the bidirectional influence of stress-sensitive hormonal systems and cognitive systems. Stress hormones can act directly on the neural substrates of attention and memory but can also have more subtle influences in children's cognitive development—for example by affecting the child's tendency to engage in the social environment. In Chapter 9, Berenbaum, Moffat, Wisniewski, and Resnick describe the organizational and activational influences of sex hormones on social and cognitive development. Their discussion emphasizes the importance of using sensitive measures of sex differences and on the use of multiple models (natural variations in hormones, genetic disorders, etc.) to fully understand the role of these hormones in normal cognitive development.

In Chapter 10, Tager-Flusberg summarizes the genetic and neural bases of developmental disorders. Even single-gene disorders can lead to widespread effects on cognition, effects that themselves can change with development. Indeed, the goal of providing a complete description and understanding of polygenic disorders such as dyslexia necessitates an interdisciplinary approach because of the multiple levels of analysis involved. Tager-Flusberg emphasizes how the study of developmental disorders of genetic origin provides a perspective distinct from that given by the study of disorders acquired through brain injury.

At the end of the book, we have also provided a glossary of the more technical terms used throughout the book. We hope this will be useful in making the chapters more accessible to those who are not specialists in the area.

UNDERSTANDING BRAIN AND BEHAVIOUR

We hope that the information provided in this book will inspire those interested in developmental psychology to further their understanding of the interface between brain and behaviour in the developing child. One main emphasis throughout the book is on integration, both with respect to integration of multiple methods and integration of domains of research that in the past have been studied in a more fragmentary way. The knowledge gained by pursuing this approach will allow for a more comprehensive understanding of the complex process of human development.

REFERENCES

Darwin, C.R. (1965). *The expression of emotions in man and animals*. Chicago: University of Chicago Press [original work published 1872].

Dutch–Belgian Fragile X Consortium (1994). Fmr1 knockout mice: A model to study fragile X mental retardation. The Dutch–Belgian Fragile X Consortium. *Cell, 78*, 23–33.

Gesell, A. (1929). *Infancy and human growth*. New York: Macmillan.

Gottlieb, G. (1992). *Individual development and evolution*. New York: Oxford University Press.

Hinde, R.A. (1974). *Biological bases of human social behaviour*. New York: McGraw-Hill.

Irwin, S.A., Galvez, R., & Greenough, W.T. (2000). Dendritic spine structural abnormalities in fragile-X mental retardation syndrome. *Cerebral Cortex, 10*, 1038–1044.

Johnson, M.H. (1997). *Developmental cognitive neuroscience: An introduction*. Oxford: Blackwell.

Johnson, M.H., & Morton, J. (1991). *Biology and cognitive development: The case of face recognition*. Oxford: Blackwell.

Lai, C.S., Fisher, S.E., Hurst, J.A., Vargha-Khadem, F., & Monaco, A.P. (2001). A forkhead-domain gene is mutated in a severe speech and language disorder. *Nature, 413*, 519–523.

McGraw, M.B. (1943). *The neuromuscular maturation of the human infant*. New York: Columbia University Press.

Nelson, C.A., & Bloom, F.G. (1997). Child development and neuroscience. *Child Development, 68*, 970–987.

O'Reilly, R., & Johnson, M.H. (1994). Object recognition and sensitive periods: A computational analysis of visual imprinting. *Neural Computation, 6*, 357–390.

Shatz, K. (1992). Dividing up the neocortex. *Science, 258*, 237–238.

Thelen, E., & Smith, L.B. (1994). *A dynamic systems approach to the development of cognition and action*. Cambridge, MA: MIT Press.

CHAPTER ONE

Mechanisms and theories of brain development

Michelle de Haan
Institute of Child Health, University College London, London, UK

Mark H. Johnson
Centre for Brain & Cognitive Development, Birkbeck College, London, UK

INTRODUCTION

Understanding the development of the cerebral cortex is central to our understanding of psychological development, as immaturity of this structure is a major limiting factor of cognitive functioning in infants and children. Genetic factors inherent to the developing cells themselves, and interactions with external factors—at the molecular, cellular, and behavioural levels—contribute to the developmental process. Even when the baby is still in the protective environment of the womb, development does not consist simply of the unfolding of a rigid "genetic plan". For example, the detailed folding patterns of the cerebral cortex present at birth can vary considerably, even between identical twins (Bartley et al., 1997). The comparatively long phase of postnatal brain development in humans compared with other primates or mammals provides an extended opportunity for later stages of brain development to be influenced by the external environment. The aim of this chapter is to outline the major events of prenatal and postnatal brain development, review current theories of how the cerebral cortex develops into its adult organization and function, and discuss how cortical injury affects development.

BASICS OF BRAIN DEVELOPMENT

The fundamental processes of brain development involve: (1) neural induction; (2) proliferation of neurons and glia; (3) cell migration; (4) cell death; (5) cell differentiation; (6) formation of synapses; and (7) pruning of synapses. For a more detailed discussion of how these processes unfold in the frontal cortex see Chapter 7.

Neural induction. Shortly after conception, a fertilized cell undergoes a rapid process of cell division that results in a cluster of proliferating cells called the blastocyst. Within a few days, the blastocyst differentiates into a three-layered structure. Development of the nervous system begins from just a few cells in the outermost layer of the blastocyst called the neural plate. By the third or fourth week of development, the edges of neural plate begin to fold in to form a hollow structure called the neural tube. The ventricles of the brain and the spinal canal develop from the hollow area inside the tube, and the cells that make up the brain develop from the layer of cells that line the tube. First the anterior, and then the posterior end of the tube closes, after which cerebrospinal fluid fills the tube and cells begin to divide quickly to form several layers.

Neural proliferation. Neurons begin to divide rapidly, or to proliferate, at approximately the sixth foetal week, and they continue to divide until approximately the 18th week. Division of cells in the neural tube produces clones, or groups of cells that result from division of a single precursor cell. Each of the neural precursor cells, or neuroblasts, gives rise to a definite and limited number of neurons. In some cases particular neuroblasts also give rise to particular types of neuron, whereas in other cases the distinctive morphology of the type of neuron arises as a product of its developmental interactions (Marin-Padilla, 1990). As the cells divide and their numbers increase, divisions of the brain become observable in the anterior part of the neural tube.

Cell migration. Neurons are not born in the exact position they will occupy in the adult brain. Instead, they must travel or migrate from the proliferative zone where they are formed to the position they will occupy in the mature brain. The most common form of migration outside the cerebral cortex is passive cell displacement. This occurs primarily in non-layered neural structures when new cells are slowly pushed further and further away from the proliferative zone by more recently born cells. This form of migration gives rise to an "outside-to-inside" spatiotemporal gradient, with the oldest cells pushed toward the surface of the brain and the most recently produced cells remaining on the inside.

The second form of migration is called active cell migration. This occurs when young cells actively travel past previously generated cells, thereby creating an "inside-to-outside" spatiotemporal gradient. Active migration occurs both in the cerebral cortex and in some subcortical areas that have a laminar structure. In active cell migration, neurons find their way to the correct position by clinging to the long fibres of "radial glia" that radiate from the inner to the outer surface of the brain. Special adhesion molecules on the surface of the migrating cell bind to similar molecules on the glial cell or nearby axons that act as chemical cues guiding the cells along the proper pathway.

One of the most striking features of the cerebral cortex is its three-dimensional organization of layers and columns of functionally similar neurons. According to the radial unit hypothesis (Rakic, 1988), this organization is determined by a combination of the timing and location of the birth of neurons. In this view, the layered structure of the cortex is determined by the timing of the birth of cells through the process of active cell migration. The radial structure of the cortex occurs because neurons from a given clone all climb up the same radial glial fibre. In this way all of the cells produced by a single neuroblast contribute to the same radial column of neurons within the cortex. This is how the two-dimensional positional information of the proliferative cells in the ventricular zone is transformed into a three-dimensional cortical structure.

Programmed cell death. At the same time that cells are proliferating and migrating, some are also dying. Programmed cell death of both neural and glial cells is part of normal development of the nervous system (Barres et al., 1992; Cowan, Fawcett, O'Leary, & Stanfield, 1984; Oppenheim, 1991). In programmed cell death, cells die as part of a gene expression-related programme of cell differentiation. Programmed cell death is characterized by cell shrinkage, rather than by the cell swelling that occurs in necrotic cell death following brain injury. Mutation of the genes involved in programmed cell death might be one mechanism responsible for the expansion of the surface area of the cerebral cortex during evolution (Rakic, 2000).

In the human telencephalon, two distinct types of programmed cell death are observable (Rakic & Zecevic, 2000). Embryonic programmed cell death occurs during proliferation and migration of neurons and is probably not related to the establishment of neuronal circuitry. Rather, it might reflect death due to errors in cell division and could play a role in elimination of transitory areas. Foetal programmed cell death occurs during neuron differentiation and synaptogenesis and might be related to the development of connections between axons and their targets. It might be one mechanism that allows the number of neurons innervating a target to match the size of the target. A small target will produce a smaller amount of chemicals to promote the survival of neurons and thus will support relatively few neurons; conversely, a larger target will produce more and thus support more neurons. In this way, the number of neurons innervating a target can be matched precisely to the size of the cell, even if this information is not pre-programmed explicitly.

Cell differentiation. Once neurons have migrated to their final positions, they further differentiate to take on their mature characteristics. One aspect of cell differentiation is dendritic arborization. The dendrites of a neuron are like antennae, picking up signals from many neurons and, if the conditions are right, passing the signal down the axon and on to other neurons. The pattern of branching of dendrites is important because it will affect the quantity and quality of signals the neuron receives. During cortical development there is an increase in size and complexity of neurons' dendritic trees. For example, by adulthood the length of the dendrites of neurons in the frontal cortex can increase over 30 times their length at birth. Dendritic branching occurs at different times in different areas and layers of the cortex. For example, dendritic trees of cells in layer 5 of the primary visual cortex are already at about 60 per cent of their maximum extent at birth. By contrast, the mean total length for dendrites in layer 3 is only about 30 per cent of maximum at birth. Dendrite branching is one of the properties of neurons that can be influenced by the environment during development. For example, laboratory animals that receive environmental stimulation show more dendritic branching than those that do not (Wallace, Kilman, Withers, & Greenough, 1992).

A second aspect of differentiation is axon guidance and target selection. The cerebral cortex consists of a large population of excitatory glutaminergic neurons that transmit their signals using the excitatory amino acid glutamate. These neurons are reciprocally connected with the thalamus, to each other, and to a smaller population of inhibitory GABAergic neurons that, in the main, provide local circuitry (Somogyi, Tamas, Lujan, & Buhl, 1998). To find their proper connections in the brain, axons often have to stretch long distances (sometimes over a metre) to reach their target. This process depends on the ability of receptors on the growth cones of axons to recognize cues in their environment, such as molecules on the membranes of neighbouring neurons or glia, and respond with appropriate directional movement. Once in position, axons form a synapse where signals can be communicated with the dendrites of the target cell. Cadherins, a family of calcium-dependent adherent proteins, might play an important role in this process in two ways (reviewed in Ranscht, 2000): (1) by controlling synapse positioning by guiding axons to target positions that express the same type of cadherin (Inoue & Sanes, 1997); and (2) by controlling the functions of the established synapses by modulating synaptic adhesion and stability (Fields & Itoh, 1996; Tanaka et al., 2000).

Synaptogenesis. Formation of synapses in humans begins in the early weeks of gestation, when synapses can be observed in the marginal zone (Zecevic, 1998). The density of synapses rapidly increases once the cortical plate is formed and, at least in layer l of the cortex, is occurring in synchrony in different parts of the cortex at 20 weeks gestation (Zecevic, 1998). Whereas in monkeys this synchrony in synaptogenesis across cortical areas continues postnatally (Rakic et al., 1986), in humans it is believed that the time of the peak of cortical synaptogenesis differs across cortical areas. For example, in parts of the human visual cortex, synaptic density reaches a peak of approximately 150 per cent of adult levels towards the end of the first year, whereas in the frontal cortex the peak synaptic density does not occur until approximately 24 months of age (Huttenlocher, 1979, 1990; Huttenlocher & Dabholkar, 1997; Huttenlocher & de Courten, 1987; Huttenlocher, de Courten, Garey, & Van der Loos, 1982).

Elimination of synapses. Elimination, or pruning, of synapses also occurs in normal development. For example, in the primary visual cortex the mean density of synapses per neuron peaks at a level higher than adult levels, and then starts to decrease at the end of the first year of life (Huttenlocher, 1990). In humans, most cortical regions and pathways appear to undergo this "rise and fall" in synaptic density, with the density stabilizing to adult levels at different ages during later childhood. The functional role of this process will be discussed further below.

The postnatal rise and fall developmental sequence can also be seen in other measures of brain physiology and anatomy. For example, positron emission tomography (PET) measures of brain metabolism show that, although there is an adult-like distribution of resting brain activity within and across brain regions by the end of the first year, the overall level of glucose uptake reaches a peak during early childhood, which is much higher than that observed in adults (Chugani, Phelps, & Mazzidta, 1987). The rates return to adult levels after about 9 years of age for some cortical regions.

DIFFERENTIATION OF THE CEREBRAL CORTEX

The majority of normal adults tend to have similar functions within approximately the same regions of cortex. How does this happen? We cannot necessarily infer from this consistency that this pattern of differentiation is intrinsically prespecified ("prewired"), because most humans share very similar pre- and postnatal environments. The protocortex and protomap hyptheses are the two main explanations of how the cerebral cortex comes to be subdivided into specialised functional areas.

Protocortex hypothesis

In this view, cortical neurons are initially equipotential and areal differences are induced by outside influences such as sensory inputs from the thalamus. One type of experiment that can test this view is to rewire thalamic inputs so that they project to different regions of the cortex than usual. If thalamic inputs determine cortical divisions, then the affected cortex should take in the characteristics associated with the new, rather than the normally intended, inputs. Results from several studies support this prediction. For example, following such rewiring, auditory cortex can take on visual representations (Sur, Garraghty, & Roe, 1988; Sur, Pallas, & Roe, 1990). A second type of experiment that tests the protocortex hypothesis is transplantation of embryonic cortex to a new location. If the hypothesis is true, then the transplanted cortex should develop characteristics consistent with its new location rather than its original one. Results of several experiments support this prediction. For example, if late embryonic visual cortex is transplanted to neonatal somatosensory cortex, this "visual" cortex will develop the functional characteristics of cells in the somatosensory cortex (O'Leary & Stanfield, 1989; Schlagger & O'Leary, 1991).

Despite the impressive results of rewiring and transplantation experiments, there are indications that the embryonic cortex is not completely equipotential. First, although transplanted or rewired cortex might look very similar to the original tissue in terms of function and structure, it is rarely absolutely indistinguishable from the original. For example, in the rewired ferret cortex, when auditory cortex takes on visual function, the mapping of the azimuth (angle right or left) is at a higher resolution (more detailed) than the mapping of the elevation (angle up or down; Roe, Pallas, Hahm, & Sur, 1990). By contrast, in the normal ferret, cortex azimuth and elevation are mapped in equal detail. Second, the timing of the transplant is also important. Although the results of some transplantation studies suggested that even "late" transplants of cortical tissue could develop connections appropriate to their new locations (O'Leary & Stanfield, 1989), it was not known how many neurons actually exhibited this capacity. More recent quantitative studies have shown that the majority of neurons show a pattern of connections consistent with their site of origin rather than their new location (Garnier, Arnault, Letang, & Roger, 1996; Garnier, Arnault, & Roger, 1997). Thus, at least in some cases, postmitotic neurons retain the characteristics of their original location. Finally, it is important to note that most of the experimental neurobiological studies on cortical plasticity have been performed on rodents or cats, and not primates, and it is clear that there are species differences. For example, although in mice cortical progenitors can integrate elsewhere in the telencephalon following transplantation, in some other species, cortical progenitors appear to be restricted in their ability to do so (Frantz & McConnell, 1996). Despite these caveats, the rewiring and transplantation studies do demonstrate that it is possible for anatomical and functional changes in axonal inputs to the cortex to modify existing divisions in the cortex or to create new ones.

Protomap hypothesis

Unlike the protocortex hypothesis, which emphasizes the importance of extrinsic factors in cell differentiation, the protomap hypothesis emphasizes the importance of intrinsic factors. In this view, cells generated within the embryonic cortical cell wall already contain some intrinsic information about their prospective species-specific cortical organization (Rakic, 1988). The hypothesized protomap involves either prespecification of the proliferative zone or intrinsic molecular markers that guide the division of cortex into particular areas. For example, neurons in the embryonic cortical plate might set up a beginning map that preferentially attracts the appropriate afferents to the appropriate locations and has a capacity to respond to this input in a specific manner.

The main line of evidence in support of this view comes from descriptions of graded or restricted patterns of gene expression in embryonic cortex (see Rubenstein et al., 1999 for a review). For example, the homeobox gene Emx2 is expressed in the proliferative zone that gives rise to cortical neurons at very early stages and is thought to play an important role in the early formation of cortical regions prior to the arrival of thalamic inputs (Gulisano, Broccoli, Pardini, & Boncinelli, 1996; Yoshida et al., 1997). Emx2 "knock-out" mice show deficits in neuron migration

(Mallamaci et al., 2000a) and changes in molecular markers and area-specific connections (Bishop, Goudreau, & O'Leary, 2000). The fact that absence of Emx2 affects area-specific molecules, such as cadherin 6, that normally show area-specific expression before the arrival of thalamic inputs supports the view that Emx2 is involved in arealization that occurs independently of the thalamus (Mallamaci et al., 2000b).

Genetically modified mice have also been used to investigate the consequences of disrupting thalamic inputs to the developing cortex. For example, Gbx-2 mutant mice, whose thalamic differentiation is disrupted and who lack cortical innervation by thalamic neurons, show normal region-specific expressions of a variety of genes (Miyashita-Lin et al., 1999). One limitation with mutant mouse models is that the mutations can cause early death and thereby limit the possible time of study of the effects of the mutation on brain development.

In summary, both the protocortex and protomap hypotheses offer accounts of how the cortex divides into areas with specific inputs, outputs, and cellular architecture. The protocortex account emphasizes epigenetic (extrinsic) factors, whereas the protomap hypothesis emphasizes genetic (intrinsic) factors. Recent reviews of the debate between the protocortex and protomap hypotheses have suggested a middle-ground view in which gradients of gene expression across the developing cortex define large-scale regions (Kingsbury & Finlay, 2001; Pallas, 2001; Ragsdale & Grove, 2001). However, with a few exceptions, these large-scale regions tend not to map onto the detailed functional areas observed in the adult mammal. Multiple dimensions of cell structure relevant to stimulus processing might be laid out such that "regions" arise combinatorily as a result of particular sensory thalamic input overlaid on large scale gradients in patterns of neurotransmitter expression, axon extensions, and neuromodulator production. For example, a region might emerge that has high visual input, high gamma-amino butyric acid (GABA), high serotonin, and short-range connections. Such a region could initially be ill-defined and lack specialization, but will be better at performing some types of computation than neighbouring regions. Subparts of this region might become "recruited" for certain computational functions (Elman et al., 1996; Johnson, 2000; Karmiloff-Smith, 1998). This process could result in the cortical region fragmenting into a series of functionally distinct areas.

For example, the development of ocular dominance columns (eye-specific cortical columns in layer 4 of the cortex) has been a central model for how experience can drive the development of modular circuitry in the cortex. In the traditional account, thalamic inputs of the two eyes initially overlap extensively in the cortex. Activity driven by visual inputs during a critical period of development then helps to sort these axons into the adult pattern of eye-specific columns. However, recent evidence shows that ocular dominance columns are present much earlier than previously suspected (before the "critical period") and at this early stage are not affected by disruption of visual input (Crowley & Katz, 2000).

These results suggest that the changes that can occur later during the critical period reflect modifications of existing columns rather than the initial creation of these columns. Intrinsic factors might thus establish the columnar organization and subsequently, activity is needed for their maintenance and plasticity.

HOW CAN EXTRINSIC FACTORS INFLUENCE CORTICAL DEVELOPMENT?

There is no doubt that genetic factors determine aspects of brain organization. Yet, detailed differences in dendritic branching and synaptic contacts are unlikely to be completely prespecified. If the approximately 10^{11} neurons that make up the brain each have 10^3 connections, the approximately 10^5 genes that mammals have could not contain sufficient information to specify all of these connections and thus some information must be determined by extrinisic factors. A variety of different representations (implemented as detailed differences in dendritic branching and synaptic contacts) can be supported by any given region of cortex early in postnatal development and external factors play a role in shaping the pattern that ultimately develops. In this sense, plasticity can be viewed as a fundamental property of the developing cortex, rather than a specialized response to injury.

Specialization by selective synapse elimination

How can inputs to the cortex determine the pattern of neural architecture? One account of how genetic and environmental factors act together in cortical development emphasizes the role of synapse elimination. In this type of model, connections between classes of cells are specified genetically but are initially labile, in that they can either stabilize or regress (e.g. Changeux, 1985; Changeux, Courrege, & Danchin, 1973). Two factors that determine what occurs are the total activity of the postsynaptic cell (which, in turn, is dependent upon its input) and competition with other cells. Thus, there is first a constructive process that generates a range of possible options, and then a mechanism for selecting among these options. At the neural level, these two stages are implemented as an exuberance of connections specified within a particular genetic envelope, followed by the selection of particular synapses, or groups of synapses. Selection is a result of either patterns of spontaneous activity within neural circuitry, and/or a result of the information structure of sensory input. This is a mechanism that allows some aspects of experience to "fine-tune" brain anatomy through selective synaptic loss. The idea that increasing cognitive capacity in childhood is related to a loss rather than a gain of synapses is consistent with findings of functional magnetic resonance imaging studies showing that the magnitude of activity during attention and memory tasks in children is larger and more widespread than in adults (reviewed in Casey, Geidd, & Thomas, 2000). Whereas the timing and extent of loss of connections or neurons might be a product of the internal environment (possibly due to genetic modification of trophic factors), the specificity or particular pattern of that loss might be determined by sensory input (Johnson & Karmiloff-Smith, 1992). By this view, there can be an intrinsically determined termination of the phase of selective loss, whereas the pattern of loss within the "sensitive period" might be determined by experience-driven neural activity.

This type of "experience-expectant" plasticity could be a mechanism of learning that is qualitatively different from the type of learning that occurs throughout the life span (Greenough & Black, 1992). It could provide a mechanism whereby aspects of the environment that are common to all members of the species can shape the brain during particular periods of development. In this way, some aspects of development need not be genetically prespecified but can be determined by commonalities in the environment of different members of a species. In this process, the synapses that are retained are those that respond to aspects of the environment that are common to all members of a species. For example, if the visual cortex is deprived of the input of pattern light by a cataract, or clouding of the lens, connections in the visual cortex and visual function will not develop normally. This shows that the input of patterned light is necessary for normal structural and functional development of the visual cortex (Maurer, Lewis, Brent, & Levin, 1999).

We should not conclude from such research that the human newborn's brain is a blank slate that absorbs information passively from the environment. Rather, the young infant appears to select appropriate aspects of the environment relevant for the further development of the cortex. In some sense, then, the infant can be said to play an active role in its own subsequent brain development. For example, human newborns have a tendency to track, and orient towards, face-like patterns (Johnson, Dziurawiec, Ellis, & Morton, 1991). This primitive response does not appear to be controlled by the same neural substrates as are involved in face processing in adults, and might be largely under the control of subcortical structures in the brain. It has been suggested (Johnson & Morton, 1991) that this primitive preferential orienting response is sufficient to ensure that the newborn looks more at faces than at other kinds of objects during the first days or weeks of life. This greater exposure to faces would then ensure the specialization of still-developing cortical circuits (see de Haan, Humphreys, & Johnson, 2002, for further discussion). Human infants have several such primitive tendencies, such as attention to speech sounds and a preference to look towards stimuli that are slightly novel relative to their previous experience ("novelty preference").

Thus, aspects of brain organization can emerge commonly in most members of the species not because the organization is genetically encoded but because the brain is shaped by aspects of environment common to all species. This time of plasticity does not last indefinitely but follows a developmental timetable. If certain synaptic connections are not laid down early in life, they are less likely to become established later in life and, once the number of neurons stabilizes at the mature level, changes in function might also stabilize or "freeze" at a particular level.

Parcellation/modularity

Some aspects of human cognitive function appear to be "encapsulated" or modular. Encapsulation refers to the fact that only the output, and not internal workings, of these modules is open to interaction with other brain systems. Visual illusions are an example of encapsulation. For example, in the Muller–Lyer illusion, even though viewers have the conscious knowledge that the two lines are the same length, they cannot help but perceive them as being of different lengths. Thus, the processing within a module is not affected by information in other parts of the system, only its end product (the lines being of different length) is accessible. Although there is evidence that the adult mind contains such encapsulated modules, there is very little evidence that they are innate. Rather, encapsulation of particular aspects of information processing might be a consequence, rather than a generator, of postnatal development (see also Johnson, 2000; Karmiloff-Smith, 1992; Patterson et al., 1999).

According to one view (Ebbesson, 1984), the process of parcellation involves the selective loss of connections between groups of neurons in an initially relatively undifferentiated brain region, resulting in the isolation of particular circuits and neuronal groups from others. This form of selectionism makes the prediction that some neural circuits will become increasingly modular with development. Some of the consequences of neural parcellation can be: (1) less informational exchange between certain neurocognitive systems with development; (2) less interference between certain neurocognitive systems with increasing age/experience; and (3) increased specificity in sensory detection (Johnson & Karmiloff-Smith, 1992; Johnson & Vecera, 1996).

Individual-specific environmental inputs

Selectionist accounts attempt to explain how environmental inputs might influence the development of an adult-like pattern of cortical organization. In these views, the rise and fall of synapse density that occurs during restricted periods of infancy and childhood provides a physiological basis through which experience can influence brain development. However, individuals continue to learn throughout the lifetime, and thus some mechanism is also needed to store information that is unique to individuals. "Experience-dependent learning" refers to changes in brain that are specific to the individual and act to optimize adaptation to the particular characteristics of their environments (Greenough & Black, 1992). For example, rats show substantial changes in their brains if they are living in an "enriched" social and physical environment; such changes are not seen if they live in relative isolation. The changes include production of new synapses and increases in complexity of the dendritic branching. Thus, by contrast to the developmental process whereby experience influences cortical organization through a process of selective loss of synapses, learning also involves creation of new synapses or modification of existing synapses by strengthening or remodelling them. Recent work also suggests that new neurons might be produced in the adult primate hippocampus and cortex (Gould, Reeves, Graziano, & Gross, 1999; Gould, Vail, Wagers, & Gross, 2001) and could play a role in learning and memory (Gross, 2000; Shors et al., 2001).

RESPONSE TO INJURY

Whether the developing cortex is initially equipotential (protocortex hypothesis) or is prespecified (protomap hypothesis) has important implications for understanding how the developing brain might respond to injury. If the protocortex hypothesis is true, then early injury might not have serious consequences, because intact areas might be able to take on the functions normally subserved by the damaged tissue. By contrast, if the protomap hypothesis is true, then early damage would be expected to cause impairments of the functions normally subserved by the damaged cortex.

A common belief is that injury early in life has less serious consequences than the same injuries sustained during adulthood. However, studies with humans with focal lesions suggest this is not always the case. Whereas in some cases the effects of focal lesions in children are less pronounced than in adults, in other cases the effects are more generalized and widespread (Vargha-Khadem, Isaacs, & Muter, 1994). This is likely because two opposing processes—a reduction in learning potential and greater functional plasticity—are both at work.

Language. In adults, damage to the left perisylvian areas that normally subserve language typically leads to difficulties in speaking, known as aphasia. By contrast, similar damage occurring between birth and 5 years of age has much less devastating consequences. For example, in one study of 16 children who sustained similar injuries in the first 5 years of life, none had any detectable dysphasic symptoms (Vargha-Khadem & Mishkin, 1997). However, three children who sustained injuries later in childhood all showed dysphasia. These results suggest that if the areas typically used for speech and language are damaged before the age of 5, other brain areas can take on these functions. However, after this time there is less adaptability and left hemisphere injury does produce a form of aphasia. In this sense, there appears to be an "increasing restriction of fate". In the first years of life there is greater plasticity because there are still options available for alternative developmental pathways. As the brain develops and different regions become specialized for different functions, such as language, there are increasingly few, or no, options left for reorganization and compensation of function (see Chapter 6 for further discussion).

Frontal lobes. By contrast to the relative plasticity of language functions in the face of early injury, damage to other areas can have serious effects even if incurred early in life. One example is injury to the frontal lobes. In adults, damage to the frontal lobes leads to impairments in some aspects of thinking collectively termed "executive function" (Temple, 1998), but might have little if any impairment on standard neuropsychological tests of intelligence (Duncan, Burgess, & Emslie, 1995; Shallice & Burgess, 1991). However, injury to the frontal lobes during infancy and childhood can lead to deficits both on tests of executive function and on standardized tests of intelligence (Garth, Anderson, & Wrennal, 1997). In fact, Vargha-Khadem, Watters, and O'Gorman (1985) concluded "Although there are likely to be differences in aetiology and extent of injuries in the different studies, the overriding conclusion that intelligence is compromised by early frontal injuries is inescapable". By contrast to the idea that the frontal lobes would show maximal plasticity because they develop relatively slowly, it appears that earlier injuries (before the age of one) might produce *greater* impairments than later injuries (Riva & Cazziniga, 1985).

Frontal lobe injuries might cause less or no reduction in intelligence in adults because standard intelligence tests tend to tap aspects of automated thinking or crystallized intelligence (Duncan et al., 1995). That is, these tests tend to tap skills that are normally well-learned and/or probe for a single correct answer (e.g. definitions of words). The frontal lobes might not be necessary for this type of thinking in adults, and instead be more necessary for controlled thinking or fluid intelligence. That is, the frontal lobes might be activated in situations where automated routines cannot be used because novel material is present or old material must be considered in new ways and/or in situations where the number and diversity of responses are important. For example, to succeed on tests of word and category fluency it is necessary to produce as many different answers as possible. As children have built-up fewer automated routines and general knowledge to "fall back on" following frontal injury, such injuries will have a more devastating impact. The influence of these injuries will become increasingly apparent with development (Banich, Cohen-Levine, Kim, & Huttenlocher, 1990).

However, it is important to note that in some cases of early injury to the frontal lobe, intelligence does appear to be relatively preserved. For example, two young adult patients who had sustained their brain damage prior to 16 months of age had histories of impaired decision making, behavioural dyscontrol, social defects, and abnormal emotion but were normal on neuropsychological measures of intellect, language, and academic achievement (Anderson, Damasio, Tranel, & Damasio, 2000). Thus, in some cases, early dysfunction in the prefrontal region might result in severe and chronic social maladjustment despite largely normal cognitive abilities.

The differing results regarding the impact of frontal lesions on intellectual development could be due to several factors. First, in many cases premorbid abilities are unknown, and it is difficult to determine whether normal scores post-injury reflect a lack of impact on intellectual functioning and whether low scores reflect a true decline. Second, the time between injury and assessment can also have an influence, as psychometric changes can occur over a long period of time and children might "grow into" their deficits (Eslinger, Grattan, Damasio, & Damasio, 1992; Williams & Mateer, 1992). Third, whether the damage is bilateral or unilateral could have an impact on the degree of recovery of function (see below). Lastly, impairments in social behaviour and executive function could interfere to varying extents with academic progress.

Bilateral versus unilateral damage. One important factor to consider when investigating the effects of brain injury in childhood is whether the damage is unilateral or bilateral. A consistent finding is that there is greater compensation following unilateral than bilateral injury. For example, children with bilateral damage to the perisylvian areas that in the left hemisphere normally subserve language show little or no development of speech and language (Vargha-Khadem et al., 1985), and children with bilateral damage to the hippocampus show a profound developmental amnesia not observed following unilateral damage (Vargha-Khadem & Mishkin, 1997). The observation that bilateral injuries result in much greater impairment than unilateral injuries points to the importance of accurately identifying the extent of damage. In some cases of apparent unilateral injury, undocumented injury in the "intact" side might be present. This could have important consequences for the extent of recovery of function. For example, in one study of the verbal abilities of epileptics following left temporal lobectomy, unexpected deficits in visual memory were related to previously undetected abnormalities (subsequently detected by MRI) in the right temporal lobe. Advances in neuroimaging techniques, which allow better visualization of brain structure, can thus play an important role in understanding structure–function relations.

Even when plasticity and compensation of function is observed, it is not necessarily without its limits and costs. This is apparent when one examines the non-verbal visuospatial abilities of children who have had sparing of linguistic function following early unilateral injury. Both non-verbal abilities and general intelligence scores are lowered in these children. This phenomenon is known as crowding—as the intact hemisphere assumes additional functions, some of its normal functions might be adversely affected. Interestingly, the crowding effect is more apparent after early left injury than after early right injury. It appears that verbal abilities tend to be spared consistently, at the cost of non-verbal abilities. Thus, with a unilateral left lesion, speech is spared and visuospatial abilities are compromised by crowding, whereas after early right lesions, speech is spared and visuospatial abilities are impaired.

More detailed study of children's visuospatial abilities following left compared with right hemisphere lesions has illustrated that, even when performance appears to be intact, the process by which this is achieved might be atypical. For example, one study of spatial grouping abilities in 4- and 6-year-olds with early unilateral brain injury found that, whereas performance accuracy was impaired only in children with right-sided lesions, the process that children with left-sided lesions used to produce accurate constructions was different from that used by typical children (Stiles, Stern, Trauner, & Nass, 1996; Vicari, Stiles, Stern, & Resca, 1998).

CONCLUSIONS

1. Development of the cerebral cortex involves both predetermined genetic influences and activity-dependent processes.
2. Activity-dependent processes begin prenatally and continue into postnatal life.
3. The primitive attentional biases of the newborn (such as the tendency to look toward faces) serve to bias the input into developing circuits. In this sense, infants can be said to be contributing actively to the later stages of their own brain specialization.
4. The developing brain can show remarkable plasticity in response to injury—in some cases, the effects of focal lesions in children are less pronounced than in adults.
5. Outcome is not always better for early- compared to later-sustained brain injuries, as in some cases the effects are more generalized and widespread when sustained early.

Some domains of cognition, such as language, appear plastic in the sense that regions of cortex are not exclusively dedicated to them from birth and other areas can take over these functions if necessary. Other aspects of development may show less adaptability. Less extensive plasticity does not necessarily imply strict genetic determinism, however, because functions more closely tied to sensory input or motor output are likely to be more restricted to the cortical regions that have the appropriate information in their input. For example, face recognition is necessarily restricted to structures on the visual "what" (ventral) pathway because it requires both visual analysis and encoding of particular items within a category. Language might be less constrained in the sense that it is less restricted to particular information processing routes within the cortex. Thus, a key point about the emergence of localization of functions within the cortex is that the restrictions on localization might be more related to which cortical routes of information processing are viable for supporting the functions, rather than being caused by prewired intrinsic circuitry within regions of cortex.

Despite impressive advances in our understanding of brain development, the question of how the functional specialization observed in the adult's cerebral cortex emerges during development remains an important issue for future research. Studying the postnatal emergence of cortical specialization for different cognitive functions offers the possibility of new perspectives not only on the study of perceptual and cognitive development in healthy human infants, but also for social development, education, and atypical developmental pathways. The use of converging methods, including animal models, computational modelling, neuroimaging, and neuropsychology, is likely to play an important role in future research in this area.

REFERENCES

Anderson, S.W., Damasio, H., Tranel, D., & Damasio, A.R. (2000). Long-term sequelae of prefrontal cortex damage acquired in early childhood. *Developmental Neuropsychology, 18*, 281–296.

Banich, M.T., Cohen-Levine, S., Kim, H., & Huttenlocher, P. (1990). The effects of developmental factors on IQ in children. *Neuropsychologia, 28*, 35–47.

Barres, B.A., Hart, I.K., Coles, H.S., Burne, J.F., Voyvodic, J.T., Richardson, W.D. et al. (1992). Cell death in the oligodendrocyte lineage. *Journal of Neurobiology, 23*, 1221–1230.

Bishop, K.M., Goudreau, G., & O'Leary, D.D. (2000). Regulation of area identity in the mammalian neocortex by Emx2 and Pax6. *Science, 288*, 344–349.

Casey, B.J., Giedd, J.N., & Thomas, K.M. (2000). Structural and functional brain development and its relation to cognitive development. *Biological Psychology, 54*, 241–257.

Changeux, J.P. (1985). *Neuronal man: The biology of mind*. New York: Pantheon Books.

Changeux, J.-P., Courrege, P., & Danchin, A. (1973). A theory of the epigenisis of neuronal networks by selective stabilization of synapses. *Proceedings of the National Academy of Sciences USA, 70*, 2974–2978.

Chugani, H.T., Phelps, M.E., & Mazziotta, J.C. (1987). Positron emission tomography study of human brain functional development. *Annals of Neurology, 22*, 487–497.

Cowan, W.M., Fawcett, J.W., O'Leary, D.D.M., & Stanfield, B.B. (1984). Regressive events in neurogenesis. *Science, 225*, 1258–1265.

Crowley, J.C., & Katz, L.C. (2000). Early development of ocular dominance columns. *Science, 290*, 1321–1324.

de Haan, M., Humphreys, K., & Johnson, M.H. (2002). Developing a brain specialized for face perception: A converging methods approach. *Developmental Psychobiology, 40*, 200–212.

Duncan, J., Burgess, P., & Emslie, H. (1995). Fluid intelligence after frontal lobe lesions. *Neuropsychologia, 35*, 261–268.

Ebbesson, S.O.E. (1984). Evolution and ontogeny of neural circuits. *Behavioral and Brain Sciences, 7*, 321–366.

Elman, J., Bates, E., Johnson, M., Karmiloff-Smith, A., Parisi, D., & Plunkett, K. (1996). *Rethinking innateness: A connectionist perspective on development*. Cambridge, MA: MIT Press.

Eslinger, P.J., Grattan, L.M., Damasio, H., & Damasio, A.R. (1992). Developmental consequences of childhood frontal lobe damage. *Archives of Neurology, 49*, 764–769.

Fields, R.D., & Itoh, K. (1996). Neural cell adhesion molecules in activity-dependent development and synaptic plasticity. *Trends in Neuroscience, 19*, 473–480.

Frantz, G.D., & McConnell, S.K. (1996). Restriction of late cerebral cortical progenitors to an upper-layer fate. *Neuron, 17*, 55–61.

Garnier, C., Arnault, P., Letang, J., & Roger, M. (1996). Development of projections from transplants of embryonic medial or lateral frontal cortex placed in the lateral frontal cortex of newborn hosts. *Neuroscience Letters, 213*, 33–36.

Garnier, C., Arnault, P., & Roger, M. (1997). Development of striatal projection from embryonic neurons from the lateral or medial cortex grafted homo- or heterotopically into the medial frontal cortex of newborn rats. *Neuroscience Letters, 235*, 41–44.

Garth, J., Anderson, V., & Wrennal, J. (1997). Executive functions following moderate to severe frontal lobe injury: impact of injury and age at injury. *Pediatric Rehabilitation, 1*, 99–108.

Gould, E., Reeves, A.J., Graziano, M.S., & Gross, C.G. (1999). Neurogenesis in the neocortex of adult primates. *Science, 286*, 548–552.

Gould, E., Vail, N., Wagers, M., & Gross, C.G. (2001). Adult-generated hippocampal and neocortical neurons in macaques have a transient existence. *Proceedings of the National Academy of Sciences USA, 98*, 10910–10917.

Greenough, W., & Black, J. (1992). Induction of brain structure by experience: Substrate for cognitive development. In M.R. Gunnar & C.A. Nelson (Eds.), *Minnesota symposia on child psychology 24: Developmental behavioral neuroscience* (pp. 155–200). Hillsdale, NJ: Lawrence Erlbaum Associates Inc.

Gross, C.G. (2000). Neurogenesis in the adult brain: Death of a dogma. *Nature Neuroscience Reviews, 1*, 67–73.

Gulisano, M., Broccoli, V., Pardini, C., & Boncinelli, E. (1996). Emx1 and Emx2 show different patterns of expression during proliferation and differentiation of the developing cerebral cortex in the mouse. *European Journal of Neuroscience, 8*, 1037–1050.

Huttenlocher, P.R. (1979). Synaptic density in human frontal cortex. Developmental changes and effects of aging. *Brain Research, 163*, 195–205.

Huttenlocher, P.R. (1990). Morphometric study of human cerebral cortex development. *Neuropsychologia, 28*, 517–527.

Huttenlocher, P.R., & Dabholkar, A.S. (1997). Regional differences in synaptogenesis in human cerebral cortex. *Journal of Comparative Neurology, 20*, 167–178.

Huttenlocher, P.R., & de Courten, C. (1987). The development of synapses in striate cortex of man. *Human Neurobiology, 6*, 1–9.

Huttenlocher, P.R., de Courten, C., Garey, L.J., & Van der Loos, H. (1982). Synaptogenesis in human visual cortex—evidence for synaptic elimination during normal development. *Neuroscience Letters, 33*, 247–252.

Inoue, A., & Sanes, J.R. (1997). Lamina-specific connectivity in the brain: Regulation by *N*-cadherin, neurotrophins, and glycoconjugates. *Science, 276*, 1428–1431.

Johnson, M.H. (2000). Functional brain development in infants: Elements of an interactive specialization framework. *Child Development, 71*, 75–81.

Johnson, M.H., Dziurawiec, S., Ellis, H.D., & Morton, J. (1991). Newborns' preferential tracking of face-like stimuli and its subsequent decline. *Cognition, 40*, 1–19.

Johnson, M.H., & Karmiloff-Smith, A. (1992). Can neural selectionism be applied to cognitive development and its disorders? *New Ideas in Psychology, 10*, 35–46.

Johnson, M.H., & Morton, J. (1991). *Biology and cognitive development: The case of face recognition*. Oxford: Blackwell.

Johnson, M.H., & Vecera, S.P. (1996). Cortical differentiation and neurocognitive development: The parcellation conjecture. *Behavioural Processes, 36*, 195–212.

Karmiloff-Smith, A. (1992). *Beyond modularity: A developmental perspective on cognitive science*. Cambridge, MA: MIT Press.

Karmiloff-Smith, A. (1998). Development itself is the key to understanding developmental disorders. *Trends of Cognitive Sciences, 2*, 389–398.

Kingsbury, M.A., & Finlay, B.L. (2001). The cortex in multidimensional space: Where do cortical areas come from? *Developmental Science, 4*, 125–156.

Mallamaci, A., Mercurio, S., Muzio, L., Cecchi, C., Pardini, C.L., Gruss, P. et al. (2000a). The lack of Emx2 causes impairment of Reelin signaling and defects of neuronal migration in the developing cerebral cortex. *Journal of Neuroscience, 20*, 1109–1118.

Mallamaci, A., Muzio, L., Chan, C.H., Parnavelas, J., & Boncinelli, E. (2000b). Area identity shifts in the early cerebral cortex of Emx2−/− mutant mice. *Nature Neuroscience, 3*, 679–86.

Marin-Padilla, M. (1990). Origin, formation and prenatal maturation of the human cerebral cortex: An overview. *Journal of Craniofacial Genetics and Developmental Biology, 10*, 137–146.

Maurer, D., Lewis, T.L., Brent, H.P., & Levin, A.V. (1999). Rapid improvement in the acuity of infants after visual input. *Science, 286*, 108–110.

Miyashita-Lin, E.M., Hevner, R., Wassarman, K.M., Martinez, S., & Rubenstein, J.L. (1999). Early neocortical regionalization in the absence of thalamic innervation. *Science, 285*, 906–909.

O'Leary, D.D.M., & Stanfield, B.B. (1989). Selective elimination of axons extended by developing cortical neurons is dependent on regional locale: Experiments utilizing fetal cortical transplants. *Journal of Neuroscience, 9*, 2230–2246.

Oppenheim, R.W. (1991). Cell death during development of the nervous system. *Annual Review of Neuroscience, 14*, 453–501.

Pallas, S.L. (2001). Intrinsic and extrinsic factors shaping cortical identity. *Trends in Neurosciences, 24*, 417–423.

Paterson, S.J., Brown, J.H., Gsodl, M.K., Johnson, M.H., & Karmiloff-Smith, A. (1999). Cognitive modularity and genetic disorders. *Science, 286*, 2355–2358.

Ragsdale, C.W., & Grove, E.A. (2001). Patterning in the mammalian cerebral cortex. *Current Opinions in Neurobiology, 11*, 50–58.

Rakic, P. (1988). Specification of cerebral cortical areas. *Science, 241*, 170–176.

Rakic, P. (2000). Radial unit hypothesis of neocortical expansion. *Novartis Foundation Symposium, 228*, 30–42.

Rakic, P., Bourgeois, J.-P., Eckenhoff, M.E., Zecevic, N., & Goldman-Rakic, P. (1986), Concurrent overproduction of synapses in diverse regions of the primate cerebral cortex. *Science, 232*: 232–235.

Rakic, S., & Zecevic, N. (2000). Programmed cell death in the developing human telencephalon. *European Journal of Neuroscience, 12*, 2721–2734.

Ranscht, B. (2000). Cadherins: Molecular codes for axon guidance and synapse formation. *International Journal of Developmental Neuroscience, 18*, 643–651.

Riva, D., & Cazzaniga, L. (1985). Late effects of unilateral lesions sustained before and after age one. *Neuropsychologia, 24*, 423–428.

Roe, A.W., Pallas, S.L., Hahm, J.O., & Sur, M. (1990). A map of visual space induced in primary auditory cortex. *Science, 250*(4982), 818–820.

Rubenstein, J.L., Anderson, S., Shi, L., Miyashita-Lin, E., Bulfone, A., & Hevner, R. (1999). Genetic control of cortical regionalization and connectivity. *Cerebral Cortex, 9*, 524–532.

Schlaggar, B.L., & O'Leary, D.D. (1991). Potential of visual cortex to develop an array of functional units unique to somatosensory cortex. *Science, 252*, 1556–1560.

Shallice, T., & Burgess, P. (1991). Deficits in strategy application following frontal lobe damage in man. *Brain, 114*, 727–741.

Shors, T.H., Miesegaes, G.L., Beylin, A., Zhao, M., Rydel, T., & Gould, E. (2001). Neurogenesis in the adult is involved in the formation of trace memories. *Nature, 410*, 372–376.

Somogyi, P., Tamas, G., Lujan, R., & Buhl, E.H. (1998). Salient features of synaptic organization in the cerebral cortex. *Brain Research, 26*, 113–135.

Stiles, J., Stern, C., Trauner, D., & Nass, R. (1996). Developmental change in spatial grouping activity among children with early focal brain injury: Evidence from a modelling task. *Brain & Cognition, 31*, 46–62.

Sur, M., Garraghty, P.E., & Roe, A.W. (1988). Experimentally induced visual projections into auditory thalamus and cortex. *Science, 242*, 1437–1441.

Sur, M., Pallas, S.L., & Roe, A.W. (1990). Cross-modal plasticity in cortical development: Differentiation and specification of sensory neocortex. *Trends in Neuroscience, 13*, 227–233.

Tanaka, H., Shan, W., Phillips, G.R., Arndt, K., Bozdagi, O., Shaprio, L. et al. (2000). Molecular modification of *N*-cadherin in response to synaptic activity. *Neuron, 25*, 93–107.

Temple, C. (1998). Executive disorders: Executive skills and the frontal lobes. In C. Temple (Ed.), *Developmental cognitive neuropsychology* (pp. 287–316). Hove, UK: Psychology Press.

Vargha-Khadem, F., Isaacs, E., & Muter, V. (1994). A review of cognitive outcome after unilateral lesions sustained during childhood. *Journal of Child Neurology, 9 (Suppl. 2)*, 67–73.

Vargha-Khadem, F., & Mishkin, M. (1997). Speech and language outcome after hemispherectomy in childhood. In I. Tuxhorn, H. Holthausen & H.E. Boenigk (Eds.), *Paediatric epilepsy syndromes and their surgical treatment* (pp. 774–784). Montrouge, France: John Libbey & Co. Ltd. Medical Books.

Vargha-Khadem, F., Watters, G., & O'Gorman, A. (1985). Development of speech and language following frontal lesions. *Brain & Language, 37*, 167–183.

Vicari, S., Stiles, J., Stern, C., & Resca, A. (1998). Spatial grouping activity in children with early cortical and subcortical lesions. *Developmental Medicine and Child Neurology, 40*, 90–94.

Wallace, C.S., Kilman, V.L., Withers, G.S., & Greenough, W.T. (1992). Increases in dendritic length in occipital cortex after 4 days differential housing in weanling rats. *Behavioural and Neural Biology, 58*, 64–68.

Williams, D., & Mateer, C.A. (1992). Developmental impact of frontal lobe injury in middle childhood. *Brain and Cognition, 20*, 196–204.

Yoshida, M., Suda, Y., Matsuo, I., Miyamoto, N., Takeda, N., Kuratani, S. et al. (1997). Emx1 and Emx2 functions in development of dorsal telencephalon. *Development, 124*, 101–111.

Zecevic, N. (1998). Synaptogenesis in Layer l of the human cerebral cortex in the first half of gestation. *Cerebral Cortex, 8*, 245–252.

CHAPTER TWO

Methods for imaging the developing brain

K.M. Thomas[1] and B.J. Casey
Sackler Institute for Developmental Psychobiology, Cornell University, New York, USA

INTRODUCTION

Historically, research in cognitive development has been restricted to the realm of observable behaviour. Following the model of ethologists and early developmental theorists, our field has profited extensively from the understanding that significant information can be learned simply by observing children behave in both natural and controlled environments. Efforts to link behavioural changes in cognitive development to changes in brain development rely heavily on the examination of postmortem specimens, observations of children known to have specific head injuries, or extrapolation from the adult neuropsychology literature. Given technological advances and refinements since the 1980s, a number of brain imaging techniques are now available for use in the *in vivo* and online examination of brain structure and function.

Investigating the neural basis of cognitive development requires sensitive measures of brain structure and function that can be used to obtain repeated observations of subject populations over an extended period of time. Single-unit recording or population-recording studies in awake, alert animals have significantly advanced our understanding of the relation between activity in particular brain regions and cognitive function, but are not possible in human subjects given the invasive nature of the recording electrodes. However, since the 1980s, technological advances have provided a number of new or refined methods for imaging brain anatomy and ongoing brain activity in human subjects, including computed tomography (CT), positron emission tomography (PET), single photon emission computed tomography (SPECT), structural and functional magnetic

[1] Kathleen Thomas has changed affiliation to: Institute of Child Development, University of Minnesota, 51 East River Road, Minneapolis, MN 55455-0345, USA.

resonance imaging (MRI), magnetoencephalography (MEG), and classic electroencephalographic (EEG) measures. Today, we can collect high-resolution images of the human brain and localize activity to specific anatomical brain regions in response to behavioural probes. However, the functional imaging techniques provide only indirect measures of neuronal activity, through scalp-recorded electrical or magnetic fields, or measures of blood flow, blood oxygenation or energy utilization (e.g. glucose metabolism), rather than direct measures of neuronal firing. In addition, some of these methods are invasive, requiring exposure to ionizing radiation and injected contrast agents, limiting their use in the study of healthy development.

This chapter focuses on three brain imaging techniques that appear to be particularly well suited for use with paediatric populations and are available to developmental investigators: (1) EEG, specifically event-related potential (ERP) measures; (2) anatomical or structural MRI; and (3) functional MRI (fMRI). The focus of the chapter will be on the basic methods used in each of these techniques, including a discussion of the utility and the limitations of each method for developmental research. Although a number of empirical studies will be described to illustrate the range of questions that can be addressed using these imaging methods, this chapter will not attempt to review the increasingly large literature applying these techniques to developmental questions.

ELECTROPHYSIOLOGICAL TECHNIQUES

Basic principles behind event-related potentials (ERPs)

One of the more traditional brain imaging techniques, the electroencephalogram (EEG), remains a useful tool in developmental science. EEG is a non-invasive and painless recording of brain electrical activity measured from the scalp surface. The ease of recording and relatively robust signal make this technique preferable for use as a functional measure of brain activity in infants and very young children for whom the demands of other imaging techniques may be too great (e.g. PET, which requires exposure to radiation, or MRI, where head motion degrades the measurable signal). Scalp-recorded electrical activity is thought to reflect the intermittent synchronization of small populations of predominantly cortical neurons (Andreassi, 1989) in response to presented sensory stimuli. By presenting subjects repeatedly with a given stimulus, and then averaging the EEG response to those stimuli, random noise is reduced and a waveform is produced reflecting the neuronal response to a particular stimulus. This averaged response is termed an evoked potential (EP) because it reflects activity evoked by a particular stimulus. Different modalities (e.g. visual or auditory) and different types of stimuli produce different sensory potentials that are labelled according to their polarity (positive peak or negative peak) and timing with respect to the stimulus, either in order of appearance (e.g. N1, N2) or in milliseconds (e.g. N19, P22) (see

Polich, 1993). Because individual EPs are thought to reflect activity of different neural sources, one application of this technique is to evaluate the integrity of sensory pathways. For example, auditory evoked potentials have been used clinically in newborn infants to assess the functioning of subcortical auditory paths (see Salamy, 1984, for developmental data). Such early sensory responses are elicited automatically by the presence of the auditory stimulus, although the observed waveforms can be modulated by higher-order processes (Regan, 1989). Similar averaged responses can be obtained for higher-level cognitive processes by comparing the responses evoked by stimuli that differ only in the cognitive events that they elicit. These event-related potentials (ERPs) reflect the precise timing of mental events such as orienting, stimulus processing and evaluation, target detection, memory updating, and semantic evaluation in the context of an individual experiment. Many authors use the terms EP and ERP interchangeably to describe any waveform that is elicited in a time-locked relation to the presentation of a stimulus.

ERP data have excellent temporal resolution. Non-random activity is measurable within milliseconds after the presentation of a stimulus, and the precise time-course of activity can be mapped out in detail. However, the spatial resolution of scalp-recorded electrical potentials is not very precise. ERPs are recorded at multiple locations simultaneously and specific components demonstrate maximal responses over particular brain regions. For example, visual stimuli tend to evoke early sensory EPs that are largest at electrodes placed over occipital scalp regions as compared to electrodes over the frontal or temporal lobes. However, in general, given the complex geometry of the brain and the potential for generators (coordinated neuronal activity) in deep brain structures, the scalp location of the maximal response is not sufficient to identify the neural source of the observed signal. This lack of spatial resolution is particularly acute when the number of recording electrodes is small, as is common in developmental studies, as typically, fewer locations are sampled across the scalp. Similarly, it is important to understand that the ERP is not the absolute electrical potential at a given location and time but rather the difference between the signal at the site of interest and the signal at a reference location. A reference location is selected to represent a relatively inactive area (e.g. earlobes), where signal is more likely to be related to ambient environmental noise than to the brain activity of interest, and all active recording sites are measured relative to this reference location. The shape and polarity of the scalp-recorded waveform is affected by the choice of reference location because changing the reference location will change its proximity to the active neural sources and hence the relative potential recorded at each electrode. A number of mathematical algorithms are now used to improve our understanding of the actual source of activity regardless of the reference used. Techniques such as dipole source modelling provide one means of generating hypotheses regarding the brain structures active at particular time points during the cognitive event, especially when used in conjunction with structural imaging techniques such as

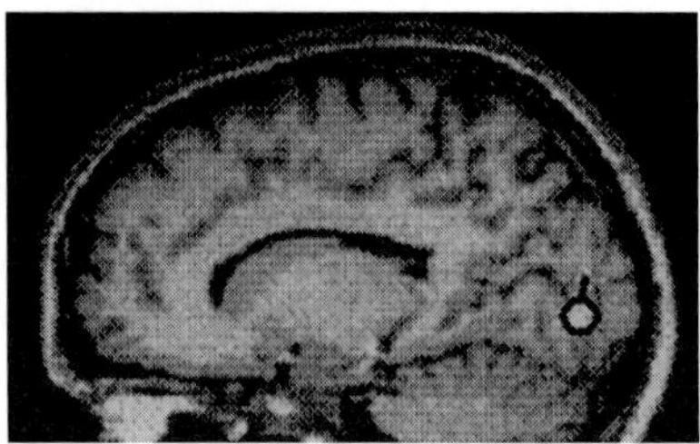
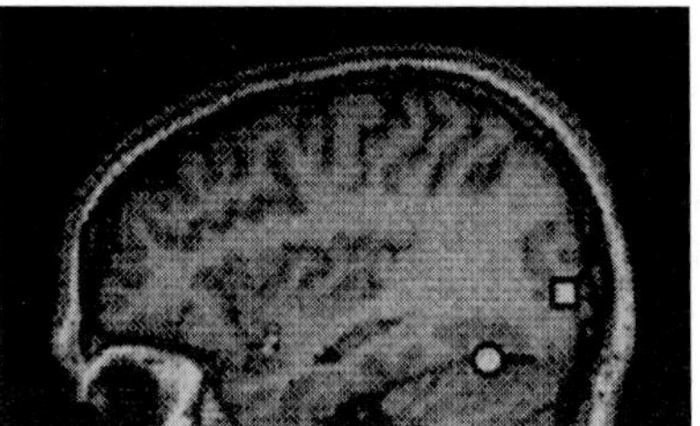

Figure 2.1. Results of an ERP dipole model of visuospatial attention in adults overlaid on a representative anatomical MRI (adapted from Martinez et al., 1999 in *Nature Neuroscience*. Reprinted with permission of Nature Publishing Group).

MRI (Fig. 2.1). However, to date there have been no published studies applying dipole source modelling to paediatric ERP data. For further discussion of reference locations and dipole modelling, see Nunez (1990) and Scherg (1990), respectively. Alternative approaches to signal localization in child populations include comparing paediatric ERP responses to adult responses with known generators (obtained through invasive clinical procedures) or animal recording studies. Such inferences can be helpful in directing further research but should be interpreted with caution given expected developmental differences in brain structure and function.

Practical challenges of ERP studies with infants and children

ERP methods are particularly well suited for studies of developmental populations. The procedure makes no demands on verbal or motor abilities, is relatively less perturbed by brief head movements, and can be accomplished within a short time frame, making fewer demands on the attention spans of young subjects. The procedure can provide exquisite temporal information regarding the timing of cognitive events in response to discrete stimuli. However, a number of practical issues arise.

First, any type of physiological recording is subject to external noise and artifact. Behavioural researchers will recognize that controlled studies of child behaviour are also subject to unintended artifact. ERP measures have several sources of artifact that are entirely unavoidable. The worst offenders are electrical potentials produced by eye movements or other muscle movements. The amplitude of scalp-recorded brain potentials is minimal compared to the magnitude of the signal produced by a muscle movement. Any muscle movement of the face and mouth, neck or eyes could show up in the recorded signal. A random muscle movement on occasional trials will probably disappear with trial averaging. On the other hand, frequently occurring or systematic movement such as blinks and saccadic eye movements will not disappear and will need to be addressed during data analysis by removing trials with movement artifact or by correcting mathematically for eye movement artifact. Experiments should be designed to minimize muscle tension over time and anticipated sources of artifact such as eye movements and blinks should be recorded deliberately to assess their impact on the observed signal. Other sources of noise include stray activity from other electrical equipment in the testing environment (fluorescent lights, computer monitors, etc.) as well as mechanical artifact when an electrode receives pressure (e.g. when subjects rest their heads against a chair back).

Although ERP techniques are non-invasive, most subjects would prefer not to wear the electrodes all day and, in fact, the conductivity of the electrodes is always time limited because the electrolyte (salt water, gel, or paste) eventually dries. When working with young subjects, a limiting factor is the child's tolerance of the electrodes, the task, and the time commitment required. A survey of the literature will reveal a somewhat higher attrition rate for infant ERP studies than for behavioural research with the same age groups. Every investigator develops tricks for minimizing this problem, but speedy and unobtrusive electrode application, engaging stimuli, and a short testing session are useful common aids.

Finally, an important practical aspect to ERP measurements is the choice of a meaningful and clear behavioural probe task. Like all functional neuroimaging techniques, the recorded ERPs are only as good as the behavioural task used to elicit the response. Electrophysiological measures are incredibly sensitive to aspects of the stimulus and its context, such as stimulus size, speed of presentation, and stimulus probability. As in behavioural research, appropriate control stimuli should be chosen to minimize unintended effects on the ERP results. Although many of the early infant ERP studies were designed to be exploratory with no clear *a priori* hypotheses, the field has advanced sufficiently for more specific questions to be tested with clear predictions regarding the components of interest.

Utility of electrophysiological measures for questions of cognitive development

Brain maturation and functional specificity. Electrophysiological techniques provide one non-invasive method for examining questions of brain maturation. For example, auditory brainstem responses show changes in latency with age (Galambos, 1982). Waveform components known to be generated in the brainstem and thalamus show rapid decreases in latency to peak response from late in the prenatal period (30 weeks gestation, measured in preterm infants) to approximately 2 years of age, at which time the response is indistinguishable from adult measures. By contrast, later peaking sensory and cognitive components thought to reflect cortical brain activity continue to show developmental changes in size (amplitude), latency to peak, and overall morphometry (shape) until early adolescence or later (Courchesne, 1978; Holcomb, Coffey, & Neville, 1992; Neville, 1995; Thomas & Nelson, 1996).

In our own work, we have examined developmental differences in a relatively simple cognitive paradigm that assesses the response to stimulus probability and stimulus novelty. We tested 8-year-olds and adults in a standard oddball paradigm with two female faces. Subjects were asked to press a button in response to one of the faces, the target face, which appeared on 20 per cent of trials. The second face, the frequent stimulus, appeared on 60 per cent of trials, with the remaining 20 per cent of trials containing novel visual patterns and objects that were never repeated. Despite the fact that behavioural performance on this task was at ceiling for both adult and 8-year-old participants, the morphology of the waveforms was distinct. Unlike adults, children demonstrated very broad and extended waveforms that took much longer to return to baseline (Fig. 2.2), suggesting an age-related difference in the scalp-recorded waveforms elicited by similar cognitive functions. These age-related changes undoubtably reflect changes in cognitive function, particularly the later peaking cognitive components. However, the age-related changes in subcortically driven responses early in childhood suggest that ERP measures can also reflect changes in brain maturation, whether in structure or functional connectivity among structures.

In a somewhat different approach, Neville and colleagues have examined the functional specificity of cortical regions that are known to be specialized for visual or auditory functions in adulthood. Using ERP measures, Neville showed that, in response to auditory stimuli, 6-month-old infants show ERP components that are equally large over auditory and visual cortices. However, between 6 and 36 months, the amplitude of the auditory ERP response decreases over visual areas while the response over temporal (auditory) areas remains unchanged (Neville, 1995).

Cognitive development. The majority of paediatric ERP studies have focused on identifying brain markers of cognitive function across development, or inferring parallel changes in brain development and cognitive development. For example, de Haan and Nelson (1997, 1999) have conducted a series of studies

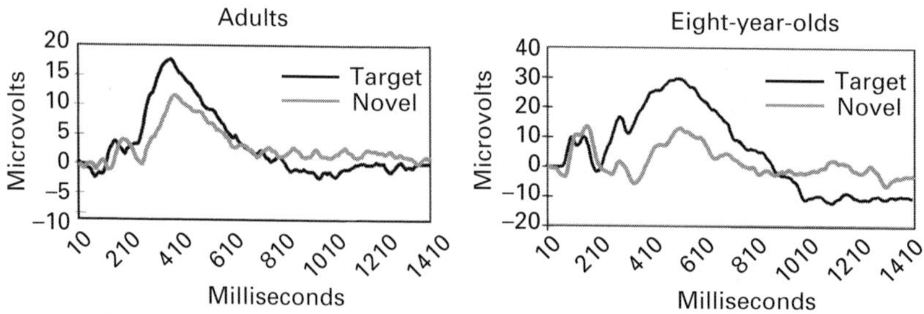

Figure 2.2. Comparison of ERP waveforms for adults and children in response to target and novel visual stimuli (adapted from Thomas & Nelson, 1996).

examining the recognition or discrimination of familiar objects such as faces or toys in infancy. Following the logic of behavioural studies, infants watch a series of pictures of a familiar stimulus and a novel stimulus. Assuming the appropriate controls are employed, differential ERP responses are presumed to reflect recognition of, or memory for, the familiar object. For example, 6-month-olds demonstrate discrimination of their own mother's face from the face of another child's mother (de Haan & Nelson, 1997). However, this discrimination is dependent on the perceptual similarity between the two faces. The infants show electrophysiological signs of recognition of mother's face only when paired with a dissimilar looking stranger. The ERP response difference goes away when infants are asked to discriminate mother from a similar looking stranger. These effects generalize to highly familiar objects such as the child's favourite toy (de Haan & Nelson, 1999), but the topography, or scalp distribution of the ERP responses differs by category (face versus object), suggesting that different neural correlates might underlie face and object recognition even as early as 6 months of age. The vast majority of paediatric ERP studies compare the electrophysiological signature of particular cognitive skills at various points in development.

ERPs also have been used to compare the brain bases of cognitive function between healthy developing infants and special populations with early brain insults or known developmental disorders. For example, deRegnier, Nelson, and colleagues (deRegnier, Georgieff, & Nelson, 1997; deRegnier et al., 2000; Nelson et al., 2000) have studied ERP measures of recognition memory in infants at risk for cognitive delays based on premature birth and/or perinatal complications. Their work suggests that group differences in cognitive function can be detected at a very young age in at-risk populations using ERP measures. A recent paper by Nelson et al. (2000) reports that infants of diabetic mothers, who are hypothesized to be at-risk for hippocampal damage due to interuterine iron deficiency, fail to show the typical ERP response differentiating the mother's face from a stranger's face at 6 months of age. Group differences in recognition memory were observed in the auditory analogue of this task (mother's voice versus stranger's voice) as early as 2 days of age (deRegnier et al., 2000).

Brain–behaviour correlations. An interesting direction in developmental ERP research has been to use the pattern of ERP responses recorded from an individual subject to predict later cognitive behaviour or skills. Behavioural measures of language and cognitive performance early in the first year typically have not proven to be reliable predictors of later skill levels in preschool and school age children. However, Molfese and Molfese (1985, 1997) have used ERP measures collected in the newborn period to discriminate the language skills of children at later ages. Molfese and Molfese (1997) used an infant's electrophysiological response during speech sound discrimination, such as /bi/ and /gi/, in a discriminant function analysis to predict which children would show high ($>$100) or low ($<$100) verbal scores on the Stanford–Binet intelligence test at 5 years of age.

Principal components analysis identified a number of important factors in the ERP data, particularly two related to a negative component occurring around 250ms after stimulus onset. Based on scores derived from these two factors during particular consonant and consonant–vowel discriminations, the authors were able to correctly classify 96 per cent of the group (8 of 9 low verbal children, and 60 of 62 high verbal children). These data suggest that early electrophysiological measures of cognitive performance might be useful in identifying children who could benefit from early intervention and remediation strategies.

A recent study by Carver and colleagues (2000) addresses whether ERP measures can predict later performance on a behavioural memory task. The authors showed 9-month-old infants how to make attractive and novel toys following a series of brief action sequences. Following an initial baseline free-play period, infants observed an experimenter completing the action sequences, but were not permitted to manipulate the toy pieces or to imitate the sequences. One week after the exposure session, in a recognition memory paradigm, infants were shown photographs of individual actions, some old and some new, and ERPs were recorded. Finally, 1 month after ERP testing, infants were allowed to manipulate the toy pieces. Both recall of previously observed event sequences as well as spontaneous completion of novel sequences were assessed. Fifty per cent of the infants failed to show behavioural recall of any of the familiar event sequences, and the other 50 per cent demonstrated long-term memory for the events (Carver & Bauer, 1999). When recall was used as a grouping variable, the pattern of ERP responses for old and new event elements clearly discriminated between infants with long-term behavioural recall and those without recall. In particular, infants who later recalled the event sequence showed differential ERP responses to old and new event elements whereas later non-recallers showed no ERP differences between previously viewed and novel elements (Fig. 2.3). Such data illustrate the utility of ERP measures in understanding the neural bases of complex behavioural phenomena such as memory consolidation and long-term recall, even when traditional behavioural measures such as verbal report are unavailable.

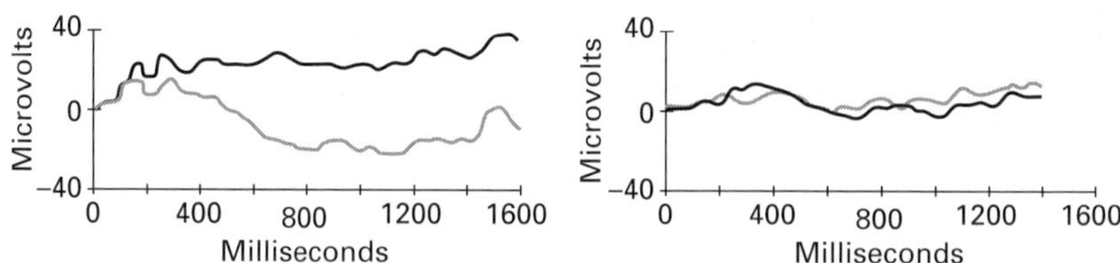

Figure 2.3. ERP waveforms in response to novel (dark line) and familiar (light line) stimuli for infants who later recalled (left panel) or did not recall (right panel) a behavioural event sequence (adapted from Carver et al., 2000).

STRUCTURAL MAGNETIC RESONANCE IMAGING (MRI) TECHNIQUES

Physiological basis of conventional MRI

Conventional magnetic resonance imaging (MRI) as applied in clinical settings can provide a number of different types of image, including high spatial resolution structural images and images of brain perfusion, based on the nuclear magnetic resonance (NMR) properties of water protons and other nuclides found in brain tissue (Young, 1988). The MRI technique relies on the fact that protons behave differently in the presence of a strong magnetic field. In the presence of an ambient magnetic field, the constantly spinning and moving protons tend to become aligned along the main axis of the field. Images are created by applying a series of brief energy pulses, radio frequency (RF) pulses, through the tissue. Each RF pulse contains enough energy to momentarily disrupt or tilt the protons in a particular plane. Measurements of the resultant change from one energy state to another are used to create images of the tissue. High resolution structural images are constructed based on measures of the energy released as pulsed protons relax back to their aligned state (called T1 relaxation). Different body tissue types demonstrate different T1 relaxation times, with lipids showing longer relaxation times than water (Bloch, 1946; Hahn, 1950). These relaxation differences are then mapped to produce T1-weighted structural images of the brain with high contrast between grey matter, white matter, and cerebrospinal fluid (Fig. 2.4). The RF field must be pulsed in such a way as to sequentially perturb multiple planes, or slices throughout the tissue, resulting in a series of in-plane images that can be stacked to recreate a 3D volume. Parameters such as slice thickness and in-plane resolution affect the length of the scanning procedure and the quality of the acquired images.

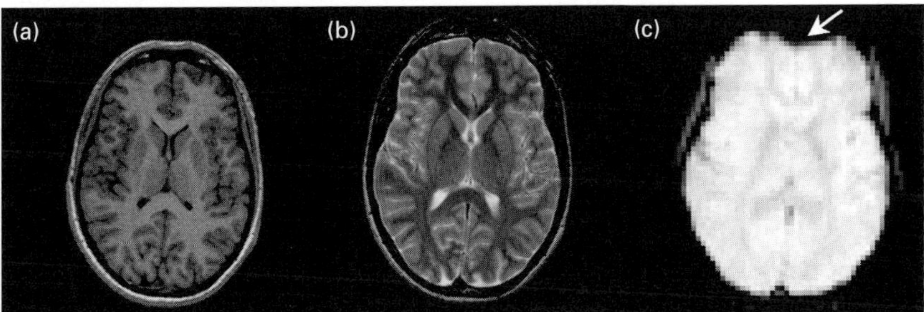

Figure 2.4. Representative magnetic resonance images of an adult brain collected in the axial plane. (a) T1-weighted anatomical image. (b) T2-weighted anatomical image. (c) T2*-weighted functional echo planar image (EPI). Signal loss due to susceptibility artifact is apparent in the T2*-weighted image at the frontal pole (arrow).

T1-weighted images are not the only type of image that can be produced using conventional scanning methods. A second measure, termed T2 relaxation, reflects energy decay as the protons gradually fall out of phase or alignment with one another despite remaining excited. T2 images reflect interactions among individual spins and local inhomogeneities in the RF-induced field that cause the nuclei to precess, or spin, at different rates and deviate from the uniform motion of the initial excitation (Bottomley, Foster, Argersinger, & Pfeiffer, 1984; Bottomley, Hardy, Argersinger, & Allen-Moore, 1987). The rate of dephasing, or loss of uniform motion, depends on the resonance of the environment (i.e. spins of neighbouring nuclei) and differs by tissue composition, producing contrast in the images (Fig. 2.4). Images can be predominantly T1-weighted or T2-weighted, depending on the specific parameters selected for the pulse sequence.

Practical challenges of MRI studies with children

Given the presence of a strong magnetic field, a number of safety concerns arise for MRI that are not an issue with other imaging techniques. In particular, the presence of any ferromagnetic materials in the scanning room could seriously injure a participant, as well as cause extensive damage to the equipment because the ambient magnetic field is always active. Items as seemingly innocuous as a paper-clip or a chair with metal legs can become dangerous projectiles in the presence of standard clinical and research magnets. Although there is no evidence of adverse effects due to exposure to magnetic fields of the strength used for most neuroimaging research (1.5–4T), some patients might have ferromagnetic medical implants or other metal objects embedded in their bodies, which would preclude their participation. Many electronic devices, including cardiac pacemakers, stop working in relatively low magnetic fields.

As with other techniques, several sources of artifact are possible. The presence of metallic or electronic devices near the magnetic field will cause inhomogeneities in the field and produce visible artifacts in the image. Therefore, if a child wears glasses or has orthodontic work such as braces or permanent retainers, the images are likely to show distortions near the object. In the case of eye glasses, plastic frames with lenses of varying prescriptions can be purchased for use in the scanner. Children with braces are best scanned at a later date when the braces have been removed. Any equipment used in the scanner or to monitor physiological activity must also be screened carefully for ferromagnetic material or RF noise.

Head motion artifact is the single most common problem when imaging children. The allowable degree of motion across a scanning session is on the order of millimetres. Any head motion will appear as blurry areas on the image or rings around the edges of the image. Techniques to reduce motion typically include foam padding around the head or a bite bar to hold the head rigid. Our group and others imaging children have had the most success using foam padding in conjunction with feedback training in a MRI simulator prior to the actual scan. In addition, children respond well when they have music, stories or videos to entertain them during the scan, or when the scan is conducted at a time when they are likely to fall asleep. In general, the youngest subjects currently scanned using these non-invasive procedures are typically 3 years or older.

Utility of conventional MRI for questions of cognitive development

Brain development. MRI-based anatomical studies have been used to examine maturational and age-related changes in brain volume. A number of segmentation techniques for parsing of large cortical regions are now semi-automated; however, quantitative volumetric measurements of individual structures such as the basal ganglia, the amygdala, or the hippocampus rely heavily on hand tracings from T1-weighted images. In addition, large sample sizes typically are required to demonstrate reliable developmental differences in healthy individuals. Several developmental differences have emerged consistently. First, total cerebral volume does not appear to change significantly beyond 5 years of age (Giedd et al., 1996a, 1996b; Reiss et al., 1996). By contrast, cortical grey matter appears to decrease significantly after 12 years (Giedd et al., 1999), whereas cerebral white matter shows an increase in volume throughout childhood and young adulthood (Caviness et al., 1996; Jernigan et al., 1991; Pfefferbaum et al., 1994; Rajapakse et al., 1996; Reiss et al., 1996). These volume changes appear to be regional in nature. Specifically, subcortical grey matter regions such as the basal ganglia decrease in volume during childhood, particularly in boys (Giedd et al., 1996a, Rajapakse et al., 1996; Reiss et al., 1996) whereas cortical grey matter in the frontal and parietal cortices does not appear to decrease until roughly puberty (Giedd et al., 1999). Similarly, white matter volume increases in dorsal prefrontal cortex, but not in more ventral prefrontal regions (i.e. orbitofrontal cortex; Reiss et al., 1996). Finally, overall volume of the temporal lobe is relatively stable across childhood (4–18 years), but hippocampal volume increases with age for females, and amygdala volume increases with age for males (Giedd et al., 1996b).

Behavioural development. One way of linking morphometric changes in the brain with behaviour is to correlate MRI-based anatomical measures with behavioural measures. For example, Casey and colleagues examined the role of the anterior cingulate cortex in the development of attention (Casey et al., 1997a). Performance during attention tasks characterized as predominantly automatic or predominantly effortful was assessed in parallel with MRI-based morphometric measures of the anterior cingulate cortex in children between 5 and 16 years of age. Children completed a behavioural task in which three stimuli that varied in shape and/or colour were presented in a row on a computer screen. The child's task was to indicate which of the three stimuli was different from the other two in a forced-choice task. Subjects were not informed as to which feature would be salient in making the discriminations. In the automatic condition, the stimuli differed on a single attribute (e.g. colour). In the controlled processing condition, the unique stimulus attribute changed from trial to trial within a block (e.g. from colour to shape). As would be expected, behavioural performance improved as a function of age (i.e. faster reaction times and higher accuracy). Volumetric measures of the right anterior cingulate cortex increased as a function of age and correlated with estimated IQ and mean reaction time on both the automatic and controlled tasks. The size of the left anterior cingulate region was not correlated with performance. When age, IQ, and total cerebral volume measures were controlled, only one significant correlation remained, between the right anterior cingulate measure and performance during the predominantly controlled attention task, but not the automatic task. This result suggests a specific relation between size of the right anterior cingulate region and performance of the controlled attention task (Fig. 2.5).

Clinical populations. Anatomical MRI has also been used to examine anatomical brain differences between healthy children and children with clinical diagnoses. De Bellis and colleagues have used quantitative MRI measures to address hypotheses of the disruption of particular anatomical circuits in childhood psychiatric disorders like post-traumatic stress disorder (PTSD; De Bellis et al., 1999) and generalized anxiety disorder (De Bellis et al., 2000). Given the hippocampal volume decreases and functional memory deficits observed in adults with PTSD, it was hypothesized that childhood PTSD would show similar decrements in hippocampal volume. In a study of 44 maltreated children with PTSD and 61 non-abused controls, hippocampal volume differences were not observed. However, total brain volume was smaller for abused children, and total brain volume was positively correlated with age of trauma onset and negatively

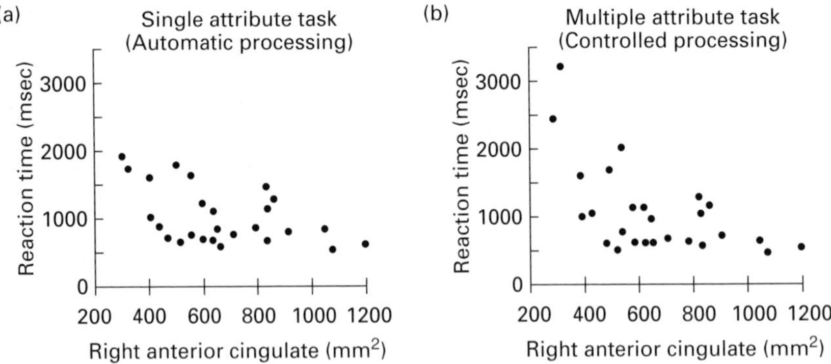

Figure 2.5. Example study illustrating the utility of correlation analyses between individual behavioural performance and brain activation (adapted from Casey et al., 1997a).

correlated with abuse duration (De Bellis et al., 1999), suggesting a more global rather than localized impact of early maltreatment. In a second study, children with diagnoses of generalized anxiety disorder were shown to have significantly larger right amygdala volume than age-matched healthy controls; other brain regions showed no group differences (De Bellis et al., 2000). These results are consistent with hypotheses of functional changes in the amygdala and related circuitry in anxiety and depressive disorders.

Changes in anatomy with behavioural and/or pharmacological treatments of childhood disorders can provide additional links between brain and behaviour. In a case study of obsessive compulsive disorder, Giedd and colleagues (Giedd et al., 1996c) used quantitative MRI to examine the relation between anatomical brain measures and changes in psychiatric symptomatology. Volumetric measures of basal ganglia structures, particularly the caudate nucleus, and globus pallidus changed with treatment and symptom severity whereas total cerebral volume and measures of frontal lobe volume were not affected.

FUNCTIONAL MAGNETIC RESONANCE IMAGING TECHNIQUES

Physiological basis of functional MRI

A relatively recent advance in conventional MRI is that of functional MRI (fMRI). Functional MRI relies on the assumption that regional changes in brain activity are associated with local haemodynamic changes in blood flow and oxygenation (Kwong et al., 1992; Ogawa, Lee, Nayak, & Glynn, 1990; Turner et al., 1991). This technique is based on the observation that haemoglobin becomes highly paramagnetic in its deoxygenated state, introducing local inhomogeneities in the applied RF magnetic field and causing dephasing of the protons in that local region. This change in energy state from the in-phase to the out of phase spin states due to local inhomogeneities is called T2* relaxation. In the case of blood oxygenation level dependent (BOLD) functional MRI, highly oxygenated areas of the brain show stronger MR signal (less disruption or inhomogeneity) in T2*-weighted images than less oxygenated regions. A basic assumption of this method of imaging is that brain areas increase their blood flow disproportionately to metabolic need when they become active, resulting in a net increase in tissue oxygenation (Fox, Raichle, Mintun, & Dence, 1988; Raichle, 1988). Maps of the MR signal intensity in these areas relative to others provide an indirect measure of the regions showing neuronal activity during the activated state. This haemodynamic change is not instantaneous, thus the observed signal change is delayed in time from the neuronal activity. It is thought that the peak haemodynamic change occurs approximately 6s after the activation. That is, the first associated activation would be expected to occur as late as 5–6s after the presentation of the stimulus. The signal change observed from the activated to the deactivated state is quite small when using this BOLD contrast, e.g. 1–2% change in a 1.5Tesla (T) ambient field. Therefore, most studies increase the power for signal detection by averaging across multiple trials of the same stimulus, as described for ERP measures. The haemodynamic signal change can be amplified by increasing the strength of the ambient magnetic field, switching, for example, to a 3T or 4T magnet rather than the 1.5T strength of the conventional clinical MRI scanner. Higher-field magnets amplify the signal change but also amplify the size of signal artifacts such as those due to motion.

Practical challenges of fMRI studies with children

In addition to the practical considerations of MRI scanning in general, other factors deserve consideration. First, the rapid image acquisition during functional scanning involves the application of gradient fields that allow for spatial coding in the image. The rapid oscillation of these gradients produces a loud auditory artifact. For example, one common functional imaging pulse sequence, echo planar imaging (EPI), produces a loud, high-pitched, repetitive beeping. Subjects are provided with ear plugs to attenuate this noise. In certain configurations, rapid gradient oscillations can induce electrical currents in the body, producing peripheral nerve stimulation, and absorption of radio frequency energy can lead to elevated body temperature and tissue heating. However, guidelines exist for determining the acceptable specific absorption rate (SAR) for different subject populations and the maximal rate and amplitude of gradient field changes to avoid these problems.

As with conventional MRI, functional scans are subject to artifacts produced by equipment or head motion. Functional MRI has the additional problem of physiological artifacts. One of the most frequently discussed is susceptibility artifact. This type of artifact is produced near the borders between tissue and air, for example, around the edges of the brain and near the sinus cavities. Susceptibility artifact appears as signal loss on the functional scan, and makes some brain regions more difficult to visualise than others. The orbital frontal cortex and temporal poles can be particularly troublesome (see Fig. 2.4). Additional sources of signal artifact are caused by blood flow in draining veins, which on the surface is indistinguishable from the haemodynamic response from neuronal activity, and artifacts caused by the mechanical motion of the chest during breathing. These sources of noise are unavoidable, but should be examined to assess their impact on the resultant functional data.

Finally, a critical component of any functional imaging method is the behavioural probe used to elicit activity. In fMRI studies, it is helpful to have some form of behavioural response from the subject during scanning both for the value of the behavioural measures, but also as a check to be sure that the child is actually completing the task as expected. Given the enclosed environment of the magnet, it is difficult to observe behaviour simply by watching the subject, and it is not uncommon for participants to fall asleep during the scan. Despite the array of exciting tasks that have been used in adult imaging research, it is often insufficient to directly apply an adult task to developmental research. Fine motor coordination is still developing in the early school years and tasks requiring multiple button presses might be impractical. Many children use visual checking methods to ensure that they are making the correct response in a behavioural task; however, when lying in the scanner, it is difficult or impossible to see one's hands. Our own research has suggested subjects do not always perform as well behaviourally in the scanner as they do outside the scanner. In addition, although adults show behavioural improvements with time in the scanner, children can actually decrease performance the longer they are in the scanner (Thomas et al., 1999). Our experience has been that children tend to show behavioural errors and move significantly more after 45–60min in the scanner.

Utility of functional MRI for questions of cognitive development

Cognitive and brain development. We have completed a number of studies using fMRI with healthy children to address cognitive domains such as attention, inhibition, and memory (Casey et al., 1995, 1997b; Thomas et al., 1999). Overall, these studies have suggested developmental differences in the size of the recruited regions, with children generally showing larger regions of activity than adults, or in the number of recruited regions, suggesting the development of more efficient networks. For example, young children appear to activate subcortical as well as cortical brain regions during saccadic eye movement tasks such as the occulomotor delayed response task (Luna, Garver, & Sweeney, 2000), whereas older children and adults tend to recruit predominantly cortical areas. Likewise, children aged 8–12 years activate both dorsal and ventral regions of prefrontal cortex during performance on a verbal working memory task, whereas adults activate predominantly dorsal regions (Casey et al., 1997b). Recently, we reported developmental differences in the way that the amygdala responds to emotional stimuli in healthy individuals. Given the literature suggesting the involvement of the amygdala and related circuitry in emotional responses to fear stimuli, we replicated an fMRI study of the amygdala response to facial expressions in a paediatric sample (Thomas et al., 2001). Adults and 8–16-year-old children watched pictures of fearful and neutral facial expressions during functional scanning of the amygdala. Our results replicated the finding that adults show a large amygdala response to fearful faces as compared to neutral faces, but we found the opposite pattern for children. Children demonstrated a larger amygdala response for neutral faces than for fearful faces, perhaps reflecting a difference in the way children and adults perceive and/or interpret different facial expressions, especially neutral faces. Further studies will be necessary to determine whether the amygdala also responds differently to other facial expressions, such as happy or sad faces, in children. Overall, children tend to show activity in the same regions activated by adult subjects, but often have additional regions or different patterns of activity in the same region.

Brain–behaviour correlations. As with structural MRI, fMRI can be used to examine anatomical correlates of behaviour. In the case of fMRI, correlations are based on changes in the MR signal measured in a given region rather than the size or volume of a structure. In addition, MR signal changes and behavioural changes are assessed simultaneously rather than in separate sessions.

One of the first published paediatric fMRI papers used a go no-go task to measure the brain bases of inhibitory control in children (Casey et al., 1997b). The task required subjects to make a behavioural response on the majority of trials, but to inhibit that response tendency when a stop signal was presented. Results indicated that activity in certain brain regions correlated significantly with behavioural task performance, regardless of the subject's age. These regions included the anterior cingulate and orbitofrontal cortices. Specifically, the more difficult the task (i.e. the more errors relative to the control task) the greater the magnitude of activity in the anterior cingulate cortex. In contrast, the better the performance (i.e. the fewer errors), the greater the volume of activity in the orbitofrontal cortex. These findings suggest that these two brain regions might be heavily involved in the development of inhibitory control and are consistent with our MRI-based anatomical study implicating the involvement of the anterior cingulate when there is competition from interfering information, as in the controlled attention task (Casey et al., 1997a). We have recently extended this go no-go task to a population of children with perinatal intraventricular haemorrhage (IVH), or bleeding into the lateral ventricles (Thomas et al., 1998). Morphometric measurements indicate that, as a group, these children show an average of 23 per cent smaller caudate nuclei than healthy control children. When we tested these children on the go no-go task, they showed more behavioural errors (false alarms) than control children. In addition, although they showed activity in the anterior cingulate and orbital frontal cortex, the signal did not correlate with behavioural performance, suggesting that disruption at the level of the basal ganglia was sufficient to disrupt the normal brain circuitry involved in task performance.

In a similar manner, we have used functional MRI to address differences in amygdala function between healthy children and children with anxiety or depression (Thomas et al., 2001). Using the face task described previously, we tested the amygdala response to fearful and neutral expressions in children with anxiety disorders (n=12) or major depression (n=5). Whereas healthy children showed large amygdala responses to neutral faces, children with anxiety disorders showed significantly greater activation to fearful expressions than to neutral expressions, perhaps reflecting a hyper-responsiveness to the fear stimuli. By contrast, data from a small sample of girls with major depression suggest a blunted amygdala response to faces in depressed children. Interestingly, across all groups of children, the degree of amygdala activity appeared to be positively correlated with each child's self-reported level of everyday anxiety.

These results illustrate some of the ways in which functional MRI results can be combined with behavioural and/or clinical information to provide additional measures of the functional significance of regional brain activation.

Remediation/Intervention. A promising avenue for paediatric neuroimaging is the study of the effects of treatment for developmental disorders such as attention deficit/hyperactivity disorder (ADHD) or dyslexia on brain function. Although a number of studies have been published addressing the brain bases of the cognitive dysfunctions in both of these disorders, the majority have studied adults who had childhood onset of the disorder (Brunswick et al., 1999; Bush et al., 1999; Eden & Zeffiro, 1998; Shaywitz et al., 1998). Studies that focus on children at or near the age when these problems first appear will be necessary to fully understand the progression of these disorders and the effects of early treatment or intervention.

As a number of behavioural studies have reported that mild to severe reading difficulties in children can be remediated successfully through targeted interventions that focus on phonological awareness and letter-sound decoding skills (Foorman et al., 1998; Torgesen, 1997; Vellutino et al., 1996; Wise, Ring, & Olsen, 2000), a logical step is to combine behavioural research with fMRI to study the impact of cognitive interventions on patterns of brain activity. McCandliss and colleagues (1999) reported preliminary results from such a study designed to examine the effectiveness of 24 behavioural intervention sessions focusing on phonological decoding skills. A group of children with reading disabilities showed an average gain of 1.4 grade levels in decoding skill after the intervention, with similar gains in phonological awareness measures. An fMRI task examining the brain response to words, pseudowords (which allow phonological decoding), and consonant strings in one of these poor readers indicated reduced activation in left perisylvian regions compared to normal readers. Prior to the intervention, the child with reading impairments showed little or no activation of the posterior superior temporal gyrus region thought to be involved in phonological skills in successful readers. However, following the 12-week (24-session) intervention, the same child showed significant increases in this brain region in response to words and pseudowords but, importantly, not for unpronouncable consonant strings, suggesting the recruitment of this brain region with behavioural improvements in phonological decoding. Case studies like this one mark a first step in more direct evaluations of the impact of cognitive and behavioural training on brain function.

Similar to these studies of dyslexia, a number of investigators have been interested in using fMRI to assess the impact of pharmacological treatments of childhood disorders such as ADHD. Vaidya et al. (1998) examined group differences between children with and without ADHD, as well as the effects of acute methylphenidate therapy on the functional brain activity observed in these children.

The study compared 10 boys (aged 8–13 years) with ADHD, and 6 boys without ADHD. Each child was scanned twice while performing the go no-go task (Casey et al., 1997b), once without medication (minimum 36h without medication) and once on medication. ADHD children took their usual dose (7.5–30mg) and control children were given 10mg of methylphenidate 2h before scanning. As expected, children with ADHD made many more behavioural false alarms than control children, even when medicated. Imaging results suggested that, off medication, ADHD children failed to show basal ganglia activity typically observed in the healthy controls during the inhibitory condition. Treatment with methylphenidate appeared to normalize the activity in the caudate and putamen for subjects with ADHD. By contrast, healthy children actually showed significantly less activity in the striatum when on the drug. Further research will be needed to assess the functional significance of these effects, as well as to address concerns such as the difference in medication history between the two groups. Paediatric fMRI techniques allow developmental disorders such as dyslexia and ADHD to be studied within the age range in which they typically first appear, and provides opportunities both for early prevention/intervention and for dynamic tracking of cortical changes associated with changes in cognitive skills.

CONCLUSIONS AND FUTURE DIRECTIONS

1. Event-related potentials (ERPs) provide a non-invasive measure for examining the temporal dynamics of cognitive events in infants and children.
2. Structural and functional magnetic resonance imaging (MRI) procedures have proven feasible in school-age children and lead the field in methods for examining morphometric brain development and the localization of cognitive processes during development.
3. Future advances in developmental cognitive neuroscience will include the combined use of these temporal and spatial brain imaging techniques to further our understanding of the complex relationship between brain development and behavioural development.
4. The exciting future of neuroimaging in developmental psychology will necessitate even more behavioural research in the development of specific and appropriate tasks to probe the neural activity associated with cognitive development.

The field of developmental cognitive neuroscience has reached an exciting era. We now have excellent methods for acquiring high resolution images of the developing brain, as well as techniques for delineating the precise timing and neural generators of cognitive activity during periods of rapid and profound cognitive development. With electrophysiological techniques such as ERPs, we can examine the electrical brain activity elicited during basic sensory processing, as well as modulations in that activity by top-down cognitive processes such as attention and learning, in infants as well as older children and adults. There is a long way to go in describing and interpreting the differences between infant, child, and adult ERPs, but this method remains one of the few neuroimaging techniques appropriate for all age levels. The temporal information provided by ERP measures allows us to pinpoint much more clearly the precise cognitive events that are changing as the child develops. By contrast, the advent of non-invasive functional MRI techniques has completely altered the questions that can be asked about the brain bases of cognition in healthy developing children. Currently, the technique has real limitations, including the lack of robust signal in the face of head or body movement, which make it most appropriate for older children. However, the ability to examine the brain regions involved in particular cognitive functions even as children are entering school or reaching adolescence holds promise for identifying some of the regions that might or might not be critical for cognitive changes at earlier ages. Clearly, the future of paediatric neuroimaging will include the combination of ERP and MRI techniques to examine both the temporal and the spatial dynamics of cognition across development, as well as the use of new imaging methodologies such as diffusion tensor imaging (Klingberg et al., 1999) and non-invasive optical imaging in infants (Chen et al., 2000). The combined use of multiple imaging methods has the potential to significantly expand our understanding of the development of both structure and function, and the precise cascade of neural events that contributes to the observed changes in behaviour and cognition. A caveat cutting across all of these techniques is the realization that a neuroimaging methodology is only as good as the behavioural paradigm used to elicit neural activity. Therefore, advances in behavioural research in cognitive development will continue to be essential in guiding the questions that are addressed in developmental cognitive neuroscience research.

REFERENCES

Andreassi, J.L. (1989). *Psychophysiology: Human behavior and physiological response* (2nd ed.). Hillsdale, NJ: Lawrence Erlbaum Associates.

Bloch, F. (1946). Nuclear induction. *Physiological Reviews, 70*, 460–474.

Bottomley, P.A., Foster, T.H., Argersinger, R.E., & Pfeiffer, L.M. (1984). A review of normal tissue hydrogen NMR relaxation times and relaxation mechanisms from 1–100 MHz. *Medical Physics, 11*, 425–460.

Bottomley, P.A., Hardy, C.J., Argersinger, R.E., & Allen-Moore, G. (1987). A review of hydrogen magnetic resonance relaxation in pathology. *Medical Physics, 14*, 1–37.

Brunswick, N., McCrory, E., Price, C.J., Frith, C.D., & Frith, U. (1999). Explicit and implicit processing of words and pseudowords by adult developmental dyslexics: A search for Wernicke's Wortshatz? *Brain, 122*, 1901–1917.

Bush, G., Frazier, J.A., Rauch, S.L., Seidman, L.J., Whalen, P.J., Jenike, M.A. et al. (1999). Anterior cingulate cortex dysfunction in attention-deficit/hyperactivity disorder revealed by fMRI and the Counting Stroop. *Biological Psychiatry, 45*(12), 1542–1552.

Carver, L.J. & Bauer, P.J. (1999). When the event is more than the sum of its parts: Long-term recall of event sequences by 9-month-old infants. *Memory, 7*, 147–174.

Carver, L.J., Bauer, P.J., & Nelson, C.A. (2000). Associations between infant brain activity and recall memory. *Developmental Science, 3*(2), 234–246.

Casey, B.J., Cohen, J.D., Jezzard, P., Turner, R., Noll, D.C., Tranior, R.J. et al. (1995). Activation of prefrontal cortex in children during a nonspatial working memory task with functional MRI. *Neuroimage, 2*, 221–229.

Casey, B.J., Trainor, R., Giedd, J., Vauss, Y., Vaituzis, C.K., Hamburger, S. et al. (1997a). The role of the anterior cingulate in automatic and controlled processes: A developmental neuroanatomical study. *Developmental Psychobiology, 30*, 61–69.

Casey, B.J., Trainor, R.J., Orendi, J.L., Schubert, A.B., Nystrom, L.E., Giedd, J.N. et al. (1997b). A developmental functional MRI study of prefrontal activation during performance of a go no-go task. *Journal of Cognitive Neuroscience, 9*(6), 835–847.

Caviness, V.S. Jr., Kennedy, D.N., Richelme, C., Rademacher, J., & Filipek, P.A. (1996). The human brain age 7–11 years: A volumetric analysis based on magnetic resonance images. *Cerebral Cortex, 6*(5), 726–736.

Chen, Y., Zhou, S., Xie, C., Nioka, S., Delivoria-Papadopoulos, M., Anday, E. et al. (2000). Preliminary evaluation of dual wavelength phased array imaging on neo-natal brain function. *Journal of Biomedical Optics, 5*(2), 194–200.

Courchesne, E. (1978). Neurophysiological correlates of cognitive development: Changes in long-latency event-related potentials from childhood to adulthood. *Electroencephalography and Clinical Neurophysiology, 45*, 468–482.

De Bellis, M.D., Casey, B.J., Dahl, R., Birmaher, B., Williamson, D., Thomas, K.M. et al. (2000). A pilot study of amygdala volumes in pediatric generalized anxiety disorder. *Biological Psychiatry, 48*(1), 51–57.

De Bellis, M.D., Keshavan, M.S., Clark, D.B., Casey, B.J., Giedd, J.N., Boring, A.M. et al. (1999). Developmental traumatology part II: Brain development. *Biological Psychiatry, 45*, 1271–1284.

de Haan, M. & Nelson, C.A. (1997). Recognition of the mother's faces by six-month-old infants: A neurobehavioral study. *Child Development, 68*, 187–210.

de Haan, M. & Nelson, C.A. (1999). Brain activity differentiates face and object processing in 6-month-old infants. *Developmental Psychology, 35*(4), 1113–1121.

deRegnier, R.-A.O., Georgieff, M.K., & Nelson, C.A. (1997). Visual event-related brain potentials in 4-month-old infants at risk for neurodevelopmental impairments. *Developmental Psychobiology, 30*, 11–28.

deRegnier, R.-A.O., Nelson, C.A., Thomas, K.M., Wewerka, S., & Georgieff, M.K. (2000). Neurophysiologic evaluation of auditory recognition memory in healthy newborn infants and infants of diabetic mothers. *Journal of Pediatrics, 137*, 777–784.

Eden, G.F. & Zeffiro, T.A. (1998). Neural systems affected in developmental dyslexia revealed by functional neuroimaging. *Neuron, 21*(2), 279–282.

Foorman, B.R., Francis, D.J., Fletcher, J.M., Schatschneider, C., & Mehta, P. (1998). The role of instruction in learning to read: Preventing reading failure in at-risk children. *Journal of Educational Psychology, 90*, 37–55.

Fox, P.T., Raichle, M.E., Mintun, M.A., & Dence, C. (1988). Nonoxidative glucose consumption during focal physiologic neural activity. *Science, 241*, 1445–1448.

Galambos, R. (1982). Maturation of auditory evoked potentials. In G.A. Chiarenza & D. Papakostopoulos (Eds.), *Clinical application of cerebral evoked potentials in pediatric medicine* (pp. 323–343). Amsterdam: Excerpta Medica.

Giedd, J.N., Blumenthal, J., Jeffries, N.O., Castellanos, F.X., Lui, H., Zijdenbos, A. et al. (1999). Brain development during childhood and adolescence: A longitudinal MRI study. *Nature Neuroscience, 2*(10), 861–863.

Geidd, J.N., Rapoport, J.L., Leonard, H.L., Richter, D., & Swedo, S.E. (1996c). Case study: Acute basal ganglia enlargement and obsessive–compulsive symptoms in an adolescent boy. *Journal of the American Academy of Child and Adolescent Psychiatry, 35*(7), 913–915.

Giedd, J.N., Snell, J.W., Lange, N., Rajapakse, J.C., Casey, B.J., Kozuch, P.L. et al. (1996a). Quantitative magnetic resonance imaging of human brain development: Ages 4–18. *Cerebral Cortex, 6*, 551–560.

Giedd, J.N., Vaituzis, A.C., Hamburger, S.D., Lange, N., Rajapakse, J.C., Kaysen, D. et al. (1996b). Quantitative MRI of the temporal lobe, amygdala, and hippocampus in normal human development: Ages 4–18 years. *Journal of Comparative Neurology, 366*(2), 223–230.

Hahn, E.L. (1950). Spin echoes. *Physiological Reviews, 80*, 580–594.

Holcomb, P.J., Coffey, S.A., & Neville, H.J. (1992). Visual and auditory sentence processing: A development analysis using event-related potentials. *Developmental Neuropsychology, 8*, 203–241.

Jernigan, T.L., Zisook, S., Heaton, R.K., Moranville, J.T., Hesselink, J.R., & Braff, D.L. (1991). Magnetic resonance imaging abnormalities in lenticular nuclei and cerebral cortex in schizophrenia. *Archives of General Psychiatry, 48*, 881–890.

Klingberg, T., Vaidya, C.J., Gabrieli, J.D., Moseley, M.E., & Hedehus, M. (1999). Myelination and organization of the frontal white matter in children: a diffusion tensor MRI study. *NeuroReport, 10*(13), 2817–2821.

Kwong, K.K., Belliveau, J.W., Chesler, D.A., Goldberg, I.E., Weisskoff, R.M., Poncelet, B.P. et al. (1992). Dynamic magnetic resonance imaging of human brain activity during primary sensory stimulation. *Proceedings of the National Academy of Sciences USA, 89*, 5675.

Luna, B., Garver, K.E., & Sweeney, J. (2000, abstract). Development in cognitive and sensorimotor systems from late childhood to adulthood. *Proceedings of the Society for Neuroscience, 26*, 1338.

Martinez, A., Anllo-Vento, L., Sereno, M.I., Frank, L.R., Buxton, R.B., Dubowitz, D.J. et al. (1999). Involvement of striate and extrastriate visual cortical areas in spatial attention. *Nature Neuroscience, 2*(4), 364–369.

McCandliss, B., Sandak, R., Beck, I., & Schneider, W. (1999). *Case studies in reading intervention: Behavioral and fMRI results in children.* Executive Meeting of the McDonnell Foundation Program in Cognitive Neuroscience, July. San Diego, CA.

Molfese, D.L. & Molfese, V.J. (1985). Electrophysiological indices of auditory discrimination in newborn infants: The basis for predicting later language performance? *Infant Behavior and Development, 8*, 197–211.

Molfese, D.L. & Molfese, V.J. (1997). Discrimination of language skills at five years of age using event-related potentials recorded at birth. *Developmental Neuropsychology, 13*(2), 135–156.

Nelson, C.A., Wewerka, S., Thomas, K.M., Tribby-Walbridge, S., deRegnier, R.-A., & Georgieff, M.K. (2000). Neurocognitive sequelae of infants of diabetic mothers. *Behavioral Neuroscience, 114*(5), 950–956.

Neville, H.J. (1995). Developmental specificity in neurocognitive development in humans. In M. Gazzaniga (Ed.), *The cognitive neurosciences* (pp. 219–231). Cambridge, MA: MIT Press.

Nunez, P.L. (1990). Physical principles and neurophysiological mechanisms underlying event-related potentials. In J.W. Rohrbaugh, R. Parasuraman, & R. Johnson (Eds.), *Event-related brain potentials: Basic issues and applications*. New York: Oxford University Press.

Ogawa, S., Lee, T.S., Nayak, A.S., & Glynn, P. (1990). Oxygenation-sensitive contrast in magnetic resonance image of rodent brain at high magnetic fields. *Magnetic Resonance in Medicine, 26*, 68–78.

Pfefferbaum, A., Mathalon, D.H., Sullivan, E.V., Rawles, J.M., Zipursky R.B., & Lim, K.O. (1994). A quantitative magnetic resonance imaging study of changes in brain morphology from infancy to late adulthood. *Archives of Neurology, 51*(9), 874–887.

Polich, J. (1993). Cognitive brain potentials. *Current Directions in Psychological Science, 2*(6), 175–179.

Raichle, M.E. (1988). Circulatory and metabolic correlates of brain function in normal humans. In V.B. Mountcastle, F. Plum, & S.R. Geiger (Eds.), *Handbook of physiology: The nervous system* (pp. 643–674). Bethesda, MD: American Psychological Society.

Rajapakse, J.C., Lenane, M.C., McKenna, K., Jacobsen, L.K., Gordon, C.T., Breier, A. et al. (1996). Brain magnetic resonance imaging in childhood-onset schizophrenia. *Archives of General Psychiatry, 53*(7), 617–624.

Regan, D. (1989). *Human brain electrophysiology: Evoked potentials and evoked magnetic fields in science and medicine*. New York: Elsevier.

Reiss, A.L., Abrams, M.T., Singer, H.S., Ross, J.L., & Denckla, M.B. (1996). Brain development, gender and IQ in children. A volumetric imaging study. *Brain, 119*, 1763–1774.

Salamy, A. (1984). Maturation of the auditory brainstem response from birth through early childhood. *Journal of Clinical Neurophysiology, 1*, 293–329.

Scherg, M. (1990). Fundamentals of dipole source potential analysis. In M. Hoke, F. Grandori, & G.L. Romani (Eds.), *Auditory evoked magnetic fields and electric potentials. Advances in audiology* (Vol. 6). New York: Karger.

Shaywitz, S.E., Shaywitz, B.A., Pugh, K.R., Fulbright, R.K., Constable, R.T., Mencl, W.E. et al. (1998). Functional disruption in the organization of the brain for reading in dyslexia. *Proceedings of the National Academy of Sciences USA, 95*, 2636–2641.

Thomas, K.M., Drevets, W.C., Dahl, R.E., Ryan, N.D., Birmaher, B., Eccard, C.H. et al. (2001). Amygdala response to fearful faces in anxious and depressed children. *Archives of General Psychiatry, 58*, 1057–1063.

Thomas, K.M., Drevets, W.C., Whalen, P.J., Eccard, C.H., Dahl, R.E., Ryan, N.D. et al. (2001). Amygdala response to facial expressions in children and adults. *Biological Psychiatry, 49*, 309–316.

Thomas, K.M., King, S.W., Franzen, P.L, Welsh, T.F., Berkowitz, A.L., Noll, D.C. et al. (1999). A developmental fMRI study of spatial working memory. *Neuroimage, 10*, 327–338.

Thomas, K.M. & Nelson, C.A. (1996). Age-related changes in the electrophysiological response to visual stimulus novelty: A topographical approach. *Electroencephalography and Clinical Neurophysiology, 98*, 294–308.

Thomas, K.M., Welsh, T.F., Eccard, C.H., Livnat, R., Pierri, J.N., & Casey, B.J. (1998, abstract). A functional MRI study of response inhibition in children with intraventricular hemorrhage. *Proceedings of the Cognitive Neuroscience Society, 10*(Suppl.), 68.

Torgesen, J.K. (1997). The prevention and remediation of reading disabilities: Evaluating what we know from research. *Journal of Academic Language Therapy, 1*, 11–47.

Turner, R., Le Bihan, D., Moonen, C.T.W., Despres, D., & Frank, J. (1991). Echo-planar time course MRI of cat brain oxygenation changes. *Magnetic Resonance in Medicine, 22*, 159–166.

Vaidya, C.J., Austin, G., Kirkorian, G., Ridlehuber, H.W., Desmond, J.E., Glover, G.H. et al. (1998). Selective effects of methylphenidate in attention deficit hyper-activity disorder: a functional magnetic resonance study. *Proceedings of the National Academy of Sciences USA, 95*(24), 14494–14499.

Vellutino, F.R., Scanlon, D.M., Sipay, E., Small, S., Pratt, A., Chen, R. et al. (1996). Cognitive profiles of difficult-to-remediate and readily remediated poor readers: Early intervention as a vehicle for distinguishing between cognitive and experimental deficits as basic causes of specific reading disability. *Journal of Educational Psychology, 88*, 601–638.

Wise, B.W., Ring, J., & Olson, R.K. (2000). Individual differences in gains from computer-assisted remedial reading with more emphasis on phonological analysis or accurate reading in context. *Journal of Experimental Child Psychology, 77*, 197–235.

Young, S.W. (1988). *Magnetic resonance imaging: Basic principles.* New York: Raven Press.

CHAPTER THREE

Neurobiological models of normal and abnormal visual development

Janette Atkinson and Oliver Braddick
Visual Development Unit, University College London, London, UK

INTRODUCTION

Since the 1980s there has been enormous progress in understanding structure–function links between visual behaviour and brain systems, but we are still relatively naïve in understanding these links in human development. There are three major reasons for this: One is the dynamic nature of development itself, with constraints in plasticity changing at different levels of the nervous system and each stage building on the preceding state of the system. The second is the paucity of information on human brain structures during development. The third is the fragmentation of approaches in looking at visual development. A synthesis drawing on psychology, paediatric neurology, neurophysiology, and ophthalmology is needed. In this chapter we attempt to bring together work on non-human species and human neuropsychology with current knowledge of human development. Our focus is visual development over the first years of life, although the plasticity shown in the adult brain can be revealing about the same processes. For example, visual neglect can be reduced in stroke patients through movements of the contralateral limb (Halligan & Marshall, 1989; Robertson & North, 1993). This example serves to highlight the close connections between visual and motor development. In studying development, we no longer find it helpful, experimentally or theoretically, to separate visual perception from visuocognitive components (including attention), or from visual control of the eyes, head, limbs, and body. Brain function does not neatly divide up into boxes called "visual perception", "spatial cognition", or "visuomotor coordination", and neither does development.

This chapter first summarizes our previous models of early visual development (Atkinson, 1984, 1992; Braddick & Atkinson, 1988) and outlines our most recent model (Atkinson, 2000), highlighting the division between dorsal and ventral cortical streams. We discuss the developmental relation between cortical and subcortical visual processing, and newer data relating these to visual action systems.

There are three conspicuous changes in visually controlled behaviour in infancy; each linked to development in a different "action" system. The first is the development of an internally driven, selective attention system using eye and head movements. Newborns show little active visual exploration; their apparently passive attentional system is driven by any high contrast stimulus in the baby's near space. By 3 months this is replaced by a system that actively selects and switches between objects of scrutiny. The second dramatic change in visual behaviour is the development of reaching, grasping, and manipulation of objects at 6–12 months of age. This behaviour is still concerned with near space. The third change, the onset of locomotion, extends the demands on visual processing and attention to more distant locations, and switches of attention between large scale features of the scene and the detailed scrutiny of objects.

A comprehensive theory of visual development should account for these three massive changes and their neural basis. At present we can only present an outline of some parts of the developmental process, drawing both on current neuroscience and on psychological insights about the nature of infants' visuospatial representations at different stages. We first outline theoretical schemes, and then present some of the supporting information on infant development.

NEUROBIOLOGICAL MODELS OF VISUAL DEVELOPMENT

Our models of the neural systems underlying visual development have been refined through progress both in the understanding of infants' visual capabilities, and in knowledge about the organization of the primate visual brain.

Two visual systems: "where?" and "what?"

Our neurobiological account starts from the idea of two visual systems, a phylogenetically older retinotectal system and a newer geniculostriate system. These two distinct routes from the retina to the brain had already been identified in the 19th century, but the functional distinction arose from studies in the 1950s and 1960s (e.g. Sprague & Meikle, 1965). Schneider (1969) showed that cortical damage in hamsters impaired pattern discrimination, whereas tectal damage impaired orienting responses to significant stimuli. He proposed that the tectal system defines "where" an object is located to trigger orienting, and newer cortical mechanisms define "what" is actually in the selected location.

Bronson's (1974) model for human visual development was based on this idea. As newborns orient by head and eye movements to conspicuous stimuli, but show little evidence of pattern discrimination, he proposed that newborn vision is controlled subcortically, with the cortex starting to mature at around 2 months postnatally. Advances in psychophysical and visual evoked potential techniques allowed a more detailed analysis of these two systems. Our first theory of visual development proposed distinct functional modules, made up of linked subcortical and cortical brain networks (Atkinson, 1984). We suggested that the subcortical networks which underpin newborn behaviour are not superseded, but come progressively under cortical executive control which modulates their function. The evidence for a developmental sequence of specific cortical modules, and their interaction with subcortical systems, is reviewed the section "Functional onset of specific cortical modules".

This model left some unanswered questions about what was changing or developing so rapidly. It also had to confront occasional glimpses of behaviour, in the first weeks of life, which seemed to require the organized neuronal specificity of the cortex, rather than subcortical systems (for example discriminative responses to faces). It still placed spatial orienting behaviour as primarily a subcortical function.

Specialized visual processing streams within the cortex

The theory based on two visual systems had to expand to at least three, given the burgeoning evidence for a major division within cortical processing. Studies in the macaque, pioneered by Zeki (1974, 1978, 1983a,b), demonstrated distinct extrastriate brain areas containing neurons responding to particular visual attributes, such as an area selective for motion information (V5, also known as MT) and a colour-specific area (V4). Combined with evidence of specific visual losses in human brain damage, this led to the idea of separate cortical modules carrying out distinct visual analyses (Zeki, 1993). These distinct areas came to be seen forming two broad, functionally distinct processing streams, the dorsal and ventral streams proposed by Ungerleider and Mishkin (1982). The dorsal stream (including V5) transmitted information to parietal lobe systems for localizing objects within a spatial array ("where") and was intimately linked to eye movement mechanisms of selective attention. The ventral stream (including V4) processed information for the temporal lobe, concerned with the "what" aspects of objects, such as form, colour and face recognition. Supporting evidence came from other studies on primates (e.g. Boussaoud, Ungerleider, & Desimone, 1990; Merigan & Maunsell, 1993; Van Essen & Maunsell, 1983) and from clinical observations of patients with specific deficits of spatial processing (e.g. Damasio & Benton, 1979), movement perception (Zihl, von Cramon, & Mai, 1983) or object recog-nition (Milner & Goodale, 1995). The new theories emphasized the role of the cortex for both "where" and "what" responses in primates, and were little concerned with the phylogenetically older subcortical tectal system.

The dorsal/ventral division has been associated with a division earlier in the visual pathway, between the parallel parvocellular and magnocellular systems. These systems are distinct morphologically at retina and lateral geniculate nucleus (LGN), project to different parts of primary visual cortex, V1, and continue within independent cortical streams to V4 and V5 (Livingstone & Hubel, 1988; Maunsell & Newsome, 1987; Van Essen & Maunsell, 1983). Parvo cells show the high acuity and wavelength selectivity needed for analysis of form and colour in the ventral stream, while the magnocellular system subserves movement perception and some aspects of stereoscopic vision associated with spatial layout in the dorsal stream. Aspects of adult psychophysical performance can be related to the functioning of the two pathways (reviewed by Merigan & Maunsell, 1993). The development of cortical functions associated with these systems, is discussed later, leading to the suggestion that parvocellular-based systems might become operational slightly earlier in development than magnocellular-based systems (Atkinson, 1992).

More detailed studies have questioned the simple distinctions between these streams. There are many interactions in visual processing between the magno and parvo systems. For example area V3, which contains many orientationally tuned neurons (for form information), projects mainly to parietal cortex (for motion analysis). Particular extrastriate areas should perhaps not be thought of as sensitive to single visual attributes but as combining information in complex analyses; for example, transforming wavelength information in V4 to yield colour constancy (Zeki, 1983b) and the response of V5 cells to the global motion of a pattern rather than its component elements (Movshon, Adelson, Gizzi, & Newsome, 1985). In development, even simple early deficits in a particular pathway can have complex consequences. For example, a motion-processing deficit related to the magnocellular stream has been hypothesized for developmental dyslexics from visual evoked potentials (Livingstone, Rosen, Drislane, & Galaburda, 1991), elevated motion coherence thresholds (Cornellissen et al., 1995; Witton et al., 1998), and motion responses of area V5 revealed by functional brain imaging (Eden et al., 1996). It is possible to imagine how an early deficit in motion processing might involve eye movement control and lead, by a developmental cascade, to impaired acquisition of reading skills.

"What?", "who?", "where?" and "how?": Multiple visual action systems

Milner and Goodale (1995) have suggested that the ventral and dorsal streams should not be primarily distinguished by their sensitivity to properties such as colour and movement. Rather, they have different behavioural functions: The ventral stream is concerned with perceptual processing for functions such as face recognition and the dorsal with controlling actions; "who" and "how" would be an alternative description to "what" and "where". Within these two broad streams, Milner and Goodale suggest loosely connected multiple modules. The idea of separate neural substrates for distinct visuomotor action systems, each consisting of linked cortical and subcortical areas, had been suggested by earlier studies, in kittens and monkeys (e.g. Hein & Held, 1967; Trevarthen, 1968; Vital-Durand, Putkonen, & Jeannerod, 1974).

There is now substantial information about many of these distinct action modules in primates. The schematic model of some of these circuits in Fig. 3.1 draws

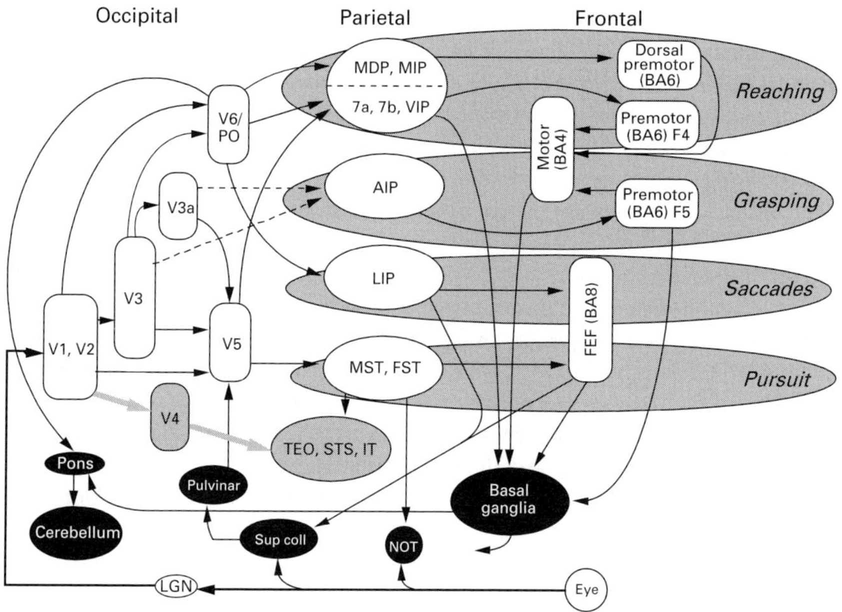

Figure 3.1. Schematic diagram of areas and connections involved in four distinct action streams in the primate brain (based on information reviewed by Milner & Goodale, 1995; Jeannerod, 1988, 1997; Rizzolatti et al., 1997). AIP = anterior intraparietal; BA = Brodmann area; BA6 = Brodmann area 6 etc.; F4, F5 = frontal areas; FEF = frontal eye field; FST = fundus of the superior temporal sulcus; IT = inferior temporal; LGN = lateral geniculate nucleus; LIP = lateral intraparietal; MDP = mediodorsal parietal; MIP = medial intraparietal; MST = middle superior temporal; NOT = nucleus of the optic tract; PO = parietal-occipital; STS = superior temporal sulcus; sup coll = superior colliculus; TEO = posterior inferior temporal; V1, V2 = visual area 1 etc.

on the extensive reviews of Milner and Goodale (1995) and Jeannerod (1997). For example, Jeannerod has argued that the dorsal stream, transmitting visual information to primary motor cortex (M1), has separate divisions for reaching and grasping. One route links the visual parieto-occipital area (PO) with dorsal premotor cortex, both directly and via areas in the intraparietal sulcus (superior parietal module). This system is important in directional coding of movements towards objects (reaching). A second route, passing from dorsal extrastriate cortex via the anterior intraparietal area to ventral premotor cortex, transforms intrinsic visual attributes of objects into the motor commands required for effective grasping.

As mentioned previously, dorsal and ventral streams might have different developmental courses. However, this analysis makes clear that different developmental timing might also occur for different modules within a stream, and this is apparent in infants' development of the multiple dorsal-stream modules controlling different actions. The major milestones of exploratory head and eye movements, directed reaching and grasping, and locomotion each involve integrated function of a different action module. Each must involve some spatial analysis of the visual layout, but the different systems need representations at different scales and with different frames of reference. For reaching and grasping, the infant needs only a representation of space near the body, and an egocentric frame of reference for matching object locations to hand actions. For locomotion, the child needs to represent the environment on a scale beyond arm's length, and with a reference frame that remains stable in space as the body moves (allocentric representation).

Some initial visual analysis of space and motion in the dorsal stream will be common to the action systems of visual exploration, manual exploration, and locomotive exploration. Elaboration of specific spatial representations, and coupling these into appropriate motor programs, follow this early processing. The developmental sequence of action systems might result from the greater complexity of integration required for some spatial representations compared to others. For example, for successful walking to a goal, mechanisms for analysing target distance and direction in the central field of view must be integrated with information about the ground surface and the direction of travel, derived from peripheral optic flow and vestibular information, to control an elaborate dynamic sequence of limb and postural movements. Reaching and grasping, by contrast, make little use of optic flow and vestibular signals and require depth and distance about the target itself, plus obstacles, in a restricted and stable zone of nearby space.

The distinction between egocentric and allocentric representations of space, which has been widely discussed in the context of development, also appears in the neuroscience of adult function. O'Keefe and Burgess (1996) have proposed models for these separate types of representation, guiding actions in nearby space on the one hand and larger scale navigation on the other, involving parietal and hippocampal circuits. Although many developmental studies have attempted to dissociate these two systems of spatial cognition and visual memory, especially using search paradigms (Newcombe & Huttenlocher, 2000), we still know little about them in neural terms.

Development of visual attention

As well as these overt action systems, there must be internal covert systems of attention and memory. Traditionally, visual attention was viewed as a unitary, supramodal mechanism subserved by separate anatomical systems from those involved in perceptual processing (La Berge & Brown, 1989; Posner, 1980; Posner & Petersen, 1990). More recently, two attentional brain systems have been postulated, a posterior system subserving spatial attention and an anterior system involved in various complex cognitive tasks (Posner & Dehaene, 1994).

An alternative approach is to consider attention as a mechanism of "selection for action" (Allport, 1989), the action being either a saccade or a bodily movement towards the object of interest. Such motor acts have been taken as indicators of a shift of *overt* attention. Rizzolatti and others (e.g. Berthoz, 1996; Rizzolatti, 1983; Rizzolatti & Camarda, 1987) have proposed a "premotor" theory of attention, according to which *covert* attention without fixating the object of interest exploits the same selection-for-action mechanism. In this theory, selective attention to a spatial location would involve activity in a number of action modules. The theory is supported by neurophysiological studies showing that parietal and frontal areas contain representations related to spatial actions, and that damage to these areas causes both inattention (neglect) and motor deficits related to particular parts of space. It is also supported by reaction time studies showing interactions between deployment of attention and the execution of motor programs (e.g. Downing & Pinker, 1985; Rizzolatti, Riggio, Dascola, & Umilta, 1987; Sheliga, Craighero, Riggio, & Rizzolatti, 1997; Sheliga, Riggio, & Rizzolatti, 1995).

Whether or not this premotor theory provides a complete account of adult attention, it is valuable in a developmental context where evidence for attention control comes from overt orienting acts. We can assess the development of attentional control in the first 3 months in terms of the latency of selecting a target for fixation (Atkinson & Braddick, 1985; Atkinson, Hood, Braddick, & Wattam-Bell, 1988a; Atkinson, Hood, Wattam-Bell, & Braddick, 1992). At this age, reaching and grasping are not well developed: the development of attentional coupling between target selection in these motor systems is discussed later in the section "Integration of subcortical orienting systems with cortical systems for attentional control of eye and head movements".

Attention is both a bottom-up and a top-down process; the target of attention is determined by "salience" arising out of stimulus processing, and by the current goals of behaviour. Developmental changes in attention-related behaviour will reflect changes in the nature of the processing and in the nature of the goals, as well as changes in the mechanisms of attention themselves.

Summary of the current developmental model

Figure 3.2 illustrates our account of the developmental sequence and the broad neural processes corresponding to it. From an initial subcortical stage, the functions of specific cortical channels develop, followed by integrative processes across channels so that the infant can build up internal representations of objects and individuals. This aspect of the developing processes takes place largely within the ventral stream, with dynamic online information contributed from the dorsal stream to control orienting by eye and head movements. Of course, colour, shape, and texture information must be integrated with motion information at a relatively early stage so that objects can be segregated from each other and from their background. These processes provide object representations that must be integrated with dorsal-stream spatial information to allow, later, emergence of the visual action systems for reaching, grasping, and locomotion. These action

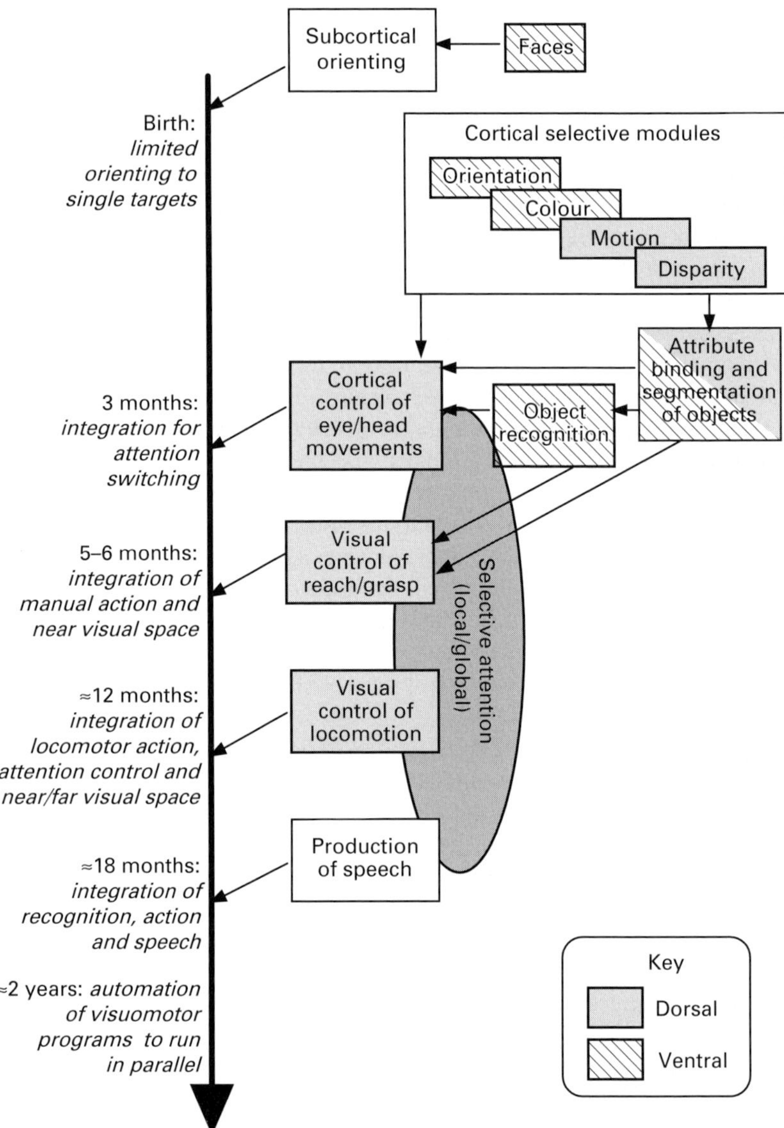

Figure 3.2. Model of the developmental sequence of visual behaviour (Lef-hand vertical line) and ventral- and dorsal-stream neural systems contributing to this (right-hand boxes).

systems combine visual attentional systems and motor systems; we do not postulate separate attentional systems.

It is oversimple, however, to show this as a linear sequence; there are likely to be important feedback loops, by which a new development can affect the way that earlier established processes work. Furthermore, a description of the sequence is only the start. We would like to be able to explain timing differences within a stage—why do some processes start to function earlier than others? How far are we seeing the unfolding of a genetically controlled maturational sequence, and how far does the developmental trajectory depend on exposure to the environment, including the kinds of exposure made possible by earlier stages?

In the following sections we outline some of these stages and the evidence for them. The level of detail, both in theory and experiment, varies greatly reflecting the depth of our knowledge.

The newborn orienting system

There is general agreement that the newborn has a "where?" system, largely under subcortical control, which orients the head and eyes to abrupt and significant changes in the world. In the visual domain these are usually changes in luminance or movement. We have studied this system using, mainly, a simple fixation shift paradigm (Atkinson & Braddick, 1985; Atkinson et al., 1992). Newborn infants make a shift of the head and eyes from a central target to a peripheral target, which appears at the moment when the central target disappears. Responses to a peripheral stimulus, when the central target continues to engage fixation, require modulation of this orienting system by cortical processes (see p. 57). In some infants who have suffered perinatal brain damage involving both cortical and subcortical areas (and in particular the basal ganglia), even the primitive orienting system might not be functional (Atkinson & Hood, 1994; Mercuri et al., 1996, 1997a,b).

This orienting system probably operates, across domains and sensory modalities, as a non-specific alerting system. The superior colliculus is strongly implicated within this system, although other subcortical circuits might be involved in different response components. The role of subcortical systems, and their interaction with the cortex, in motion processing is discussed later.

FUNCTIONAL ONSET OF SPECIFIC CORTICAL MODULES

Cortical stimulus selectivity: Orientation

Primate research has shown highly specific stimulus selectivity in cortical neurons, and the development of such selectivity forms the main line of evidence for visual cortical development. For example, many cells in the primary visual cortex respond best to contours of a particular orientation (Hubel & Wiesel, 1977) and such orientation tuning is not generally found in subcortical parts of the visual pathways (except from cortical feedback, e.g. Sillito, Cudeiro, & Murphy, 1993). Tests of orientation selectivity in the infant can measure this aspect of cortical development.

Such a test is the orientation-reversal visual evoked potential (VEP) or visual event-related potential (VERP). The VEP is a stimulus-related electrical signal arising from mass neural activity, measured non-invasively from the surface of the head. It can be identified as a statistically reliable, repetitive signal at a frequency related to the alternation of stimuli of two different orientations. With a suitable stimulus sequence, this signal provides evidence for orientation-selective mechanisms. We first found just such a response to an orientation change (OR-VEP) in 6–8-week-olds but not in newborns (Braddick, 1993; Braddick et al., 1986).

Behavioural indicators of orientation discrimination can also provide evidence for such mechanisms. Using paired, static grating patterns in a habituation–recovery test, both Slater and colleagues (Slater, Morison, & Somers, 1988) and ourselves (Atkinson et al., 1988b) showed discrimination performance by newborns between gratings oriented at 45 degrees and 135 degrees. This newborn performance might seem at odds with the VEP evidence for later emergence of selectivity. However, the VEP test, unlike the discrimination test, requires the use of dynamically alternating gratings. When the same dynamic frequencies are used for each test, behavioural and VEP results are in line (Braddick, 1993; Hood, Atkinson, Braddick, & Wattam-Bell, 1992). Infants show orientation selectivity for stimuli alternating at 3 reversal/s by 1 month of age, but only respond to 8 reversal/s at around 2 months. This is not simply an overall improvement of response to rapidly changing stimuli; the simpler pattern-reversal VEP response can be seen for either frequency at birth. Rather, the mechanism generating the orientation-reversal response has its own temporal sensitivity, which matures rapidly in the early weeks of life. It is possible that the development of the orientation-reversal response for high temporal frequencies reflects an increasing contribution of the magnocellular system, which is known to respond better than the parvo system to rapidly changing stimuli (Derrington & Lennie, 1982). Other reasons for believing that this system, which provides the main input for motion processing, lags behind the parvocellular in its contribution to cortical development (Atkinson, 1992) are discussed later.

The orientation-reversal VEP, as well as being an index of normal visual cortical development, has proved to be a sensitive indicator of cortical function and deficit in the development of at-risk infants (Atkinson et al., 1994; Mercuri et al., 1998, 1999).

Directional selectivity

A second kind of selectivity, found in cortical cells but not at earlier levels in the visual pathway, is selectivity for specific directions of motion. It is important to distinguish this from a non-specific response to motion, which could simply reflect sensitivity to local contrast or luminance changes. Such a sensitivity is implied by infants' preference for moving over static stimuli (Volkmann & Dobson, 1976), but does not necessarily indicate any ability to encode the direction of motion.

True direction selectivity can be approached in a similar way to orientation selectivity, isolating the response of direction-selective neurons with a "designer stimulus". This is a moving random dot pattern, whose direction reverses four times a second, embedded in a sequence of "jumps" in which the dots are replaced with a new random pattern. The jumps control for responses to stimulus transients that could arise in non-directional neurons. Using this method, a significant directional response was first found at a median age of 10 weeks in normal infants (Wattam-Bell, 1991).

A converging approach is to use behavioural discrimination, indicated either by habituation–recovery or by preferential looking. In the latter method, one side of the screen contains motion contrast between oppositely moving regions. This structure can be detected only by a visual system sensitive to difference in direction. A series of experiments using these behavioural measures show a slightly earlier onset of direction selectivity than the VEP measures, at around 7–8 weeks (Braddick, 1993; Wattam-Bell, 1996a). Further experiments showed that the absence of the response in younger infants was not a consequence: (1) of testing an inappropriate speed; (2) of no preference for motion-defined structure, even if direction selectivity was present (Wattam-Bell, 1996b,c); or (3) of an inability to compare directional signals across the field (Wattam-Bell, 1996d). On the contrary, motion-defined structure seems necessary to evoke directional discriminations at 8 weeks, a finding supporting the view that object segmentation is key aspect of perceptual development and of the motion system.

In summary, a range of techniques provide converging evidence that cortical direction selectivity does not emerge before 7–8 weeks, significantly later than orientation selectivity. Evidence that a distinct, subcortical system sensitive to motion direction operates from birth will be discussed in a later section.

Cortical binocularity

A third feature of visual cortical organization, not found lower in the visual pathway, is binocularity. That is, cortical neurons integrate inputs from the two eyes, and respond specifically when they receive correlated images. Binocular neurons are generally disparity-selective, that is, they respond optimally to a particular positional relationship (disparity) between left and right eye image elements, providing the substrate for stereoscopic depth perception.

One way to test the development of cortical binocularity is to examine responses specific to binocular correlation. A random-dot correlogram is a dynamic display, which alternates between the right- and left-eye images being identical and being opposite in contrast (anticorrelated). Extensive studies have shown that VEP responses to dynamic correlograms are absent at birth and normally appear between 8–20 weeks, with a median age around 13 weeks (Braddick et al., 1980, 1983; Wattam-Bell, Braddick, Atkinson, & Day, 1987). A related display, with one half containing large correlated and anticorrelated checks, can be used in a preferential looking test. VEP and preferential looking tests on the same infants show onsets of binocularity by the different measures within 2 weeks of each other (Smith, 1989; Smith, Atkinson, Braddick, & Wattam-Bell, 1988).

Sensitivity to stereo disparity provides a slightly different approach, but the results are very similar. Behavioural studies with a wide variety of disparity-defined stimuli (Birch, 1993; Birch, Gwiazda, & Held, 1982; Fox, Aslin, Shea, & Dumais, 1980; Held, Birch, & Gwiazda, 1980; Smith, 1989; Smith et al., 1988), concur in finding an onset of cortical binocular processing, typically between 12 and 16 weeks of age.

There is a close relationship between binocular processing and precise alignment of the two eyes; both are required if sensitivity to stimulus correlation and disparity is to be revealed. It might be, therefore that a lack of oculomotor control conceals cortical binocular connectivity that is established from an early age. However, the evidence is against this: many infants before 8 weeks show appropriate adjustments of binocular alignment (Aslin, 1993; Hainline & Riddell, 1995, 1996); in congenitally strabismic infants who cannot align their eyes, disparity sensitivity shows a similar age of onset when the stimuli are corrected for their misalignment (Birch, 1993; Birch & Stager, 1985); and stimuli designed to be insensitive to eye alignment give a similar age of onset for normal infants (Birch, Gwiazda, & Held, 1983). In summary, a very wide body of data shows cortical binocular interaction becoming functional on average between 12 and 16 weeks, albeit with significant individual variations.

Relationship between cortical selective properties

Figure 3.3 schematizes the development of these three areas of cortical function. There is a period between 1 and 4 months of age when the visual cortex is undergoing very rapid qualitative and quantitative development in neuronal selectivity. In this period a dramatic increase begins in the number of synapses in visual cortex (Huttenlocher et al., 1982); presumably these synapses provide the rich connectivity upon which selective cortical processing depends. However, the various aspects of selectivity do not emerge together; rather, there is a clear developmental ordering, with orientation selectivity first, followed by direction selectivity, and then selectivity to binocular relations. The latter two aspects of selectivity are associated with input to the cortex from the magnocellular pathway, and processing within the cortex by the dorsal stream (Livingstone & Hubel, 1988), suggesting that the initial development of this pathway might be slower than that of the parvocellular–ventral pathway that specializes in form and colour processing. Two other relevant factors are the need for temporal precision and for spatially extended connections. Effective motion processing requires consistent timing of visual transmission to the cortex, which is likely to depend on the progressive myelination of the visual pathway to a greater degree than static pattern processing. Motion and disparity processing both require the comparison of information

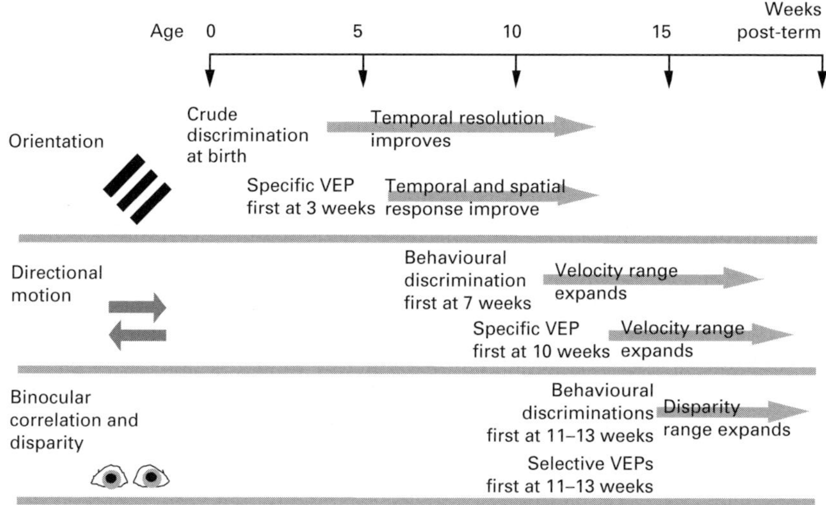

Figure 3.3. Summary of development of cortical selective systems. Ages are approximate. VEP, visual evoked potential.

between separate positions and hence the establishment of orderly horizontal connections in cortex. After the initial onset, infants' directional sensitivity develops to progressively greater displacements (Wattam-Bell 1992, 1996a) and binocular sensitivity develops to progressively greater disparities (Wattam-Bell, 1995). This suggests that the range of these connections, increasing with age, might be a limiting factor in the development of these functions.

Cortical–subcortical relations: The case of motion

We have proposed that the visual behaviour of the newborn is mediated by subcortical systems, which come under cortical control in the course of development. Visual motion processing provides an example where this relation can be examined. We discussed earlier evidence that cortical directional processing begins at around 8 weeks of age. However, with uniform movement of a large part of the field of view, even newborns show optokinetic nystagmus (OKN)—the eyes follow the motion and flick back in a repetitive sequence. Such responses, acting to stabilize the retinal image, occur in the visual system of virtually every species. Because the response matches the direction of stimulus motion, it implies the existence of some directional mechanism from birth.

However, this early directionality has an asymmetry, which gives insight into its basis. In infants under 2–3 months, when viewing with one eye alone, OKN can only be driven by a nasalwards movement (i.e. towards the nose), and not in the opposite, temporalwards direction (Atkinson, 1979; Atkinson & Braddick, 1981).

This matches a subcortical pathway in the cat (Hoffman, 1981); each eye projects to the contralateral midbrain nucleus of the optic tract (NOT) where the neurons respond only to the nasalwards direction of motion for that eye. The response to temporalwards motion depends on signals carried from binocular cortical neurons by a descending pathway to the NOT. In newborns, only the subcortical pathway is presumed to operate; the newborn can respond in both directions only because each eye drives the response in one direction. The development of the cortical pathway from 2–3 months is needed to establish the full, bidirectional response for each eye.

Recent evidence suggests that a more complex account is needed of the developing cortical–subcortical interactions in this system. One line comes from children who have undergone the surgical removal of one cerebral hemisphere to relieve intractable epilepsy. Two infants that we studied (Braddick et al., 1992) following surgery at 5 and 8 months of age, showed marked asymmetry of OKN with both binocular and monocular stimulation, with good responses only to movement in the direction towards the decorticate half-field (e.g. for right to left movement if the right hemisphere was removed). If a subcortical system alone could sustain OKN at this age, binocular OKN should be possible in both directions, as these children had intact subcortical systems on both sides. This result suggests either that the subcortical response is programmed to drop out as the cortical system develops (and does so even if the cortex is faulty) or that the intact cortex suppresses subcortical responses on the other side. More recently, we studied a child who was hemispherectomized even earlier, at age 13 weeks (Morrone et al., 1999). By 10 months of age, this patient showed a dominance of OKN towards the damaged half field, like our earlier patients. However, shortly after surgery, each eye showed OKN in the nasalwards direction, like a normal newborn. This case argues that a purely subcortical directional mechanism *can* operate in early infancy, independent of the immature or damaged cortex. However, this appears to be a transient stage of development. Before the end of the first year OKN comes to depend on cortical directional mechanisms and, even if these are disrupted, the subcortical system can no longer sustain the optokinetic response.

A second line of evidence on cortical mechanisms associated with OKN comes from asymmetries of the VEP to monocular movement. Norcia (1996), Norcia, Hamer, and Orel-Bixler (1990), and Norcia et al. (1991) have shown that young infants' viewing an oscillating grating with one eye, show unbalanced VEP responses to the movements in nasal and temporal directions. Our own data show that this asymmetry, if tested at a rate of 6 reversals/s, has almost entirely disappeared by 5 months of life (Braddick, Mercuri, Atkinson, & Wattam-Bell, 1998). Because the VEP is a cortically generated response, these results imply that early directional asymmetry is not exclusively subcortical, and raise the possibility that the directional OKN response of newborns might have a cortical basis. However, the relation between monocular OKN and VEP asymmetries is not straightforward. It is the VEP response to the temporalwards motion that is larger than the nasalwards, i.e. the opposite of the OKN asymmetry (Mason, Braddick, Wattam-Bell, & Atkinson, 2001). The mechanisms of the two asymmetries might be linked, possibly by an inhibitory or compensatory relation, but the asymmetrical cortical response cannot drive OKN directly. Overall, the hypothesis that newborn OKN has a subcortical mechanism still provides the best account, especially given recent data from Birch, Fawcett, and Stager (2000) that the VEP asymmetry was absent in the youngest infants (under 5 weeks). However, the developing cross-talk between cortical and subcortical systems must be quite complex. When other domains of subcortical visual function are explored to the same extent as directional responses, similarly complex relationships to cortical development may be revealed.

DEVELOPMENT OF INTEGRATION ("BINDING") AND SEGMENTATION PROCESSES

The twin processes of integration and segmentation are necessary for the infant to define surfaces and objects, and understand the dynamic spatial layout of the visual world. Both involve the interaction of information from different selective modules (e.g. motion, orientation, disparity), and also interaction across locations within a module to recognize coherence and discontinuity in a particular attribute.

We have demonstrated the existence of binding/segmentation processes in the orientation system by 2 months of age (Atkinson & Braddick, 1993). Infants showed preferential looking to a patch defined by contrast between oriented textures. This ability has also been demonstrated in older infants using a slightly different stimulus (Sireteanu & Rieth, 1993).

The sensitivity to motion-defined structure, described earlier, also reflects segmentation and binding for common motion and is the basis of a number of our motion studies (e.g. Wattam-Bell, 1992). "Second order" motion is the perceived motion of an area defined by its static or dynamic texture, and this can also be demonstrated in infants at the onset of directional sensitivity (Braddick, Atkinson, & Hood, 1996a).

INTEGRATION OF SUBCORTICAL ORIENTING SYSTEMS WITH CORTICAL SYSTEMS FOR ATTENTIONAL CONTROL OF EYE AND HEAD MOVEMENTS

The crude subcortical system, described earlier, will orient to a single salient target. However, it works much less effectively when a peripheral stimulus appears but the central target remains visible (Atkinson & Braddick, 1985; Atkinson et al., 1992). Disengagement from one object to switch attention to another appears to require cortical modulation of the orienting system (probably by parietofrontal systems)—a modulation whose effects can be mapped by varying the interval between offset of one target and onset of another (Hood & Atkinson, 1993). More complex cortical modulation can be seen in the development of "inhibition of return" (Hood, 1993). The cortical contribution to attention is vulnerable to brain damage (Atkinson & Hood, 1994; Braddick et al., 1992; Hood & Atkinson, 1990; Mercuri et al., 1996); in infants with either focal lesions or diffuse hypoxic–ischaemic damage, we have identified "sticky fixation"—an inability to easily switch visual attention from one target to another, similar to that sometimes seen in adult stroke patients with "visual neglect".

DEVELOPMENT OF REACHING AND GRASPING ACTION MODULES

The visual action systems controlling reaching and grasping, from 4 to 6 months onwards, require two kinds of visual processing. First, the location of the object, laterally and in distance, must be identified. Second, visual analysis must determine whether the object is a suitable target for reaching.

For the first, the co-occurrence of the development of binocularity around 4 months (Braddick, 1996) and the emergence of visually guided reaching suggests that binocular disparity information is a key input to the reaching module. Supporting this, we find that binocular information is critical in determining the kinematics of infants' reaches (Braddick, Atkinson, & Hood, 1996b).

From 6 to 9 months, reaching appears as a quite compulsive behaviour for small objects presented within arm's length. This behaviour raises the question of what visual information an infant uses to determine that an object is graspable and hence a suitable target for reaching. The same information also needs to be processed by the distinct module that controls the shaping and timing of the grasp (Jeannerod, 1997). However, infants who do not show the preshaping of the hand that indicates grasp preparation, still need information about object size and shape as an input for the selection of a reaching target. Graspability is probably computed by the anterior intraparietal (AIP) area in the grasping module of Fig. 3.1, but feeds into the reaching module to determine target selection.

The development of distinct visuomotor modules, and their ultimate integration, is illustrated by experiments that combine preferential looking with preferential reaching (Newman, Atkinson, & Braddick, 2001). Preferential looking, extensively used to analyse infants' visual information processing, depends on the orienting response of head and eyes towards the most salient object or region in the visual field. Presentation of paired stimuli allows the relative salience of these stimuli to be assessed at a given stage of development. Depending on the development of the various cortical modules, salience is a function of luminance, colour, motion, or depth contrast, and of spatial structure defined by such contrast. It also depends on novelty (as in habituation tests) and on the special significance of certain stimuli such as faces. Salience, so defined, is computed by the cortical modules, which contribute to the orienting system (providing output through the superior colliculus). When presented with two 3D objects, similar in shape and surface but different in size, infants tend to orient to the larger object (King et al., 1996; Newman et al., 2001).

However, reaching is only an appropriate response for objects that are small enough to be grasped. Thus, target size as well as location must be computed by the modules that provide visual information to control this response (Pryde, Roy, & Campbell, 1998). This computation is not necessarily possible at the age when the motor schema of reaching becomes available but, when it is possible, it will preferentially direct reaching to the smaller of two objects, when the larger is beyond the span of the infant's hand.

Thus the visuomotor systems for orienting and reaching might be driven by different visual information from the same pair of objects. Work by King and Newman in our group showed that these systems interact differently at different ages. Figure 3.4 schematizes possible organizations of this interaction at each stage. Infants' first reaches (up to 8 months), do not show a significant preference between large and small objects. However, reaching is predominantly directed to the object they initially fixate. We infer that processing of the visual attributes signifying graspability is not yet linked into a visuomotor module for reaching, and that there is at this stage coupling between this system and that determining orienting (stage 1).

Between 8 and 12 months, a strong preference emerges for reaching for the smaller object that is within the span of the infant's hand (i.e. graspable). Thus an effective visual analysis of graspability has developed and provides an input to the reaching control system. At this age there is some decoupling of reaching and initial orienting—infants are more likely than previously to first fixate one object and then reach for another. This decoupling can be manipulated through visual salience: A schematic face on one object increases preference for looking at that object, without altering graspability and hence without a corresponding increase in the reaching preference (Newman, 2001; Newman et al., 1999).

After 12 months, reaching becomes less selective towards the smaller object, perhaps because reaching behaviour has become less compulsive, and also because the infant can grasp larger objects. At the same time, reaching and initial looking become more congruent again. It appears that the orienting and reaching systems can be integrated into a single goal-directed behaviour.

This example could serve as a model for the development of other visuomotor modules. Initially, the visual computation needed to guide a particular action is immature, and the specificity of the visuomotor module is crude. As the specialized visual processing develops, the visuomotor module becomes functional, but it might not be well integrated with other behaviours that have their own visual control. Eventually, the new module comes to function effectively alongside established visuomotor modules, entraining them into coordinated behavioural sequences when required.

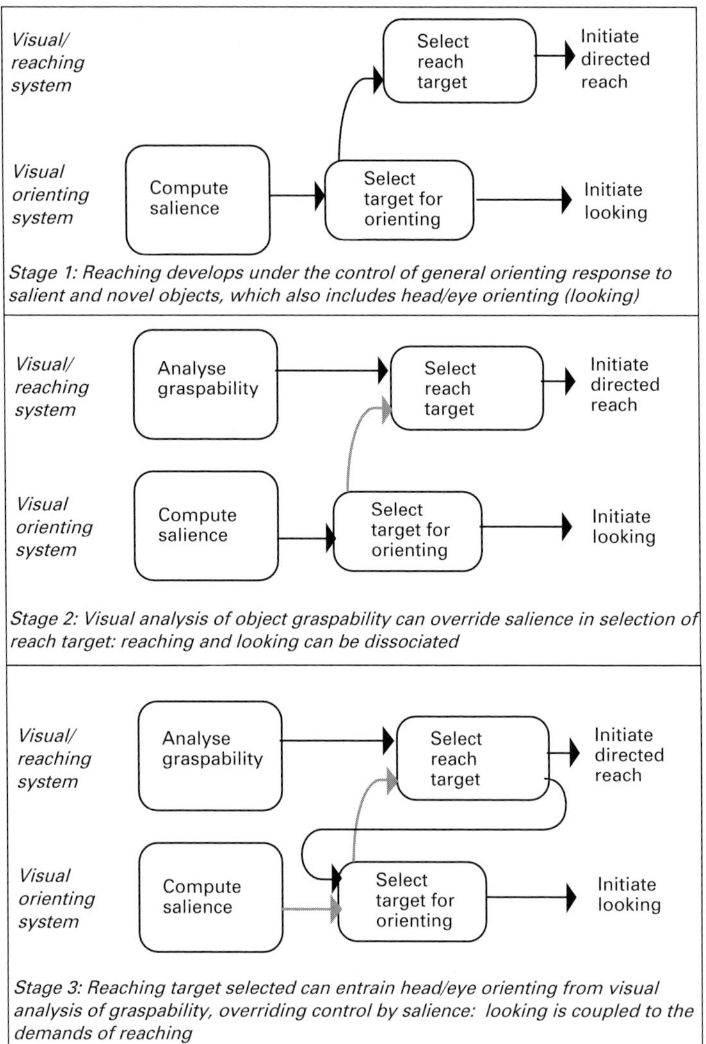

Figure 3.4. Suggested stages in the development of action systems controlling looking and reaching, and their interaction (based on the preferential reaching/preferential looking experiments of Newman, 2001; Newman et al., 1999).

Development of locomotion and shifts of scale/distance

Such integration must be required in the development of locomotion. For instance, an object is processed in far space as a target for locomotion, and brought into near space as a target for reaching. The child must become able to switch attention from near to far, and to engage the visual processes required at each scale. Other visual behaviour also requires such shifts, e.g. joint attention invoked by an adult's pointing gesture, also achieved around the beginning of the second year (Butterworth & Grover, 1990). The challenge remains for further research to characterize and understand these integration and switching processes.

ABNORMAL DEVELOPMENT OF DORSAL AND VENTRAL STREAMS

The broad division between the dorsal and ventral functions is reflected in abnormal development. We have studied development with tasks designed to compare the two streams in several groups of young children with atypical developmental profiles—children with Williams syndrome (WS), autism, and perinatal brain damage resulting in focal lesions and hemiplegia. A general finding has been that, in abnormal development, the dorsal stream is more likely to be affected than the ventral. This has led us to a general hypothesis of "dorsal stream vulnerability" (Atkinson et al., 2002, in press; Spencer et al., 2000).

Ventral and dorsal stream processing in children with Williams Syndrome

Children with Williams syndrome typically show a very uneven profile of neuropsychological development, with relatively strong expressive language abilities, combined with unusual semantics, good face recognition, but spatial cognition severely impaired (see, for example, Atkinson et al., 2001; Bellugi et al., 1988, 1990, 1994, 1999; Bertrand, Mervis, & Eisenberg, 1997; Karmiloff-Smith, 1998; Klein & Mervis, 1999; Pezzini et al., 1999). They reach motor milestones later than typically developing children, often being delayed in learning to walk and in fine motor skills. On a standardized test of motor function (Motor ABC; Henderson & Sugden, 1992) they show an average delay of at least 2 years (Atkinson et al., 1996). Problems that persist into later life include uncertainty when negotiating stairs or uneven surfaces (Atkinson et al., 1996) and difficulty with the use of everyday tools.

This profile is consistent with ventral processes (e.g. face recognition), being relatively unimpaired but abnormal development of dorsal function for visual control of action. We have explored this possibility in several ways. First, we have compared two tests that both require global integration by extrastriate visual areas—motion coherence thresholds, which are believed to depend on dorsal stream area V5, and form coherence thresholds, which relate to the kind of integration performed by neurons in ventral stream area V4. The independence of the brain areas involved in these tasks has been demonstrated by functional imaging (Braddick et al. 2000). Many (but by no means all) children with Williams syndrome find considerable difficulty with the motion task relative to the form task (Atkinson et al., 2002, in press). These Williams syndrome children are found right across the age range from 4 years to adulthood. This pattern is also found in some younger, typically developing children (4–5 years) and so, although the results are in line with the "dorsal vulnerability" hypothesis, they suggest a more general delay with ability never approaching adult levels, but asymptoting at the 4–5 year level.

Other tasks look more directly at visual control of action. The post-box task is based on a striking dissociation found in Goodale, Milner, Jakobson, and Carey's (1991) testing of a ventral-stream-impaired patient. She could accurately post a card through an oriented slot (dorsal control of action) but failed on perceptual matching of the slot orientation (ventral processing for perception and recognition). We found that children with Williams syndrome showed much greater inaccuracy in posting the card than when matching its orientation to the slot, compared to the relative skills of normally developing children (Atkinson et al., 1997). This result supports the account of a dorsal stream deficit, although again the degree of deficit was quite varied between individuals.

As discussed in earlier sections (see Fig. 3.1), the dorsal stream is not a unitary channel but contains functionally and anatomically distinct pathways related to different action systems. Consequently, particular aspects of dorsal stream function could be selectively impaired in Williams syndrome, or might display atypical patterns of linkage. In our group, Newman (2001), has explored this issue by comparing children with Williams syndrome and normally developing children over a wide age range, on several novel visuomotor tasks involving planning, reaching, and grasping.

One task compared the control of action with perceptual judgement of object size. In normal adults, the opening of the hand during a reaching movement is finely calibrated to the target size (Jeannerod, 1988), but this is absent or impaired in patients with parietal damage (Goodale et al., 1993; Jakobson et al., 1991). In Newman's tests, children selected a square to match a sample and picked it up, giving a matching estimate, a measurement of hand aperture, and data on the kinematics of reaching, from a single action. Children with Williams syndrome showed greater matching errors than normally developing children at any age. They also showed markedly less adjustment of grip aperture to target size, leading to smaller mean apertures (in contrast to adults in whom visual or proprioceptive information is degraded, who compensate with an increase in aperture; Berthier et al., 1996; Haggard & Wing, 1995; Jakobson & Goodale, 1991).

Detailed reaching behaviour was also different in children with Williams syndrome: they made slower reaches, with more movement segments, suggesting that they were less able to programme accurately the reach as a whole. These results suggest that children with Williams syndrome are controlling their reaches less automatically than typically developing children, with greater use of online visual feedback control. There appears to be a continuing immaturity in Williams syndrome in the dorsal stream modules controlling reaching and grasping. However, the matching data show problems in Williams syndrome in both "ventral" and "dorsal" aspects of the task.

Visual information in motor planning

Programming the target location of a reach is just one aspect of motor planning based on dorsal-stream visual information. Preparation of an object-oriented movement requires two other forms of planning. Object-based planning uses dorsal-stream analysis of the object's visual properties to prepare the grasping action—scaling grip aperture to object size is one example. End-state planning also involves the intended use or end-state of the object. For example, in picking up a screwdriver, different grips must be chosen for applying it to a screw or for giving the handle to another person. This requires the ability to predict the positions of the object and the limb at the end of the movement. End-state planning probably involves integration of dorsal stream information with prefrontal areas involved in inhibiting inappropriate actions and coordinating the elements of action sequences.

In the post-box task (Atkinson et al., 1997), children with Williams syndrome often found their hands in awkward postures as they rotated the card, suggesting poor end-state planning. This was tested explicitly by Newman (2001), using a handle rotation task adapted from Rosenbaum et al. (1992). The child has to grasp a handle and turn it through 180 degrees, to direct a pointer to a particular target. A simple stereotypical strategy is to use the same grip (thumb upwards) on every trial. A second strategy involves object-based planning: the thumb is placed towards the pointer (the focus of attention in the task) whether this is up or down. Neither strategy leads consistently to a comfortable end-state. In normal development between ages 4 and 8, children move from the second strategy to full end-state planning (Smyth & Mason, 1997). Even the youngest normal children in our study (3 years) showed the thumb-towards bias, and most typically developing children showed end-state planning by 7 years.

Children with Williams syndrome show more mixed patterns, unrelated to either chronological or mental (vocabulary) age. Many reach stereotypically using thumb-up grip regardless of target or pointer position. Others showed inconsistent grip choices, with many, for instance, equally likely to choose a thumb-towards or thumb-away grip. Both patterns are very rare in typically developing children over 4 years. The children with Williams syndrome either do not attempt end-state planning or are unable to make the spatial transformations required to predict the end-state correctly.

Overall, these studies found subtle and variable deficits in the use of dorsal-stream information to control manual action, although not necessarily dissociated from ventral-stream performance. The deficits were most striking beyond the early stages of visual processing for actions, in the use of visuospatial information for end-state planning. There might well be a "cascade" effect, with early abnormalities in the dorsal pathway affecting later development of complex feedback loops involved in visuomotor planning, which remain apparent even if the lower level effects are overcome. The individual variability highlights how adaptive strategies can lead to differently configured systems even if from a common initial developmental deficit, and might indicate possible goals of remediation.

CONCLUSIONS

We have discussed the example of Williams syndrome because it illustrates how analysis in terms of visuomotor modules is a necessary and helpful way to consider the development of visual information processing in the brain. The function of the visual system is to enable effective interaction with the environment. The perspective presented here sees the processes of visual development, both normal and abnormal, as built around this interaction, which combines aspects of what have been traditionally considered perception, cognition, and motor control. From this perspective, the main conclusions we have argued are:

1. The cortical systems underlying vision develop in two-way interaction with subcortical systems.
2. Cortical development shows the staged development of subsystems within the dorsal and ventral streams.
3. The dorsal stream shows greater vulnerability during development.
4. Behavioural milestones depend on the emergence of distinct visuomotor modules.
5. These modules first differentiate, then become coupled for integrative behaviour.
6. The development of spatial attention is intimately linked with target selection and planning in visual-motor systems.

ACKNOWLEDGEMENTS

We thank the Medical Research Council, University of Cambridge, and University College London for support of the research whose results are described in this chapter. We thank the many members of the Visual Development Unit who have contributed to it, our academic and clinical collaborators in paediatrics and ophthalmology, and the families whose participation has made this research possible. We thank the Williams Syndrome Foundation for their support and cooperation.

REFERENCES

Allport, A. (1989). Visual attention. In M.I. Posner (Ed.), *Foundations of cognitive science*. Cambridge, MA: MIT Press.

Aslin, R.N. (1993). Infant accommodation and convergence. In K. Simons (Ed.), *Early visual development: Normal and abnormal*. New York: Oxford University Press.

Atkinson, J. (1979). Development of optokinetic nystagmus in the human infant and monkey infant: An analogue to development in kittens. In R.D. Freeman (Ed.), *Developmental neurobiology of vision* (NATO Advanced Study Institute Series). New York: Plenum Press.

Atkinson, J. (1984). Human visual development over the first six months of life. A review and a hypothesis. *Human Neurobiology, 3*, 61–74.

Atkinson, J. (1992). Early visual development: Differential functioning of parvocellular and magnocellular pathways. *Eye, 6*, 129–135.

Atkinson, J. (2000). *The developing visual brain*. Oxford: Oxford University Press.

Atkinson, J. Anker, S., Macpherson, F., Nokes, L., Andrew, R., & Braddick, O. (2001). Visual and visuo-spatial development in young children with Williams Syndrome. *Developmental Medicine and Child Neurology, 43*, 330–337.

Atkinson, J., & Braddick, O.J. (1981). Development of optokinetic nystagmus in infants: An indicator of cortical binocularity? In D.F. Fisher, R.A. Monty, & J.W. Senders (Eds.), *Eye movements: Cognition and visual perception*. Hillsdale, NJ: Lawrence Erlbaum Associates Inc.

Atkinson, J., & Braddick, O.J. (1985). Early development of the control of visual attention. *Perception, 14*, A25.

Atkinson, J., & Braddick, O.J. (1993). Visual segmentation of oriented textures by infants. *Behavioural Brain Research, 49*, 123–131.

Atkinson, J., Braddick, O., Anker, S., Curran, W., & Andrew, R. (in press). Neurobiological models of visuo-spatial cognition in young Williams syndrome children: Measures of dorsal stream and frontal function. *Developmental Neuropsychology.*

Atkinson, J., Braddick, O., Anker, S., Ehrlich, D., Macpherson, F., Rae, S. et al. (1996). *Development of sensory, perceptual, and cognitive vision and visual attention in young Williams Syndrome children*. Presentation and poster at the Seventh International Professional Conference on Williams syndrome, King of Prussia, PA. July 1996.

Atkinson, J., Braddick, O., Lin, M.H., Curran, W., Guzzetta, A., & Cioni, G. (1999). Form and motion coherence: Is there a dorsal stream vulnerability in development? *Investigative Ophthalmology and Visual Science, 40*, S395.

Atkinson, J., & Hood, B. (1994). Deficits of selective visual attention in children with focal lesions. *Infant Behaviour and Development, 17*, 423.

Atkinson, J., Hood, B., Braddick, O.J., & Wattam-Bell, J. (1988a). Infants' control of fixation shifts with single and competing targets: Mechanisms of shifting attention. *Perception, 17*, 367–368.

Atkinson, J., Hood, B., Wattam-Bell, J., Anker, S., & Tricklebank, J. (1988b). Development of orientation discrimination in infancy. *Perception, 17*, 587–595.

Atkinson, J., Hood, B., Wattam-Bell J., & Braddick, O.J. (1992). Changes in infants' ability to switch visual attention in the first three months of life. *Perception, 21*, 643–653.

Atkinson, J., King, J., Braddick, O.J., Nokes, L., Anker, S., & Braddick, F. (1997). A specific deficit of dorsal stream function in Williams' syndrome. *NeuroReport*, 8, 1919–1922.

Atkinson, J., Weeks, F., Anker, S., Rae, S., Macpherson, F., & Hughes, C. (1994). VEP and behavioural measures for delayed visual development in VLBW infants. *Strabismus, 2*, 42.

Bellugi, U., Bihrle, A., Trauner, D., Jernigan, T., & Doherty, S. (1990). Neuropsychological, neurological, and neuroanatomical profile of Williams syndrome children. *American Journal of Medical Genetics (Suppl.), 6*, 115–125.

Bellugi, U., Lichtenberger, L., Mills, D., Galaburda, A., & Korenberg, J.R. (1999). Bridging cognition, the brain, and molecular genetics: Evidence from Williams syndrome. *Trends in Neurosciences, 22*, 197–207.

Bellugi, U., Sabo, H., & Vaid, J. (1988). Spatial deficits in children with Williams syndrome. In J. Stiles-Davis, M. Kritchevsky, & U. Bellugi (Eds.), *Spatial cognition: Brain bases and development*. Hillsdale NJ: Lawrence Erlbaum Associates Inc.

Bellugi, U., Wang, P.P., & Jernigan, T.L. (1994). Williams syndrome: An unusual neuropsychological profile. In S.H. Broman & J. Grafman (Eds.), *Atypical cognitive deficits in developmental disorders: Implications for brain function* (pp. 23–56). Hillsdale NJ: Lawrence Erlbaum Associates Inc.

Berthier, N.E., Clifton, R.K., Gullapati, V., McCall, D.D., & Robin, D.J. (1996). Visual information and object size in the control of reaching. *Journal of Motor Behaviour, 28*(3), 187–197.

Berthoz, A. (1996). Neural basis of decision in perception and the control of movement. In A.R. Damasio, H. Damasio, & Y. Christen (Eds.), *Neurobiology of decision making*. Berlin: Springer.

Bertrand J., Mervis C.B., & Eisenberg J.D. (1997). Drawing by children with Williams syndrome: A developmental perspective. *Developmental Neuropsychology, 13*, 41–67.

Birch, E.E. (1993). Stereopsis in infants and its developmental relation to visual acuity. In K. Simons (Ed.), *Early visual development: Normal and abnormal*. New York: Oxford University Press.

Birch, E.E., Fawcett, S., & Stager, D. (2000). Co-development of VEP motion response and binocular vision in normal infants and infantile esotropes. *Investigative Ophthalmology & Visual Science, 41*, 1719–1723.

Birch, E.E., Gwiazda, J., & Held, R. (1982). Stereoacuity development for crossed and uncrossed disparities in human infants. *Vision Research, 22*, 507–513.

Birch, E.E., Gwiazda, J., & Held, R. (1983). The development of vergence does not account for the development of stereopsis. *Perception, 12*, 331–336.

Birch, E.E., & Stager, D.R. (1985). Monocular acuity and stereopsis, in infantile esotropia. *Investigative Ophthalmology and Visual Science, 26*, 1624–1630.

Boussaoud, D., Ungerleider, L.G., & Desimone, R. (1990). Pathways for motion analysis: Cortical connections of the medial superior temporal and fundus of the superior temporal visual areas in the macaque. *Journal of Comparative Neurology, 296*, 462–495.

Braddick, O.J. (1993). Orientation- and motion-selective mechanisms in infants. In K. Simons (Ed.), *Early visual development: Normal and abnormal* (pp. 163–177). New York: Oxford University Press.

Braddick, O.J. (1996). Binocularity in infancy. *Eye, 10*, 182–188.

Braddick, O.J., & Atkinson, J. (1988). Sensory selectivity, attentional control, and cross-channel integration in early visual development. In A. Yonas (Ed.), *20th Minnesota Symposium on Child Psychology*. Hillsdale, NJ: Lawrence Erlbaum Associates Inc.

Braddick, O., Atkinson, J., & Hood, B. (1996b). Monocular vs binocular control of infants' reaching. *Investigative Ophthalmology and Visual Science, 37*, S290.

Braddick, O., Atkinson, J., & Hood, B. (1996a). Striate cortex, extrastriate cortex, and colliculus: Some new approaches. In F. Vital-Durand, O. Braddick, & J. Atkinson (Eds.), *Infant vision*. Oxford: Oxford University Press.

Braddick O., Atkinson J., Hood B., Harkness W., Jackson G., & Vargha-Khadem F. (1992). Possible blindsight in babies lacking one cerebral hemisphere. *Nature, 360*, 461–463.

Braddick, O.J., Atkinson J., Julesz B., Kropfl W., Bodis-Wollner I., & Raab, E. (1980). Cortical binocularity in infants. *Nature, 288*, 363–365.

Braddick, O., Mercuri, E., Atkinson, J., & Wattam-Bell, J. (1998). Basis of the naso-temporal asymmetry in infants' VEPs to grating displacements. *Investigative Ophthalmology and Visual Science, 39*, S884.

Braddick, O.J., O'Brien, J.M.D., Wattam-Bell, J., Atkinson J. & Turner, R. (2000). Form and motion coherence activate independent, but not dorsal/ventral segregated, networks in the human brain. *Current Biology, 10*, 731–734.

Braddick, O.J., Wattam-Bell, J., & Atkinson, J. (1986). Orientation-specific cortical responses develop in early infancy. *Nature, 320*, 617–619.

Braddick, O.J., Wattam-Bell, J., Day, J. & Atkinson, J. (1983). The onset of binocular function in human infants. *Human Neurobiology, 2*, 65–69.

Bronson, G.W. (1974). The postnatal growth of visual capacity. *Child Development, 45*, 873–890.

Butterworth, G., & Grover, L. (1990). Joint visual-attention, manual pointing, and preverbal communication in human infancy. In J.M. Jeannerod (Ed.), *Attention and performance XIII* (pp. 605–624). Cambridge MA: MIT Press.

Cornelissen, P., Richardson, A., Mason, A., Fowler, S., & Stein, J. (1995). Contrast sensitivity and coherent motion detection measured at photopic luminance levels in dyslexics and controls. *Vision Research, 35*, 1483–1494.

Damasio, A.R., & Benton, A.L. (1979). Impairment of hand movements under visual guidance. *Neurology, 29*, 170–178.

Derrington, A.M., & Lennie, P. (1982). The influence of temporal frequency and adaptation level on receptive-field organization of retinal ganglion cells in cat. *Journal of Physiology, 333*, 343–366.

Downing, C.J., & Pinker, S. (1985). The spatial structure of visual attention. In M.I. Posner & O.S.M. Marin (Eds.), *Attention and performance XI* (pp. 171–187). Hillsdale, NJ: Lawrence Erlbaum Associates Inc.

Eden, G.F., Vanmeter, J.W., Rumsey, J.M., Maisog, J.M., Woods, R.P., & Zeffiro, T.A. (1996). Abnormal processing of visual motion in dyslexia revealed by functional brain imaging. *Nature, 382*, 66–69.

Fox, R., Aslin, R.N., Shea, S.L., & Dumais, S.T. (1980). Stereopsis in human infants. *Science, 207*, 323–324.

Goodale, M.A, Milner, A.D., Jakobson, L.S., & Carey, D.P. (1991). A neurological dissociation between perceiving objects and grasping them. *Nature, 349*, 154–156.

Goodale, M.A, Murphy, K.J., Meenan J., Racicot, C.I., & Nicholle, D.A. (1993). Spared object perception but poor object calibrated grasping in a patient with optic ataxia. *Society of Neuroscience Abstracts, 19*, 775.

Haggard, P., & Wing, A.M. (1995). Remote responses to perturbation in human prehension. *Neuroscience Letters, 122*, 103–108.

Halligan, P., & Marshall, J. (1989). Laterality of motor response in visuo-spatial neglect: A case study. *Neuropsychologia, 27*, 1301–1307.

Hainline, L., & Riddell, P. (1995). Binocular alignment and vergence in early infancy. *Vision Research, 35*, 3229–3236.

Hainline, L., & Riddell, P. (1996). Eye alignment and convergence in young infants. In F. Vital-Durand, O. Braddick, & J. Atkinson (Eds.), *Infant vision*. Oxford: Oxford University Press.

Hein, A., & Held, R. (1967). Dissociation of the visual placing response into elicited and guided components. *Science, 158*, 190–192.

Held, R., Birch, E.E., & Gwiazda J. (1980). Stereoacuity of human infants. *Proceedings of the National Academy of Sciences of the USA, 77*, 5572–5574.

Henderson, S.E., & Sugden, D.A. (1992). *The movement ABC manual*. London: The Psychological Corporation.

Hoffmann, K.-P. (1981). Neuronal responses related to optokinetic nystagmus in the cat's nucleus of the optic tract. In A. Fuchs & W. Becker (Eds.), *Progress in oculomotor research* (pp. 443–454). New York: Elsevier.

Hood, B. (1993). Inhibition of return produced by covert shifts of visual attention in 6-month-old infants. *Infant Behaviour and Development, 16*, 255–264.

Hood, B., & Atkinson, J. (1990). Sensory visual loss and cognitive deficits in the selective attentional system of normal infants and neurologically impaired children. *Developmental Medicine and Child Neurology, 32*, 1067–1077.

Hood, B., & Atkinson, J. (1993). Disengaging visual attention in the infant and adult. *Infant Behaviour and Development, 16*, 405–422.

Hood, B., Atkinson, J., Braddick, O.J., & Wattam-Bell, J. (1992). Orientation selectivity in infancy: Behavioural evidence for temporal sensitivity. *Perception, 21*, 351–354.

Hubel, D.H., & Wiesel, T.N. (1977). Functional architecture of macaque monkey visual cortex. *Proceedings of the Royal Society of London B, 198*, 1–59.

Huttenlocher, P.R., de Courten, C., Garey, L.J., & van der Loos, H. (1982). Synaptogenesis in human visual cortex – evidence for synapse elimination during normal development. *Neuroscience Letters, 33*, 247–252.

Jakobson, L., & Goodale, M.A. (1991). Factors affecting higher-order movement planning: A kinematic analysis of human prehension. *Experimental Brain Research, 86*, 199–208.

Jakobson, L.S., Archibald, Y.M., Carey, D.P., & Goodale, M.A. (1991). A kinematic analysis of reaching and grasping movements in a patient recovering from optic ataxia. *Neuropsychologia, 29*, 803–809.

Jeannerod, M. (1988). *The neural and behavioural organization of goal directed movements*. Oxford: Oxford University Press.

Jeannerod, M. (1997). *The cognitive neuroscience of action*. Oxford: Blackwell.

Karmiloff-Smith, A. (1998). Development itself is the key to understanding developmental disorders. *Trends in Cognitive Sciences, 2*, 389–398.

King, J.A., Atkinson, J., Braddick, O.J., Nokes, L., & Braddick, F. (1996). Target preference and movement kinematics reflect development of visuomotor modules in the reaching of human infants. *Investigative Ophthalmology and Visual Science, 37*, S526.

Klein B.P., & Mervis C.B. (1999). Contrasting patterns of cognitive abilities of 9- and 10-year-olds with Williams syndrome or Down syndrome. *Developmental Neuropsychology, 16*, 177–196.

LaBerge, D., & Brown, V. (1989). Theory of attentional operations in shape identification. *Psychological Review, 96*, 101–124.

Livingstone, M., & Hubel, D.H. (1988). Segregation of form, color, movement and depth: Anatomy, physiology and perception. *Science, 240*, 740–749.

Livingstone, M.S., Rosen, G.D., Drislane, F.W., & Galaburda, A.M. (1991). Physiological and anatomical evidence for a magnocellular defect in developmental dyslexia. *Proceedings of the National Academy of Sciences of USA, 88*, 7943–7947.

Mason, A.J.S., Braddick, O.J., Wattam-Bell, J., & Atkinson, J. (2001). Directional motion asymmetry in infant VEPs – which direction? *Vision Research, 41*, 201–211.

Maunsell, J.H.R., & Newsome, W.T. (1987). Visual processing in monkey extrastriate cortex. *Annual Review of Neuroscience, 10*, 363–401.

Mercuri, E., Atkinson, J., Braddick, O., Anker, S., Nokes, L., Cowan, F., Rutherford, M., Pennock, J., & Dubowitz, L. (1996). Visual function and perinatal focal cerebral infarction. *Archives of Disease in Childhood, 75*, F76–F81.

Mercuri, E., Atkinson, J., Braddick, O., Anker, S., Nokes, L. Cowan, F. et al. (1997a). Basal ganglia damage in the newborn infant as a predictor of impaired visual function. *Archives of Disease in Childhood, 77*, F111–F114.

Mercuri, E., Atkinson, J., Braddick, O., Anker, S., Cowan, F., Rutherford, M. et al. (1997b). Visual function in full term infants with hypoxic–ischaemic encephalopathy. *Neuropediatrics, 28*, 155–161.

Mercuri, E., Braddick, O., Atkinson, J., Cowan, F., Anker, S., Andrew, R. et al. (1998). Orientation-reversal and phase-reversal visual evoked potentials in full-term infants with brain lesions: A longitudinal study. *Neuropaediatrics, 29*, 1–6.

Mercuri, E., Haataja, L., Guzzetta, A., Anker, S., Cowan, F., Rutherford, M. et al. (1999). Visual function in term infants with hypoxic–ischaemic insults: Correlation with neurodevelopment at 2 years of age. *Archives of Diseases in Childhood, 80*, F99–F104.

Merigan, W.H., & Maunsell, J.H.R. (1993). How parallel are the primate visual pathways? *Annual Review of Neuroscience, 16*, 369–402.

Milner A.D., & Goodale, M.A. (1995). *The visual brain in action*. Oxford: Oxford University Press.

Morrone, M.C., Atkinson, J., Cioni, G., Braddick, O.J., & Fiorentini. A. (1999). Developmental changes in optokinetic mechanisms in the absence of unilateral cortical control. *NeuroReport, 10*, 1–7.

Movshon J.A., Adelson, E.H., Gizzi, M.S., & Newsome, W.T. (1985). The analysis of moving visual patterns. In C. Chagas, R. Gattass, & C.G. Gross (Eds.), *Pattern recognition mechanisms, Pontificae Academiae Scientiarum Scripta Varia, 54*, 117–151. Vatican City: Pontifica Academia Scientiarum.

Newcombe, N.N., & Huttenlocher, J. (2000). *Making space*. Cambridge MA: MIT Press.

Newman, C. (2001). *The planning and control of action in normal infants and children with Williams syndrome*. PhD Thesis, University of London.

Newman, C., Atkinson, J., & Braddick, O. (2001). The development of reaching and looking preferences in infants to objects of different sizes. *Developmental Psychology, 37*, 561–572.

Newman, C., Mason, A.J.S., Andrew, R., Braddick, O.J., & Atkinson, J. (1999). *infants' reaching and looking preferences for objects varying in size and visual pattern: A cross sectional and longitudinal study*. Paper presented at the Child Vision Research Society Conference, London, June 1999.

Norcia, A.M. (1996). Abnormal motion processing and binocularity: Infantile esotropia as a model system for effects of early interruptions of binocularity. *Eye, 10*, 259–265.

Norcia A.M., Garcia H., Humphry R., Holmes A., Hamer R.D., & Orel-Bixler D. (1991). Anomalous motion VEPs in infants and in infantile esotropia. *Investigative Ophthalmology and Visual Science, 32*, 346–439.

Norcia A.M., Hamer R.D., & Orel-Bixler, D. (1990). Temporal tuning of the motion VEP in infants. *Investigative Ophthalmology and Visual Science, (Suppl.), 31*, 10.

O'Keefe J., & Burgess, N. (1996). Geometric determinants of the place fields of hippocampal neurones. *Nature, 381*, 425–428.

Pezzini, G., Vicari, S., Volterra, V., Milani, L., & Ossella, M.T. (1999). Children with Williams syndrome: Is there a single neuropsychological profile? *Developmental Neuropsychology, 15*, 141–155.

Posner, M.I. (1980). Orienting of attention. *Quarterly Journal of Experimental Psychology, 32*, 3–25.

Posner, M.I., & Dehaene, S. (1994). Attentional networks. *Trends in Neurosciences, 17*, 75–79.

Posner, M.I., & Petersen, S.E. (1990). The attention system of the human brain. *Annual Review of Neuroscience, 13*, 25–42.

Pryde, K.M., Roy, E.A., & Campbell, K. (1998). Prehension in children and adults: The effect of object size. *Human Movement Science, 17*, 743–752.

Rizzolatti, G. (1983). Mechanisms of selective attention in mammals. In J.-P. Ewwert, R.R. Capranica, & D.J. Ingle (Eds.), *Advances in vertebrate neuroethology* (pp. 261–297). Amsterdam: Elsevier.

Rizzolatti, G., & Camarda, R. (1987). Neural circuits for spatial attention and unilateral neglect. In M. Jeannerod (Ed.), *Neurophysiological and neuropsychological aspects of spatial neglect* (pp. 289–213). Amsterdam: Elsevier.

Rizzolatti, G., Fogassi, L., & Gallese, V. (1997). Parietal cortex: From sight to action. *Current Opinion in Neurobiology, 7*, 562–567.

Rizzolatti, G., Riggio, L., Dascola, I., & Umilta, C. (1987). Reorienting attention across the horizontal and verical meridians: Evidence in favour of a premotor theory of attention. *Neuropsychologia, 25*, 31–40.

Robertson, I.H., & North, N. (1993). Active and passive activation of left limbs: Influence on visual and sensory neglect. *Neuropsychologia, 31*, 293–300.

Rosenbaum, D.A., Vaughan, J., Barnes, H.J., Marchak, F., & Slotta, J.D., (1992). Timecourse of movement planning: Selection of handgrips for object manipulation. *Journal of Experimental Psychology: Learning, Memory and Cognition, 18*, 1058–1073.

Schneider, G.E. (1969). Two visual systems: brain mechanisms for localization and discrimination are dissociated by tectal and cortical lesions. *Science, 163*, 895–902.

Sheliga, B.M., Craighero, L., Riggio, L., & Rizzolatti, G. (1997). Effects of spatial attention on directional manual and ocular responses. *Experimental Brain Research, 114*, 339–351.

Sheliga, B.M., Riggio, L., & Rizzolatti, G. (1995). Spatial attention and eye movements. *Experimental Brain Research, 105*, 261–275.

Sillito, A.M., Cudeiro, J., & Murphy, P.C. (1993). Orientation sensitive elements in the corticofugal influence on center-surround interactions in the dorsal lateral geniculatenucleus. *Experimental Brain Research, 93*, 6–16.

Sireteanu, R., & Rieth, C. (1993). Texture segmentation in infants and children. *Behavioural Brain Research, 49*, 133–139.

Slater, A.M., Morison, V., & Somers, M. (1988). Orientation discrimination and cortical function in the human newborn. *Perception, 17*, 597–602.

Smith, J. (1989). *The development of binocular vision in normal and strabismic infants.* PhD Thesis, University of Cambridge.

Smith, J., Atkinson, J., Braddick, O.J., & Wattam-Bell, J. (1988). Development of sensitivity to binocular correlation and disparity in infancy. *Perception, 17*, 365.

Smyth, M.M., & Mason, U.M. (1997). Planning and execution of action in children with and without developmental co-ordination disorder. *Journal of Child Psychology and Psychiatry, 38*, 1023–1027.

Spencer J., O'Brien, J., Riggs, K., Braddick, O., Atkinson, J., & Wattam-Bell, J. (2000). Motion processing in autism: Evidence for a dorsal stream deficiency. *NeuroReport, 11*, 2765–2767.

Sprague, J.M., & Meikle, T.H. (1965). The role of the superior colliculus in visually guided behavior. *Experimental Neurology, 11*, 115–146.

Trevarthen, C.B. (1968). Two mechanisms of vision in primates. *Psychologishe Forschung, 31*, 299–337.

Ungerleider, L.G., & Mishkin, M. (1982). Two cortical visual systems. In D.J. Ingle, M.A. Goodale, & R.J.W. Mansfield (Eds.), *Analysis of visual behavior* (pp. 549–586). Cambridge, MA: MIT Press.

Van Essen, D.C., & Maunsell, J.H.R. (1983). Hierarchical organization and functional streams in visual cortex. *Trends in Neurosciences, 6*, 370–375.

Vital-Durand, F., Putkonen, P.T.S., & Jeannerod, M. (1974). Motion detection and optokinetic responses in dark reared kittens. *Vision Research, 14*, 141–142.

Volkmann F.C., & Dobson, V. (1976). Infant responses of ocular fixation to moving visual stimuli. *Journal of Experimental Child Psychology, 22*, 86–99.

Wattam-Bell, J. (1991). The development of motion-specific cortical responses in infants. *Vision Research, 31*, 287–297.

Wattam-Bell, J. (1992). The development of maximum displacement limits for discrimination of motion direction in infancy. *Vision Research, 32*, 621–630.

Wattam-Bell, J. (1995). Stereoscopic and motion Dmax in adults and infants. *Investigative Ophthalmology & Visual Science, 36*, S910.

Wattam-Bell, J. (1996a). The development of visual motion processing. In F. Vital-Durand, O. Braddick, & J. Atkinson (Eds.), *Infant vision*. Oxford: Oxford University Press.

Wattam-Bell, J. (1996b). Visual motion processing in one-month-old infants: Preferential looking experiments. *Vision Research, 36*, 1679–1685.

Wattam-Bell, J. (1996c). Visual motion processing in one-month-old infants: Habituation experiments. *Vision Research, 36*, 1671–1677.

Wattam-Bell, J. (1996d). Infants' discrimination of absolute direction of motion. *Investigative Ophthalmology and Visual Science, 37*, S917.

Wattam-Bell, J., Braddick, O.J., Atkinson J., & Day, J. (1987). Measures of infant binocularity in a group at risk for strabismus. *Clinical Vision Sciences, 1*, 327–336.

Witton, C., Talcott, J.B., Hansen, P.C., Richardson, A.J., Griffiths, T.D., Rees, A. et al. (1998). Sensitivity to dynamic auditory and visual stimuli predicts nonword reading ability in both dyslexic and normal readers. *Current Biology, 8*, 791–797.

Zeki, S. (1974). Functional organization of a visual area in the posterior bank of the superior temporal sulcus of the rhesus monkey. *Journal of Physiology, 236*, 549–573.

Zeki, S. (1978). Functional specialization in the visual cortex of the rhesus monkey. *Nature, 274*, 423–428.

Zeki, S. (1983a). The distribution of wavelength and orientation selective cells in different areas of monkey visual cortex. *Proceedings of the Royal Society B, 217*, 449–470.

Zeki, S. (1983b). Color coding in the cerebral cortex – the reaction of cells in monkey visual cortex to wavelengths and colors. *Neuroscience, 9*, 741–765.

Zeki, S. (1993). *A vision of the brain*. Oxford: Blackwell Scientific.

Zihl, J., von Cramon, D., & Mai, N. (1983). Selective disturbance of motion vision after bilateral brain damage. *Brain, 106*, 313–340.

CHAPTER FOUR

The development of visual attention and the brain

John E. Richards
Department of Psychology, University of South Carolina, USA

INTRODUCTION

Attention shows development throughout the lifespan. In the early period of infancy, attention is directed primarily to salient characteristics of the environment and, by 2 or 3 years of age, comes under subject-directed control. The attention system comes under control of the child's executive functioning and is used in the service of cognitive, social, and emotional tasks. Some aspects of attention show gradual development over the entire period of childhood and adolescence, and then follow the course of other cognitive changes in the adult period. Many of these changes in attention are based upon age-related changes in brain areas involved in attention.

This chapter presents a neurodevelopmental perspective on the development of visual attention, focusing on research done with infants and very young children, because of the wealth of studies showing brain–attention relations in this age range. The primary focus is on visual attention, again because of the broad set of theories and empirical studies in this area. However, the comments about infants and young children should generalize to other ages, and the comments about visual attention should generalize to other sensory systems. First, two influential neurodevelopmental models of visual attention that relate the development of visual attention to changes in the brain are reviewed; a recent model that relates a general arousal/attention system to the development of visual attention is also presented. Second, three research areas that illustrate the role that brain development plays in the changes that occur in infant attention are examined. These areas will show the role that developmental change in a general attention/arousal system has on infant recognition memory, developmental changes in covert orienting and attention and their relation to brain development, and saccade planning. Some implications of the role of brain development in visual attention are discussed.

NEURODEVELOPMENTAL MODELS OF VISUAL ATTENTION

Two influential models that relate the development of visual behaviour in young infants to concurrent changes in the brain are Bronson's "two visual systems" (1974, 1997) and Johnson's model emphasizing the role of the primary visual cortex (1990, 1995; Johnson, Gilmore, & Csibra, 1998; Johnson, Posner, & Rothbart, 1991). Bronson was the first to take a specific hypothesis about neural systems developed in adult and animal studies and apply it to infant visual behaviour. His model was well received and many research studies interpreted their results in light of his model. Johnson took an established model of eye movement control (Schiller, 1985) and knowledge of the development of the primary visual area and presented a model that showed how infant visual behaviour was governed by changes in neural systems. Johnson's model and similar models have generated a wide body of behavioural, psychophysiological, and neuropsychological research in infants and young children. Although both neurodevelopmental models were concerned with a variety of visual behaviour, I use these models in this chapter in their application to visual attention. Also, in this section I present a model I have been using to guide my research that relates developmental changes in a general attention/arousal system to visual attention development.

Bronson's two visual systems.

The most influential theory of developmental change in visual behaviour controlled by brain development is that of Gordon Bronson (1974, 1997; see also Karmel & Maisel, 1975; Maurer & Lewis, 1979; Salapatek, 1975). Bronson's theory postulated two systems in the brain (e.g. Schneider, 1969) that control visual behaviour. The primary visual system has excellent visual acuity and is devoted to fine pattern visual analysis. The secondary visual system has poor visual acuity and responds to stimulus location and movement. It is dedicated to the detection and localization of targets in the periphery. The primary visual system is over-represented in the fovea and primary visual cortex and the secondary system is represented equally across the retina and in other areas of the brain involved in visual behaviour (e.g. the superior colliculus). According to Bronson, the secondary visual system is phylogenetically older and exists relatively mature at birth. Thus, newborn infant visual behaviour should respond primarily to movement, stimulus location, and peripheral visual information, but not to fine visual detail. The cortical components of the primary visual system show major developmental changes from 1 to 2 months of age until well into the second year. Thus, sensitivity to fine visual detail, attention to forms and objects, and memory for patterns should begin about 2 months of age and increase rapidly from 2 to 12 months. According to this model, the development of the brain areas involved in vision is directly responsible for changes in the infant's visual behaviour and visual attention.

Bronson's neurodevelopmental model of infant visual behaviour explained the findings of many studies on infant visual attention. The propensity of newborn infants to be extremely sensitive to motion and peripheral visual stimuli, and the later onset of detailed pattern discrimination, were consistent with this model. The model distinguished correctly between the control of peripheral orienting by subcortical neural systems, and visual attention involved in infant recognition memory and attention controlled by higher cortical visual systems. It captured to some extent the development patterns of those systems. However, the model was too simplistic. Several brain systems control visual behaviour. These systems, and the subsystems and brain areas involved in them, show developmental changes such as myelination, synaptic generation, neural innervation, synaptic pruning, and neurotransmitter development (see Chapter 1). Many specifics of the "two visual systems" (Schneider, 1969) are now held to be incorrect or incomplete in explaining the role of the brain in visual behaviour and visual attention.

Johnson's development of primary visual area (V1)

Several models from the 1990s relate development in the brain areas controlling visual behaviour to developmental changes in infant and child visual behaviour. The prototype of these models is that developed by Mark Johnson (Johnson, 1990, 1995; Johnson et al., 1991, 1998). Johnson posits that development in the layers of the primary visual cortex acts as a limiting factor for visual behaviour and visual attention controlled by brain systems. Johnson uses Schiller's (1985, 1998) model of the neural pathways for short-latency reflex saccades, smooth pursuit eye movements, attention-directed saccades, and inhibitory relations between attention-directed and reflexive eye movements. The short-latency reflex saccade pathway is primarily subcortical and mature at birth. The other pathways each have connections in various layers of the primary visual cortex before projecting to other cortical areas (e.g. area MT for smooth pursuit eye movements; areas MT, parietal cortex, frontal eye fields for attention-directed saccades). Specific developmental changes in the layers of the primary cortex from birth to about 6 months act as a gateway for the onset of these eye movements in young infants. Figure 4.1 shows the changes in the primary visual cortex that act as the gateway for these neural pathways. The changes in the primary visual cortex are posited to be responsible for the dates of the onset of smooth pursuit eye movement, "sticky fixation", attention-directed saccades, and other infant visual behaviour.

Johnson's model has been influential in generating research on visual attention in infants and young children and on other neurodevelopmental models of infant visual attention (see Chapter 3; also Hood, 1995; Hood, Atkinson, & Braddick, 1998; Maurer & Lewis, 1998; Richards, 2000a; Richards & Casey, 1992; Richards & Hunter, 1998). This model explains the general phenomena explained by Bronson's model of the early sensitivity to peripheral stimuli and later sensitivity

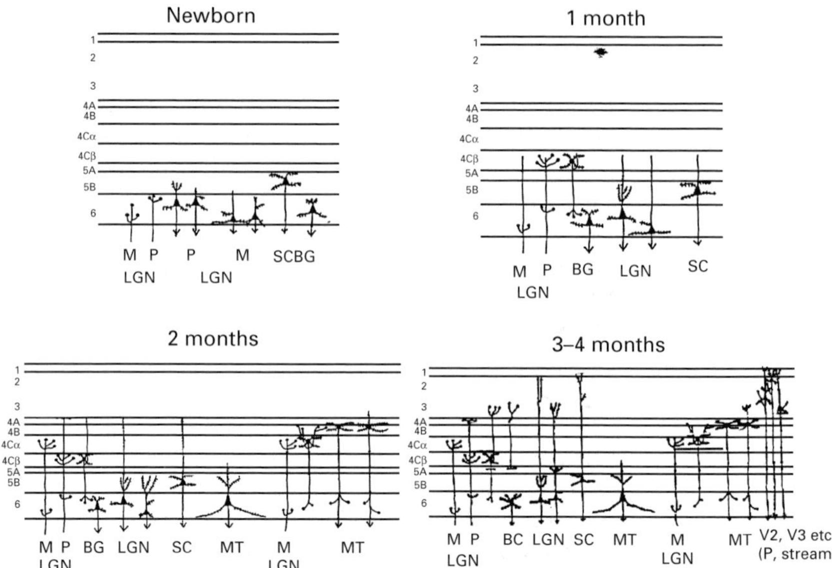

Figure 4.1. Developmental changes in the layers of the primary visual cortex and the connections to areas of the brain controlling eye movement. From Johnson (1995).
M = magnocellular; P = parvocellular; LGN = lateral geniculate nucleus; SC = superior colliculus; BG = basal ganglia; MT = medial temporal.

to fine visual detail, object and form, and recognition memory. It also explains several other developmental changes (e.g. smooth pursuit initiation, "sticky fixation", attention-directed eye movements) and makes predictions about visual behaviour and visual attention in the young infant and into early childhood. Some of the details of the model are in dispute (see Richards & Hunter, 1998) and the interpretation of the role of the frontal cortex in saccade planning has been questioned (Canfield, Smith, Brezsnyak, & Snow, 1997; Smith & Canfield, 1998; Wentworth & Haith, 1998; Wentworth, Haith, & Karrer, 2001). None the less, Johnson's neurodevelopmental model and similar models have been influential in explaining the role of the brain in the development of visual attention and visual behaviour.

The development of general arousal/attention

In several places (Berg & Richards, 1997; Richards, 2000a; Richards & Casey, 1992; Richards & Hunter, 1998), I have presented a model where infants' heart rate changes during stimulus presentation are used to distinguish phases of attention. Recently, this model was explicated as showing the relation between the development of a general arousal/attention system in the brain and brain systems

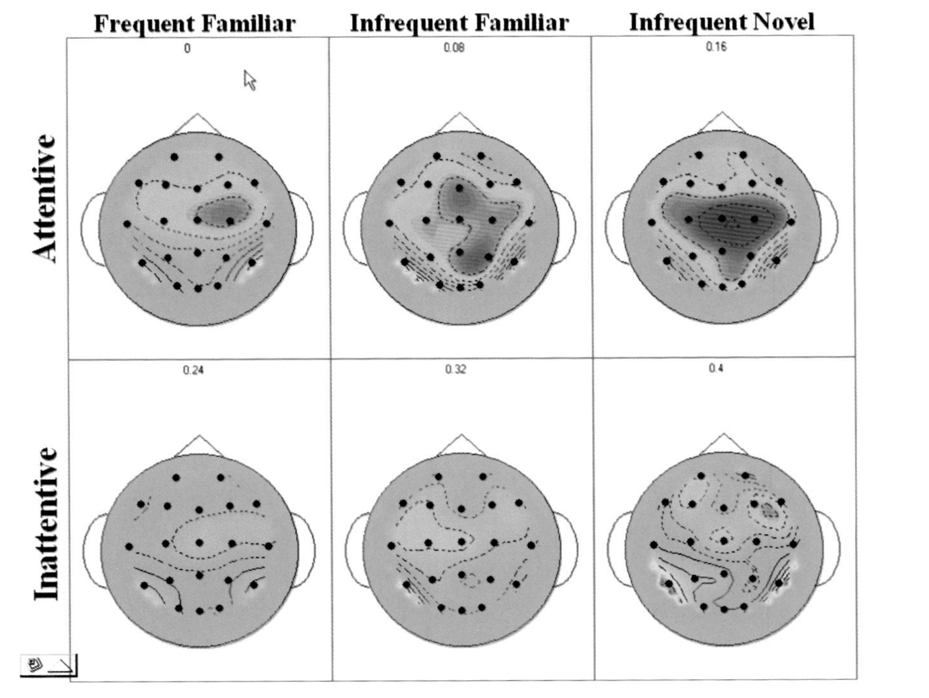

Plate 1. A topographical mapping of the Nc component that occurs during sustained attention and inattention for the frequent familiar, infrequent familiar, and infrequent novel stimuli. The data in each figure represent an 80ms average of the ERP for the Nc component at the maximum point of the ERP response. The data are plotted with a cubic spline interpolation algorithm, with an averaged electrode reference, and represent absolute amplitude of the ERP (from Richards, 2000c).

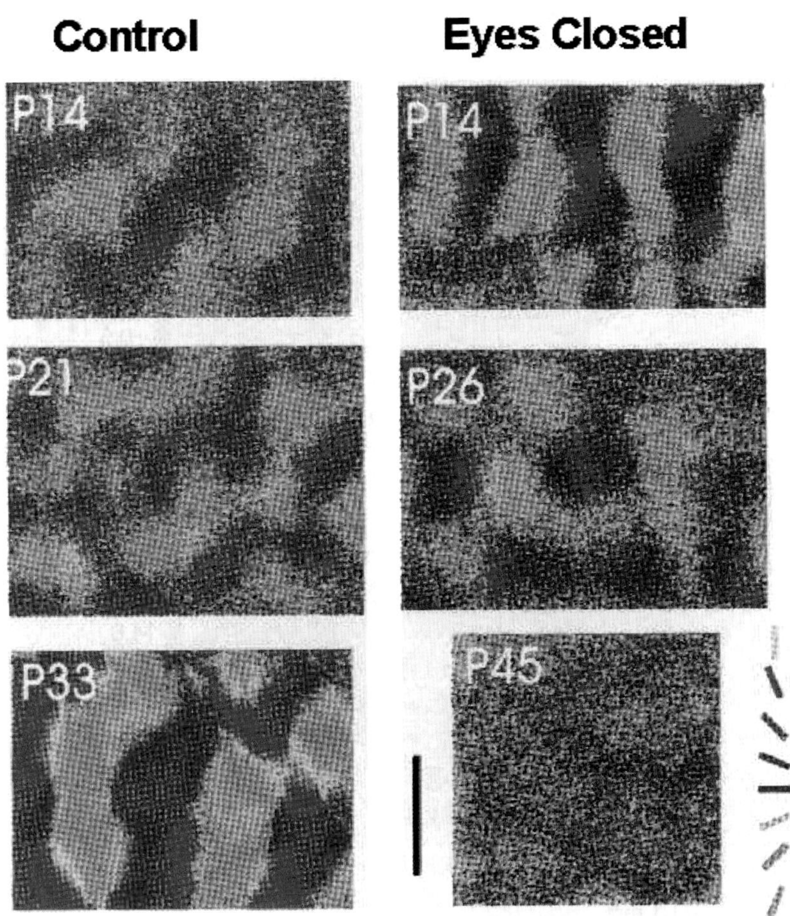

Plate 8. Left: Visual cortex is composed of columns of cells responsive to lines of different orientation (see colour code at right). In normal developing cats, a dramatic sharpening of the borders occurs between postnatal (P) days 21 and 33. In cats whose eyes have been sutured shut, the orientation columns develop normally until P26 and then their responses deteriorate rapidly. Patterned stimulation is only necessary for maintenance, not for formation, of the orientation columns (reprinted with permission from Crair et al. (1998). Science, 279, p.566. Copyright 1998 American Association for the Advancement of Science).

involved in specific cognitive activities (Richards, 2000a). One aspect of attention is the arousal associated with energized cognitive activity. This arousal is associated with increased performance on cognitive tasks and the sustaining of performance over extended periods of time. This arousal system is based upon neuroanatomical connections between the mesencephalic reticular activity system and the cortex (Heilman, Watson, Valenstein, & Goldberg, 1987; Mesulam, 1983; see Fig. 1 in Richards, 2000a). It probably uses the noradrenergic and cholinergic neurotransmitter systems (Robbins & Everitt, 1995; see Fig. 2 in Richards, 2000a) to heighten arousal and increase attentive cognitive performance. The heart rate changes occurring during infant attention index this general arousal/attention system and thus provide an indirect measure of the brain areas controlling sustained attention.

There are three interesting aspects of this arousal system for the present chapter. First, it affects a wide range of modalities, sensory systems, cognitive systems, and cognitive processes. Thus its energizing aspect could affect visual attention or attention to other stimulus modalities. This general system might influence a specific system in the brain that has selective properties, so that this arousal could be accompanied by modality-specific attentive behaviour (e.g. stimulus modality effects on the blink reflex; Richards, 1998, 2000b). In this case, the "arousal" system might actually inhibit modalities or cognitive processes that interfere with the specific cognitive processes currently engaged. Second, there are dramatic developmental changes in this arousal system at least through the first year of life. This is seen, for example, by a change in the level of the heart rate response during attention (Richards, 1989), changes in the effect of this system on selective attention systems (Richards, 1998), and changes in the effect of this system on brain responses during attention (Richards, 2000c). The effect of the development of this system will be discussed in the next section. Third, this model is complementary, rather than competitive, to models such as those of Johnson or Bronson. Richards (2000a) distinguished between the general arousal/attention system and its development, and the development of specific attention systems. The Johnson model, for example, was concerned primarily with the development of several systems involved in eye movement control and visual behaviour. Such specific systems develop concurrently with this general system to influence infant visual attention (see eye movement studies by Richards & Holley, 1999). A full treatment of the effects of brain development on visual attention in infants and children must deal with many brain areas and cognitive systems.

Measuring "neuro" in neurodevelopmental models

One weakness in the neurodevelopmental models of visual attention is the lack of direct measures of brain activity in developing human infants. The most common manner in which neurodevelopmental models are tested is with the "marker task".

These are behavioural tasks for which brain areas have been well specified using animal, invasive, or neuropsychological preparations. Johnson (1997) proposes that such tasks can be used with infants and young children. Developmental change in the behaviour on the tasks is inferred to represent developmental changes in the brain area controlling their functioning. This indirect method allows inferences to be made about brain development without the concomitant invasive measurement techniques used in animals, adults, or with neuropsychological patients. However, careful theoretical and empirical links must be made between the brain system and cognitive behaviours for this approach to work. In several examples (see the sections "Covert orienting and attention" and "Saccade planning") it can be shown that this method can be deceptive in its claims supporting neurodevelopmental models of visual attention.

An approach that provides a more direct measurement of brain function is the use of psychophysiological measures (see Chapter 2). Two measures of brain activity have been used that are derived from electrical potential activity occurring on the scalp: the electroencephalogram (EEG) and scalp-recorded event-related potentials (ERPs). The electrical activity occurring on the scalp consists of changing electrical voltages that are caused by action potentials summed over large numbers of neurons, synapses, neural pathways, and neural systems. The spontaneous electrical activity occurring on the scalp, the EEG, has been used as a measure of arousal during task performance (Bell, 1998; Ray, 1990) and is thought to reflect the underlying cognitive processes occurring in the brain related to task performance. However, EEG activity is difficult to link to specific cortical areas and attempts to do so require theoretical linkages (neural generators, skull and scalp conductance, electrical changes on the scalp; see Chapter 2). It has been rarely used in studies of attention development.

Scalp-recorded electrical activity can be related to specific experimental events or cognitive processes. The resulting ERPs might provide a non-invasive and direct measure of functioning within specific brain areas (Hillyard, Mangun, Woldroff, & Luck, 1995). ERPs are derived by averaging EEG changes over multiple experimental (or cognitive) events. The averaging process eliminates or attenuates the spontaneous activity in the EEG and results in electrical potential changes related to specific events. The ERP has varying positive and negative electrical waves that are referred to as "components". These components are hypothesized to be controlled by specific neural areas and psychological processes (Hillyard et al., 1995; Swick, Kutas, & Neville, 1994). Current methods using high-density EEG recording (Tucker, 1993; Tucker et al., 1994) and cortical source localization (Huizenga & Molenaar, 1994; Nunez, 1990; Scherg, 1990; Scherg & Picton, 1991) can be used with ERP to identify cortical areas involved in cognitive processes (see the section "Saccade planning"). Cortical source localization analysis allows the ERP to be used as a direct measure of the cortical areas involved in cognitive processes and experiment events (Richards, 2000c; see Chapter 2 for further discussion of localization of the sources of

ERP components). This chapter emphasizes areas of study in which the measurement of the ERP in infants and children help to confirm the neurodevelopmental models of visual attention.

Not all psychophysiological measures are so direct. For example, I have used heart rate changes during visual attention in infants and preschool children as a measure of the general arousal system (see studies in Richards, 2000a). As with behavioural marker tasks, the relation between the neural system governing arousal/attention (Heilman et al., 1987; Mesulam, 1983) and heart rate control are well known. Yet, it is only the theoretical and empirical linkages found in animal studies or invasive studies with other populations that allow the inferences to be made when using this measure in infants. In this respect, heart rate is a "behavioural marker task" similar to eye movements, reaction time, novelty preference, or habituation. Several other psychophysiological measures have the same indirect measurement status as do heart rate and behavioural tasks—e.g. electromyogram (EMG; Richards, 1998); electro-oculogram (EOG; Richards & Hunter, 1997).

AROUSAL/ATTENTION SYSTEM AND RECOGNITION MEMORY

This section reviews studies showing how the general arousal/attention system affects the development of infant recognition memory. As in the previous section, I have used changes in infant heart rate during stimulus presentation to distinguish phases of infant attention (Richards, 2000a; Richards & Casey, 1992; Richards & Hunter, 1998). These phases are the automatic interrupt, stimulus orienting, sustained attention, and attention termination. These attention phases differ in the type of behaviour and cognitive processes that occur and in heart rate changes that occur when they are in effect. Figure 4.2 depicts the heart rate changes occurring during these phases of attention and Table 4.1 has a list of some of the cognitive processes occurring in these phases. For example, stimulus orienting is a period at the beginning of stimulus processing when the infant evaluates stimulus novelty and decides whether to allocate further mental resources to the stimulus. It is characterized by a rapid deceleration of heart rate and lasts 1–5s. Sustained attention maintains the level of information processing initiated in stimulus orienting and continues processing the stimulus. This phase of attention is quite variable. It can be quite short (2–3s) or long (60–120s), depending on the state of the infant, the complexity of visual information in the stimulus, and individual differences between infants. Heart rate during this phase continues at a lower level than during prestimulus levels. Finally, during attention termination the heart rate returns to its prestimulus level. During this phase the infant does not process information in the stimulus and the sensitivity to any new stimulus can be attenuated.

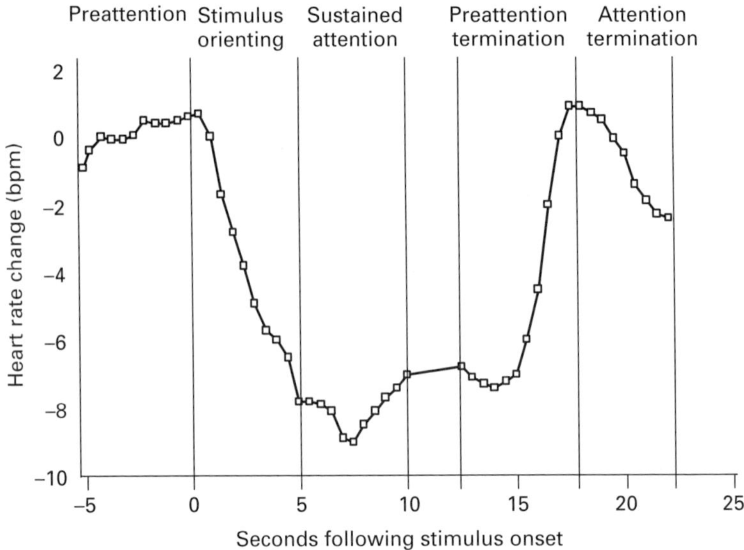

Figure 4.2. Average heart rate change as a function of stimulus presentation following stimulus onset for the heart rate defined attention phases for infants from 3 to 6 months of age (from Richards & Casey, 1991, Heart rate variability during attention phases in young infants. *Psychophysiology, 28*, 43–53. Cambridge University Press, 1991 © The Society for Psychophysiological Research. Reprinted with permission.)

TABLE 4.1.
Heart rate and behaviour/cognitive processes in heart-rate-defined attention phases (see full description in Richards & Casey, 1992)

Phase	*Heart rate change*	*Behaviour and cognitive processes*
Automatic interrupt	Biphasic heart rate change Deceleration–acceleration < 1s duration	Detect transient change in environment Startle reflex Automatically engaged
Stimulus orienting	Large heart rate deceleration 1–5s duration	Evaluate stimulus novelty Process preliminary information Make decision to suspend processing, or continue extended processing
Sustained attention	Heart rate below prestimulus Variable duration	Detailed information processing Subject-controlled Developmental and individual differences occur
Atttention termination	Heart rate return to prestimulus level 5–7s duration	No information processing Insensitivity to new stimulation "Refractory period"

Of primary interest to this chapter are the phases of sustained attention, attention termination, and the time after attention termination but before attention is re-engaged. The heart rate slows down and remains below the prestimulus level during sustained attention (see Fig. 4.2). During this time the infant is engaged in subject-controlled processing of stimulus information. This phase of attention represents the energizing of cognitive processes, i.e. the arousal phase of the general arousal/attention system (Richards, 2000a). Alternatively, during the attention termination phase the heart rate has returned to its prestimulus level. Infants can continue to direct fixation towards the stimulus for periods of time without a re-engagement of attention. These periods represent inattentiveness, and the infant is not processing stimulus information. This represents the lack of arousal of the arousal/attention system in the brain (Richards, 2000a). There are several reviews of the relation between these heart rate changes and infant and child behaviour (Berg & Richards, 1997; Richards, 1995, 2000a; Richards & Casey, 1992; Richards & Hunter, 1998; Richards & Lansink, 1998).

The relation between the heart-rate-defined attention phases and infant recognition memory has been shown in three studies using "behavioural markers" of infant recognition memory. Two studies have shown that a familiarization stimulus presented for only 5 or 6s results in recognition memory (Frick & Richards, 1999; Richards, 1997). In these studies, we presented 3- to 6-month-old infants with a *Sesame Street* film that elicited sustained attention (heart rate slowing in Fig. 4.2). A familiarization stimulus was then presented for 5 or 6s followed by the *Sesame Street* film. On "no exposure" trials the *Sesame Street* film was played continuously. Then, about 10s later, the paired-comparison procedure (Fagan, 1974) was used to test for a preference for the novel stimulus that would indicate recognition memory for the familiarized pattern. The infants looked longer at the novel stimulus in the test phase on the 5s or 6s exposure trials than on no-exposure trials. In fact, the infants looked at the novel stimulus on these 5s or 6s exposure trials for as long as they did on control trials with a traditional 20s exposure trial. These results imply that the acquisition of stimulus information by young infants occurs primarily when the infant is in a highly aroused state, i.e. sustained attention. We have also shown that infants distribute their fixations to the novel and familiar stimuli in the test phase of the paired-comparison task depending on their attention state (Richards & Casey, 1990). Novelty preference (fixation on the novel stimulus) occurred primarily during sustained attention, whereas no preference (fixation equally likely on novel or familiar stimulus) occurred during attention termination.

Recently, we have begun to study how developmental changes in the arousal/attention system affect infant recognition memory using direct measures of brain activity (Richards, 2000c). This study uses a common procedure in which brief visual stimuli are presented in an "oddball" procedure (Courchesne, 1977, 1978; Nelson & Collins, 1991, 1992; see reviews by Nelson, 1994, 2000, Nelson & Dukette, 1998). This procedure consists of the presentation of one stimulus relatively frequently and an "oddball" stimulus that is presented relatively infrequently. We use Nelson's modification of the procedure to familiarize the infant with these two stimuli ("frequent familiar", "infrequent familiar") before the brief presentations and to present a series of novel stimuli relatively infrequently ("infrequent novel") during the brief presentations.

The ERP is used as a direct measure of brain activity in the procedure. The ERP has components such as the P1 (or "P100"), N1, P2, N2, P3 (or "P300"), and various slow waves that differ for adult and infant participants (see Nelson, 1994; Nelson & Monk, 2000; Nelson & Dukette, 1998 or de Haan & Nelson, 1997, for a review of these components). The studies of the recognition of briefly presented visual stimuli find two types of components in this task. First, there is a large negative component occurring about 400–800ms after stimulus onset. This negative component is primarily located in the central leads and has been labelled the Nc ("*N*egative *c*entral"; Courchesne, 1977, 1978; Courchesne, Ganz, & Norcia, 1981). In most studies, the Nc component is larger to the infrequently presented stimuli and has been hypothesized to represent a general attentive or alerting to the presence of a novel stimulus. However, if the frequently presented and infrequently presented stimuli are already familiar to the infant, the Nc component does not differ (Nelson & Collins, 1991, 1992).

The second type of ERP activity found in these studies are slow waves occurring from 800 to 1500ms after stimulus presentation. Negative slow waves are found in response to the infrequent novel stimuli and positive slow waves are found in response to the infrequent familiar stimuli. Thus, infants are sensitive to novelty *per se* and to the frequency of the stimulus presentation. At the youngest testing ages (about 4 months), these later waves do not differ but by 6 months of age (Nelson & Collins, 1991) or 8 or 12 months (Nelson & Collins, 1992; Nelson & deRegnier, 1992) these three stimulus presentation procedures result in differing ERP potential shifts.

The results of the study I am conducting show that attention to the visual stimuli enhances the Nc component (Richards, 2000c). Infants at 4.5, 6, or 7.5 months of age have been tested in this study. Sustained attention is elicited in the infants with a *Sesame Street* film and the brief visual stimuli are overlaid upon the movie during sustained attention or during inattentive periods. Figure 4.3 shows the ERP changes from the 10–20 recording montage for the frequent familiar, infrequent familiar, and infrequent novel stimuli. The Nc component occurring 400–700ms after stimulus presentation can be seen clearly in these graphs. This component is approximately equivalent for the three presentation procedures. Plate 1 shows topographical potential maps of the Nc for the three presentation methods during attentive and inattentive periods. The response during attention is a widespread negative response in the central area of the scalp for the three presentation methods. The response during inattention is weaker or absent. There is a difference in the breadth of the response for the two infrequent conditions and the frequent condition, whereas the amplitude of the response is the same. The similarity between these three topographical maps suggests that the Nc response is an

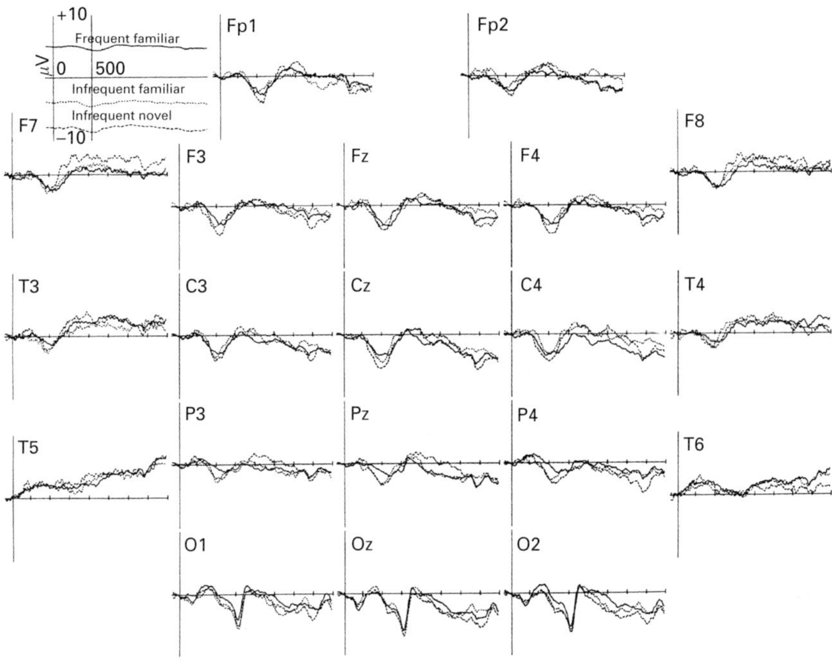

Figure 4.3. The ERP in response to the frequent familiar, infrequent familiar and infrequent novel presentations for 4- to 7.5-month-old infants. These recordings are from the 10–20 electrodes (+Oz). The Nc component occurs 400–700 ms after stimulus onset and the slow waves occur 800–1500ms after stimulus presentation (from Richards, 2000c).

orienting response that is greater during attention but is not closely related to stimulus novelty or recognition memory. The Nc response is larger when the general arousal system is energized ("sustained attention") than when the arousal system is not active ("inattention").

This study also shows developmental changes in the Nc component consistent with the development of the general arousal/attention system, and shows some effect of attention on the slow wave components. Plate 2 shows the changes over the three testing ages for the Nc response for attentive and inattentive periods. There was a clear increase in the amplitude of the Nc component during attentive periods over the three testing ages. The response during the inattentive periods changed only slightly. This finding is consistent with the model that the general arousal/attention system continues developing into the second half of the first year. There was some effect of attention on the late slow waves. In general, this difference consisted of larger slow waves during attention than inattention, but primarily for the oldest ages in the study. The youngest ages showed inconsistent patterns for the slow wave activity.

These studies show that the arousal aspect of sustained attention invigorates the acquisition of stimulus information (Richards, 1997; Frick & Richards, 2001) and the exhibition of recognition memory (Richards, 2000c; Richards & Casey, 1990). The study using the ERP measures has two broad implications. First, it implies that the Nc component is a manifestation of the general arousal/attention system of the brain. This interpretation suggests that such an ERP measure might provide a direct measure of this brain system, complementing heart rate, which is an indirect measure of this general arousal/attention system. Second, this study shows the interaction between the general attention system and a specific system supporting recognition memory. The enhancement of the slow waves during sustained attention demonstrates how the general system invigorates specific brain areas occurring during recognition memory. The facilitative effect of sustained attention on infant recognition memory (Frick & Richards, 2001; Richards, 1997) could occur because specific brain areas responsible for information acquisition or recognition are enhanced during sustained attention.

COVERT ORIENTING AND ATTENTION

One aspect of infant attention that has been studied with direct measures of brain activity is covert orienting and attention. Shifts of visual attention can occur without moving the eyes to a new location—"covert attention". Covert orienting of attention implies that attention and eye movements are partially independent, and that information can be processed in peripheral locations when the eyes remain fixed in a central location. The spatial cueing procedure developed by Posner (Posner, 1980; Posner & Cohen, 1984) can be used to measure covert orienting and attention. The participant's fixation is held at a central location and a peripheral cue and target are presented. If the target follows the cue in the same location at very short intervals, the response to the target is faster than if the cue and target are in a different location, i.e. facilitation. Alternatively, if the cue and target are separated by longer intervals the response to the target is slower in the cued location than in other locations, i.e. inhibition of return. Facilitation and inhibition of return are behavioural indices that attention was shifted to the cued location in the absence of specific eye movements. Hood (1993, 1995; Hood & Atkinson, 1991) developed a version of this task appropriate for infant participants. Figure 4.4 is a schematic illustration of the procedure used for infant participants (adapted from Hood, 1995; used in Richards, 2000d,e, 2001a,b). The spatial cueing procedure used with infant participants presents a central stimulus that engages fixation in the centre location and then presents a cue simultaneous with the central stimulus, followed by a delay, and then presents the target without the central stimulus.

Studies of covert orienting in young infants find that infants do not show consistent facilitation until about 4 to 6 months of age, but the results are not entirely consistent across studies. Hood and Atkinson (1991, reported in Hood, 1995)

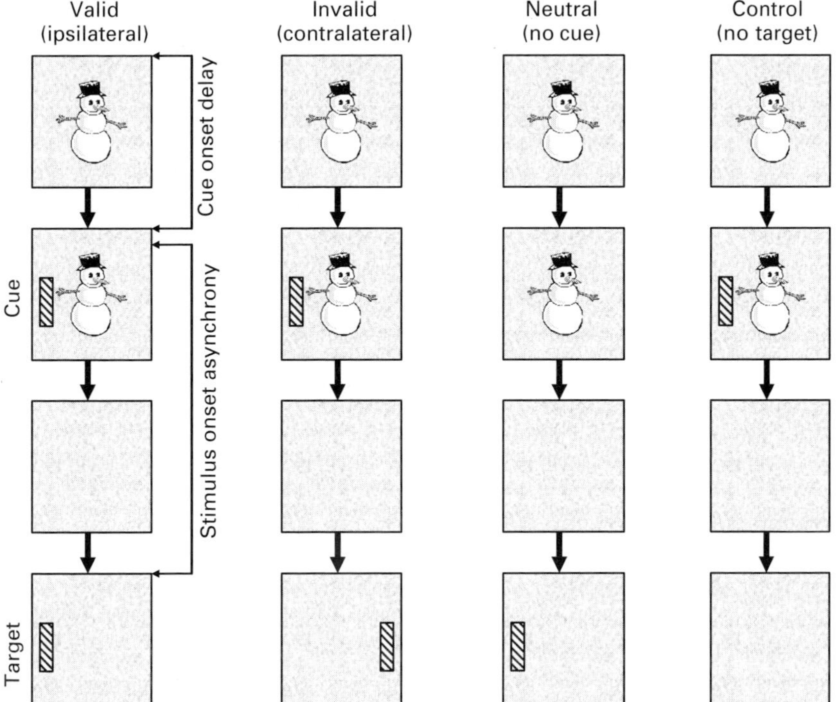

Figure 4.4. The spatial cueing procedure used by Richards in several studies (Richards, 2000d,e, 2001b, c) and adapted from Hood (1995). The ipsilateral cue-target condition is called a "valid" trial, the contralateral condition is called an "invalid" trial, and the no-cue control condition is a "neutral" trial. The no-target control condition provides control for spontaneous looking to the periphery of the cued location.

used the spatial cueing procedure shown in Fig. 4.4 with 100 or 600 ms cue-target asynchronies. The 3-month-old infants showed no evidence of facilitation of a saccade to the target at either delay interval. Conversely, Richards (2000d, e), using this paradigm, did find facilitation of the reaction time of the saccade towards the target for 3-month-old infants at short cue-target delay asynchronies. Similarly, a study by Butcher and colleagues using bilateral targets found that, from about 6 to 16 weeks of age infants would look more frequently and faster to the cued target location than to an uncued location (Butcher, Kalverboer, & Geuze, 1999). A similar study by Johnson and Tucker (Johnson & Tucker, 1996) did not find such effects with 2-month-old infants. However, by 4 or 6 months of age, nearly all studies report that at short cue-target delays a saccade to the cued side occurs faster than a saccade to an uncued or neutral location (Hood, 1993, 1995; Hood & Atkinson, 1991; Johnson, Posner, & Rothbart, 1991; Johnson & Tucker, 1996; Richards, 2000d,e, 2001a).

Almost no studies find inhibition of return after covert shifts of attention in the first 3 months, and some studies have reported inhibition of return around 4 months of age. Infants show inhibition of return following overt localization shifts from the newborn age. That is, if an overt fixation shifts from a central location to a peripheral location and then back to the central location, there is a lower probability of shifting back to the same location in the presence of bilateral targets and the shifts to that same location take longer to occur (Simion, Valenza, Umilta, & Barba, 1995; Valenza, Simion, & Umilta, 1994; however, see also Clohessy, Posner, Rothbart, & Vecera, 1991). In the spatial cueing procedure where an overt shift of fixation does not occur, infants at 2 and 3 months of age do not show inhibition of return, whereas infants at 4 months of age and beyond do (Butcher et al., 1999; Clohessy et al., 1991; Hood, 1993, 1995; Hood & Atkinson, 1991; Johnson et al., 1991; Johnson & Tucker, 1996; Richards, 2000d,e, 2001a). These findings imply that the mechanism for inhibiting the return of attention to the recently attended location might exist at birth but that the infants do not show covert shifts of attention in the spatial cueing procedure that would result in facilitation or inhibition of return.

Facilitation and inhibition of return in the spatial cueing paradigm have been explained in neurophysiological terms by those studying adults and those studying infants. Inhibition of return is thought to be mediated by the superior colliculus (Rafal, 1998). Overt fixation shifts, or merely planning to make an eye movement, activate pathways in the superior colliculus and inhibition of return results after that activation. The neurodevelopmental approach would approve this explanation, because the pathways governing eye movements that involve the superior colliculus are mature at birth (Hood, 1993, 1995; Johnson, 1990, 1995; Richards & Hunter, 1998; Simion et al., 1995; Valenza et al., 1994). Thus, newborn infants should and do show inhibition of return after overt eye movements. Covert orienting or covert shifting of attention can result in inhibition of return when the participant shifts attention, activates the pathways of the superior colliculus, but inhibits the final motor pathway for the saccade. Such enhancement and inhibition is hypothesized to be controlled by a "posterior attention network" (Posner, 1995; Posner & Petersen, 1990). This network includes the parietal cortex, regions of the thalamus projecting to the parietal cortex (e.g. pulvinar), frontal eye fields, and the superior colliculus. The changes in shifts of covert attention must therefore be due to changes in cortical areas involved in the posterior attention network, particularly cortical areas such as the parietal cortex and the frontal eye fields (Hood, 1993, 1995; Johnson et al., 1991, 1998; Johnson & Tucker, 1996).

I have begun to study the development of cortical involvement in covert orienting using direct measures of brain activity (Richards, 2000d, 2001a,b,c). In one of these studies, infants were tested in the spatial cueing procedure (see Fig. 4.4). The goal of this study was to examine the "P1 validity effect" in young infants. The "P1" is an ERP component that consists of a large positive deflection in EEG about 100 ms alter stimulus presentation. The "N1" is a large negative deflection in EEG closely following the P1 component. Studies with adult participants have shown that the P1 and N1 ERP components are enhanced on the valid trials (cue validly predicts target) relative to invalid trials or neutral trials (see studies in Hillyard et al., 1995). These early ERP components reflect sensory and perceptual processes. The P1 validity effect suggests that covert attention to the cue enhances the early stages of information processing. The studies with infants (Richards, 2000d) found that the spatial relation between the cue and target significantly affected the ERP to the target onset. There was a larger ERP component amplitude occurring at about 135 ms when the cue and target were in the ipsilateral hemifields ("valid trials") than when the cue and target were in the contralateral fields ("invalid trials"). Figure 4.5 (top panels) shows the ERP response of

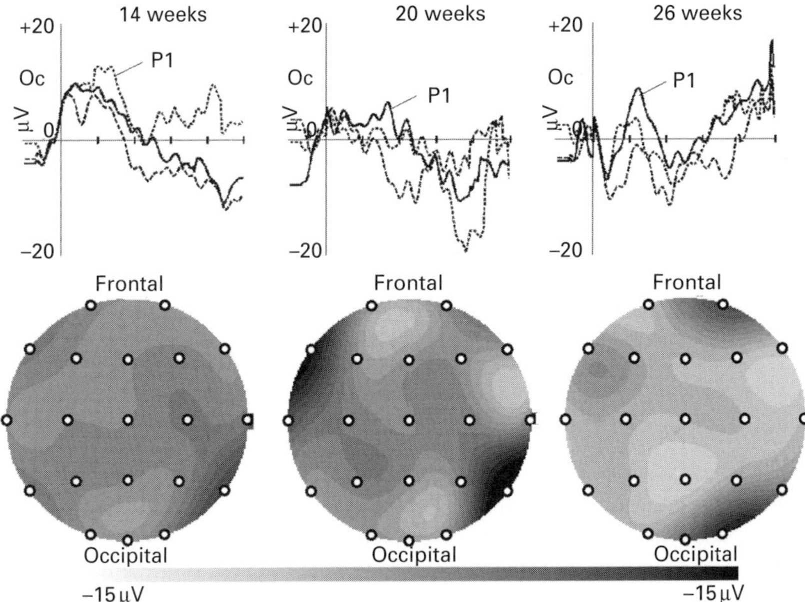

Figure 4.5. Top: ERP responses on the contralateral occipital electrode to the peripheral stimulus onset when it was presented as a target. The responses are presented separately for the three testing ages, and separately for the valid (solid line), invalid (small dashes), and no-cue control (long dashes) trials. The data are presented as the difference from the ERP on the no-stimulus control trial. The approximate locations of the P1 and N1 components are identified on each figure.
Bottom: Topographical scalp potential maps for the P1 effect for the three testing ages. These maps plot the difference between the valid and no-cue control trials for the peak potential occurring between 50 and 200 ms after peripheral stimulus onset, which on the average occurred about 135 ms after peripheral stimulus onset (from Richards, 2000d, Localizing the development of covert attention in infants using scalp event-related potentials. *Developmental Psychology*, *36*, 91–108. Copyright © 2000 by the American Psychological Association. Reprinted with permission.)

the contralateral occipital electrode for the ipsilateral, contralateral, and no-cue control trials plotted separately for 14-, 20-, and 26-week-old infants (Richards, 2000d). The validity effect on this positive ERP component did not occur (or was very small) in the 14-week-old infants, occurred at larger levels in the 20-week-old infants, and was at its largest in the 26-week-old infants. The topographical maps shown in Fig. 4.5 (bottom panels) show that this effect was localized to the contralateral occipital area for the oldest infants, showed a wider spread over the cortex for the 20-week-olds, and was very small for the youngest infants. The results from this study indicate that infants were shifting attention to the cued location covertly and that this early sensory–perceptual gating occurs in infant attention as it does in adult attention.

The findings from this study shed some light on the development of covert attention and orienting in young infants. There was an interesting developmental dissociation in this study between the facilitation effect that occurred at all three ages, the inhibition of return effect that gradually increased over the three testing ages, and the increasing amplitude of the P1 validity effect over the three testing ages. It suggests that the infants at the youngest testing ages (i.e. 3 months) might show covert orienting to the exogenous peripheral target, but that this orienting occurs as a result of reflexive saccadic programming rather than a shift of attention (Hillyard et al., 1995; Hopfinger & Mangun, 1998). Alternatively, at 4.5 and 6 months of age the infants were shifting attention appropriately, resulting in facilitation, inhibition of return, and the P1 validity effect. The direct measurement of brain activity afforded by the ERP results supports the neurodevelopmental models that suggest that there is an increasing involvement in this age range of cortical attention areas that affect infant attentive behaviour.

SACCADE PLANNING

Primates have several types of eye movements that have been shown to be controlled by specific areas of the brain. Two of these in particular, reflexive saccades and voluntary saccades, have been examined in neurodevelopmental models and empirical studies of infant visual attention. The neural basis of these two types of eye movements has been outlined by Schiller (1985, 1998). "Reflexive saccades" are eye movements that occur in response to the sudden onset of peripheral stimuli. These eye movements are controlled by several subcortical neural areas (retina, lateral geniculate nucleus, superior colliculus) and perhaps by the primary visual area. "Voluntary saccades" are eye movements that are under voluntary control and are affected by attention. Consistent with their voluntary nature and the role of attention in these eye movements, there are several areas of the cortex that affect these eye movements. Of particular interest are the parietal cortex and frontal eye fields. Johnson's neurodevelopmental model (Johnson, 1990, 1995; Johnson et al., 1991, 1998) emphasizes the role of the primary visual cortex in delaying these attention-directed eye movements until the fourth or fifth post-natal month. Thus, it can be predicted that reflexive saccades occur predominantly (exclusively?) in the first few postnatal months followed by the onset of voluntary eye movements by about the fourth or fifth postnatal months.

Saccade planning has been studied in non-human primates and human adults. For example, when monkeys are trained to make a saccadic eye movement from a fixation point to a target in a location to which attention has been directed, activity in the frontal eye fields (and sensorimotor eye fields) precedes the eye movements (Boch & Goldberg, 1989; Bruce & Goldberg, 1984, 1985; Hanes & Schall, 1996; Hanes, Thompson, & Schall, 1995; Schall, 1991a,b, 1995; Schall & Hanes, 1993; Schall, Hanes, Thompson, & King, 1995). In human adults, cortical influence on saccade planning has been studied with EEG occurring in advance of the saccadic eye movement, "presaccadic ERP". This activity includes an early negativity occurring up to 1s prior to saccade onset, a positive component occurring 30–300ms prior to saccade onset, and a "spike potential" occurring just prior to saccade onset (Balaban & Weinstein, 1985; Becker, Hoehne, Iwase, & Kornhuber, 1973; Csibra, Johnson, & Tucker, 1997; Kurtzberg & Vaughan, 1980, 1982; Moster & Goldberg, 1990; Weinstein, Balaban, & Ver Hoeve, 1991). Several of these presaccadic ERP components differ when adults make voluntary eye movements to targeted locations from when adults make reflexive saccades to unexpected peripheral targets.

A number of recent studies have examined these presaccadic ERP changes in infants. An interesting series of studies is that of Csibra, Johnson, and Tucker (Csibra et al., 1997; Csibra, Tucker, & Johnson, 1998; Csibra, Tucker, Volein, & Johnson, 2000), who used a procedure in 6-month-old infants, 12-month-old infants, and adults in which a cue in an unexpected peripheral location was presented. The infants and adults showed the typical "gap effect" in which a fixation-target temporal gap resulted in shorter saccadic reaction time than did a fixation-target pair that overlapped. The presaccadic ERP in these studies was recorded with 64 channels. Figure 4.6 (top panel) shows the presaccadic ERP at the Pz electrode for the participants at different ages. There was a clear spike potential for the adults, a smaller one for the 12-month-olds, and no spike potential for the youngest infants. The topographical potential maps for the 12-month-olds and adults are shown in Fig. 4.6 (bottom panels). A clear spike potential is distributed primarily contralateral to the eye movement over the parietal area. The presumed origin of the spike potential is the parietal cortex and these results suggest that saccade planning by this area is developing throughout the early part of childhood.

I have found in three studies some provocative results for 3- to 6-month-old infants making eye movements to an expected location (Richards, 2000d, 2001a,b). These studies involved the spatial cueing procedure (see Fig. 4.4) in which a cue predicted the upcoming target location, did not predict the location, or no cue occurred. I argued that in the case of the cue predicting the target location, the infant could "plan" to make a saccade to the location in which the cue occurred (Richards, 2001c). Alternatively, if a target occurred in an unexpected

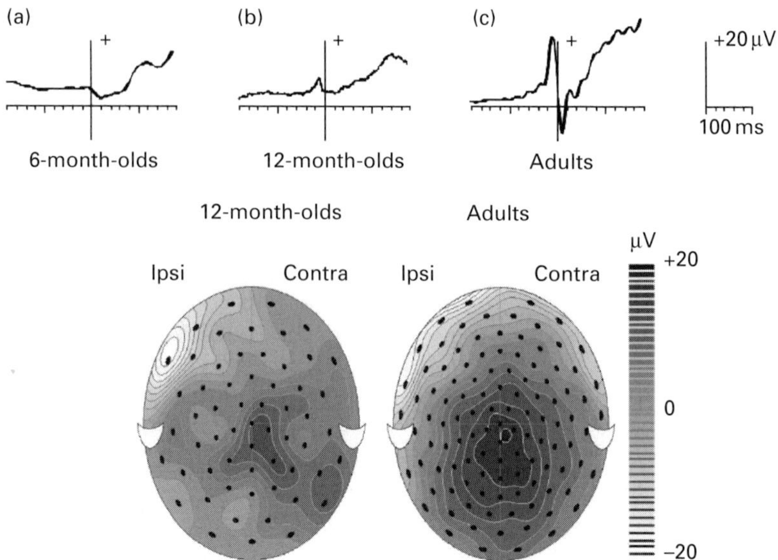

Figure 4.6. The presaccadic ERP to an unexpected peripheral target in 6- and 12-month-old infants and adults. Top: The ERP at the Pz electrode immediately preceding the saccade to the target. Bottom: Topographical potential map for the spike potential in 12-month-old infants and in adults (from Csibra et al., 2000).

location (i.e. contralateral to the cue, or no cue occurred) then the infant must make a reflexive saccade. The ERP that occurred immediately before the infant made a saccade to the target was recorded. Figure 4.7 shows the ERP changes for 4 of 40 electrode sites and Fig. 4.8 shows topographical maps at about 50 and 300ms preceding saccade onset. On the trials in which the cue predicted the location of the target, there was a large positive presaccadic potential that occurred about 50ms before the saccade occurred (Fig. 4.7, top panels). This ERP component occurred primarily over the frontal areas (Fig. 4.8, left figure). For trials on which there was no target and the infant made an eye movement, or for which the target appeared in a location that was unexpected given the cued location, this presaccadic ERP component did not occur. Alternatively, on the trials on which the infant made a saccade to the location predicted by the target *whether the target was there or not,* there was a positive potential occurring over the parietal cortex (Fig. 4.8, right figure), compared with eye movements to targets occurring in unexpected locations (Fig. 4.7, bottom panels). These results suggest that the infant first plans to make a saccade to an expected peripheral location (parietal cortex), uses the expected target to guide the planned saccade (frontal cortex), and then makes the saccade.

The results from one of these studies (Richards, 2001a) and from recently collected data with 128 electrodes were used to identify the area of the cortex

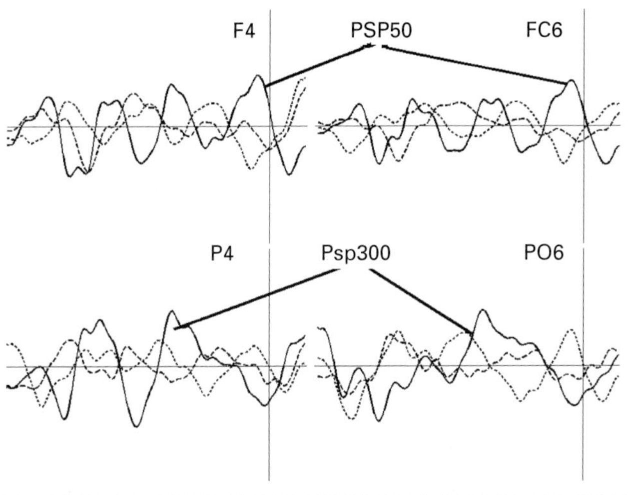

Figure 4.7. The ERP responses for 4 of 40 electrode locations. The presaccadic ERP for F4 and FC6 show a large presaccadic positive ERP component that occurred about 50ms before saccade onset for cued-exogenous saccades (PSP50). The presaccadic ERP for P4 and PO6 show a large presaccadic positive ERP component that occurred about 300ms before saccade onset for the cued-exogenous and endogenous saccades (PSP300) (from Richards, 2001b, Cortical indices of saccade planning following covert orienting in 20-week-old infants. *Infancy*, *2*, 135–157. Reprinted with permission of Lawrence Erlbaum Associates.)

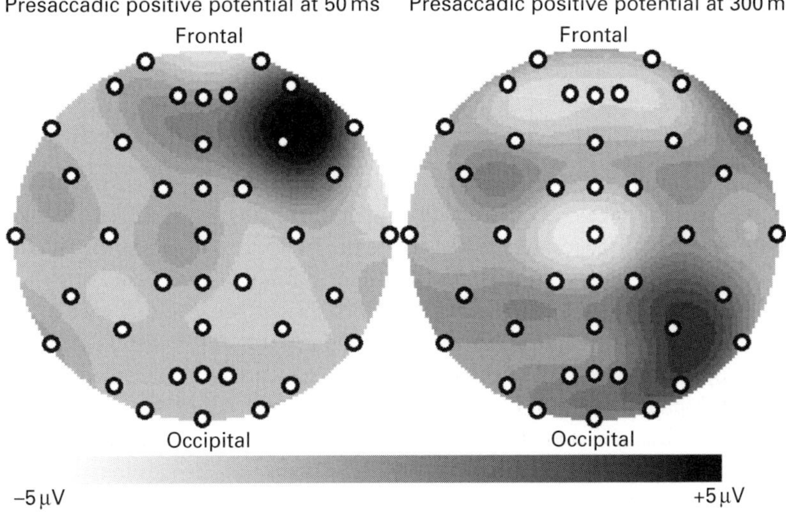

Figure 4.8. Topographical scalp potential maps for the PSP50 and PSP300 components for the difference between the cued-exogenous and the combined endogenous and cued-exogenous saccades (left) and for the difference between the combined cued-exogenous and endogenous, and the cued-exogenous saccades (right). The maps were plotted as if the infant were making a saccade towards the left side (from Richards, 2001b, Cortical indices of saccade planning following covert orienting in 20-week-old infants. *Infancy*, *2*, 135–157. Reprinted with permission of Lawrence Erlbaum Associates.)

involved in this presaccadic activity (Richards, 2001b). "Equivalent current dipole analysis" ("brain electrical source analysis"; Huizenga & Molenaar, 1994; Nunez, 1990; Scherg, 1990, 1992; Scherg & Picton, 1991; see also Chapter 2) hypothesizes specific locations for a neural generator of the recorded ERP activity and compares the activity generated on the scalp by the hypothesized dipole with the recorded cortical potentials. Plate 3 (top left figure) shows the topographical scalp potential map for presaccadic ERP potential occurring about 50 ms before the saccade to the expected location (i.e. Fig. 4.7 top panels; Fig. 4.8, left panel). A current dipole located in the area of the frontal eye fields (Plate 3 bottom figures) was used to generate a topographical map of this effect (Plate 3 top right figure). The hypothesized cortical dipole generated a scalp potential map that closely mapped the recorded ERP. This analysis is consistent with the interpretation that the eye movements to the target in the planned location involve cortical areas that control planned eye movements. These results also show that the brain areas controlling planned saccades can be measured directly with scalp-recorded ERPs.

CONCLUSIONS

1. Developmental changes in attention are caused by changes in the brain.
2. Infant recognition memory development parallels brain–attention development.
3. Neurodevelopment bases of covert orienting and eye movement planning can be examined directly in young infants.
4. New techniques in recording and quantification of EEG and ERP will result in more studies using direct methods of brain measurement in the study of attention development.

Attention shows development over the human lifespan, and much of that development is due to concomitant changes in the brain areas controlling attention. This chapter has emphasized neurodevelopmental models of visual attention in the first 6 to 12 months of infancy. This was chosen because of explicit neurodevelopment models that relate changes in the brain areas involved in vision to developmental changes in infant visual behaviour and visual attention. Such neurodevelopmental approaches to infant behaviour could be discussed that related brain changes to other sensory systems or to higher cognitive functions (Colombo, 1995; Ruff & Rothbart, 1996). Developmental changes in attention that occur in children, adolescents, and adults could probably use such models, although these models are rare at this time. The chapter emphasized the use of direct measures of brain activity, such as scalp-recorded ERP changes that occur in tasks requiring visual attention.

A major shift now occurring in this area of research is the use of high-density EEG and ERP for the identification of specific cortical areas involved in attention. The high-density ERP recording increases the resolution of ERP even if used without topographical methods or cortical source analysis. Such enhanced resolution, along with quantitative techniques, will allow the identification of specific scalp sites or spatiotemporal localizing of such effects. Perhaps the brightest light on this horizon is the ability to pinpoint specific areas of the cortex that generate the scalp-recorded EEG/ERP with equivalent current dipole analysis or associated cortical source techniques. The study reported in this chapter identifying the frontal eye fields as the likely source for the presaccadic ERP effects in infant planned saccades is such an example. This is particularly critical for infants and very young children for whom other neuroimaging techniques are still not feasible (see Chapter 2). Such techniques should lead to a better understanding of the relation between brain development and the development of visual attention in infants and children.

ACKNOWLEDGEMENT

The writing of this chapter was supported by a grant from the National Institute of Child Health and Human Development, R01-HD19842.

REFERENCES

Atkinson, J., & Braddick, O. (2001). Visual development. In M. de Haan & M.H. Johnson (Eds.), *The cognitive neuroscience of development*. Hove, UK: Psychology Press.

Balaban, C.D., & Weinstein, J.M. (1985). The human pre-saccadic spike potential: Influences of a visual target, saccade direction, electrode laterality and instructions to perform saccades. *Brain Research, 347*, 49–57.

Becker, W., Hoehne, O., Iwase, K., & Kornhuber, H.H. (1973). Cerebral and ocular muscle potentials preceding voluntary eye movements in man. *Electroencephalography and Clinical Neurophysiology Supplement, 33*, 99–104.

Bell, M.A. (1998). In J.E. Richards (Ed.), *Cognitive neuroscience of attention: A developmental perspective* (pp. 287–316). Hillsdale, NJ: Lawrence Erlbaum Associates Inc.

Berg, W.K., & Richards, J.E. (1997). Attention across time in infant development. In P.J. Lang, R.F. Simons, & M.T. Balaban (Eds.), *Attention and orienting: Sensory and motivational processes* (pp. 347–368). Mahwah, NJ: Lawrence Erlbaum Associates Inc.

Boch, R.A., & Goldberg, M.E. (1989). Participation of prefrontal neurons in the preparation of visually guided eye movements in the rhesus monkey. *Journal of Neurophysiology, 61*, 1064–1084.

Bronson, G.W. (1974). The postnatal growth of visual capacity. *Child Development, 45*, 873–890.

Bronson, G.W. (1997). The growth of visual capacity: Evidence from infant scanning patterns. In C. Rovee-Collier & L.P. Lipsitt (Eds.), *Advances in infancy research* (Vol. 11, pp. 109–141). Greenwich, CT: Ablex.

Bruce, C.J., & Goldberg, M.E. (1984). Physiology of the frontal eye fields. Special issue: The frontal lobes –uncharted provinces of the brain. *Trends in Neurosciences, 7*, 436–441.

Bruce, C.J., & Goldberg, M.E. (1985). Primate frontal eye fields: I. Single neurons discharging before saccades. *Journal of Neurophysiology, 53*, 603–635.

Butcher, P.R., Kalverboer, A.F., & Gueze, R.H. (1999). Inhibition of return in very young infants: A longitudinal study. *Infant Behaviour and Development, 22*, 303–319.

Canfield, R.L., Smith, E.G., Brezsnyak, M.E., & Snow, K.L. (1997). Information processing through the first year of life. *Monographs of the Society for Research in Child Development*, Serial No 250.

Casey, B.J., & Thomas, K.M. (2002). Methods in cognitive neuroscience. In M. de Haan & M.H. Johnson (Eds.), *The cognitive neuroscience of development*. Hove, UK: Psychology Press.

Clohessy, A.B., Posner, M.I., Rothbart, M.K., & Vecera, S.P. (1991). The development of inhibition of return in early infancy. *Journal of Cognitive Neuroscience, 3*, 345–350.

Colombo, J. (1995). On the neural mechanism underlying developmental and individual differences in visual fixation in infancy: Two hypotheses. *Developmental Review, 15*, 97–135.

Courchesne, E. (1977). Event-related brain potentials: Comparison between children and adults. *Science, 197*, 589–592.

Courchesne, E. (1978). Neurophysiological correlates of cognitive development: Changes in long-latency event-related potentials from childhood to adulthood. *Electroencephalography and Clinical Neurophysiology, 45*, 468–482.

Courchesne, E., Ganz, L., & Norcia, A.M. (1981). Event-related brain potentials to human faces in infants. *Child Development, 52*, 804–811.

Csibra, G., Johnson, M.H., & Tucker, L.A. (1997). Attention and oculomotor control: A high-density ERP study of the gap effect. *Neuropsychologica, 35*, 855–865.

Csibra, G., Tucker, L.A., & Johnson, M.H. (1998). Neural correlates of saccade planning in infants: A high-density ERP study. *International Journal of Psychophysiology, 29*, 201–215.

Csibra, G., Tucker, L.A., Volein, A., & Johnson, M.H. (2000). Cortical development and saccade planning: The ontogeny of the spike potential. *NeuroReport, 11*, 1069–1073.

de Haan, M., & Nelson, C.A. (1997). Recognition of the mother's face by six-month-old infants: A neurobehavioural study. *Child Development, 68*, 187–210.

Fagan, J.F. (1974). Infant recognition memory: The effects of length of familiarization and type of discrimination task. *Child Development, 59*, 1198–1210.

Frick, J., & Richards, J.E. (2001). Individual differences in infants' recognition of briefly presented visual stimuli. *Infancy, 2*, 331–352.

Hanes, D.P., & Schall, J.D. (1996). Neural control of voluntary movement initiation. *Science, 274*, 427–430.

Hanes, D.P., Thompson, K., & Schall, J.D. (1995). Relationship of presaccadic activity in frontal eye field and supplementary eye field to saccade initiation in macaque: Poisson spike train analysis. *Experimental Brain Research, 103*, 85–96.

Heilman, K.M., Watson, R.T., Valenstein, E., & Goldberg, M.E. (1987). Attention: Behaviour and neural mechanisms. In V.B. Mountcastle, F. Plum, & S.R. Geiger (Eds.), *Handbook of physiology* (pp. 461–481). Bethesda, MD: American Physiological Society.

Hillyard, S.A., Mangun, G.R., Woldroff, M.G., & Luck, S.J. (1995). Neural systems mediating selective attention. In M.S. Gazzaniga (Ed.), *Cognitive neurosciences* (pp. 665–682). Cambridge, MA: MIT Press.

Hood, B.M. (1993). Inhibition of return produced by covert shifts of visual attention in 6-month-old infants. *Infant Behaviour and Development, 16*, 245–254.

Hood, B.M. (1995). Shifts of visual attention in the human infant: A neuroscientific approach. *Advances in Infancy Research, 10*, 163–216.

Hood, B.M., & Atkinson, J. (1991). *Shifting covert attention in infants.* Paper presented at the meeting of the Society for Research in Child Development, Seattle, WA, April 1991.

Hood, B.M., Atkinson, J., & Braddick, O.J. (1998). Selection-for-action and the development of orienting and visual attention. In J.E. Richards (Ed.), *Cognitive neuroscience of attention: A developmental perspective* (pp. 219–250). Hillsdale, NJ: Lawrence Erlbaum Associates Inc.

Hopfinger, J., & Mangun, G.R. (1998). Reflexive attention modulates processing of visual stimuli in human extrastriate cortex. *Psychological Science, 9*, 441–447.

Huizenga, H.M., & Molenaar, P.C.M. (1994). Estimating and testing the sources of evoked potentials in the brain. *Multivariate Behavioural Research, 29*, 237–262.

Johnson, M.H. (1990). Cortical maturation and the development of visual attention in early infancy. *Journal of Cognitive Neuroscience, 2*, 81–95.

Johnson, M.H. (1995). The development of visual attention: A cognitive neuroscience perspective. In M.S. Gazzaniga (Ed.), *The cognitive neurosciences* (pp. 735–747). Cambridge, MA: MIT Press.

Johnson, M.H. (1997). *Developmental cognitive neuroscience*. London: Blackwell.

Johnson, M.H., Gilmore, R.O., & Csibra, G. (1998). Toward a computational model of the development of saccade planning. In J.E. Richards (Ed.), *Cognitive neuroscience of attention: A developmental perspective* (pp. 103–130). Hillsdale, NJ: Lawrence Erlbaum Associates Inc.

Johnson, M.H., Posner, M.I., & Rothbart, M.K. (1991). Components of visual orienting in early infancy: Contingency learning, anticipatory looking and disengaging. *Journal of Cognitive Neuroscience, 3*, 335–344.

Johnson, M.H., & Tucker, L.A. (1996). The development and temporal dynamics of spatial orienting in infants. *Journal of Experimental Child Psychology, 63*, 171–188.

Karmel, B.Z. & Maisel, E.G. (1975). A neuronal activity model for infant visual attention. In L.B. Cohen & P. Salapatek (Eds.), *Infant perception: From sensation to cognition* (Vol. 1, pp. 77–131). New York: Academic Press.

Kurtzberg, D., & Vaughan, H.G. (1980). Differential topography of human eye movement potentials preceding visually triggered and self-initiated saccades. In H.H. Kornhuber & L. Deecke (Eds.), *Motivation, motor and sensory processes of the brain* (pp. 203–208). Amsterdam: Elsevier Science Publishers.

Kurtzberg, D., & Vaughan, H.G. (1982). Topographic analysis of human cortical potentials preceding self-initiated and visually triggered saccades. *Brain Research, 243*, 1–9.

Maurer, D., & Lewis, T.L. (1979). A physiological explanation of infants' early visual development. *Canadian Journal of Psychology, 33*, 232–252.

Maurer, D., & Lewis, T.L. (1991). The development of peripheral vision and its physiological underpinnings. In M.J.S. Weiss & P.R. Zelazo (Eds.), *Newborn attention: Biological constraints and the influence of experience* (pp. 218–255). Norwood, NJ: Ablex Publishing Co.

Maurer, D., & Lewis, T.L. (1998). Overt orienting toward peripheral stimuli: Normal development and underlying mechanisms. In J.E. Richards (Ed.), *Cognitive neuroscience of attention: A developmental perspective* (pp. 51–102). Hillsdale, NJ: Lawrence Erlbaum Associates Inc.

Mesulam, M.M. (1983). The functional anatomy and hemispheric specialisation for directed attention. *Trends in Neuroscience, 6*, 384–387.

Moster, M.L., & Goldberg, G. (1990). Topography of scalp potentials preceding self-initiated saccades. *Neurology, 40*, 644–648.

Nelson, C.A. (1994). Neural correlates of recognition memory in the first postnatal year. In G. Dawson & K.W. Fischer (Eds.), *Human behaviour and the developing brain* (pp. 269–313). New York: Guilford Press.

Nelson, C.A., & Collins, P.F. (1991). Event-related potential and looking-time analysis of infants' responses to familiar and novel events: Implications for visual recognition memory. *Developmental Psychology, 27*, 50–58.

Nelson, C.A., & Collins, P.F. (1992). Neural and behavioural correlates of visual recognition memory in 4- and 8-month-old infants. *Brain and Cognition, 19*, 105–121.

Nelson, C.A., & deRegnier, R.A. (1992). Neural correlates of attention and memory in the first year of life. *Developmental Neuropsychology, 8*, 119–134.

Nelson, C.A., & Dukette, D. (1998). In J.E. Richards (Ed.), *Cognitive neuroscience of attention: A developmental perspective* (pp. 327–362). Hillsdale, NJ: Lawrence Erlbaum Associates Inc.

Nelson, C.A., & Monk, C. (2001). The use of event-related potentials in the study of cognitive development. In C.A. Nelson & M. Luciana (Eds.), *Handbook of developmental cognitive neuroscience* (pp. 125–136). Cambridge, MA: MIT Press.

Nunez, P.L. (1990). Localization of brain activity with electroencephalography. *Advances in Neurology, 54*, 39–65.

Posner, M.I. (1980). Orienting of attention. *Quarterly Journal of Experimental Psychology, 32*, 3–25.

Posner, M.I. (1995). Attention in cognitive neuroscience: An overview. In M.S. Gazzaniga (Ed.), *Cognitive neurosciences* (pp. 615–624). Cambridge, MA: MIT Press.

Posner, M.I., & Cohen, Y. (1984). Components of visual orienting. In H. Bouma & D.G. Bouwhis (Eds.), *Attention and performance X* (pp. 531–556). Hillsdale, NJ: Lawrence Erlbaum Associates Inc.

Posner, M.I., & Petersen, S.E. (1990). The attention system of the human brain. *Annual Review of Neuroscience, 13*, 25–42.

Rafal, R.D. (1998). The neurology of visual orienting: A pathological disintegration of development. In J.E. Richards (Ed.), *Cognitive neuroscience of attention: A developmental perspective* (pp. 181–218). Hillsdale, NJ: Lawrence Erlbaum Associates Inc.

Ray, W.J. (1990). Electrical activity of the brain. In J.T. Cacioppo & L.G. Tassinary (Eds.), *Principles of psychophysiology: Physical, social, and inferential elements* (pp. 385–412). Cambridge: Cambridge University Press.

Richards, J.E. (1989). Development and stability in visual sustained attention in 14, 20, and 26 week old infants. *Psychophysiology, 26*, 422–430.

Richards, J.E. (1995). Infant cognitive psychophysiology: Normal development and implications for abnormal developmental outcomes. In T.H. Ollendick & R.J. Prinz (Eds.), *Advances in Clinical Child Psychology* (Vol 17, pp. 77–107). New York: Plenum Press.

Richards, J.E. (1997). Effects of attention on infants' preference for briefly exposed visual stimuli in the paired-comparison recognition-memory paradigm. *Developmental Psychology, 33*, 22–31.

Richards, J.E. (1998). Development of selective attention in young infants. *Developmental Science, 1*, 45–51.

Richards, J.E. (2000a). Attention in young infants: A developmental psychophysiological perspective. In C.A. Nelson & M. Luciana (Eds.), *Developmental cognitive neuroscience*. Cambridge, MA: MIT Press.

Richards, J.E. (2000b). Development of multimodal attention in young infants: Modification of the startle reflex by attention. *Psychophysiology, 37*, 1–11.

Richards, J.E. (2000c). *The effect of attention on the recognition of brief visual stimuli: An ERP study*. Paper presented at the International Conference on Infancy Studies, Brighton, UK, July, 2000.

Richards, J.E. (2000d). Localizing the development of covert attention in infants using scalp event-related-potentials. *Developmental Psychology, 36*, 91–108.

Richards, J.E. (2000e). *The development of covert attention to peripheral targets and its relation to attention to central visual stimuli*. Paper presented at the International Conference for Infancy Studies, Brighton, UK, July 2000.

Richards, J.E. (2001a). Cortical indices of saccade planning following covert orienting in 20-week-old infants. *Infancy, 2*, 135–157.

Richards, J.E. (2001b). *Using high-density EEG recording to localize cortical sources of infant attention*. Paper presented at the Society for Research in Child Development, Minneapolis, MN, April 2001.

Richards, J.E., & Casey, B.J. (1990). Infant visual recognition memory performance as a function of heart rate defined phases of attention. *Infant Behaviour and Development, 13*, 585.

Richards, J.E., & Casey, B.J. (1991). Heart rate variability during attention phases in young infants. *Psychophysiology, 28*, 43–53.

Richards, J.E., & Casey, B.J. (1992). Development of sustained visual attention in the human infant. In B.A. Campbell, H. Hayne, & R. Richardson (Eds.), *Attention and information processing in infants and adults* (pp. 30–60). Mahwah, NJ: Lawrence Erlbaum Associates Inc.

Richards, J.E., & Holley, F.B. (1999). Infant attention and the development of smooth pursuit tracking. *Developmental Psychology, 35*, 856–867.

Richards, J.E., & Hunter, S.K (1997). Peripheral stimulus localization by infants with eye and head movements during visual attention. *Vision Research, 37*, 3021–3035.

Richards, J.E., & Hunter, S.K. (1998). Attention and eye movement in young infants: Neural control and development. In J.E. Richards (Ed.), *Cognitive neuroscience of attention: A developmental perspective* (pp. 131–162). Mahwah, NJ: Lawrence Erlbaum Associates Inc.

Richards, J.E., & Lansink, J.M. (1998). Distractibility during visual fixation in young infants: The selectivity of attention. In C. Rovee-Collier, L. Lipsitt, & H. Hayne (Eds.), *Advances in infancy research* (Vol. 13, pp. 407–444). Norwood, NJ: Ablex Publishing Co.

Robbins, T.W., & Everitt, B.J. (1995). Arousal systems and attention. In M.S. Gazzaniga (Ed.), *Cognitive neurosciences* (pp. 703–720). Cambridge, MA: MIT Press.

Ruff, H.A., & Rothbart, M.K. (1996). *Attention in early development*. New York: Oxford University Press.

Salapatek, P. (1975). Pattern perception in early infancy. In L. Cohen & P. Salapatek (Eds.), *Infant perception*. New York: Academic Press.

Schall, J.D. (1991a). Neuronal activity related to visually guided saccadic eye movements in the supplementary motor area of rhesus monkeys. *Journal of Neurophysiology, 66*, 530–558.

Schall, J.D. (1991b). Neuronal activity related to visually guided saccades in the frontal eye fields of rhesus monkeys: Comparison with supplementary eye fields. *Journal of Neurophysiology, 66*, 559–579.

Schall, J.D. (1995). Neural basis of saccade target selection. *Reviews in the Neurosciences, 6*, 63–85.

Schall, J.D., & Hanes, D.P. (1993). Neural basis of saccade target selection in frontal eye field during visual search. *Nature, 366*, 467–469.

Schall, J.D., Hanes, D.P., Thompson, K.G., & King, D.J. (1995). Saccade target selection in frontal eye field of macaque: I. Visual and premovement activations. *Journal of Neuroscience, 15*, 6905–6918.

Scherg, M. (1990). Fundamentals of dipole source potential analysis. In F. Grandori, M. Hoke, & G.L. Romani (Eds.), *Auditory evoked magnetic fields and potentials* (pp. 40–69). Basel: Karger.

Scherg, M. (1992). Functional imaging and localization of electro-magnetic brain activity. *Brain Topography, 5*, 103–111.

Scherg, M., & Picton, T.W. (1991). Separation and identification of event-related potential components by brain electrical source analysis. In C.H.M. Brunia, G. Mulder, & M.N. Verbaten (Eds.), *Event-related brain research* (pp. 24–37). Amsterdam: Elsevier.

Schiller, P.H. (1985). A model for the generation of visually guided saccadic eye movements. In D. Rose & V.G. Dobson (Eds.), *Models of the visual cortex* (pp. 62–70). New York: John Wiley.

Schiller, P.H. (1998). The neural control of visually guided eye movements. In J.E. Richards (Ed.), *Cognitive neuroscience of attention: A developmental perspective* (pp. 3–50). Mahwah, NJ: Lawrence Erlbaum Associates Inc.

Schneider, G. (1969). Two visual systems. *Science, 163*, 895–902.

Simion, F., Valenza, E., Umilta, C., & Barba, B.D. (1995). Inhibition of return in newborns is temporo-nasal asymmetrical. *Infant Behaviour and Development, 18*, 189–194.

Smith, E.G., & Canfield, R.L. (1998). *Two-month-olds make predictive saccades: Evidence for early frontal lobe function.* Paper presented at the International Society for Infant Studies conference, Atlanta, GA.

Swick, D., Kutas, M., & Neville, H.J. (1994). Localizing the neural generators of event-related brain potentials. In A. Kertesz (Ed.), *Localization and neuroimaging in neuropsychology. Foundations of neuropsychology* (pp. 73–121). San Diego: Academic Press.

Tucker, D.M. (1993). Spatial sampling of head electrical fields: The geodesic sensor net. *Electroencephalography and Clinical Neurophysiology, 87*, 154–163.

Tucker, D.M., Liotti, M., Potts, G.F., Russell, G.S., & Posner, M.I. (1994). Spatiotemporal analysis of brain electrical fields. *Human Brain Mapping, 1*, 134–152.

Valenza, E., Simion, F., & Umilta, C. (1994). Inhibition of return in newborn infants. *Infant Behaviour and Development, 17*, 293–302.

Weinstein, J.M., Balaban, C.D., & VerHoeve, J.N. (1991). Directional tuning of the human presaccadic spike potential. *Brain Research, 543*, 243–250.

Wentworth, N., & Haith, M.M. (1998). Infants' acquisition of spatiotemporal expectations. *Developmental Psychology, 34*, 247–257.

Wentworth, N., Haith, M.M., & Karrer, R. (2001). Behavioural and cortical measures of infants' visual expectations. *Infancy, 2*, 175–196.

CHAPTER FIVE

A cognitive neuroscience perspective on early memory development

Charles A. Nelson
Institute of Child Development and Department of Pediatrics, University of Minnesota, USA

Sara J. Webb
Institute of Child Development, University of Minnesota, USA

INTRODUCTION

It is difficult to date a historical interest in memory development. Clearly Freud was enamoured by the topic, as it lay at the route of his speculation that early life experiences have a profound and central role in many aspects of one's day-to-day adult life (Freud, 1965). Indeed, many attribute to Freud the notion that we fail to remember the events that transpire during our first few years of life (the concept of infantile amnesia) because we repress these early memories. Although such speculation was then, and remains, without empirical support, this view of early memory continues to dominate some schools of psychoanalytic thought and psychotherapeutic practice (e.g. it is behind the movement to help patients "recover" early childhood memories). Further, it has weaved its way into some contemporary views of attachment theory (e.g. the concept of inner working models, whereby infants develop a mental representation of their attachment relationship with their primary caretaker; see Bowlby, 1969).

Although clinically relevant, approaching how memory develops by studying how (and why) early memories are forgotten might not be the most fruitful avenue to pursue with regard to how early memories are formed and stored. For this reason, several investigators have formulated more developmentally oriented and/or sensitive approaches to the concept of infantile amnesia and early memory development. For example, Howe and Courage (1993, 1997) argue that the failure to recall the events from our infancy is not due to encoding or retrieval errors, or indeed any fundamental immaturity in the memory system *per se*; rather, they argue that the infant lacks what they refer to as the "cognitive self". With the emergence of the self at around the second year of life comes true autobiographical memory; that is, the ability to place oneself into one's memories (e.g. memories that happened to *me*). By contrast, our group (see Nelson & Carver, 1998, for a discussion) has adopted a more neurobiological (rather than phenomenological) perspective, and suggested that infantile amnesia might well be due to immaturity in the inferotemporal structures to which the hippocampus and rhinal cortex are intimately connected. Thus, we fail to remember the events from the first few years of life primarily because these events are not laid down in those regions of the brain that eventually give rise to conscious recollection of long-term memories.

The approach we adopt in this chapter complements and extends those of other investigators (for an overview, see Cowan, 1997). It does so by considering the neural bases of memory development. In our estimation, only by understanding the relation between changes in the brain and changes in memory will we be able to provide a complete account of the ontogeny of memory. The premise upon which this claim is made is that most accounts of memory development operate at the descriptive, rather than the mechanistic, level. Thus, changes in memory capacity or retrieval ability are accounted for without benefit of explaining what underlying brain systems make such changes possible. By contrast, our approach attempts to consider the relation between changes in the brain and changes in memory. This bidirectional perspective takes into consideration how changes in the brain influence changes in memory behaviour and, conversely, how changes in behaviour can influence changes in the brain. In so doing we hope to be able to provide a more synthetic view of the memory ability of the developing child.

We begin our chapter by briefly reviewing the history of interest in the relation between brain and memory. We then summarize a model put forward several years ago by one of us (Nelson, 1995) that focuses specifically on the neural bases of memory. We update and expand this model in two ways. To update the model, we begin our discussion by considering new evidence that bears on the neural systems thought to underlie the recognition of novel stimuli, and on the development of explicit memory in general. Here we emphasize new work in developmental neuroscience, in cognitive neuroscience, and in studies with children with pre- or perinatal brain injury. Second, we expand this discussion to include a type or form of memory that benefited from only cursory discussion in the original model, specifically, the neural underpinnings of the development of implicit memory. We conclude by offering some suggestions for future research endeavours.

HISTORY OF THE STUDY OF BRAIN–BEHAVIOUR RELATIONS

Karl Lashley spent many years attempting to answer the question of how memory is organized in the brain. He taught animals a specific task and then systematically removed different pieces of cortex to establish where memory was stored. No matter how much cortex he removed, however, he could not find a specific part in which the memory "engram" was located. In 1950 he wrote:

> This series of experiments ... has discovered nothing directly of the real nature of the engram. I sometimes feel, in reviewing the evidence on the localization of the memory trace, that the necessary conclusion is that learning just is not possible. (Lashley, 1950)

Subsequent research (some of which will be reviewed below) made the reasons for Lashley's failure clear: many regions and structures in the brain are crucial to the formation of memory. In addition, although memories appear to be stored in the cortex, that storage seems to be organized in a distributed and redundant way.

Donald Hebb (one of Lashley's students) went on to develop a model of memory that has influenced research since the time it was first published in 1949. Hebb distinguished between short-term and long-term memory. He argued that short-term memory was an active process of limited duration, leaving no traces in the brain. By contrast, long-term memory (for example, remembering the name of your first teacher) was produced by structural changes in the nervous system. Hebb believed that these structural changes resulted from repeated activation of a loop of neurons in the cortex. Repeated activation of the neurons comprising the loop would cause the synapses between them to become functionally connected. Once connected, these neurons would constitute what Hebb called a cell assembly, and an excitation of neurons in any part of the assembly would activate the complete loop. Hebb posited that these structural changes probably occurred at synapses and took the form of some growth process or metabolic change that increased each neuron's effect on the next. Impressively, during the time Hebb was developing his theory, relatively little was known about synapses or processes such as inhibition.

The idea of cell assemblies acknowledged the fact that memories are not simply static records (such as a photograph) but, rather, are products of a change in neurons and molecules in the brain, and that memory is a process involving the interaction of many such neurons and molecules. Contemporary research in the molecular biology of memory (see Beggs et al., 1999, for a review) represents a tribute to Hebb's early theories.

CONTEMPORARY VIEWS OF MEMORY

Most cognitive neuroscientists agree that memory is not a unitary trait; rather, there are different "types" of memory or different memory "systems". Sherry and Schacter (1987) define a memory system as an interaction among acquisition, retention, and retrieval mechanisms that is characterized by certain rules of operation. Thus, if one proposes multiple memory systems, those systems must have different rules of operating. The current nomenclature in the memory literature refers to a dissociation between explicit (or declarative) memory and implicit (or non-declarative) memory (but see Roediger, Weldon, & Challis, 1989). The former typically refers to memory that can be declared, that can be brought to mind as an image or proposition, that exists in some time frame, and that is memory of which we are consciously aware (although, as discussed by Nelson, 1997, and Nelson & Carver, 1998, the extent to which this last criterion applies to the non- or preverbal organism remains unclear). Examples of explicit memory typically include the ability to recall events, objects, or places. Explicit memory can occur on a rapid time frame, in as little as one trial and, under certain circumstances, might involve some aspect of "self".

By contrast, implicit memory refers to a number of different subtypes of memory, although, collectively, all are distinct from explicit memory (and thus some investigators refer to this "type" as non-declarative memory). Not surprisingly, then, all forms of implicit memory are assumed to be unconscious, to require multiple trials to acquire, and might not involve the "self" at all. As described in detail later in this chapter, there are a number of types of implicit memory, such as habits, skills, procedures, conditioning, and priming. In many implicit memory paradigms, participants apply prior information to the test situation, without needing to recall the actual learning experience. For example, a subject's faster or more accurate identification of the test items relative to similar but unstudied items is taken as evidence of priming, whereas faster manual responses to a repeating pattern are taken as evidence of procedural learning. In the adult memory literature, researchers have proposed that explicit and implicit memory are dissociable in a number of ways, however, these terms might be more descriptive in nature, specifying the retrieval circumstances and do not necessarily refer to a specific memory system (see Schacter & Tulving, 1994).

THE DEVELOPMENT OF MEMORY SYSTEMS: A PRÉCIS

Although the literature on adult memory "systems" is vast, there is a relative paucity of information on when in development these systems emerge. Drawing heavily on work in adult cognitive neuroscience, behavioural neuroscience, and developmental neuroscience, Nelson (1995, 1997) has proposed a neurobiologically based model of memory development. In this model implicit and explicit memory can be distinguished from one another early in life (see Table 5.1). Nelson (1995, 1997) proposed that within the first few months of life a form of explicit memory termed "pre-explicit" memory makes its appearance. This type of memory largely reflects the infant's (possibly obligatory) response to novelty, and is often observed in such paradigms as the visual paired comparison procedure or the habituation procedure. The hippocampus is probably the major structure that subserves novelty responses (discussed later). As infants approach 1 year of age, development of regions within the inferior temporal cortex (such as area TE)

TABLE 5.1 The major memory systems and developmental tasks

General system	*Subsystems*	*Tasks*	*Neural systems related to tasks*
Implicit memory (non-declarative memory)	Procedural learning	Serial reaction time (SRT) task	Striatum, supplementary motor association, motor cortex, frontal cortex
		Visual expectation paradigm (VExP)	Frontal cortex, motor areas
	Conditioning	Conditioning	Cerebellum, basal ganglia
	Perceptual representation system	Perceptual priming paradigms	Modality dependent: parietal cortex, occipital cortex, inferior temporal cortex, auditory cortex
Explicit memory	Pre-explicit memory	Novelty detection in habituation and paired comparison tasks	Hippocampus
	Semantic (generic knowledge)	Semantic retrieval, word priming, and associative priming	Left prefrontal cortex, anterior cingulate hippocampal cortex
	Episodic (autobiographical)	Episodic encoding	Left prefrontal cortex, left orbitoprefrontal cortex
		Recall and recognition	Right prefrontal, anterior cingulate, parietal, cerebellum, hippocampal cortex

makes possible the emergence of more sophisticated forms of explicit memory, such as the ability to recognize a novel object in the delayed non-match to sample (DNMS) task, and to recognize objects in one modality (e.g. vision) that were originally presented in another (e.g. haptic). As these cortical regions mature (as, too, the connections between them and the medial temporal lobe), dramatic improvements in explicit memory are observed. Finally, as children move from the transition from preschool (ages 3–4 years) to school age (ages 5–6 years), development in regions of the prefrontal cortex makes possible the child's use of strategies and improved mnemonic ability.

The development of the implicit memory system is more difficult to define, because implicit memory refers to a heterogeneous set of abilities that might involve a number of neural systems, each of which has its own developmental trajectory. However, there might be several processes available to infants early in the first year of life that underlie these implicit tasks. First, by 2 to 3 months of age, we suggest that a perceptual representation system (Mandler, 1988; Schacter, 1992) is functional and allows infants and young children to take advantage of the perceptual similarities between learning and test on priming tasks and instrumental conditioning paradigms. This system might be a precursor to Schacter's (1994) perceptual representation system, which operates at a presemantic level and is based on the perceptual modality of the test items. This system represents information about the form and structure, but not the meaning or associative properties of words and objects (Schacter, 1994). It is likely that these processes involve the neural systems within their representative perceptual system, i.e. visual processing of stimuli within the occipital and parietal cortices. Second, based on results from the visual expectancy paradigm and classical conditioning tasks, by 2 months infants are able to take advantage of contingencies in their environment and develop expectations for certain events. Young infants can also be guided by rule-based behaviour without needing to possess an awareness of the relationship between the concepts. This system would allow children to develop motor responses that were adaptive to repeated experiences.

In the sections that follow, we elaborate and update this model of memory development. We begin with a discussion of explicit memory, and then progress to a discussion of implicit memory.

THE DEVELOPMENT AND NEURAL BASES OF PRE-EXPLICIT AND EXPLICIT MEMORY

Recognition memory and novelty preferences

The vast majority of the literature on infant memory is predicated on the infant's ability to recognize a previously seen (or felt, or heard) stimulus as inferred by a preference for a novel stimulus. For example, in the habituation procedure, infants are presented with a single stimulus repeatedly until their looking time declines to half or less than that observed in the beginning of the session. Immediately or following a delay, infants are presented with pictures of the same stimulus, followed by a picture of a novel stimulus. Longer looking to the novel stimulus is taken as evidence of recognition memory. Similarly, in the visual paired comparison (VPC) procedure, infants are initially familiarized to a pair of identical stimuli for a set period of time (e.g. 30 to 60s, depending on age). Either immediately after familiarization, or after a delay, test trials are presented in which the familiar stimulus is paired simultaneously with a novel stimulus for two, counterbalanced (left, right positions reversed) trials. Again, longer looking to the novel stimulus permits the inference that the infant has recognized the previously seen (familiarized) stimulus. In the DNMS task, infants are presented with a sample stimulus for a set period of time, and then, following some delay, are presented with a pair of stimuli, one of which is familiar and the other novel. Correct reaching (or looking) to the novel stimulus is taken as evidence of recognition memory.

Although all three of these tasks depend on the subject responding differentially to the novel versus familiar stimuli, the time course of development differs among them. For example, although novelty preferences have been observed in both the VPC and habituation tasks at or shortly after birth (Pascalis & de Schonen, 1994; Pascalis, de Schonen, Morton, & Deruelle, 1995), performance on the classic reaching version of the DNMS task is much slower to mature, with children not performing well on this task until after the fourth year of life (Overman, Bachevalier, Sewell, & Drew, 1993). As discussed by Nelson (1995, 1997), requirements other than novelty preferences likely contribute to this different developmental timetable.[1]

In the original formulation of his model, Nelson (1995) speculated that novelty preferences depend disproportionately on the hippocampus (see Plate 4). For example, Bachevalier and colleagues (Bachevalier, Brickson, & Haggar, 1993) demonstrated that when the hippocampus is lesioned in newborn monkeys, novelty preferences are perturbed. More recent investigations with human adults (using neuroimaging procedures such as PET or fMRI) and mature monkeys support this claim. For example, Zola et al. (2000) selectively lesioned just the hippocampus (and *not* the surrounding cortex) in mature cynomolgus monkeys using radio frequency ablation or ibotenic acid. Animals were tested on both the DNMS and VPC tasks with varying delays. The authors reported that across both procedures, at all delays except one, recognition memory was impaired. The exception was for the 1s delay in the VPC procedure. From this, the authors concluded that: (1) the hippocampus is critically involved in recognition memory; and (2) the detection of novelty *per se* might not depend on the hippocampus. (For discussion of similar conclusions obtained in rats, see Honey, Watt, & Good, 1998; Wan, Aggleton, & Brown, 1999.)

The conclusion that the hippocampus might not mediate novelty responses *per se* is at odds with the conclusion drawn by Nelson in his original formulation. However, this discrepancy could be accounted for by two observations. First, the original inference that novelty preferences are mediated by the hippocampus depended on data in which both the hippocampus and surrounding cortex were lesioned (see Bachevalier et al., 1993). Thus, it is possible that more than just the hippocampus is involved in responding to novelty, or that the hippocampus actually mediates visual recognition memory, which is *inferred* by novelty preferences. Alternatively, it might also be the case that the hippocampus *is* involved in mediating novelty responses, but only in the juvenile animal, not the mature animal. This interpretation makes sense in light of the greater proclivity for responding to novelty in infant versus adult animals (including humans).

Support for the idea that the hippocampus supports recognition memory via responding to novelty can be found in the human adult neuroimaging literature. For example, Strange et al. (1999) reported that the left hippocampus responds disproportionately to novelty, whereas both left and right posterior hippocampus showed greatest activation to increasing familiarity. A similar finding that the hippocampus is involved in encoding has also been reported by Fernández et al.

---

[1] It should be noted that recognition memory for the mother's voice has also been demonstrated at birth using an operant conditioning procedure. Here it has been argued that *in utero* exposure to the mother's voice during the last weeks of pregnancy facilitates recognition at birth.

(1998). These findings are in agreement with other investigators, who have also reported that the hippocampus is critically involved in mediating novelty responses (Dolan & Fletcher, 1997; Tulving et al., 1996). Again, as stated above, it is difficult to disentangle perturbations in visual recognition memory from perturbations in responding to novelty *qua* novelty, because novelty preferences are used to infer memory. Zola et al. (2000) argued that hippocampal lesions did not affect novelty preferences at 1s delays, and thus, that impairment (i.e. decline in performance) at subsequent delays was due to problems in memory, not novelty detection. However, an alternative interpretation is that the perceptual support provided by the VPC procedure (in which both the familiar and novel stimuli are presented simultaneously) facilitated recognition at the 1s delay; that is, that infants could discriminate these stimuli due to some iconic store rather than need to compare the novel stimulus to one stored in memory. This could occur through iconic stores in short memory or through a perceptual representation system (see the section on Priming, p. 110).

Collectively, it is difficult to determine if lesions of the hippocampus impair visual recognition memory by knocking out novelty preferences or because they actually perturb memory *per se*. Speaking to this issue is a series of studies reported by Nelson and Collins (1991, 1992) with 4-, 6-, and 8-month-old infants. These authors initially familiarized infants to two stimuli. During the test trials that followed, infants saw one of these stimuli presented on 60 per cent of the trials ("frequent-familiar"), and the other on a random 20 per cent of the trials ("infrequent-familiar"). On each of the remaining 20 per cent of the trials a different (unique) stimulus was presented ("infrequent-novel"). Based on recordings of event-related potentials (ERPs), at 4 months infants were unable to distinguish among these three classes of events. At 6 months their ERPs differentiated both the novelty information (i.e. the response to the infrequent-novel stimuli differed from their response to the two classes of familiar stimuli) and the probability information (i.e. their ERPs distinguished between the two types of familiar stimuli). By contrast, at 8 months infants' ERPs distinguished the stimuli only at the level of novel versus familiar; that is, the ERPs were identical to the two classes of familiar stimuli, both of which differed from the response to the novel stimuli. From these findings the authors concluded that, sometime after the first half year of life, infants could, in fact, dissociate novelty from recognition memory.

To argue that from an early age the hippocampus mediates novelty preferences and thus recognition memory begs the question whether this structure is sufficiently mature early in life to do this. Indeed, it is known from histochemical, radiological, and anatomical studies that the hippocampus matures very early in the primate (see Serress, 2001, for a review). But, as we also know that mature forms of explicit memory (for a review, see Eichenbaum et al., 1999) depend on more than just the hippocampus, Nelson speculated that memory evaluated in paradigms that depend on novelty responses (without delays or where simple stimuli need to be encoded) probably reflects a primitive form of explicit memory that he called "pre-explicit" memory.

Pre-explicit memory can be distinguished from explicit memory in two respects. First, the latter depends on a more distributed system than just the hippocampus; particularly important components to this system are the entorhinal and perirhinal cortices (Plate 5), lesions of which have recently been shown to greatly affect explicit memory in the mature monkey (Murray & Mishkin, 1998).

Second, most tests of explicit memory depend on more than simple novelty preferences. For example, cross-modal recognition memory depends on the ability to recognize a stimulus as familiar, having initially encoded this stimulus in another sensory modality. In addition, when delays are imposed between initial presentation and test (such as in the VPC or DNMS tasks), infants must be able to compare the new stimulus to one stored in memory; that is, they cannot distinguish novel from familiar stimuli based on perceptually available information. Overall, then, what additionally distinguishes pre-explicit from explicit memory (aside from being hippocampally based versus dependent on a more distributed medial temporal lobe network) is that the former subserves novelty detection and the latter subserves memory *qua* memory.

THE ROLE OF THE PREFRONTAL CORTEX IN THE DEVELOPMENT OF EXPLICIT MEMORY

Deferred imitation task

Nelson speculated that the transition from pre-explicit to explicit memory is made as infants approach the end of the first year of life. It is during this period of time, for example, that infants are able to tolerate increasingly longer delays between initial exposure to a stimulus and subsequent tests of recognition. In addition, in the original proposal, the deferred imitation paradigm was thought to reflect this more mature form of explicit memory. In this paradigm, infants are presented with a set of objects that when shown together form an event. An example might be placing a marble into a cup and then shaking the cup to make a rattle. Bauer and colleagues have made extensive use of this procedure and have reported that, as infants make the transition from the first to the second year of life, they are able to: (1) remember increasingly longer events sequences; and (2) tolerate increasingly long delays (Bauer & Mandler, 1989, 1992; for a review, see Bauer, 1997). As memory for these events does not depend on actually performing the action sequences themselves, but simply on observing them, Bauer has argued that the deferred imitation task is not dependent on skilled motor activity but, rather, reflects a form of recall memory. And, based on work by McDonough, Mandler, McKee, and Squire (1995) in which adults with bilateral lesions of medial temporal lobe structures (including the hippocampus) performed poorly on this task, Nelson (1995) suggested that this paradigm reflects a form of explicit memory.

One problem with this view is that more than simple memory might be involved in the deferred imitation task. First, infants must encode not just the object properties but also the actual order in which events occur. Such sequencing ability has historically been viewed as a function subserved by the prefrontal cortex (in the context of development, see the discussion by Luciana & Nelson, 1998). Indeed, it has long been known that lesions of the frontal cortex perturb the ability to reproduce a sequence of events in the correct order (Lepage & Richer, 1996). Second, in addition to sequencing the object, the participants must also encode the motoric actions performed on the objects. The frontal cortex might also be involved in the mapping of motoric responses onto a particular set of stimuli, similar to a serial reaction time task and could involve a frontobasal ganglia circuit. For example, Nishitani and Hari (2000) found that observation (and imitation) of manual actions activated the left inferior prefrontal cortex as well as the premotor cortex and the occipital cortex. The supplementary motor area has also been implicated in motor sequencing and might encode the numerical order of components (Clower & Alexander, 1998). Thus, the task is likely to engage a number of developing systems and their interactions.

Episodic encoding and retrieval

In an update on his original proposal, Nelson (1997) suggested that much of the development in explicit memory beyond the preschool years (age 3–4 years) is probably due to development of structures in the prefrontal cortex that facilitate the use of strategies.[2] For example, it is well known that one of the major transitions in memory once children begin formal schooling is an improvement in their meta-memory skills (for a discussion, see Kail, 1990). Thus, it is at this age that children become aware that things can be forgotten and that, to remember complex material, strategies must be employed. As a result, children learn to rehearse material, to chunk material, etc. Although not formally studied, it is surmised that, like the development of other problem-solving abilities subserved by the prefrontal cortex (see Luciana & Nelson, 1998, for a discussion), the ability to develop effective strategies for remembering more information and more complex information is also subserved by this region.

In general, there are qualitative differences between a child's encoding processes and later adult encoding strategies. For example, development occurs in children's ability to take advantage of semantic encoding. By 5 years of age, children show

[2] It should be obvious at this point in our discussion of memory development that little has been said of changes in memory—or in brain development—between the ages of 1 or 2 years and 3 or 4 years. The reason is simply that this has historically been uncharted territory and, thus, little is known about the transition from infancy to the preschool period, both behaviourally and neurologically.

increased performance on explicit tasks when the stimuli are originally encoded in a semantic manner ("deep" encoding). Performance on explicit tasks and on semantic priming paradigms improves as children have a larger semantic knowledge-base and as they are able to take better advantage of deeper encoding procedures. It is probable that children are also able to use this knowledge to make detailed searches during recall tasks. Also, as the general knowledge-base expands, representation amongst and between concepts changes, facilitating a higher level of encoding and easier recall (Chi & Koeske, 1983). These individual systems might allow children consciously to create mental representations and to become aware of their own memory.

From a cognitive neuroscience perspective, these changes in encoding and retrieval abilities are likely to be driven by structures in the frontal cortex. Several adult memory theories propose that the frontal cortex is lateralized in its proficiency in encoding and retrieving explicit memories. This includes a retrieval-associated right hemisphere proposal as well as an encoding-associated left hemisphere proposal. For example, the right prefrontal cortex (PFC) has been implicated in semantic associations as well as in non-verbal post-retrieval monitoring (Fletcher et al., 1998; Opitz, Mecklinger, Friederici, & von Cramon, 1999). On the other hand, Tulving et al. (1996) propose that the left frontal cortex becomes involved with encoding novel stimuli as well as when encoding is manipulated (also see Frey & Petrides, 1999). There are two caveats to this theory. First, there is little support for a completely dichotomous view of PFC activation, as bilateral activation of the PFC seems to be the rule, not the exception. Second, these studies all used adult participants and thus do not speak to the developmental role of the frontal cortex in explicit encoding and recall.

Summary

Overall, an element of the explicit memory system—in this case, pre-explicit memory—makes its appearance shortly after birth, although, not surprisingly, such memory ability is quite limited. Thus, infants show robust evidence of visual recognition memory when the task depends on novelty preferences, and when the interval between familiarization and test is of short duration. As infants approach a year of age, other structures in the formal explicit memory system, notably the inferotemporal cortex and rhinal cortex, begin to elaborate their connections with the hippocampus. In so doing, infants' proficiency in more demanding memory tasks improves, as does their ability to remember material over longer periods of time. In addition, as infants leave infancy, gradual changes in the prefrontal cortex enable them to remember sequences of events and eventually, in childhood, to develop strategies. The latter will eventually result in something that resembles the adult memory system, and is typically observed before children reach adolescence.

We should stress that changes in pre-explicit and explicit memory are not the only types of memory developing over the first few years of life—dramatic changes are also occurring in non-declarative forms of memory. It is this topic to which we next turn our attention.

THE DEVELOPMENT AND NEURAL BASES OF IMPLICIT MEMORY

Implicit memory has been defined as an evolutionarily "early" system (Reber, 1992), as dominating infant memory in the first 2 years of life (Schacter & Moscovitch, 1984), and as having a different developmental time course than explicit memory (Nelson, 1995, but see Rovee-Collier, 1997b). However, despite these proposals, few studies have investigated the developmental time-course of implicit memory, even though the neural structures thought to be involved in implicit memory mature early within the first year (Nelson, 1995, 1997). Structures that lie outside the medial temporal lobe, such as the cerebellum (conditioning), extrastriate occipital cortex, and inferior temporal cortex (visual priming, pattern learning, prototype learning), the striatum/basal ganglia (procedural learning and, in animals, habit learning), and frontal cortex (puzzle learning, conceptual fluency judgements) have been implicated in tests of implicit memory (see Squire, 1994). However, most implicit memory tasks require behavioural responses such as accuracy, reaction time, and stimulus categorization, which require subjects to be able to understand verbal instructions and respond motorically to stimuli. Because of these task requirements, few experiments have been adapted for a preverbal subject population. To further elaborate on the development of the implicit memory system, we will highlight three areas that have been used to test implicit memory in infants and young children: priming, procedural learning, and conditioning.

Priming

The priming paradigm is a well-known test of implicit memory, largely due to its use as a comparison to tests of recall and recognition. Priming refers to improvement in detecting or processing a perceptual object based on a recent experience (Tulving & Schacter, 1990). Perceptual priming is thought to act through the retrieval of the perceptual features of the representation at test, unlike conceptual priming and non-verbal explicit memory tasks, which are assumed to tap-in to semantic features (Weldon, Roediger, & Challis, 1989). Jacoby and colleagues (Jacoby, Baker, & Brooks, 1989) propose that priming will be maximized when the perceptual memory trace is similarly activated at study and test.

Schacter (1990, 1992) has proposed that perceptual priming is based on a perceptual representation system that is sensitive to the form and structure of the stimulus and is possibly based within the neural structures that process stimulus form and structure at a presemantic level. From this, one would assume that subjects could be primed to a number of image types. For example, facial priming would depend on the specificity and development of the neural system that supports facial recognition (e.g. the fusiform gyrus, superior temporal sulcus).

In a recent study in our laboratory (Webb & Nelson, 2001), we employed ERPs during a perceptual priming paradigm. In this study, 6-month-old infants were shown brief presentations of upright and inverted faces, some of which repeated 8 to 12 images later. When comparing the first, novel presentation of a face to the repeated or primed presentation, we found that primed images differed from novel images at the mid-latency negative component (Nc; see Nelson, 1994, and Nelson & Monk, 2001, for discussion of infant ERP components). Unlike ERP tests of object recognition/familiarity, we did not find any differentiation as reflected in positive slow wave activity (which has been interpreted by us as reflecting a form of explicit memory). In our study, the lack of significant effects of repetition at this component further strengthens the hypothesis that infants were not using explicit memory structures during this paradigm. Further experiments will help to elucidate whether these responses reflect a mature response (equivalent to adult performance) or whether they represent early efficacy.

To investigate perceptual priming in older children (over 3 years of age), a number of researchers have employed the picture fragment completion task. In this task, participants are shown fragmented pictures at encoding, these pictures consist of a standard number of stages ranging from the incomplete to the complete picture. To document implicit savings, subjects must show faster or earlier identification of the previously seen stimuli during the test phase. A number of researchers have documented equivalence across ages for priming on fragment pictures for 3-, 5-, and 7-year-olds (Parkin & Streete, 1988), 3-year-olds, 5-year-olds, and adults (Drummey & Newcombe, 1995), 4-, 5-, and 10-year-olds (Hayes & Hennessy, 1996), 4-year-olds, 6-year-olds, and adults (Russo, Nichelli, Gibertoni, & Cornia, 1995), 8- and 12-year-olds (DiGiulio, Seidenberg, O'Leary, & Raz, 1994; also on degraded words) as well as children who are learning disabled and normal 7- and 12-year-olds (Lorbasch & Worman, 1989). Although there are age-related trends in many of these studies, i.e. older subjects showed increased ease of identifying pictures on the learning phase as well as at the test phase (old versus new), in general they suggest that the system supporting perceptual priming is relatively mature by 3 years of age.

Several functional neuroimaging studies (PET and fMRI) with adult participants on priming tasks might give us a better idea of the neural structures involved in the tasks illustrated above. Repetition of items during the task can lead to decreases in the amount of activation present in specific brain areas, however, this appears to be selective depending on task overlap across repetition (Schacter & Buckner, 1998). Using a word stem completion task, primed words were produced more quickly and showed reduced activity in posterior perceptual processing areas (Schacter et al., 1996; Buckner et al., 1995). Similar results were found for object naming (Martin et al., 1995) and object categorization tasks (Buckner & Koustaal, 1998). The most consistent finding is blood flow decreases in extrastriate occipital regions, area BA19 (Squire et al., 1992; Buckner et al., 1995; Schacter et al., 1996). Additionally, more recent results using single trial fMRI have located areas extending into the inferior temporal cortex and left dorsal lateral prefrontal cortex (BA44; Buckner et al., 1998) in an object classification task. Further, a patient with a right posterior lesion has shown selective deficits in perceptual priming (Gabrieli et al., 1995) as has a right occipital lobe lesion patient (Fleischman, Vaidya, Lange, & Gabrieli, 1997), whereas amnesic patients with bilateral limbic system lesions have normal or near normal implicit retrieval (Graf & Schacter, 1985; Shimamura & Squire, 1984).

If perceptual priming depends on the integrity of the perceptual system used to process the stimulus, then priming should follow a developmental trajectory that is similar to that individual sensory system. For example, the visual cortex shows rapid development between the second and fourth postnatal months. Physically, the shape and structure of the eye and the retina are undergoing massive transformations. In the cortex, the maximum dendritic arborization and peak number of axon spines occurs at about 5 postnatal months (Michel & Garey, 1984) and the peak of synaptogenesis occurs between the fourth and nineteenth postnatal months, depending on the layer examined (Huttenlocher & de Courten, 1987). Given this profile, one might propose that the infant would be sensitive to priming as early as the second postnatal month, but that changes in the way in which visual images are processed might lead to increases in the infant's ability to use prior visual experience. In general, this fits with the results to date, with functional visual priming found in 6-month-olds (Webb & Nelson, 2001) and mature priming in 3-year-olds (Parkin & Streete, 1988) when the visual system is also largely mature. For auditory priming, these ages would probably decrease as the auditory system shows a faster developmental trajectory.

Procedural learning

Implicit learning according to Buchner and Wippich (1998) refers to the acquisition of knowledge about the structural properties of the relations between objects or events. Similar to implicit memory, of which implicit learning is thought to be a subset, knowledge acquisition is incidental. The most common task used to assess procedural learning is the Serial Reaction Time task (SRT task). Similar to most priming tasks, the SRT task cannot be used with younger participants because it necessitates the ability to understand and follow directions and to be able to make somewhat consistent and accurate motor movements. We will briefly discuss some SRT results with children; Nelson (1995) posited that the visual expectation task (VExP) might be a developmental precursor to the SRT task.

In the VExP task, infants are presented with predictable and unpredictable sequences of pictures in two locations. Infants are then assessed on their ability to predict or anticipate the sequences of target stimuli by shifting their visual attention. Like the SRT task, in which subjects are presented with several possible spatial locations, learning is measured by a decrease in reaction time to target fixation and the percentage of anticipatory eye movements to the target location. In early studies, Haith and colleagues (Haith, Hazan, & Goodman, 1988; Haith & McCarty, 1990; Haith, Wentworth, & Canfield, 1993) found reliable decreases in reaction times to alternating series and increases in anticipatory eye movements during the interstimulus intervals. Within a 2-min testing session, 2-month-old infants can form expectations for the reappearance of an alternate side event (R–L) and 3-month-olds' anticipations are seen to asymmetrical sequences (e.g. R–R–L; Canfield & Haith, 1991). Moreover, Canfield, Smith, Brezsnyak, and Snow (1997) found that between 2 and 12 months of age, infants produced greater percentages of anticipatory eye movements and increased facilitation of reaction time for predictable events with age.

Using the SRT task, Thomas and Nelson (2001) tested 4-, 7-, and 10-year-old children. Each subject participated in 5 blocks of 100 trials of a 10-item sequence; on blocks 1 and 4, the trials occurred in a random pattern. Similar to the results found in priming, older subjects demonstrated faster reaction times across all blocks. In general, sequence-specific learning was found as reaction times decreased across the sequence blocks and increased during the random blocks. A caveat to these results is that a greater percentage of the younger subjects did not show sequence specific learning. For 4-year-olds, approximately 25–30 per cent of the participants failed to show reaction time improvements across the sequence blocks.

Research with animals and adults has led to the proposal of a basal-ganglia–prefrontal-cortex system underlying the SRT task, which has been supported by patient and PET/fMRI studies. In the primate brain, the basal ganglia (Plate 6) send efferents to the motor and prefrontal cortices. These striatal circuits are thought to modulate movement and cognition, in particular, the timing of movements, motor planning, and execution. The prefrontal cortex (Fig. 5.1), on the other hand, is thought to be necessary for the arbitrary mapping of a set of stimuli onto a set of responses (Dieber et al., 1997). Unlike the SRT task, very little attention has been paid to the VExP outside infancy research and almost nothing is known about its neural circuitry. However, Posner, Rothbart, Thomas-Thrapp, and Gerardi (1998) have proposed that sequence learning in the VExP is associated with brain mechanisms related to covert visual orienting and might be represented by a fronto-executive attention network. Similar to the SRT task, all but the most simple sequences (R–L) will require higher-order information processing as well as motor areas related to eye movements. However, the VExP requires less coordination of output, because the infant does not need to map the stimuli display onto a response output. Because of these slight variations, the neural circuitry in this task might be different.

Unlike priming, which seems to be dependent on individual perceptual systems, procedural learning involves a more complex network of interwoven systems. However, similar to priming, infants do show sequence learning as early as 2 months of age. The improvements in this ability might occur with maturation

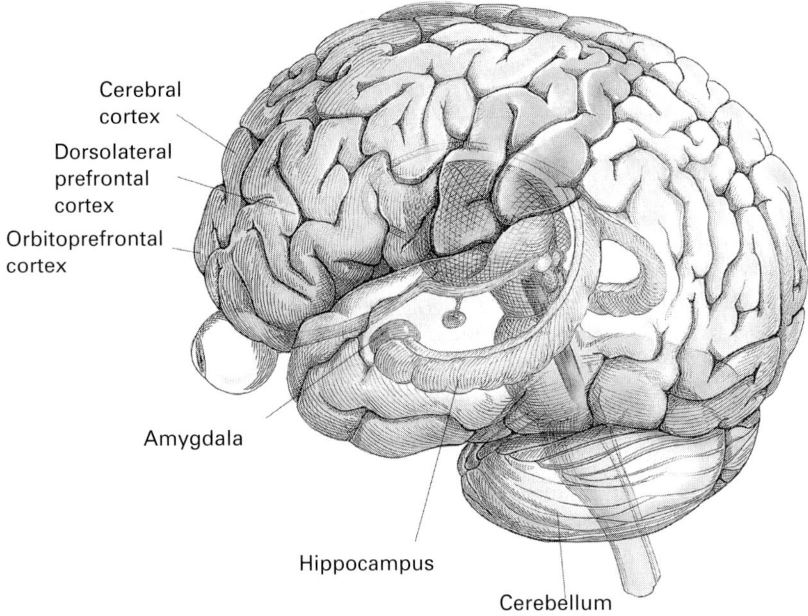

Figure 5.1. The prefrontal cortex, in particular, the dorsolateral and orbitofrontal cortices (from *Brain, Mind and Behaviour* by Floyd Bloom, Charles A. Nelson, Arlyne Lazerson © 1985, 1988, 2001 by Educational Broadcasting Corporation with permission of Worth Publishers).

of the individual neural systems as well as increased interconnectivity. Thus, we cannot claim that the procedural learning system is mature, simply that the system is functional shortly after birth.

Conditioning

Conditioning paradigms are traditionally associated with animal models of learning and memory. Conditioned learning allows the organism to anticipate an event by detecting its precursor signal (Balleine & Dickinson, 1998). In general, the participant learns the contingency between two previously unrelated stimuli or responses. There are two types of conditioning. First, in classical conditioning, a neutral cue (conditioned stimulus; CS) acquires the ability to elicit anticipatory responses as a result of its predictive association with an unconditioned stimulus (UCS) and unconditioned response (UR). Unto itself, the first stimulus does not evoke a response from the subject, however, the second stimulus does evoke a reflexive response. When the two stimuli and response are paired over time, the UR becomes associated with the neutral cue. The second, instrumental conditioning, involves the association of a novel stimulus with a motor response by the participant, which then leads to either a pleasurable outcome or the avoidance of an aversive outcome. Unlike classical conditioning, in instrumental conditioning the subject has control over the action that leads to the reward. However, in both cases, the subject does not need to consciously learn the contingency in order for the events to be associated.

Classical conditioning. Studies suggest that newborn infants are able to acquire a conditioned response. In an olfactory condition experiment, Sullivan et al. (1991) found conditioned responses (head turning) if the interstimulus interval between the CS (odour) and the UCS (tactile stimulation) was of a long duration (30s). Similarly, using the eye-blink-conditioning paradigm, Little, Lipsitt, and Rovee-Collier (1984) were able to condition 10-, 20-, and 30-day-old infants (with interstimulus intervals of 1500ms).

These results suggest that the mechanisms involved in conditioned learning are functional by birth. As the system matures, the time needed between the CS and UCS decreases; however, children at 7 years of age require longer interstimulus intervals than adults (Ohlrich & Ross, 1968). In addition, there seems to be an inverted "U"-shaped function, as both young infants and older adults need longer latencies to acquire the contingency behaviour (Woodruff-Pak & Jaeger, 1998). It is possible that the longer CS presentation and interstimulus interval needed during development reflect longer response latencies in the mechanical or biological properties of the response system.

Most of the work done on the neurobiological underpinnings of classical conditioning has been modelled on amnesiac patients and animal models. First, studies with patient populations have shown that the cerebellum is essential for both the acquisition and retention of (simple) classical conditioning and that no other forebrain structure, including the hippocampus, is required. For example, amnesiacs are able to acquire the eye-blink conditioned response (Woodruff-Pak, 1993), whereas patients with cerebellar lesions, particularly in the lateral cerebellum, are impaired (Woodruff-Pak, Papka, & Ivry, 1996). Consequently, changes across development might be due to the integrity of the cerebellar Purkinje cells. As we do not have a firm picture of the developmental of the cerebellum in humans, these are but speculations as to the possible mechanisms.

Instrumental conditioning. In an instrumental behaviour task, the subject must learn a stimulus–response mechanism as well as the contingency between the response and the reward (Balleine & Dickinson, 1998). Because this task requires an intentional motoric response (unlike classical conditioning, which relies on reflexive responses), it is likely that the developmental trajectory will be somewhat delayed. The principal operant task used with young infants is the mobile conjugate reinforcement task (2 to 6 months of age) and the train reinforcement task (6 to 18 months of age). In the former task, the subjects are placed in front of a novel mobile, on which they can perform a particular behaviour. The subjects must learn that their response, e.g. kicking, will control the rate of revolution of the mobile.

Rovee-Collier and colleagues have demonstrated improvements in retention of the mobile conjugate reinforcement task across the first year of life (see Rovee-Collier, 1997b, for a review). In general, 3-month-olds remember the behaviour for approximately 1 week, 6-month-olds for 2 weeks, 9-month-olds for 6 weeks, and 12-month-olds for 8 weeks (Hartshorn et al., 1998). After intervals longer than this, the infant no longer responds to the mobile with the learned behaviour. In general, the infant's memory for this learned behaviour is highly unstable; slight changes in the context or the mobile pattern, such as the insertion of a novel object at test, and the infant will not exhibit any retention (Butler & Rovee-Collier, 1989; Rovee-Collier, Patterson, & Hayne, 1985).

To date, little is known about the neuroscientific basis of the mobile conjugate reinforcement task. However, some parallels can be drawn to work with other goal-directed instrumental conditioning paradigms in animals and patients as well as conditioned motor learning tasks. Balleine and Dickinson (1998) suggest that instrumental behaviour involves the learning of the contingency between the response and the reward as well as the acquisition of the incentive value of the reward (i.e. the properties that make the reward rewarding). Following a neurotoxic lesion to either the prelimbic (PL) area of the prefrontal cortex (implicated in the control of purposeful action; Goldman-Rakic, 1994) or the insular cortex (IC, implicated in gustatory processing), animals were trained to press a lever and pull a chain for food pellets. Animals with PL lesions failed to show sensitivity to the reward-specific contingencies, whereas animals with IC lesions did not respond to the motivational manipulations of the food reward.

In a PET experiment by Deiber and colleagues (1997), in which subjects performed a conditional spatial motor learning task, researchers found decreases in activation in the premotor cortex (PMC), prefrontal cortex (PFC), and parietal cortex as well as increases in the cerebellum and portions of the basal ganglia (putamen). The results found in the PFC resemble those seen in motor sequence learning tasks, as well as other skill learning tasks. Activation in the PMC and basal ganglia probably reflects (conditional) motor learning and parallel decreases in the dorsal and rostral PMC areas were associated with the decreases found in the PFC. Similar to the results seen for the SRT task, the authors have proposed a PMC–PFC circuit.

Summary

Theoretically, researchers have proposed that implicit memory is functional at an earlier age and follows a different developmental trajectory than explicit memory. For example, most of the empirical studies of priming and recognition memory with children have put forward the idea that implicit memory is stable throughout childhood, whereas explicit memory shows improved functioning across the same ages. However, although this is true for certain priming studies, it is not implicit memory *per se* that is stable across these ages, but the representational memory system underlying perceptual priming. This system represents information about the form and structure, but not the meaning or associative properties of words and objects (Schacter, 1994) and would allow children to discriminate particulars of an item or a language, prior to assigning meaning to the item or sound (Church & Fisher, 1998). Moreover, this system would allow matches across different instances, without being limited to the particular context. By 4 months of age, we suggest that a visual/perceptual representation system (Schacter, 1992) is functional and allows infants to take advantage of the perceptual similarities between learning and test on priming tasks and instrumental conditioning paradigms.

Similarly, based on results from the VExP paradigm and classical conditioning tasks, by birth infants are able to take advantage of contingencies in their environment and develop expectations for certain events. Infants and children can be guided by rule-based behaviour without needing to possess an awareness of the relationship between the concepts. DiGiulio et al. (1994) suggests that these rule-guided processes, such as those typically described in procedural memory tasks, might allow infants to demonstrate various motor, perceptual, and cognitive skills without needing to be aware of the contingencies. This system would allow children to develop motor responses that were adaptive to their individual experiences. Although it has been proposed that this system involves a frontal lobe/executive system, it is likely that the cerebellum and the striatum are important in the timing of movements, motor planning, and motor execution.

This system undergoes a long period of developmental improvement, because infants and children are not able to take advantage of more complex contingencies. The procedural system that underlies instrumental conditioning and procedural learning also has a prolonged time course related to the intricacies of the motor task. Although young infants can map a motor response onto a stimulus, as the mapping becomes more complex and as more planning is needed to initiate the motor response, improvements in performance will extend into late childhood. Although children do not need to be aware of the contingencies, improvements in frontal lobe/working memory functions can allow children to take advantage of more complex rule-based paradigms and make more hypotheses about the structure of events.

PLASTICITY IN MEMORY SYSTEMS

The development of memory ability clearly involves more than just the coming online of underlying neural circuits; such circuits are most likely also modified by experience (for a discussion, see Nelson, 2000). Until recently, relatively little was known about the plasticity of the developing explicit memory system. However, this has begun to change with a series of reports published by Vargha-Khadem and colleagues. For example, these authors have reported that children who, as infants, suffered significant bilateral damage to the hippocampus, grow up to suffer from persisting deficits in episodic memory but show relative sparing of semantic memory (Gadian et al., 2000; Vargha-Khadem et al., 1997). Thus, such children develop normal language, near-normal vocabularies, and in most respects function normally in the world, despite frank damage to their episodic memory capacity. Moreover, this group has also reported that a single representative subject, "Jon", shows: (1) ERP evidence of impaired recollection in the face of intact recognition (Düzel, Vargha-Khadem, Heinze, & Mishkin, 2001); and (2) hippocampal activation (as inferred from fMRI) during memory retrieval, despite having considerable hippocampal volume reduction (Maguire, Vargha-Khadem, & Mishkin, 2001). The authors have suggested that one potential cause of such sparing in memory function has to do with the fact that the entorhinal cortex is relatively spared. This hypothesis remains to be evaluated. None the less, these findings are intriguing in that they point to a developmental dissociation between episodic and semantic memory and the lack of plasticity in explicit memory.

Similar to the explicit memory system, little is known about the plasticity of the implicit memory system. In a preliminary report, Thomas and colleagues (Thomas, Livnat, Eccard, & Casey, 1999), found that children who experienced varying degrees of intraventricular haemorrhage (IVH) at birth were likely to demonstrate slower reaction times and less sequence-specific knowledge during a serial reaction time task than full-term controls. In addition, these children are more likely to make errors in accuracy and are less likely to show explicit knowledge of the task. More severe IVH is known to damage brain tissue adjacent to the lateral ventricles, such as those involved in the basal ganglia, putamen, and caudate—structures that are known to be involved in procedural learning. As children were tested 5–10 years after this damage occurred (most IVHs typically occur within the first days of life), these findings suggest a relative lack of plasticity in memory circuits.

Unfortunately, in neither body of work do we know for certain what circuits were reorganized based on experience, nor do we have a clear picture of the mechanisms underlying such reorganization. Ideally, future investigations will focus on these questions, because understanding how memory circuits are modified by experience would greatly expedite our knowledge of memory development *per se*.

CONCLUSIONS

We believe it is clear from the literature reviewed here that the memory systems observed in the adult have their ontogeny in the infancy period. From this review we have drawn several conclusions:

1. A form of explicit memory called "pre-explicit" memory emerges shortly after birth. Pre-explicit memory gives way to explicit memory as infants

approach 1 year of age. Explicit memory undergoes continued refinements over the next decade of life, made possible, in part, by changes in the medial temporal lobe and prefrontal cortex.

2. Some forms of implicit memory also appear very early in life. Contrary to previous speculation (Schacter, & Moscovitch, 1984), the implicit memory system does, in fact, develop over the first years of life.
3. There appears to be greater plasticity in the explicit memory system than in the implicit memory system, although this conclusion is based on very few data.

These conclusions notwithstanding, many challenges lie ahead. First, although we have described the development of memory as reflecting independence of memory systems, it seems likely that these systems interact in everyday life. For example, memory is probably a dynamic system, such that developmental increases in motor and perceptual systems, as well as in short-term, working, and semantic memory, will lead to increases in the ability to encode and retrieve prior events and items in both explicit and implicit tasks. Thus, although we claim that several systems are functional by 6 months of age (i.e. novelty preference, priming, procedural learning), these systems undergo massive changes in the first years of life.

Second, many of our claims about the neural bases of memory are based on studies with animals or adult humans with brain damage. If our knowledge of early memory development is to increase, it is essential that we improve the methods whereby memory and its associated neural circuitry is studied in the human child.

Finally, it is essential that we undertake a systematic examination of the role of experience in influencing the development of the structures and circuits that lead to changes in memory performance across age.

ACKNOWLEDGEMENTS

The writing of this chapter was made possible, in part, by grants from the NIH (NS34458), the John D. and Catherine T. MacArthur Foundation, and the James S. McDonnell Foundation (through their support of a research network on early experience and brain development) to the first author, and from the NIH (MH12132) to the second author.

REFERENCES

Bachevalier, J., Brickson, M., & Hagger, C. (1993). Limbic-dependent recognition memory in monkeys develops early in infancy. *NeuroReport, 4*, 77–80.

Balleine, B., & Dickinson, A. (1998). Goal directed instrumental action: Contingency and incentive learning and their cortical substrates. *Neuropharmacology, 37*, 407–419.

Bauer, P.J. (1995). Recalling past events: From infancy to early childhood. *Annals of Child Development, 11*, 25–71.

Bauer, P.J. (1997). Development of memory in early childhood. In N. Cowan (Ed.), *The Development of Memory in Childhood* (pp. 83–111). Hove, UK: Psychology Press.

Bauer, P.J., & Mandler, J.M. (1989). One thing follows another: Effects of temporal structure on 1- to 2-year-olds' recall of events. *Developmental Psychology, 25*, 197–206.

Bauer, P.J., & Mandler, J.M. (1992). Putting the horse before the cart: The use of temporal order in recall of events by one-year-old children. *Developmental Psychology, 28*, 441–452.

Beggs, J.M., Brown, T.H., Byrne, J.H., Crow, T., LeDoux, J.E., LeBar, K. et al. (1999). Learning and memory: Basic mechanisms. In M.J. Zigmond, F.E. Bloom, S.C. Landis, J.L. Roberts, & L.R. Squire (Eds.), *Fundamental neuroscience* (pp. 1411–1454). New York: Academic Press.

Bloom, F., Nelson, C.A., & Lazerson, A. (2001). *Brain, mind and behavior* (3rd ed.). New York: Worth Publishers.

Bowlby, J. (1969). *Attachment and Loss*. New York: Basic Books.

Buchner, A., & Wippich, W. (1998). Differences and commonalities between implicit learning and implicit memory. In M. Stadler & P. Frensch (Eds.), *Handbook of implicit learning* (pp. 3–46). London: Sage Publications.

Buckner, R., Goodman, J., Burock, M., Rotte, M., Koutstaal, W., Schacter, D. et al. (1998). Functional-anatomic correlates of object priming in humans revealed by rapid presentation event-related fMRI. *Neuron, 20*, 285–296.

Buckner, R.L., & Koutstaal, W. (1998). Functional neuroimaging studies of encoding, priming, and explicit memory retrieval. *Proceedings of the National Academy of Sciences USA, 95*, 891–898.

Buckner, R., Petersen, S.E., Ojemann, J.G., Miezin, F.M., Squire, L.R., & Raichle, M.E. (1995). Functional anatomical studies of explicit and implicit memory retrieval tasks. *Journal of Neuroscience, 15*, 12–29.

Butler, J., & Rovee-Collier, C. (1989). Contextual gating of memory retrieval. *Developmental Psychobiology, 22*, 533–552.

Canfield, R., & Haith, M. (1991). Young infants' visual expectations for symmetric and asymmetric stimulus sequences. *Developmental Psychology, 27*, 198–208.

Canfield, R., Smith, E., Brezsnyak, M., & Snow, L.K. (1997). Information processing through the first year of life: A longitudinal study using the Visual Expectation Paradigm. *Monographs of the Society for Research in Child Development, 62*(2), 1–145.

Chi, M., & Koeske, R. (1983). Network representation of a child's dinosaur knowledge. *Developmental Psychology, 19*, 29–39.

Church, B., & Fisher, C. (1998). Long-term auditory word priming in preschoolers: Implicit memory support for language acquisition. *Journal of Memory and Language*, 39, 523–542.

Clower, W.T., & Alexander, G.E. (1998). Movement sequence-related activity reflecting numerical order of components in supplementary and presupplementary motor areas. *Journal of Neurophysiology, 80*, 1562–1566.

Cowan, N. (1997). *The development of memory in childhood*. Hove, UK: Psychology Press.

Deiber, M., Wise, S.P., Honda, M., Catalan, M.J., Grafman, J., & Hallett, M. (1997). Frontal and parietal networks for conditional motor learning: A positron emission tomography study. *Journal of Neurophysiology, 78*, 977–991.

DiGiulio, D., Seidenberg, M., O'Leary, D., & Raz, N. (1994). Procedural and declarative memory: A developmental study. *Brain and Cognition, 25*, 79–91.

Dolan, R.J., & Fletcher, P.C. (1997). Dissociating prefrontal and hippocampal function in episodic memory encoding. *Nature, 388*, 6642, 582–585.

Drummey, A., & Newcombe, N. (1995). Remembering versus knowing the past: Children's explicit and implicit memories for pictures. *Journal of Experimental Child Psychology, 59*, 549–565.

Düzel, E., Vargha-Khadem, F., Heinze, H.J., & Mishkin, M. (2001). Brain activity evidence for recognition without recollection after early hippocampal damage. *Proceedings of the National Academy of Sciences USA, 98*, 8101–8106.

Eichenbaum, H.B., Cahill, L.F., Gluck, M.A., Hasselmo, M.E., Keil, F.C., Martin, A.J. et al. (1999). Learning and memory: Systems analysis. In M.J. Zigmond, F.E. Bloom, S.C. Landis, J.L. Roberts, & L.R. Squire (Eds.), *Fundamental neuroscience* (pp. 1455–1486). New York: Academic Press.

Fernández, G., Weyerta, H., Schrader-Bölsche, Tendolkar, I., Genderikus, G.O.M., Smid, C.T. et al. (1998). Successful verbal encoding into episodic memory engages the posterior hippocampus: A parametrically analyzed functional magnetic resonance imaging study. *The Journal of Neuroscience, 18*, 1841–1847.

Fleischman, D., Vaidya, CJ., Lange, KL., & Gabrieli, JD. (1997). A dissociation between perceptual explicit and implicit memory processes. *Brain and Cognition, 35*, 42–57.

Fletcher, P., Shallice, T., Frith, U., Frackowiak, R., & Dolan, R. (1998). The functional roles of prefrontal cortex in episodic memory. II Retrieval. *Brain, 121*, 1249–1256.

Freud, S. (1965). *The psychopathology of everyday life* (A. Tyson, Trans.). New York: Norton.

Frey, S., & Petrides, M. (1999). Re-examination of the human taste region: A positron emission tomography study. *European Journal of Neuroscience, 11*(8), 2985–2988.

Gabrieli, J., Fleischman, D., Keane, M., Reminger, S., & Morrel, F. (1995). Double dissociation between memory systems underlying explicit and implicit memory in the human brain. *Psychological Science, 6*, 76–82.

Gadian, D.G., Aicardi, J., Watkins, K.E., Porter, D.A., Mishkin, M., & Vargha-Khadem, F. (2000). Developmental amnesia associated with early hypoxic–ischaemic injury. *Brain, 123*, 499–507.

Goldman-Rakic, P. (1994). The issue of memory in the study of prefrontal function. In A.M. Thiery et al. (Eds.), *Motor and cognitive functions of the prefrontal cortex* (pp. 112–121). Berlin: Springer-Verlag.

Graf, P., & Schacter, D. (1985). Implicit and explicit memory for new associations in normal subjects and amnesic patients. *Journal of Experimental Psychology: Learning, Memory, and Cognition, 11*, 501–518.

Haith, M., Hazan, C., & Goodman, G. (1988). Expectation and anticipation of dynamic visual events by 3.5-month-old babies. *Child Development, 59*, 467–479.

Haith, M., & McCarty, M. (1990). Stability of visual expectations at 3.0 months of age. *Developmental Psychology, 26*, 68–74.

Haith, M.M., Wentworth, N., & Canfield, R. (1993). The formation of expectations in early infancy. In C. Rovee-Collier & L.P. Lipsitt (Eds.), *Advances in infancy research* (pp. 251–297). New Jersey: Ablex Press.

Hartshorn, K., Rovee-Collier, C., Gerhardstein, P, Bhatt, R., Klein, P., Aaron, F. et al. (1998). Developmental changes in the specificity of memory over the first year of life. *Developmental Psychobiology, 33*, 61–78.

Hayes, B., & Hennessy, R. (1996). The nature and development of nonverbal implicit memory. *Journal of Experimental and Child Psychology, 63*, 22–43.

Hebb, D.O. (1949). *The organization of behaviour*. New York: Wiley.
Honey, R.C., Watt, A., & Good, M. (1998). Hippocampal lesions disrupt an associative mismatch process. *The Journal of Neuroscience, 18*, 2226–2230.
Howe, M.L., & Courage, M.L. (1993). On resolving the enigma of infantile amnesia. *Psychological Bulletin, 113*, 305–326.
Howe, M.L., & Courage, M.L. (1997). The emergence and early development of autobiographical memory. *Psychological Review, 104*, 499–523.
Huttenlocher, P., & de Courten, C. (1987). The development of synapses in striate cortex of man. *Human Neurobiology, 6*, 1–9.
Jacoby, L., Baker, J.G., & Brooks, L.R. (1989). Episodic effects on picture identification: Implications for theories of concept learning and theories of memory. *Journal of Experimental Psychology: Learning, Memory, & Cognition, 15*, 275–281.
Kail, R. (1990). *The development of memory in children* (3rd ed.). New York: W.H. Freeman & Co.
Lashley, K.S. (1950). *In search of the engram. Society of Experimental Biology Symposium. No. 4: Physiological Mechanisms of Animal Behaviour.* Cambridge: Cambridge University Press.
Lepage, M., & Richer, F. (1996). Inter-response interference contributes to the sequencing deficit in frontal lobe lesions. *Brain, 119*, 1289–1295.
Little, A., Lipsitt, LP., & Rovee-Collier, C. (1984). Classical conditioning and retention of the infant's eyelid response: Effects of age and interstimulus interval. *Journal of Experimental Child Psychology, 37*, 512–524.
Lorbasch, T., & Worman, L. (1989). The development of explicit and implicit forms of memory in learning disabled children. *Contemporary Education Psychology, 14*, 67–76.
Luciana, M., & Nelson, C.A. (1998). The functional emergence of prefrontally-guided working memory systems in four- to eight-year-old children. *Neuropsychologia, 36*, 272–293.
Maguire, E.A., Vargha-Khadem, F., & Mishkin, M. (2001). The effects of bilateral hippocampal damage on the fMRI regional activations and interactions during memory retrieval. *Brain, 124*, 1156–1170.
Mandler, J. (1988). How to build a baby: On the development of an accessible representational system. *Cognitive Development, 3*, 113–136.
Martin, A., Haxby, J.V., Lalonde, F.M., Wiggs, C.L., & Ungerleider, L.G. (1995). Discrete cortical regions associated with knowledge of color and knowledge of action. *Science, 270* (5233), 102–105.
McDonough, L., Mandler, J.M., McKee, R.D., & Squire, L.R. (1995). The deferred imitation task as a nonverbal measure of declarative memory. *Proceedings of the National Academy of Sciences USA, 92*, 7580–7584.
Michel, A., & Garey, L. (1984). The development of dendritic spines in the human visual cortex. *Human Neurobiology, 3*, 223–227.
Murray, E.A., & Mishkin, M. (1998). Object recognition and location memory in monkeys with excitotoxic lesions of the amygdala and hippocampus. *Journal of Neuroscience, 18*, 6568–6582.
Nelson, C.A. (1994). Neural correlates of recognition memory in the first postnatal year of life. In G. Dawson & K. Fischer (Eds.), *Human behaviour and the developing brain* (pp. 269–313). New York: Guilford Press.
Nelson, C.A. (1995). The ontogeny of human memory: A cognitive neuroscience perspective. *Developmental Psychology, 31*, 723–735.

Nelson, C.A. (1997). The neurobiological basis of early memory development. In N. Cowan (Ed.), *The development of memory in childhood* (pp. 41–82). Hove, UK: Psychology Press.

Nelson, C.A. (2000). Neural plasticity and human development: The role of early experience in sculpting memory systems. *Developmental Science, 3*, 115–130.

Nelson, C.A., & Carver, L.J. (1998). The effects of stress and trauma on brain and memory: A view from developmental cognitive neuroscience. *Development & Psychopathology, 10*, 793–809.

Nelson, C.A., & Collins, P.F. (1991). Event-related potential and looking time analysis of infants' responses to familiar and novel events: Implications for visual recognition memory. *Developmental Psychology, 27*, 50–58.

Nelson, C.A., & Collins, P.F. (1992). Neural and behavioural correlates of recognition memory in 4- and 8-month-old infants. *Brain and Cognition, 19*, 105–121.

Nelson, C.A., & Monk, C. (2001). The use of event-related potentials in the study of cognitive development. In C.A. Nelson & M. Luciana (Eds.), *Handbook of developmental cognitive neuroscience* (pp. 125–136). Cambridge, MA: MIT Press.

Nishitani, N., & Hari, R. (2000). Temporal dynamics of cortical representation for action. *Proceedings of the National Academy of Sciences USA, 97*, 913–918.

Ohlrich, E., & Ross, L.E. (1968). Acquisition and differential conditioning of the eyelid response in normal and retarded children. *Journal of Experimental Child Psychology, 6*, 181–193.

Opitz, B., Mecklinger, A., Friederici, A., & von Cramon, D. (1999). The functional neuroanatomy of novelty processing: Integrating ERP and fMRI results. *Cerebral Cortex, 9*, 379–391.

Overman, W.H., Bachevalier, J., Sewell, F., & Drew, J. (1993). A comparison of children's performance on two recognition memory tasks: Delayed nonmatch-to-sample versus visual paired-comparison. *Developmental Psychobiology, 26*, 345–357.

Parkin, A., & Streete, S. (1988). Implicit and explicit memory in young children and adults. *British Journal of Psychology, 79*, 361–369.

Pascalis, O., & de Schonen, S. (1994). Recognition memory in 3- to 4-day-old human neonates. *NeuroReport, 5*, 1721–1724.

Pascalis, O., de Schonen, S., Morton, J., & Deruelle, C. (1995). Mother's face recognition by neonates: A replication and extension. *Infant Behaviour and Development, 18*, 79–95.

Posner, M., Rothbart, M., Thomas-Thrapp, L., & Gerardi, G. (1998). The development of orienting to locations and objects. In R. Wright et al. (Eds.), *Visual attention. Vancouver studies in cognitive science* (Vol. 8, pp. 269–288). New York: Oxford University Press.

Reber, A.S. (1992). The cognitive unconscious: An evolutionary perspective. *Consciousness and Cognition, 1*, 93–133.

Roediger, H., Weldon, M., & Challis, B. (1989). Explaining dissociations between implicit and explicit measures of retention: A processing account. In H.R. Roediger &. F. Craik (Eds.), *Varieties of memory and consciousness: Essays in honor of Endel Tulving* (pp. 3–41). Hillsdale, NJ: Lawrence Erlbaum Associates Inc.

Rovee-Collier, C. (1997a). Development of memory in infancy. In N. Cowan (Ed.), *The development of memory in childhood* (pp. 5–39). London: University College London Press.

Rovee-Collier, C. (1997b). Dissociations in infant memory: Rethinking the development of implicit and explicit memory. *Psychological Review, 104*, 467–498.

Rovee-Collier, C., Patterson, J., & Hayne, H. (1985). Specificity in the reactivation of infant memory. *Developmental Psychobiology, 18*, 559–574.

Russo, R., Nichelli, P., Gibertoni, M., & Cornia, C. (1995). Developmental trends in implicit and explicit memory: A picture completion study. *Journal of Experimental Child Psychology, 59*, 566–578.

Schacter, D. (1990). Perceptual representation systems and implicit memory: Toward a resolution of the multiple memory systems debate. *Annals of the New York Academy of Sciences, 608*, 543–571.

Schacter, D. (1992). Priming and multiple memory systems. *Journal of Cognitive Neuroscience, 4*, 244–256.

Schacter, D. (1994). Implicit knowledge: New perspectives on unconscious processes. *International Review of Neurobiology, 37*, 271–284; discussion 285–288.

Schacter, D., Alpert, N.M., Savage, C.R., Rauch, S.L., & Albert, M.S. (1996). Conscious recollection and the human hippocampal formation: Evidence from positron emission tomography. *Proceedings of the National Academy of Sciences USA, 93*, 321–325.

Schacter, D., & Buckner, R.L. (1998). On the relations among priming, conscious recollection, and intentional retrieval: Evidence from neuroimaging research. *Neurobiology of Learning & Memory, 70*, 284–303.

Schacter, D., & Moscovitch, M. (1984). *Infants, amnesiacs, and dissociable memory systems*. New York: Plenum.

Schacter, D., & Tulving, E. (1994). What are the memory systems of 1994? In D. Schacter & E. Tulving (Eds.), *Memory systems 1994* (pp. 1–38). Cambridge, MA: Bradford Press.

Seress, L. (2001). Morphological changes of the human hippocampal formation from midgestation to early childhood. In C.A. Nelson & M. Luciana (Eds.), *Handbook of developmental cognitive neuroscience*. Cambridge, MA: MIT Press.

Sherry, D., & Schacter, D. (1987). The evolution of multiple memory systems. *Psychological Review, 94*, 439–454.

Shimamura, A., & Squire, LR. (1984). Paired-associate learning and priming effects in amnesia: A neuropsychological study. *Journal of Experimental Psychology: General, 113*, 556–570.

Squire, L.R. (1994). Declarative and nondeclarative memory: Multiple brain systems supporting learning and memory. In D.L. Schacter & E. Tulving (Eds.), *Memory systems 1994* (pp. 203–231). Cambridge, MA: MIT Press.

Squire, L.R., Ojemann, J.G., Miezin, F.M., Petersen, S.E., Videen, T.O., & Raichle, M.E. (1992). Activation of the hippocampus in normal humans: A functional anatomical study of memory. *Proceedings of the National Academy of Sciences USA, 89*, 1837–1841.

Strange, B.A., Fletcher, P.C., Henson, R.N.A., Friston, K.J., & Dolan, R.J. (1999). Segregating the functions of the human hippocampus. *Proceedings of the National Academy of Sciences USA, 96*, 4034–4039.

Sullivan, R.M., Taborsky-Barba, S., Mendoza, R., Itano, A., Leon, M., Cotman, C.W. et al. (1991). Olfactory classical conditioning in neonates. *Pediatrics, 87*(4), 511–518.

Thomas, K.M., Livnat, R., Eccard, C.H., & Casey, B.J. (1999, April). *Implicit learning and perinatal complications: A serial reaction time study with children*. Poster presented at the biennial meeting of the Society for Research in Child Development, Albuquerque, New Mexico.

Thomas, K., & Nelson, C. (2001). Serial reaction time learning in pre-school and school-aged children. *Journal of Experimental Child Psychology, 79*, 364–387.

Tulving, E., Markowitsch, H.J., Craik, F.E., Habib, R., & Houle S. (1996). Novelty and familiarity activations in PET studies of memory encoding and retrieval. *Cerebral Cortex, 6*, 71–79.

Tulving, E., & Schacter, D.L. (1990). Priming and human memory systems. *Science, 247* (4940), 301–306.

Vargha-Khadem, F., Gadian, D.G., Watkins, K.E., Connelly, A., Van Paesschen, W., & Mishkin, M. (1997). Differential effects of early hippocampal pathology on episodic and semantic memory. *Science, 277*, 376–380.

Wan, H., Aggleton, J.P., & Brown, M.W. (1999). Different contributions of the hippocampus and perirhinal cortex to recognition memory. *The Journal of Neuroscience, 19*, 1142–1148.

Webb, S., & Nelson, C.A. (2001). Neural correlates of perceptual priming in human adults and infants. *Journal of Experimental Child Psychology, 79*, 1–22.

Weldon, M.S., Roediger, H.L., & Challis, B.H. (1989). The properties of retrieval cues constrain the picture superiority effect. *Memory & Cognition, 17*, 95–105.

Woodruff-Pak, D. (1993). Eyeblink classical conditioning in H.M.: Delay and trace paradigms. *Behavioural Neuroscience, 107*, 911–925.

Woodruff-Pak, D., & Jaeger, M. (1998). Predictors of eyeblink classical conditioning over the adult age span. *Psychology of Aging, 13*, 193–205.

Woodruff-Pak, D., Papka, M., & Ivry, R. (1996). Cerebellar involvement in eyeblink classical conditioning in humans. *Neuropsychology, 10*, 443–458.

Zola, S.M., Squire, L.R., Teng, E., Stefanacci, L., Buffalo, E.A., & Clark, R.E. (2000). Impaired recognition memory in monkeys after damage limited to the hippocampal region. *The Journal of Neuroscience, 20*, 451–463.

CHAPTER 6

Neural substrate of speech and language development

Christiana M. Leonard
McKnight Brain Institute, University of Florida, USA

INTRODUCTION

The human ability to communicate in sentences sets us apart from other animals. The "nativist" position holds that such a unique ability must depend on a unique human module—the language acquisition device—that enables us to apply syntactic rules. An alternative position is presented in this chapter. In this view, language learning obeys general laws of cognitive and motor development. Recent research has demonstrated that seemingly rule-guided behaviour can emerge from simple neural networks sensitive to statistical associations in the input. Words, concepts, and sentences might simply emerge from social reinforcement of children's attempts to imitate and to generalize from experience.

This chapter uses studies of cortical organization, evolution, and development to generate hypotheses about the neural substrate for language development. Neurophysiological work in non-human primates has identified "mirror neurons" in the frontal lobe. These multimodal neurons fire when the animal is performing or viewing a particular goal-directed action, or when it is viewing the target of the action. Auditory feature detectors and mirror neurons could participate in phonological loops to mediate language acquisition.

Human language is unique because humans have: (1) more cortical processing areas biased to code distributional and combinatorial features of auditory input; (2) a sensorimotor system capable of complex vocal imitation; (3) a long period of immaturity; (4) caretakers who focus attention on useful environmental features, shape and reward useful actions, and protect the child from adverse results of sensorimotor experimentation; and (5) a powerful drive for task mastery. Individual differences in the asymmetry, size, and plasticity of cortical maps, as well as the quantity and quality of linguistic input, interact to shape language development. The chapter is divided into four parts covering early language development; human cortical specializations for language; cortical organization and cortical development.

> How is it possible for speakers of two distinctly different dialects to understand each other?...Linguistic systems are so structured that the listener has to respond to many linguistic events in two or more ways simultaneously. He must recognize that the sound or combination of sounds he hears may have several different meanings or significances depending on linguistic context. He must...select the significance intended by the speaker and reject the nonapplicable ones. Only human languages among communication systems show this paradoxical ambivalence between phonology (sound structure) and grammar. No other means of human or animal communication is so structured... to learn what is significant and what is not significant, what constitutes contrast and what constitutes equivalence at the various levels of organisation of language requires a kind of learning that is uniquely human. (Smith, 1980, p. *xxvi*)

Language acquisition is a special case of vocal learning—a species-specific behavioural strategy that unfolds as the infant learns what constitutes contrast and what constitutes equivalence. In the first stage of language development, children reach behavioural mastery by building up a system of implicit linguistic procedures, "a set of constraints for attending to, processing, and representing linguistically relevant input, biases that constrain the way in which the child represents objects and events in the world" (Karmiloff-Smith, 1992, p. 47). In the second stage, these implicit representations undergo redescription and become linguistic objects of attention, themselves. Children can not only talk *in* sentences but talk *about* sentences; they can articulate a linguistic system of rules.

Because complex rules of grammar are used by 3-year-olds (long before they can formulate such rules explicitly) Chomsky proposed that the human brain has a specific language acquisition device (LAD) (Chomsky, 1965). The recent identification of a genetic mutation in a family with severe speech and language disorders (Lai et al., 2001) has been taken as support for this "nativist" position. An innate LAD is proposed because linguistic input is described as too degenerate to support accurate generalization. Recent research demonstrating that linguistic input is rich, not degenerate, has challenged the nativist position. Seemingly rule-guided behaviour can emerge from simple neural networks sensitive to statistical associations in the input (Elman et al., 1996; Jusczyk, 1997; Mehler & Cristophe, 2000; Saffran, Aslin, & Newport, 1996). Many linguistic rules can be described in terms of contrasts and equivalences. Word and sentence learning might emerge from social reinforcement of children's attempts at more powerful generalization (Karmiloff-Smith, 1992; MacWhinney, 1998).

Humans strive to generalize and understand; chimpanzees do not. They have a surprising lack of curiosity into how tools work (Povinelli & Dunphy-Lelii, 2001). The drive for understanding might fuel, as well as profit from, language acquisition. Children who use language to help themselves master tasks achieve more successful performance (Clark, 1997). The use of cultural artifacts such as words and paper extends our reach into the environment, producing a qualitative difference in behavioural mastery and the scope of generalization. Clark suggests that small changes in neural organization, which allow the production and interaction with such artifacts, can enable huge leaps in cognitive control. Perhaps the complex rules of grammar are simply another cultural artifact, created by the human drive for understanding. Innate knowledge of these rules does not help us learn language, they are our attempt to explain and understand what it is we have learned. The rules are, in a sense, an epiphenomenon (McClelland & Seidenberg, 2000).

Another theoretical shift is affecting views of language development. The distinctions between perception, cognition, and action that have dominated artificial intelligence and cognitive science are eroding (Clark, 1997). Writing and speaking require refined control of the digits and the vocal apparatus, as well as refined thought. It is perhaps no accident that the species with the most well developed and precise motor control of the digits, tongue, and larynx is the one with the highest cognitive attainments, or that cognitive and motor delay go hand in hand in development (Diamond, 2000; Trauner, Wulfeck, Tallal, & Hesselink, 2000).

The view that language learning obeys general laws of cognitive and motor development is by no means universally accepted (Marcus, 1999; Pinker, 1994). This chapter takes this view, because neural mechanisms underlying development of goal-oriented sensorimotor sequences can be investigated in animals. In some respects, language resembles an oral spear (J. Pettigrew, private communication). In a manual throw, a goal-oriented recasting of visual and somatosensory input shapes the coordinated movements of fingers, wrist, and shoulder. In a verbal hurl, goal-oriented recasting of oral, acoustic, and visual input shapes syllables, words, and phrases. If learning to produce meaningful utterances has similarities to learning to grasp and throw, then evidence about developmental changes in the neural mechanisms for grasp can help generate hypotheses about the neural changes underlying language acquisition.

This chapter argues that studies of cortical organization, evolution, and development can generate hypotheses about the neural substrate for language. Human language is unique because humans have: (1) more cortical processing areas biased to code distributional and combinatorial features of auditory input; (2) a sensorimotor system capable of complex vocal imitation; (3) a long period of immaturity; (4) caretakers who focus attention on useful environmental features, shape and reward useful actions, and protect the child from adverse results of sensorimotor experimentation; and (5) a powerful drive for task mastery. Recent research suggests that motor and sensory impairments, reduced cortical area, and reduced maternal input all compromise language development (Eckert, Lombardino & Leonard, 2001; Hart & Risley, 1995; Leonard et al., 2001; Trauner et al., 2000; Yoshinaga-Itano, Sedey, Coulter, & Mehl, 1998). The basic research supporting this argument will be presented in four sections covering early language development; human cortical specializations for language; cortical organization, and cortical development.

EARLY LANGUAGE DEVELOPMENT

According to the principles discovered by Charles Darwin, organisms adapt to their ecological niches by developing novel behavioural strategies. Improved stimulus sensitivity, differentiated motor control, and the elaboration of more complex mechanisms for selecting appropriate actions (attention, goal-setting, memory) all contribute to the success of behavioural modifications. A new behavioural strategy can monopolize a food source, facilitate predator avoidance, and improve the survival rate of offspring. Although ontogeny does not precisely recapitulate phylogeny, developmental changes in skill share many common features with evolutionary adaptations. The similarities suggest that similar cortical modifications could accompany both evolution and development.

Language is a novel, species-specific behavioural strategy. All humans but no non-human primates combine sounds to form complex messages. Oral communication by language has enabled humans to develop elaborate social mechanisms for environmental control. During development, there is a similar progression (Berk & Garvin, 1984; Clark, 1997; Jusczyk, 1997). Strategies become ever more complex as the ability to parse, represent, imitate, and create a speech stream improves. In this view, these early stages of language development are characterized by a bottom-up assembly of increasingly flexible auditory–action schemata, rather than guided by a top-down application of formal rules.

What develops?

At birth, infants have little voluntary control of their motor apparatus and a relatively undifferentiated perceptual landscape. But auditory learning occurs even in the womb, when infants adapt to familiar stories and voices (Jusczyk, 1997). At birth, infants can discriminate approximately 200 phonemes. By 2 months of age, they confuse foreign languages with similar rhythmic stress patterns and distinguish this group from their own (Mehler & Cristophe, 2000). Their perceptual space distorts in order to distinguish linguistic contrasts and confuse equivalencies (Kuhl et al., 1997).

In all cultures, adults use baby talk (parentese) when talking to infants. Baby talk emphasizes acoustic parameters that confer meaning to sounds in the native language (Fernald, 1993). Infants prefer baby talk. The perceptual amplification produced by selective attention to this distorted input warps their perceptual landscape (Kuhl et al., 1997). Large acoustic differences *between* sounds within a phoneme category are confused (the perceptual magnet effect) whereas small acoustic differences *across* a phoneme boundary are discriminated (categorical perception). Categorical perception is a general property of the mammalian auditory system (Kuhl & Miller, 1975). The perceptual magnet effect is not (Kuhl, 1991), and its strength might vary among individuals (Aaltonen et al., 1997). Differences in how accurately individuals distinguish contrasts and equivalencies could underlie individual differences in the rate of language development (Kraus et al., 1996; Tallal et al., 1996; Wright, 2000; Wright et al., 1997).

Both categorical perception and the magnet phenomenon can be demonstrated in 8-month-old infants at the time they are babbling and producing their first words. Babbling involves the matching of heard and produced sounds and does not develop normally in the absence of auditory input (Jusczyk, 1997). Babbling progresses from the production of isolated vowel-like sounds to sequences of syllables (stop consonants combined with an open, central vowel), to the alternation of different consonantal segments.

Experimentation with different combinations and attention to the parental response can guide initial linguistic output. Vihmann hypothesizes that each child has an articulatory filter, "a phonetic template which renders similar patterns in adult speech unusually salient or memorable" (Vihmann, 1993). Such templates might be a requirement for successful vocal imitation. Such imitation is a rare phenomenon in biology—only dolphins, parrots, and songbirds share this capacity with humans (Doupe & Kuhl, 1999).

The emergence of complex organization

The final stage of babbling coincides with a marked increase in vocal imitation of words, the precursor to the so-called "vocabulary burst", an exponential increase in words and phrase length that occurs some time in the second year. Exposure to and practice in the native language clearly shape phonology. But in an organism fitted by evolution with appropriate mechanisms for selective attention and reinforcement learning, exposure, and practice might be sufficient to drive the production of meaningful sequences of sounds as well. Although this possibility was ridiculed when originally proposed (Chomsky, 1959; Skinner, 1957), and still is not accepted by many psycholinguists, support comes from three completely different scientific traditions: experimental psycholinguistics, longitudinal studies of child development, and computer simulation.

In a critical psycholinguistic experiment, Saffran and her colleagues demonstrated that 8-month-old infants can use statistical associations in auditory input to shape their expectations about speech (Saffran et al., 1996). After exposure for just 2min to a stream of nonsense syllables, the infants were able to recognize novel sequences. Such rapid storage of statistical probabilities would be a useful asset in segmenting fluent speech into words and phrases.

A recent longitudinal study reveals darker implications of environmental sensitivity. In their book *Meaningful differences*, Hart and Risley (1995) describe how, during monthly home visits, they recorded every word spoken to 42 children between 9 months and 3 years of age. At every stage, the number of words spoken by the child reflected the cumulative number of words that had been directed to the child. Children from professional homes heard three times as many words and had vocabularies three times the size of children from impoverished homes.

At 4 years of age, the difference in words heard between a professional and a poor family had accumulated to the incredible total of 20 million words.

Children with larger vocabularies use more complicated sentences and perform better on standardized tests. Although correlation does not necessarily indicate causation, and simple exposure is certainly not the only difference between the families, other experiments demonstrate equally strong effects of differing linguistic environments in children from otherwise equivalent backgrounds (Huttenlocher, 1998). Furthermore, the findings are consistent with animal data on the crucial role played by sensory stimuli in neural organization during development (Crair, Gillespie, & Stryker, 1998; Greenough & Alcantara, 1993).

Computer simulations give the same message—complex structures emerge from sensitivity to statistical properties of the input (Elman et al., 1996; Harm & Seidenberg, 1999; Seidenberg, 1997). Burgess and Lund fed 3 million words collected from Internet news groups into a high dimensional memory model, which recorded the frequency of co-occurrence for each word and its five nearest backwards and forwards neighbours (Burgess, 1998). A vector was then formed for the 50,000 most frequent words by concatenating the number of forwards and backwards co-occurrences. When a similarity metric was applied to the vectors, words with similar uses clustered together. Verbs clustered with verbs, concrete nouns with concrete nouns, abstract nouns with abstract nouns, and prepositions with prepositions. These clusters can be regarded as primitive representations of meaningful semantic and syntactic categories. If plastic cortical mechanisms stored the frequencies of word sequences, a thesaurus of contrasts and equivalences would be created that could assist in generating and decoding of novel sentences without recourse to a system of formal rules. This experiment suggests (to modellers and neurobiologists, but not, it is important to emphasize, to supporters of the nativist position) that infants receive all the information they need to become linguistic experts.

Hypothetical cortical loops

What neural structures mediate these effects of language exposure? This chapter proposes that perceptual maps and frontal cortex action-sequence maps participate in a phonological loop to mediate this learning. The term "phonological loop" refers to a hypothetical neural circuit that holds sound images in short-term memory (Baddeley, 1986). It is composed of an articulatory rehearsal process and a phonological store. This loop could have evolved to facilitate learning the sound patterns of new words (Baddeley, Gathercole, & Papagno, 1998). As the frequency of word imitation by individual children predicts the rate of vocabulary development, it is possible that imitation allows words to be held in a short-term store while long-term traces and associations with meaning are laid down. The next section describes anatomical specializations for auditory processing and action representation that could provide the neural substrate for this phonological loop.

CORTICAL ANATOMY

Figure 6.1 shows a simplified surface view of a human left cerebral hemisphere. The two largest sulci are the central sulcus (CS), which separates the frontal lobe from the parietal lobe, and the Sylvian fissure (lateral sulcus), which separates the frontal and parietal lobes from the temporal lobe. The lobes posterior to the central sulcus map physical and perceptual features of the environment. The frontal lobes contain maps of responses (Funahashi, Bruce, & Goldman-Rakic, 1989; Passingham, 1993). The anterior bank of the central sulcus contains primary motor cortex, which conveys motor commands to brainstem and spinal cord centres. More anterior regions, which extend onto the medial wall (Fig. 6.2) contain representations of complex goal-oriented actions (Picard & Strick, 1996; Rizzolatti, Fogassi, & Gallese, 2000). The medial areas are active during motor learning. The presupplementary motor area (PreSMA) is more active during the learning of new sensorimotor sequences, whereas the supplementary motor area (SMA) is more active during their storage and execution (Nakamura, Sakai, & Hikosaka, 1999). Between the SMA and PreSMA is a specialized area, the supplementary eye fields (SEF), which is devoted to the control of goal-oriented saccades (Grosbras et al., 1999) that play a prominent role in visual attention.

Almost all information from the internal and external environment reaches the cortex through relays in the thalamus. There is a topographic gradient of thalamic projections to the cortex. Nuclei in the anterior thalamus project to frontal and medial (response selection) cortex, whereas nuclei in the posterior thalamus project to occipital, parietal, and temporal (perceptual) cortex. The cortical targets of thalamic nuclei are called primary projection areas. Primary areas project to secondary or association areas. For example, primary auditory cortex on Heschl's gyrus sends projections to the planum temporale and superior temporal sulcus (STS) (Fig. 6.3).

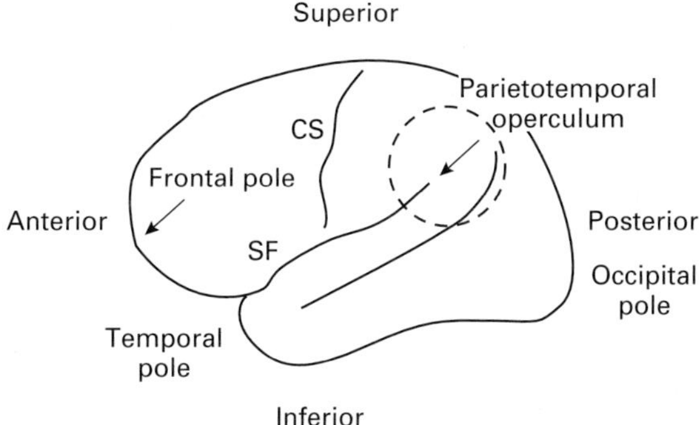

Figure 6.1. Schematic lateral view of the left hemisphere. CS, central sulcus; SF, Sylvian fissure (lateral sulcus). There is no boundary between the parietal and temporal lobes. The areas of the parietal and temporal lobes that cover the insula are called the opercula (lids).

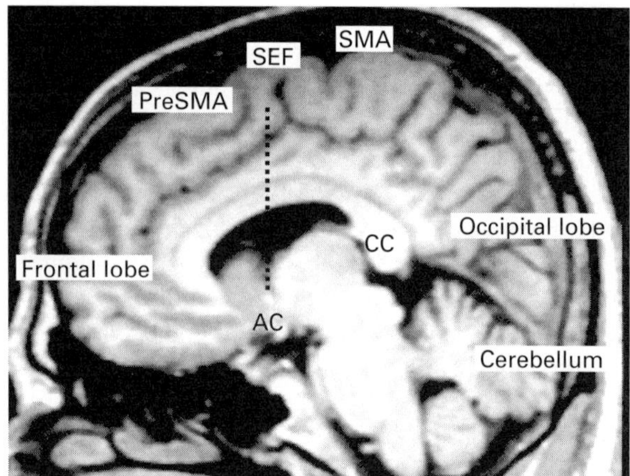

Figure 6.2. An MRI of the medial surface showing the supplementary motor area (SMA) and the presupplementary motor area (PreSMA). AC = anterior commisure; CC = corpus callosum; SEF = supplementary eye field.

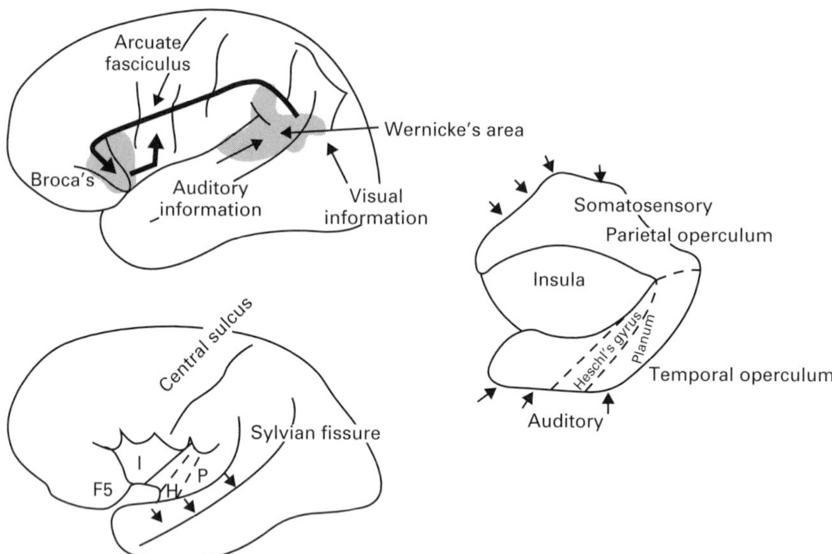

Figure 6.3. Top left: Schematic view of information flow from posterior sensory areas to frontal response areas through the inferior temporofrontal loop. The dotted regions show where brain damage causes fluent (Wernicke's) and non-fluent (Broca's) aphasia. These regions are conceptual rather than anatomical. Bottom left: The Sylvian fissure has been pulled out and down in the direction of the arrows to reveal the insula (I) and the auditory cortex (H,P) on the superior surface of the temporal lobe. The region of the frontal operculum indicated as F5 contains mirror neurons in the monkey. It is thought that these neurons play a crucial role in imitation learning. Right: Enlarged view of Heschl's gyrus and planum temporale.

The connections between anterior and posterior cortex are also arranged topographically. Perisylvian frontal regions (called Broca's area on the left) are connected with perisylvian parietal and temporal regions (called Wernicke's area on the left) whereas more superior frontal regions are connected with more superior parietal regions.

In the monkey, a region of ventral premotor cortex (F5) that is specialized for the production of mouth and hand movements might be a homologue for the human Broca's area (Rizzolatti et al., 2000). The transcortical input to this region originates in inferior parietal and superior temporal cortex, possible homologues for Wernicke's area. Many neurons in F5 fire when the monkey reaches for and grasps objects. The same neurons also fire at the *sight* of a graspable object—or even the sight of another individual grasping an object. This property of generalization between self and non-self stimulated the designation "mirror neurons" (Rizzolatti et al., 2000). Rizzolatti speculates that F5 has enlarged in the primate line as the role of imitation has increased. The circuits guiding the development of visual grasp in monkeys might have been coopted to support the development of human phonological grasp—the phonological loop that supports vocal imitation of auditory input. The properties of neurons in this region provide a potential neural mechanism for the representation of meanings and intentions. If the same neuron fires during goals and actions, the signal could represent the intention to throw a particular targeted linguistic message.

Functional lateralization

Disorders of language (aphasia) occur after damage to the perisylvian region in the left hemisphere (Benson, 1993). Damage to the right hemisphere has more subtle effects on the perception and production of emotional prosody, pragmatics, and the interpretation of metaphors and ambiguity (Chiarello, 1999). After damage to the left anterior perisylvian region, speech is non-fluent but semantically appropriate (Kimura, 1993). After left posterior damage, speech is fluent but filled with semantic errors. Comprehension can be impaired after either anterior and posterior damage.

Functional asymmetries are more difficult to demonstrate in medial cortex for technical reasons. Early reports of anteromedial control of species specific emotional vocalizations in the monkey did not describe asymmetries (Jurgens, Maurus, Ploog, & Winter, 1967). An isolated report in the bat demonstrated that medial cortex contains a topographic representation of frequencies used in echolocation, an auditory means of locating prey (Gooler & O'Neill, 1987). This field might be an auditory homologue to a lateralized visual control region that locates targets in humans. Control of memory guided and intentional saccades appear to rest in the left supplementary eye field (Grosbras et al., 1999).

Hand preference and functional lateralization

The left hemisphere is responsible for skilled hand movements as well as language in almost all right-handers (Kimura, 1993). In non-right-handers, hemispheric lateralization of skilled movements and language is variable (Rasmussen & Milner, 1975). There are interesting avian parallels for lateralized control of skilled movements. The left hemisphere controls most elements in birdsong (Nottebohm, Stokes, & Leonard, 1976) whereas the right hemisphere is responsible for more accurate grain pecking (Rogers, 2000). Non-human primates do not show a right-hand bias that is generalized over a variety of skilled actions (Corballis, 1991). The fact that both right-handedness and language are unique human specializations suggests that the cortical specializations for skilled hand and oral movements evolved together in the primate line.

Neurobiological bases for functional lateralization

There are marked interindividual and interspecies differences in the size and shape of auditory structures in the human left and right hemisphere. In monkeys, the two Sylvian fissures are of equal length, whereas in chimpanzees there is a slight leftwards asymmetry (Yeni-Komshian & Benson, 1976) because of asymmetry of the planum temporale (Gannon et al., 1998). The prominent bump formed by Heschl's gyrus and the terminal ascending branch of the Sylvian fissure (planum parietale) are not found in monkeys and are rare in chimpanzees (Fig. 6.4).

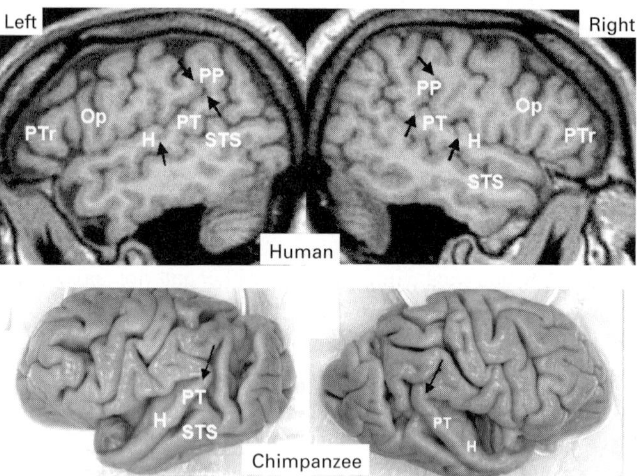

Figure 6.4. Top: Sagittal MRI images demonstrating typical leftwards asymmetry of the planum temporale (PT) and rightwards asymmetry of the planum parietale (PP) in a right-handed human. Heschl's gyrus (H) is a prominent bulge (larger on the left) that contains primary auditory cortex. In the frontal lobe, Broca's area is composed of the pars triangularis (PTr) and pars opercularis (Op). The asymmetries in these anterior structures and the superior temporal sulcus (STS) are less reliable. Bottom: Photographs of a chimpanzee brain demonstrating small Heschl's gyri and absent planum parietale (by permission of Todd Preuss).

In humans, Heschl's gyrus and the planum temporale are approximately 30 per cent larger on the left (Geschwind & Levitsky, 1968; Penhune, Zatorre, MacDonald, & Evans, 1996; Steinmetz, Rademacher, & Huang, 1989) and the planum parietale is longer on the right (Leonard et al., 1993; Steinmetz, Ebeling, Huang, & Kahn, 1990; Witelson & Kigar, 1992). The cellular structure of the perisylvian region is also asymmetric with more widely spaced cellular columns on the left than the right (Galuske, Schlote, Bratzke, & Singer, 2000; Seldon, 1985). In the frontal lobe, there are leftward asymmetries of cell and region size in Broca's area (Foundas et al., 1996; Foundas, Eure, Luevano, & Weinberger, 1998a; Hayes & Lewis, 1995). Anatomical asymmetries, like functional asymmetries, are more reliable in right- than non-right-handers.

There are also structural asymmetries in the human medial cortex. Two sulci associated with voluntary behaviour are more common in the left hemisphere than the right (Ono, Jubik, & Abernathy, 1990)—the paracingulate sulcus, a site of language generation (Crosson et al., 1999; Paus et al., 1996) and the lateral paracentral sulcus, which is activated during voluntary saccades (Grosbras et al., 1999). Non-human primates do not appear to have a paracingulate sulcus (Preuss & Leonard, unpublished data; Fig. 6.5).

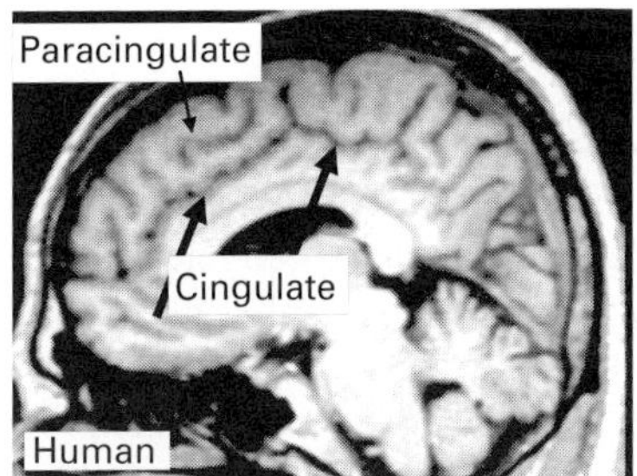

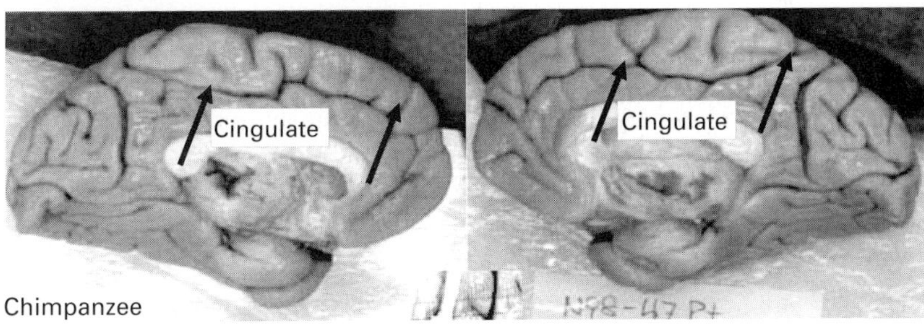

Figure 6.5. Top: Parasagittal MRI image demonstrating prominent paracingulate and cingulate sulci. Bottom: The chimpanzee has prominent cingulate sulci in both hemispheres but no discernible paracingulate sulci. The paracingulate sulcus was not visible in either hemisphere in the three other specimens examined (by permission of Todd Preuss).

Functional asymmetries

Imaging studies demonstrate asymmetries in functional activation during speech and music processing (Binder et al., 1995; Szymanski, Rowley & Roberts, 1999; Zatorre, Evans, Meyer, & Gjedde, 1992; Zatorre, Meyer, Gjedde, & Evans, 1996). These asymmetries might result from different perceptual biases in the two hemispheres. Left hemisphere damage affects the discrimination of tone duration whereas right hemisphere damage affects pitch (Robin, Tranel, & Damasio, 1990). Asymmetrical effects of cortical damage have also been demonstrated in rats and monkeys (Fitch, Miller, & Tallal, 1997). The left hemisphere is more active when processing short-duration sounds (Belin et al., 1998). The left hemisphere has a perceptual bias for categorizing, i.e. naming stimuli, whereas the right hemisphere distinguishes fine gradations (Kosslyn, Gazzaniga, Galaburda, & Rabin, 1999).

There is some evidence that asymmetrical linguistic and perceptual biases are associated with structural asymmetries. Imaging studies have shown a correlation between the degree of structural asymmetry in the planum temporale and functional dominance for language (Foundas et al., 1994; Tzourio et al., 1998). Enhanced structural asymmetry predicts enhanced cognitive and verbal skills (Eckert & Leonard, 2002; Eckert et al., 2001; Leonard et al., 1996; Rumsey et al., 1997). Musicians with exceptionally great leftwards asymmetry of the planum tend to have perfect pitch (an example of a naming bias) and to have initiated musical training in childhood (Schlaug, Jancke, Huang, & Steinmetz, 1995). Anomalous development of planar asymmetry (absent or extreme leftward asymmetry) might be a risk factor for the development of reading and language impairments (Eckert & Leonard, 2000; Galaburda et al., 1985; Leonard et al., 2001). Individual differences in the morphology of the supramarginal gyrus and pars triangularis have also been related to learning disabilities (Clark, 1997; Gauger, Lombardino, & Leonard, 1997; Habib & Robichon 1996). Structural and functional asymmetry are less prominent in non-right-handers (Foundas et al., 1998a; Foundas, Hong, Leonard, & Heilman, 1998b; Foundas, Leonard, & Heilman, 1995; Steinmetz, Volkmann, Jancke, & Freund, 1991; Witelson & Kigar, 1992). Reduced left hemisphere dominance (as indicated by an elevated incidence of mixed handedness) is a risk factor for language and learning disabilities. This relationship is additional evidence that the lateral biases for the controls of verbal and manual tools share common neural substrates.

Although structural and perceptual asymmetries are present at birth (Molfese, Freeman, & Palermo, 1975; Witelson & Paillie, 1973), brain damage does not cause aphasia in children (Bates et al., 1997; Dennis & Whitaker, 1976). The mechanisms of cortical neuroplasticity that could be responsible for the sparing of language after early brain damage will be covered in the next two sections.

CORTICAL ORGANIZATION

Posterior cortex contains a series of topographically organized maps that represent dimensions of environmental information (Allman, 1987; Kaas, Hacket, & Tramo,

1999; Sereno et al., 1995). Each primary projection area contains a point-to-point map of a sensory receptor array. The primary visual area contains a complete "retinotopic" map of the opposite visual field. The primary somatosensory area contains "somatotopic" maps of sensory receptors from the contralateral body, and the primary auditory area contains a "tonotopic" map of the cochlea. The posteromedial part of the auditory map is optimally sensitive to high frequencies whereas the anterolateral part of the map is optimally sensitive to low frequencies (Plate 7, top).

Maps in "association cortex"

Allman and Kass (1971) transformed our understanding of cortical processing with their discovery that association cortex, like primary cortex, contains topographically ordered maps. Each primary map projects in a point-to-point fashion to many secondary maps. Each column in the secondary map retains its retino- or tono- or somatotopic label but, in addition, acquires new sensitivities. In vision, the areas that code object features are called the "what" system, and the areas that code spatial location in different frames of reference form the "where" or "how" system (Goodale & Humphrey, 1998).

Many critical aspects of auditory stimuli can be signalled not by spatial organization but by temporal properties of the firing pattern (Cheung, Bedenbaugh, Nagarajan, & Schreiner, 2001; Middlebrooks, Clock, Xu, & Green, 1994) (see Plate 7). In auditory cortex, maps of abstract auditory features such as latency cross the tonotopic map in primary auditory cortex, (Cheung et al., 2001; Mendelson & Schreiner, 1990; Middlebrooks, Dykes, & Merzenich, 1980). Auditory cortex can be "when" or "how fast" cortex, rather than "what", "where", or "how" cortex (Belin & Zatorre, 2000). A few studies have investigated auditory cortical responses to species specific stimuli (Rauschecker, Tian, & Hauser, 1995; Steinschneider, Schroeder, Arezzo, & Vaughan, 1993). As in visual cortex (Felleman & Van Essen, 1991), there could be multiple superimposed maps of meaningful auditory contrasts. Although it is reasonable to suppose that asymmetrical auditory specializations correspond to asymmetrical auditory maps, no such asymmetries have been investigated.

Frontal lobe response areas

The frontal lobe response selection regions that lie anterior to the central sulcus receive topographic projections from nuclei in the anterior thalamus. These nuclei relay information from the globus pallidus and cerebellum, rather than from sensory receptors. There is a gross somatotopic organization, with separated regions governing mouth, hand, and eye movements. All regions of frontal cortex receive input from parietal and temporal association cortex. The parietal cortex "where" system projects to more dorsal frontal regions whereas the temporal cortex "what" system projects more ventrally. Auditory cortex projections are also segregated, with anterior regions projecting more ventrally than caudal regions (Romanski et al., 1999).

The segregation of afferent input to different frontal regions allows different frontal areas to select responses on the basis of different types of information (Passingham, 1993). Frontal regulation of goal-oriented saccades is best understood. There is a topographic map of intended targets for voluntary saccades in dorsolateral prefrontal cortex (Funahashi et al., 1989). Neurons within this region code different sensory aspects of the goal (Kikuchi-Yorioka & Sawaguchi, 2000). The mirror neurons described in F5 might also be organized into maps of targets for oral, verbal, and manipulative behaviours. If a saccade is a throw with the eyes, then, by analogy, other goal-oriented skills could be topographically mapped in other frontal regions.

Evolution and differentiation of cortical maps

One of the fundamental differences among organisms is in the dimensionality and resolution of their cortical maps. Species-specific "hard-wired" maps evolve as adaptations to an evolutionary niche. Bats that identify their prey with ultrasonic calls have enlarged maps for the frequency modulated echos they use to pinpoint locations. Novel anatomical specializations have evolved to support learned vocal communication systems in other species: songbirds have a song control system of unique forebrain nuclei that are absent in species that do not learn their songs (Doupe & Kuhl, 1999; Nottebohm et al., 1976). In some species, the females (who do not sing) actually lack specialized structures present in the male.

How do cortical maps adapt to facilitate the evolution and development of species-specific behaviours? There are both specific and non-specific mechanisms. A non-specific increase in brain size is the hallmark of primate development and evolution. The human brain is three times larger than that of the chimpanzee, despite similar body size and protein diversity (Preuss, 2000). Although most of the increase in cortical size is associated with non-specific increases in map size (Finlay, Hersman, & Darlington, 1998), some cortical expansion could also be associated with specific changes in map number, distortion, and superposition that facilitated manipulation of the oral spear. Unfortunately, there are no comparative data on map number, for the only system in which maps have been enumerated is monkey vision (Felleman & Van Essen, 1991). Progress is being made in counting human visual maps with fMRI (Sereno et al., 1995).

Cortical columns do not appear to vary in size among organisms from rat to human (Jones, 1990). Cortical maps, on the other hand, vary tremendously in gross size both between and within species. Human primary visual cortex varies four fold between individuals (Stensaas, 1974). Stimulus discriminability is improved in large maps because there are more cells with non-overlapping receptive fields. Another way that evolutionary changes in maps could facilitate the emergence of language is through changes in map superposition. Connectionist models conceptualize stimulus recognition and discrimination in terms of the satisfaction of multiple constraints. Map superposition by the addition of new stimulus dimensions could provide a neurobiological "AND" gate to satisfy multiple constraints. The superposition of maps of different auditory features could allow context to influence phoneme perception, for example.

Another fundamental principle of cortical organization is map distortion. V1 is not a true map of the visual environment. The cortical representations of objects that fall on the fovea (the 5 degrees of central vision) are greatly enlarged relative to those in the retinal periphery, because photoreceptors are densely concentrated in the fovea. Because the number of projections depends on the number of receptors, the cortical region representing the fovea is much larger than that for the retinal periphery. Species that do not depend on fine discrimination of objects for survival do not have the same degree of foveal magnification in V1. The maps of face and object features in the ventral "what" pathway have even greater foveal magnifications.

In auditory cortex, some regions of the tonotopic map are expanded. Humans have an expansion of the low- and medium-frequency ranges used in speech discrimination. Animals that depend on high frequencies for communication or prey detection have expanded cortical regions for high frequencies. One way of identifying the function of a particular cortical region is by determining the region of the perceptual dimension that is amplified. Auditory maps in the human cochlea and cortex could be distorted so that the number of cells coding discrimination of linguistically significant auditory contrasts is increased. Small localized map distortions could provide the neurobiological substrates for perceptual contrasts and equivalencies. Innate predispositions for such distortions could be amplified by sensory experience during development. Changes in map size could occur through structural changes in individual cellular arborizations that accompany changes in neuronal sensitivity. Individual differences in the rate of language acquisition could be related to the extent of these local map distortions.

Summary

Mammals that occupy different ecological niches have distinct perceptual and motor cortical maps. Evolutionary variation in cortical mapping functions that accompanied the evolution of language have involved changes in: (1) map number; (2) gross map size—column number and spacing; (3) map specificity and superposition; and (4) map distortion—regional expansion and contraction. Developmental changes in mapping properties involve similar mechanisms. Map number, specificity, and relative size are probably set to a large extent by genetic predispositions translated as topographic gradients of neurotrophic factors (Rubenstein & Beachy, 1998), but map distortion tuning can be greatly influenced by experience and practice (Crair et al., 1998; Hubel, Wiesel, & LeVay, 1977; Recanzone, Schreiner, & Merzenich, 1993).

Allman has suggested that cortical maps might have evolved in the same way as the homeobox genes for body segment organization (Allman, 1987). These conserved genes have duplicated many times during evolution. Each time a homeobox gene duplicates, the copy becomes slightly modified to modulate development of a new body or brain segment. By analogy, Allman suggests, gene duplication could trigger map duplication and/or superposition. The new map could develop new stimulus-filtering properties while the original map retains its original function. Map expansion and distortion have probably been fostered by a different mechanism involving developmental gene regulation by transcription factors.

CORTICAL DEVELOPMENT

The stages of language development occur postnatally after conclusion of the major stages of cortical differentiation: neuron birth, migration, axon elongation, synaptic formation, and myelination. Although a few cortical neurons might be formed during adulthood, their role in behavioural plasticity is unclear. Events during the last phase of neural development—that of synaptic stabilization, enlargement, and pruning, are probably the neural modifications that accompany the development of language skills. For technical reasons, it has been difficult to test or document this assumption. The near eradication of childhood disease means that developing brains are rarely available for postmortem study. Although advances in imaging make the non-invasive study of human brain development theoretically possible, current techniques lack the resolution and reliability necessary to study the development of microscopic structures such as synapses and the arborization of their associated axonal and dendrite terminals. Technical improvements in diffusion-weighted imaging, a non-invasive magnetic resonance imaging technique (Conturo et al., 1999), hold promise, but implementation in large longitudinal studies is only beginning.

There are very few studies of human brain development (see Elman et al., 1996, for a review). Most of these studies have concluded that frontal regions mature slowly and trail primary sensory regions (Huttenlocher & Dabholkar, 1997; Yakovlev & Lecours, 1967). By contrast, animal studies suggest that each of the five phases of synaptic development occurs simultaneously in all regions of the cortex (Bourgeois, Goldman-Rakic, & Rakic, 2000). This unexpected finding is consistent with the idea that there are no boundaries between perceptual, motor, and cognitive modules and that development proceeds through the elaboration of widespread cortical loops. The first three phases of synaptic development occur prenatally and are only weakly susceptible to modification by experience or experimental manipulation. The fourth phase is the synaptic loss referred to as pruning. Pruning occurs over a protracted period, slowing down towards the close of puberty (Bourgeois et al., 2000). Synaptic stability during this period is modifiable by experience.

The process of synaptic pruning can be traced indirectly by magnetic resonance imaging because it is accompanied by a gradual shrinking and "drying-out" of the cortex. Drying-out reflects a change in the distribution of water in white and grey matter. As cortical neurons become committed to specific circuits, ineffective synapses drop out, remaining synapses enlarge and become wrapped by glia, and myelin wrapping of the axons increases. Myelination in cortical regions where perceptual inputs converge continues to increase into adulthood (Benes, Turtle, Khan, & Farel, 1994) Whether neurons are actually lost during the stages of pruning and myelination is controversial. At the scale presently visible with magnetic resonance imaging, developmental changes appear to be gradual. Grey matter is replaced by white matter at an average rate of 1 per cent a year, with no evidence for more than modest regional differences (Giedd et al., 1999; Paus et al., 1996; Reiss et al., 1996). Cortical complexity in the frontal lobe and asymmetry in the Sylvian fissure increase into the second decade (Blanton et al., 2001). These anatomical changes may underlie functional changes in map properties.

Sensory plasticity

What are the mechanisms by which experience changes map distortion to emphasize perceptual contrasts? Neural responses to sensory stimuli form "tuning curves". The peak of the tuning curve defines the place on a stimulus dimension that evokes maximal firing. This place is called "the optimal stimulus". In primary auditory cortex, each cortical column is optimally sensitive to a characteristic auditory frequency. Cells and columns vary in the breadth and amplitude of their tuning curves. Cells with narrow and sharply peaked tuning curves discriminate sounds better than cells with broad, low-amplitude tuning curves.

Tuning curves sharpen with experience. At birth, tuning curves are broad, that is, cells generalize over broad regions of a dimension. The precision of the mapping is a function of experience and can undergo modest changes even in the adult with a few hours of reinforced exposure (Recanzone et al., 1993). If receptors or muscles are removed, or their activity is stopped with chemical inhibitors, cells change their properties to match the new input.

The general principles that govern tuning-curve sharpening in sensory maps probably govern development of cortical regions subserving language function. Sensory exposure during early development shapes both the developing brain and the behavioural repertoire. These processes have been studied in avian model systems (Bottjer & Johnson, 1992; Doupe & Kuhl, 1999; Knudsen, 1999). In mammals, our understanding of sensory neurodevelopment comes mainly from visual studies in kittens (Wiesel, 1982). At birth, most cells are tuned to horizontal and vertical lines. If diagonals are seen, the number of cells tuned to diagonals increases and the number of cells tuned to horizontal and vertical decreases (an example of map distortion) (Leventhal & Hirsch, 1975). There is a sensitive period when environmental modification has peak potential to alter map properties. At the height of the sensitive period for vision, the effect of a 1-hour environmental modification can be detected. Later, large environmental modifications have only modest effects.

Competition between inputs shapes sensory neuroplasticity during the sensitive period (Crair, 1999). If one eye is sutured closed, the dendrites on unstimulated cortical cells shrink, synapses are lost, and, later, when that eye is opened, the cells no longer fire to visual stimulation. If both eyes are closed, the cells are protected. Similarly, in an edgeless visual environment, cells will remain capable of being stimulated by lines of all orientations, although the tuning curves might be flatter. If only horizontal lines are provided, eventually no cells responsive to lines of other orientations will remain. Cells can retain their innate tuning potential only during brief periods of deprivation. Cellular tuning properties for orientation survive a 3-week period of binocular deprivation but, subsequently, cortical organization degenerates (Crair et al., 1998) (Plate 8).

A startling parallel developmental plasticity in human language has recently been demonstrated in hearing impaired children (Yoshinaga-Itano et al., 1998). Children whose impairment was identified and remediated with hearing amplification and parental counselling before the age of 6 months had normal levels of language function at 3 years of age. Comparable improvement could not be demonstrated when remediation was introduced after the age of 6 months. Evidence from our laboratory suggests that deaf children have smaller Heschl's gyri than controls (Eckert & Gauger, unpublished data). Thus it is possible that auditory cortical maps shrink in the absence of auditory and linguistic input early in development.

A neuronal mechanism for developmental neuroplasticity

A mechanism for developmental neuroplasticity was proposed by Hebb in 1949, in his psychological classic entitled *The organization of behavior*. Hebb tried to account for the retroactive ability of reinforcement by postulating what is now called "a Hebbian synapse". A Hebbian synapse is an excitatory synapse that becomes stronger (more likely to trigger an action potential) with repeated stimulation. A synaptic receptor with such properties has now been discovered—the postsynaptic *N*-methyl-D-aspartate (NMDA) receptor for glutamate, the excitatory transmitter used by most cortical neurons. NMDA receptors allow weak inputs to gain control of cell depolarization. The presence of glutamate alone is not sufficient to open ion channels in the NMDA receptor because the channel is normally blocked by magnesium. When the cell is depolarized in the presence of glutamate, however, the magnesium pops off, allowing calcium to flow in. Calcium entry triggers a cascade of chemical events that increase the size and number of non-NMDA glutamate synapses on the cell. The increased number of synapses increases the probability of future action potentials. This is the neurobiological substrate of "strengthening the connection".

Recent discoveries have identified developmental changes in the NMDA receptor that could terminate the sensitive period for developmental neuroplasticity

(Flint et al., 1997). The temporal gradients of change could differ in different maps and in the two hemispheres, and could be regulated by sensory input. Variation in these gradients could contribute to individual differences in the developmental timetable for language and reading milestones, language function after early damage, and the ability to acquire a second language.

There has been considerable discussion concerning the importance of early stimulation and the existence of a critical 3-year "window of opportunity" when enrichment is particularly important for children. The neurobiological data concerning critical periods come from animals. Developmental timetables cannot be translated directly from animals to humans because human foetal and infant development occurs over such a long timespan. In a recent startling example of human uniqueness, it has been discovered that the human pyramidal tract makes synapses with spinal cord motor neurons for the hand during foetal life, almost a year before the emergence of independent finger movements (Eyre et al., 2000). In monkeys, by contrast, such synapses are formed 3 months postnatally, at the time that independent finger movements appear. Such comparative studies demonstrate that each species has a unique developmental trajectory.

The boundaries of critical or sensitive periods must be different for different abilities and behaviours and, probably, different children. In the case of hearing impairment, the data are compelling. In the case of early brain injury, however, only the end of puberty seems to close the window for hemispheric transfer of language function and the acquisition of a second language without an accent (Bates et al., 1997; Johnson & Morton, 1991). For each behavioural domain, there is probably a period of peak sensitivity to input that is flanked by regions of declining sensitivity, based on the maturational stage of the circuits involved (Huttenlocher & Dabholkar, 1997), and, probably, individual differences.

The neural basis of language development

Individual-specific mapping starts during the last trimester of pregnancy when cortex differentiates and the foetus becomes able to hear and respond to the mother's voice. Reorganization continues through infancy and childhood into puberty. Sounds produced during the babbling period are variable because of perceptual and vocal immaturity. During the transition from "playing with sound" to intentional production of words, the variety decreases and the frequency of simpler sounds increases. Infants apparently have "difficulty in handling the processing demands of generating the appropriate articulatory routines from a stored representation of the sound pattern while trying simultaneously to convey a specific message" (Jusczyk, 1997, p. 182). During this period there are large individual differences, as infants experiment in the use of different routines (Boysson-Bardies, 1999). By 3 years of age these differences have receded as the routines approximate the sounds of the native language.

The neural substrate for these circuits must involve the auditory cortex that codes phonemes, the motor cortex that controls the mouth and throat, and a premotor region (possibly the mirror neuron region) where the perceptual and motor patterns for particular phonemes move into register. Neural circuits coding infrequently heard and produced syllables would simply drop out during this period, as they do during song crystallization (Doupe & Kuhl, 1999). In the songbird, neurons in a forebrain region interposed between auditory and motor regions lose their sensitivity to elements that are not selected for the bird's own song during the subsong "babbling" period. Such experience-dependent neural plasticity in human cortex could underlie the loss of sensitivity to phonemes not found in the native language.

One of the most dramatic phenomena in language development is the vocabulary burst. What are the neural mechanisms that could underlie such rapid development? Words are meaningful sequences of syllables. Learning to produce syllable sequences might require participation of neurons in the PreSMA (Hikosaka et al., 2000). The attachment of meaning to syllables probably requires the establishment of circuits between the planum, the superior temporal sulcus (STS), and the parietal cortex. The initiation of meaningful word production is thus dependent on the maturation of synapses in at least three circuits: the vocal–imitation–planum–F5 loop responsible for babbling; an F5–PreSMA–SMA loop responsible for sequence learning and production; and a planum–STS–parietal cortex loop that attaches meaning to sounds. During the babbling stage, synapses might stabilize independently in these three loops. A critical mass of connections is required before synchronous firing in all three loops enables imitation and understanding. The circuit is only as functional as its weakest link. Once activity in these circuits has started to synchronize, the vocabulary burst can be initiated. By analogy, later development of conversational facility and apparent grammatical rules could involve the same kind of circuit-joining and synchronization between superior frontal cortex, anterior cingulate, and anterior temporal regions implicated in complex cognition (Binder et al., 1995).

The developmental changes in neural circuitry that are hypothesized to participate in the vocabulary burst have been demonstrated in animals and do not require unique human mechanisms. Features of this hypothesis could therefore be tested in animal models. There has been a small amount of study of developmental differences in the developmental effects of cortical lesions (Bachevalier, 1991; Goldman-Rakic, 1987), but the research has not been directed at pinpointing the locus or timing of developmental changes. Neuroethological research of this type is generally conducted on non-mammalian and invertebrate species whose brain organization is fundamentally different (for an example, see Rogers, 2000). Little empirical evidence is available on the sequences of cortical circuit development and their relation to the appearance of novel behaviours in mammals.

Nature and nurture

Individual-specific maps of the sensory environment internalize the effects of the unique environment in the uterus, the home, the day-care centre, and school. The epigenetic interaction between species-specific constraints and individual-specific experiences is commonly referred to as the "nature–nurture" problem. Studies of cortical neurobiology in animals suggest that nature endows us with a restricted range of map types with preset biases amplifying features to which attention should be paid. Nurture provides the sensory experiences that shape the development of a "native" language by inducing distortion of the auditory maps on Heschl's gyrus and auditory cortex. The space devoted to representing features useful for the discrimination of meaningful auditory contrasts presumably expands.

During "normal" development, those preset biases will facilitate the storage and imitation of human communication gestures important for survival. The preset biases will be modified by the actual distribution of stimuli in the environment, however. Even if a map were pretuned to devote a large amount of space to linguistic contrasts, this space would shrink in the absence of reciprocal communicative interactions between parent and child, punctuated by parentese and babbling. Conversely, infants with smaller initial biases might compensate in linguistically enriched environments.

Initial neural predispositions might shape the development of learning (Molfese, 2000). Auditory evoked responses to syllables recorded at birth distinguished different types of reading disability 8 years later. Reduced auditory cortex asymmetry and size might be responsible for the differences in auditory evoked activity. The innate predisposition for language processing to be performed in the left perisylvian region could rest on a structural asymmetry—there is simply more space in left hemisphere auditory cortex for neural columns devoted to auditory features that mark linguistic contrasts. During development, the neurons in this space mature and develop properties that improve discrimination of contrasts in the native language. Meanwhile, homologous right hemisphere regions develop sensitivity to other acoustic features of the environment and the space devoted to linguistic contrasts shrinks. Interhemispheric connections from the left hemisphere might actually inhibit right hemisphere responsiveness to language (Geschwind & Galaburda, 1987). Increasing functional asymmetry is associated with a loss of neuroplasticity and an increased probability of aphasia after left hemisphere lesions. After early lesions, the left and right hemisphere contains uncommitted maps whose properties can be modified to emphasize linguistic contrasts. As development proceeds, maps stabilize, and the effects of a left hemisphere lesion become catastrophic.

SUMMARY

1. The idea that language depends on unique human specializations has limited neurobiological research.
2. Language development can be viewed as a particularly skilled form of vocal learning.

3. The unique properties of human language stem from an urgent human drive to understand and generalize.
4. The neural correlates of language acquisition can be conceptualized as experience-induced differentiation, distortion, and superposition of cortical sensory and response maps.
5. Research on cortical neuroplasticity in appropriate animal models has the potential to contribute essential insights into this mysterious product of human evolution.

ACKNOWLEDGEMENTS

This chapter was written with the support of National Institute of Deafness and Communication Disorders grant R01 DC002922. The author is grateful to Purvis Bedenbaugh, Mark Eckert, John Kuldau, Lise Eliot, and Ben Burkley for helpful criticism.

REFERENCES

Aaltonen, O., Eerola, O., Hellstrom, A., Uusipaikkla, E., & Lang, A. (1997). Perceptual magnet effect in the light of behavioral and psychophysiological data. *Journal of the Acoustical Society of America, 101*, 1090–1105.

Allman, J. (1987). Maps in context: Some analogies between visual cortical and genetic maps. In L. Vaina (Ed.), *Matters of intelligence* (pp. 369–393). Dordrecht, The Netherlands: D. Reidel.

Allman, J., & Kaas, J. (1971). A representation of the visual field in the caudal third of the middle temporal gyrus of the owl monkey (*Aotus trivirgatus*). *Brain Research, 31*, 85–101.

Bachevalier, J. (1991). An animal model for childhood autism: Memory loss and socio-emotional disturbances following neonatal damage to the limbic system in monkeys. In C. Tamminga & S. Schulz (Eds.), *Advances in neuropsychiatry and psychopharmacology* (pp. 129–140). New York: Raven Press.

Baddeley, A. (1986). *Working memory*. New York: Oxford.

Baddeley, A., Gathercole, S., & Papagno, C. (1998). The phonological loop as a language learning device. *Psychological Review, 105*, 158–173.

Bates, E., Thal, D., Aram, D., Eisele, J., Nass, R., & Trauner, D. (1997). From first words to grammar in children with focal brain injury. *Developmental Neuropsychology, 33*, 447–476.

Belin, P., & Zatorre, R. (2000). “What,” “where,” and “how” in auditory cortex. *Nature Neuroscience, 3*, 965–966.

Belin, P., Zilbovicius, M., Fontaine, A., Crozier, S., & Thivard, L. (1998). Lateralisation of speech and auditory temporal processing. *Journal of Cognitive Neuroscience, 10*, 536–540.

Benes, F., Turtle, M., Khan, Y., & Farol, P. (1994). Myelination of a key relay zone in the hippocampal formation occurs in the human brain during childhood, adolescence, and adulthood. *Archives of General Psychiatry, 51*, 477–484.

Benson, D. (1993). Aphasia. In K. Heilman & E. Valenstein (Eds.), *Clinical neuropsychology* (pp. 17–36). New York: Oxford University Press.

Berk, L., & Garvin, R. (1984). Development of private speech among low-income Appalachian children. *Developmental Psychology, 20*, 271–286.

Binder, J., Rao, S., Hammeke, T., Frost, J., Bandettini, P.A., Jesmanowicz, A. et al. (1995). Lateralized human brain language systems demonstrated by task subtraction functional magnetic resonance imaging. *Archives of Neurology, 52*, 593–601.

Blanton, R.E., Levitt, J.G., Thompson, P.M. Narr, K.L., Capetillo-Cunliffe, L., Nobel, A. et al. (2001). Mapping cortical asymmetry and complexity patterns in normal children. *Psychiatry Research, 107*, 29–43.

Bottjer, S., & Johnson, F. (1992). Matters of life and death in songbird forebrain. *Journal of Neurobiology, 23*, 1172–1191.

Bourgeois, J.-P., Goldman-Rakic, P., & Rakic, P. (2000). Formation, elimination, and stabilisation of synapses in the primate cerebral cortex. In M. Gazzaniga (Ed.), *The new cognitive neurosciences* (pp. 45–53). Cambridge, MA: MIT Press.

Boysson-Bardies, B. (1999). *How language comes to children*. Cambridge MA: MIT Press.

Burgess, C. (1998). From simple associations to the building blocks of language: Modeling meaning in memory with the HAL model. *Behavior Research Methods, Instruments, & Computers, 30*, 188–198.

Cheung, S., Bedenbaugh, P., Nagarajan, S., & Schreiner, C. (2001). Functional organisation of squirrel monkey primary auditory cortex: responses to pure tones. *Journal of Neurophysiology, 85*, 1732–1749.

Chiarello, C. (1999). Parallel systems for processing language: Hemispheric complementarity in the normal brain. In M. Banich & M. Mack (Eds.), *Mind, brain, & language: Multidisciplinary perspectives*. Mahwah, NJ: Lawrence Erlbaum Associates Inc.

Chomsky, N. (1959). A review of B.F. Skinner's *Verbal Behavior*. *Language, 35*, 26–58.

Chomsky, N. (1965). *Aspects of a theory of syntax*. Cambridge, MA: MIT Press.

Clark, A. (1997). *Being there: Putting brain, body, and world together again*. Cambridge, MA: MIT Press.

Conturo, T., Lori, N., Cull, T., Akbudak, E., Snyder, A., Shimony, J. et al. (1999). Tracking neuronal fiber pathways in the living human brain. *Proceedings of the National Academy of Science, 96*, 10422–10427.

Corballis, M. (1991). *The lopsided ape*. New York: Oxford.

Crair, M. (1999). Neuronal activity during development: Permissive or instructive? *Current Opinion in Neurobiology, 9*, 88–93.

Crair, M., Gillespie, D., & Stryker, M. (1998). The role of visual experience in the development of columns in cat visual cortex. *Science, 279*, 566–570.

Crosson, B., Sadek, J., Bobholz, J., Gokcay, D., Mohr, C., Leonard, C. et al. (1999). Medial frontal activity during word generation is centered within the paracingulate sulcus: An fMRI study of functional anatomy in 28 individuals. *Cerebral Cortex, 9*, 307–316.

Dennis, M., & Whitaker, H. (1976). Language acquisition following hemidecortication: Linguistic superiority of the left over the right hemisphere. *Brain and Language, 3*, 404–433.

Diamond, A. (2000). Close interrelation of motor development and cognitive development and of the cerebellum and prefrontal cortex. *Child Development, 71*, 44–56.

Doupe, A., & Kuhl, P. (1999). Birdsong and speech: Common themes and mechanisms. *Annual Review of Neuroscience, 22*, 567–631.

Eckert, M., & Leonard, C. (2000). Structural imaging in dyslexia: The planum temporale. *Mental Retardation and Developmental Disabilities Research Reviews, 6*, 198–206.

Eckert, M., & Leonard, C. (2002). Developmental disorders: dyslexia. In K. Hugdahl (Ed.), *Brain asymmetry* Cambridge, MA: MIT Press.

Eckert, M., Lombardino, L., & Leonard, C. (2001). Tipping the environmental playground: Who is at risk for reading failure. *Child Development, 72*, 988–1001.

Elman, J., Bates, E., Johnson, M., Karmiloff-Smith, A., Parisi, D., & Plunkett, K. (1996). *Rethinking innateness: A connectionist perspective on development*. Cambridge, MA: MIT Press.

Eyre, J., Miller, S., Clowry, G., Conway, E., & Watts, C. (2000). Functional corticospinal projections are established prenatally in the human foetus permitting involvement in the development of spinal motor centres. *Brain, 123*, 51–64.

Felleman, D., & Van Essen, D. (1991). Distributed hierarchical processing in the primate cerebral cortex. *Cerebral Cortex, 1*, 1–47.

Fernald, A. (1993). Human material vocalizations to infants as biologically relevant signals: An evolutionary perspective. In P. Bloom (Ed.), *Language acquisition* (pp. 51–94). Cambridge, MA: MIT Press.

Finlay, B., Hersman, M., & Darlington, R. (1998). Patterns of vertebrate neurogenesis and the paths of vertebrate evolution. *Brain, Behavior and Evolution, 52*, 232–242.

Fitch, R., Miller, S., & Tallal, P. (1997). Neurobiology of speech perception. *Annual Review of Neuroscience, 20*, 331–353.

Flint, A., Maisch, U., Weishaupt, J., Kriegstein, A., & Monyer, H. (1997). N2A subunit expression shortens NMDA receptor synaptic currents in developing neocortex. *Journal of Neuroscience, 17*, 2469–2476.

Foundas, A., Eure, K., Luevano, L., & Weinberger, D. (1998a). MRI asymmetries of Broca's Area: The pars triangularis and pars opercularis. *Brain and Language, 64*, 282–296.

Foundas, A., Hong, K., Leonard, C., & Heilman, K. (1998b). Hand preference and MRI asymmetries of the central sulcus. *Neuropsychiatry, Neuropsychology, and Behavioral Neurology, 11*, 65–71.

Foundas, A., Leonard, C., Gilmore, R., Fennell, E., & Heilman, K. (1994). Planum temporale asymmetry and language dominance. *Neuropsychologia, 32*, 1225–1231.

Foundas, A., Leonard, C., Gilmore, R., Fennell, E., & Heilman, K. (1996). Pars triangularis asymmetry and language dominance. *Proceedings of the National Academy of Science USA, 93*, 719–722.

Foundas, A., Leonard, C., & Heilman, K. (1995). Morphological cerebral asymmetries and handedness: The pars triangularis and planum temporale. *Archives of Neurology, 52*, 501–508.

Funahashi, S., Bruce, C., & Goldman-Rakic, P. (1989). Mnemonic coding of visual space in the monkey's dorsolateral prefrontal cortex. *Journal of Neurophysiology, 61*, 331–349.

Galaburda, A., Sherman, G., Rosen, G., Aboitiz, F., & Geschwind, N. (1985). Developmental dyslexia: Four consecutive cases with cortical anomalies. *Annals of Neurology, 18*, 222–233.

Galuske, R., Schlote, W., Bratzke, H., & Singer, W. (2000). Interhemispheric asymmetries of the modular structure in human temporal cortex. *Science, 289*, 1946–1949.

Gannon, P., Holloway, R., Broadfield, D., & Braun, A. (1998). Asymmetry of chimpanzee planum temporale: Humanlike pattern of Wernicke's brain language area homolog. *Science, 279*, 220–222.

Gauger, L., Lombardino, L., & Leonard, C. (1997). Brain morphology in children with specific language impairment. *Journal of Speech Hearing & Language Research, 40*, 1272–1284.

Geschwind, N., & Galaburda, A. (1987). *Cerebral lateralisation: Biological mechanisms, association and pathology*. Cambridge, MA: MIT Press.

Geschwind, N., & Levitsky, W. (1968). Human brain: Left–right asymmetries in temporal speech region. *Science, 161*, 186–187.

Giedd, J., Blumenthal, J. Jeffries, N., Castellanos, F., Liu, H., Zijdenbos, A. et al. (1999). Brain development during childhood and adolescence: A longitudinal MRI study. *Nature Neuroscience, 2*, 861–863.

Goldman-Rakic, P. (1987). Development of cortical circuitry and cognitive function. *Child Development, 58*, 642–691.

Goodale, M., & Humphrey, G. (1998). The objects of action and perception. *Cognition, 67*, 181–207.

Gooler, D., & O'Neill, W. (1987). Topographic representation of vocal frequency demonstrated by microstimulation of anterior cingulate cortex in the echolocating bat (*Pheronotus parneli parneilli*). *Journal of Comparative Physiology A, 161*, 283–294.

Greenough, W., & Alcantara, A. (1993). The roles of experience in different developmental information stage processes. In B. de Boysson-Bardies, S. De Schonen, P. Juscyk, P. McNeilage & J. Morton (Eds.), *Developmental neurocognition* (pp. 3–16). Dordrecht, The Netherlands: Kluwer.

Grosbras, M., Lobel, E., Van de Moortele, D., LeBihan, D., & Berthoz, A. (1999). An anatomical landmark for the supplementary eye fields in human revealed with functional magnetic resonance Imaging. *Cerebral Cortex, 9*, 705–711.

Habib, M., & Robichon, F. (1996). Parietal lobe morphology predicts phonological skills in developmental dyslexia. *Brain and Cognition, 32*, 139–142.

Harm, M., & Seidenberg, M. (1999). Phonology, reading acquisition and dyslexia: Insights from connectionist models. *Psychological Review, 106*, 491–528.

Hart, B., & Risley, T. (1995). *Meaningful differences*. Baltimore, MD: Paul Brookes.

Hayes, T., & Lewis, D. (1995). Anatomical specialisations of the anterior motor speech area. *Brain and Language, 49*, 289–308.

Hebb, D. (1949). *The organisation of behavior*. New York: Wiley.

Hikosaka, O., Sakai, K., Nakahara, H., Lu, X., Miyachi, S., Nakamura, K. et al. (2000). Neural mechanisms for learning of sequential procedures. In M. Gazzaniga (Ed.), *The new cognitive neurosciences* (pp. 553–572). Cambridge, MA: MIT Press.

Hubel, D.H., Wiesel, T.N., & LeVay, S. (1977). Plasticity of ocular dominance columns in monkey striate cortex. *Philosophical Transactions of the Royal Society, 278*, 377–409.

Huttenlocher, J. (1998). Language input and language growth. *Preventive Medicine, 27*, 195–199.

Huttenlocher, P.R., & Dabholkar, A.S. (1997). Regional differences in synaptogenesis in human cerebral cortex. *Journal of Comparative Neurology, 387*, 167–178.

Johnson, M., & Morton, J. (1991). *Biology and cognitive development: The case of face recognition*. Oxford: Blackwell.

Jones, E. (1990). Modulatory events in the development and evolution of primate neocortex. In E. Jones (Ed.), *The cerebral cortex* (pp. 311–362). New York: Plenum Press.

Jurgens, U., Maurus, M., Ploog, D., & Winter, P. (1967). Vocalisation in the squirrel monkey (*Saimiri sciureus*) eliced by brain stimulation. *Experimental Brain Research, 4*, 114–117.

Jusczyk, P. (1997). *The discovery of spoken language*. Cambridge, MA: MIT Press.

Kaas, J., Hacket, T., & Tramo, M. (1999). Auditory processing in primate cerebral cortex. *Current Opinion in Neurobiology, 9*, 164–170.

Karmiloff-Smith, A. (1992). *Beyond modularity: A developmental perspective on cognitive science*. Cambridge, MA: MIT Press.

Kikuchi-Yorioka, Y., & Sawaguchi, T. (2000). Parallel visuospatial and audiospatial working memory processes in the monkey dorsolateral prefrontal cortex. *Nature Neuroscience, 3*, 1075–1076.

Kimura, D. (1993). *Neuromotor mechanisms of human communication*. New York: Oxford Press.

Knudsen, E. (1999). Mechanisms of experience-dependent plasticity in the auditory localisation pathway of the barn owl. *Journal of Comparative Physiology A, 185*, 305–321.

Kosslyn, S., Gazzaniga, M., Galaburda, A., & Rabin, C. (1999). Hemispheric specialisation. In M. Zigmond, F. Bloom, S. Landis, J. Roberts, & L. Squire (Eds.), *Fundamental neuroscience* (pp. 1521–1542). San Diego: Academic Press.

Kraus, N., McGee, T.J., Carrell, T.D., Zecker, S.G., Nicol, T.G., & Koch, D.B. (1996). Auditory neurophysiologic responses and discrimination deficits in children with learning problems. *Science, 273*, 971–973.

Kuhl, P. (1991). Human adults and human infants show a "perceptual magnet effect" for the prototypes of speech categories, monkeys do not. *Perception & Psychophysiology, 50*, 93–107.

Kuhl, P., Andruski, J., Chistovich, I., Chistovich, L., Kozhevnikova, E., Ryskina, V. et al. (1997). Cross-language analysis of phonetic units in language addressed to infants. *Science, 277*, 684–686.

Kuhl, P., & Miller, J. (1975). Speech perception by the chinchilla; voiced–voiceless distinction in alveolar plosive consonants. *Science, 190*, 69–72.

Lai, C. S., Fisher, S. E., Hurst, J. A., Vargha-Khadem, F., & Monaco, A. P. (2001). A fork-head-domain gene is mutated in a severe speech and language disorder. *Nature, 413*, 519–523.

Leonard, C., Eckert, M., Lombardino, L., Oakland, T., Kranzler, J., Mohr, C. et al. (2001). Anatomical risk factors for phonological dyslexia. *Cerebral Cortex, 11*, 148–157.

Leonard, C., Lombardino, L., Mercado, L., Browd, S., Breier, J., & Agee, O. (1996). Cerebral asymmetry and cognitive development in children: A magnetic resonance imaging study. *Psychological Science, 7*, 79–85.

Leonard, C., Voeller, K.S., Lombardino, L., Morris, M.K., Alexander, A., Andersen, H. et al. (1993). Anomalous cerebral structure in dyslexia revealed with magnetic resonance imaging. *Archives of Neurology, 50*, 461–469.

Leventhal, A.G., & Hirsch, H.V. (1975). Cortical effect of early selective exposure to diagonal lines. *Science, 190*, 902–904.

Marcus, G.F. (1999). Connectionism: With or without rules? *Trends in Cognitive Sciences, 3*, 168–170.

McClelland, J.L., & Seidenberg, M.S. (2000). Why do kids say goed and brang? (review of Pinker: Words & Rules). *Science, 287*, 47–48.

MacWhinney, B. (1998). Models of the emergence of language. *Annual Reviews of Psychology, 49*, 199–227.

Mehler, J., & Cristophe, A. (2000). Acquisition of languages: Infant and adult data. In M. Gazzaniga (Ed.), *The new cognitive neurosciences* (pp. 897–907). Cambridge, MA: MIT Press.

Mendelson, J., & Schreiner, C. (1990). Functional topography of cat primary auditory cortex: Distribution of integrated excitation. *Journal of Neurophysiology, 64*, 1442–1459.

Middlebrooks, J., Clock, A., Xu, L., & Green, D. (1994). A panoramic code for sound location by cortical neurons. *Science, 264*, 842–844.

Middlebrooks, J., Dykes, R., & Merzenich, M. (1980). Binaural response-specific bands in primary auditory cortex (AI) of the cat: Topographical organisation orthogonal to isofrequency contours. *Brain Research, 181*, 31–48.

Molfese, D. (2000). Predicting dyslexia at 8 years of age using neonatal brain responses. *Brain and Language, 72*, 238–245.

Molfese, D.L., Freeman, R., Jr., & Palermo, D. (1975). The ontogeny of brain lateralisation for speech and nonspeech sounds. *Brain and Language, 2*, 356–368.

Nakamura, K., Sakai, K., & Hikosaka, O. (1999). Effects of local inactivation of monkey medial frontal cortex in learning of sequential procedures. *Journal of Neurophysiology, 82*, 1063–1068.

Nottebohm, F.F., Stokes, T.M., & Leonard, C.M. (1976). Central control of song in the canary. *Journal of Comparative Neurology, 165*, 457–486.

Ono, M., Jubik, S., & Abernathy, C. (1990). *Atlas of the cerebral sulci*. New York: Thieme.

Passingham, R. (1993). *The frontal lobes and voluntary behavior*. Oxford: Oxford University Press.

Paus, T., Tomaiuolo, F., Otaky, N., MacDonald, D., Petrides, M., Atlas, J. et al. (1996). Human cingulate and paracingulate sulci; pattern, variability, asymmetry, and probabilistic map. *Cerebral Cortex, 6*, 207–214.

Penhune, V.B., Zatorre, R.J., MacDonald, J.D., & Evans, A.C. (1996). Interhemispheric anatomical differences in human primary auditory cortex; probabilistic mapping and volume measurement from magnetic resonance scans. *Cerebral Cortex, 6*, 661–672.

Picard, N., & Strick, P. (1996). Motor areas of the medial wall: A review of their location and functional activations. *Cerebral Cortex, 6*, 342–353.

Pinker, S. (1994). *The language instinct*. New York: William Morrow.

Povinelli, D.J., & Dunphy-Lelii, S. (2001). Do chimpanzees seek explanations? Preliminary comparative investigations. *Canadian Journal of Experimental Psychology, 55*, 185–193.

Preuss, T. (2000). What's human about the human brain? In M. Gazzaniga (Ed.), *The new cognitive neurosciences* (pp. 1219–1234). Cambridge, MA: MIT Press.

Rasmussen, T., & Milner, B. (1975). Clinical and surgical studies of the cerebral speech areas in man. In K.J. Zulch, O. Creutzfeldt, & G.C. Galbraith (Eds.), *Otfrid Foerster symposium on cerebral localisation* (pp. 238–257). New York: Springer Verlag.

Rauschecker, J., Tian, B., & Hauser, M. (1995). Processing of complex sounds in the macaque nonprimary auditory cortex. *Science, 268*, 111–114.

Recanzone, G., Schreiner, C., & Merzenich, M. (1993). Plasticity in the frequency representation of primary auditory cortex following discrimination training in adult owl monkeys. *Journal of Neuroscience, 13*, 87–103.

Reiss, A.L., Abrams, M.T., Singer, H.S., Ross, J.L., & Denckla, M.B. (1996). Brain development, gender and IQ in children: A volumetric imaging study. *Brain, 119*, 1763–1774.

Rizzolatti, G., Fogassi, L., & Gallese, V. (2000). Cortical mechanisms subserving object grasping and action recognition: A new view on the cortical motor functions. In M. Gazzaniga (Ed.), *The new cognitive neurosciences* (pp. 539–552). Cambridge, MA: MIT Press.

Robin, D., Tranel, D., & Damasio, H. (1990). Auditory perception of temporal and spectral events in patients with focal left and right cerebral lesions. *Brain and Language, 39*, 539–555.

Rogers, L. (2000). Evolution of hemispheric specialisation: Advantages and disadvantages. *Brain and Language, 73*, 236–253.

Romanski, L., Tian, B., Fritz, J., Mishkin, M., Goldman-Rakic, P., & Rauschecker, J. (1999). Dual streams of auditory afferents target multiple domains in the primate prefrontal cortex. *Nature Neuroscience, 2*, 1131–1136.

Rubenstein, J., & Beachy, P. (1998). Patterning of the embryonic forebrain. *Current Opinion in Neurobiology, 8*, 18–26.

Rumsey, J., Donahue, B., Brady, D., Nace, K., Giedd, J., & Andreason, P. (1997). A magnetic resonance imaging study of planum temporale asymmetry in men with developmental dyslexia. *Archives of Neurology, 54*, 1481–1489.

Saffran, J., Aslin, R., & Newport, E. (1996). Statistical learning by 8-month-old infants. *Science, 274*, 1926–1928.

Schlaug, G., Jancke, L., Huang, Y., & Steinmetz, H. (1995). *In vivo* evidence of structural brain asymmetry in musicians. *Science, 267*, 699–701.

Seidenberg, M. (1997). Language acquisition and use; learning and applying probabilistic constraints. *Science, 275*, 1559–1603.

Seldon, H. (1985). The anatomy of speech perception: Human auditory cortex. In A. Peters & E. Jones (Eds.), *Cerebral cortex* (pp. 273–327). New York: Plenum.

Sereno, M., Dale, A., Reppas, J., Kwong, K., Belliveau, J., Brady, T. et al. (1995). Borders of multiple visual areas in humans revealed by functional magnetic resonance imaging. *Science, 268*, 889–893.

Skinner, B. (1957). *Verbal behavior*. New York: Appleton Century Crofts.

Smith, H.L. Jr. (1980). Dialects of English. In W. Morris (Ed.), *The American Heritage Dictionary of the English Language* (pp xxv–xxx). Boston, MA: Houghton Mifflin.

Steinmetz, H., Ebeling, U., Huang, Y., & Kahn, T. (1990). Sulcus topography of the parietal opercular region: An anatomic and MR study. *Brain and Language, 38*, 515–533.

Steinmetz, H., Rademacher, J., & Huang, Y. (1989). Cerebral asymmetry: MR planimetry of the human planum temporale. *Journal of Computer Assisted Tomography, 13*, 996–1005.

Steinmetz, H., Volkmann, J., Jancke, L., & Freund, H.-J. (1991). Anatomical left-right asymmetry of language related temporal cortex is different in left- and right-handers. *Annals of Neurology, 29*, 315–319.

Steinschneider, M., Schroeder, C., Arezzo, J., & Vaughan, H.G. (1993). Speech-evoked activity in primary auditory cortex: Effects of voice onset time. *Electroencephalography and Clinical Neurophysiology*, 1–14.

Stensaas, S. (1974). The topography and variability of primary visual cortex in man. *Journal of Neurosurgery, 40*, 747–755.

Szymanski, M., Rowley, H., & Roberts, T. (1999). A hemispherically asymmetrical MEG response to vowels. *NeuroReport, 10*, 2481–2486.

Tallal, P., Miller, S., Bedi, G., Byma, G., Wang, X., Nagarajan, S.S. et al. (1996). Language comprehension in language-learning impaired children improved with acoustically modified speech. *Science, 271*, 81–84.

Trauner, D., Wulfeck, B., Tallal, P., & Hesselink, J. (2000). Neurological and MRI profiles of children with developmental language impairment. *Developmental Medicine and Child Neurology, 42*, 470–475.

Tzourio, N., Crivello, F., Mellet, E., Nkanga-Ngila, B., & Mazoyer, B. (1998). Functional anatomy of dominance for speech comprehension in left handers vs right handers. *Neuroimage, 8*, 1–16.

Vihmann, M. (1993). Variable paths to early word production. *Journal of Phonetics, 21*, 61–82.

Wiesel, T. (1982). Postnatal development of the visual cortex and the influence of environment. *Nature, 299*, 583–591.

Witelson, S., & Kigar, D. (1992). Sylvian fissure morphology and asymmetry in men and women: Bilateral differences in relation to handedness in men. *Journal of Comparative Neurology, 323*, 326–340.

Witelson, S., & Paillie, W. (1973). Left hemisphere specialisation for language in the newborn: Neuroanatomical evidence of asymmetry. *Brain, 96*, 641–646.

Wright, B. (2000). Nonlinguistic perceptual deficits associated with reading and language disorders. *Current Opinion in Neurobiology, 10*, 482–488.

Wright, B., Lombardino, L., King, W., Puranik, C., Leonard, C., & Merzenich, M. (1997). Auditory temporal and spectral processing in children with language impairments. *Nature, 387*, 176–178.

Yakovlev, P., & Lecours, A.-R. (1967). The myelogenetic cycles of regional maturation of the brain. In A. Minkowski (Ed.), *Regional development of the brain in early life* (pp. 3–70). Oxford: Blackwell.

Yeni-Komshian, G., & Benson, D. (1976). Anatomical study of cerebral asymmetry in the temporal lobe of humans, chimpanzees, and Rhesus monkeys. *Science, 192*, 387–389.

Yoshinaga-Itano, C., Sedey, A., Coulter, D., & Mehl, A. (1998). Language of early- and later-identified children with hearing loss. *Pediatrics, 102*, 1161–1171.

Zatorre, R., Evans, A., Meyer, E., & Gjedde, A. (1992). Lateralisation of phonetic and pitch discrimination in speech processing. *Science, 256*, 846–849.

Zatorre, R., Meyer, E., Gjedde, A., & Evans, A. (1996). PET Studies of phonetic processing of speech: Review, replication and reanalysis. *Cerebral Cortex, 6*, 21–30.

CHAPTER SEVEN

The neural and functional development of human prefrontal cortex

Monica Luciana
Department of Psychology, University of Minnesota, Minneapolis, USA

INTRODUCTION

The behavioural functions of the human frontal lobe have been of interest to neuroscientists for decades, ever since the infamous case of Phineas Gage highlighted that this region of the brain was crucial for behavioural regulation independent of general intelligence (Harlow, 1868). Because the frontal lobe is believed to modulate relatively high-level information processing, including abstract reasoning skills, flexibility of behaviour under changing circumstances, and inhibition of inappropriate responses, it would seem to represent a critical neural substrate for behaviours that we tend to think of as being "adult" or "mature" in nature. Indeed, one prominent theorist has suggested that we have need of a concept of "working intelligence" (Jasper, 1995) to account for the types of behaviour that are deficient in individuals with frontal lobe damage. Many of these deficiencies (poor judgement, lack of planning, inattention, socially inappropriate behaviour) are considered normative in early infant and child development, perhaps reflecting immaturity of the frontally guided executive systems that control them. Yet relatively little is known about the lifespan neural development of the human frontal lobe, and available information on the time-course of its physiological and structural maturation does not always correspond to that of functional changes as they emerge. The goal of this chapter is to review current conceptualizations of frontal lobe development from both a neural and a functional standpoint. Controversies in interpreting available data will be mentioned. The chapter will first review general principles of cortical development and their applications to the development of the frontal lobe. Next, behavioural functions controlled by the frontal lobe will be described. Studies examining the development of these abilities in humans will be reviewed, and, finally, speculations as to the neural mechanisms underlying observed patterns of behavioural development will be considered.

OVERVIEW OF PREFRONTAL DEVELOPMENT

In the primate, the frontal cortex is defined as the cortex anterior to the central fissure, an expanse of tissue that includes the precentral gyrus (or primary motor cortex, Brodmann's area 4; see Fig. 7.1). The term "prefrontal cortex" (PFC) describes all regions of the frontal lobe that lie anterior to the motor strip. Traditionally, the prefrontal cortex has also been defined as the projection field of the dorsomedial thalamus (Goldman-Rakic & Porrino, 1985; Rose & Woolsey, 1948; Walker, 1940). The prefrontal cortex is not viewed as a unitary structure, and several functional divisions have been proposed. These divisions generally include the dorsal region (Brodmann's areas 6, 8, 9, and 46) and the ventral region (Brodmann's areas 11, 12, 13, 25, 32, 45, and 10). In the mature primate, the prefrontal cortex is reciprocally connected with numerous cortical and subcortical structures, including the superior temporal cortex, posterior parietal cortex, cingulate gyrus, thalamus, and caudate nucleus (Cavada & Goldman-Rakic, 1989; Selemon & Goldman-Rakic,1988).

The basic sequence of events underlying the development of the primate cortex is extensively described in Chapter 1. This sequence includes a phase of neural induction, the proliferation of neurons and glia, cellular migration, differentiation, the formation of synapses, and synaptic pruning. These events have not been described thoroughly in the human foetus because of methodological limitations, but they are being increasingly examined in non-human primates. It is generally believed that a parallel sequence of events occurs in both species (Goldman-Rakic, Bourgeois, & Rakic, 1997). The first four phases (neural induction, proliferation of neurons, migration, and differentiation) occur during the prenatal period. Synaptogenesis begins prenatally but continues into infancy. Synaptic pruning begins during early adolescence and continues well into adulthood.

Neurons destined for both posterior and prefrontal association cortical regions develop in the proliferative zone of the neural tube between embryonic day 40 and embryonic day 100 in the rhesus macaque (Rakic, 1974, 1995). As this proliferative phase is being completed, migration begins, and an intermediate zone forms between the ventricular zone of the neural tube and the marginal zone that has been the target of developing cellular processes. By 8–10 weeks after conception, this intermediate zone forms the cortical plate (CP) and an underlying subplate zone. The subplate zone is a secondary and transiently present locus of continued cell proliferation as well as a holding area for incoming subcortical afferents (Kostovic & Rakic, 1990; Rakic, 1977, 1995). In the primate, the subplate zone in the frontal cortex is as much as four times wider than what has been observed in other cortical areas, such as the occipital cortex (Rakic, 1995). Rakic (1995) speculates that the wider subplate is necessary to accommodate the relatively greater number of afferent fibres that form between the developing frontal cortex and other cortical regions (Kostovic & Rakic, 1980). As neurons continue to migrate to their final destinations, the cortical plate will eventually develop into

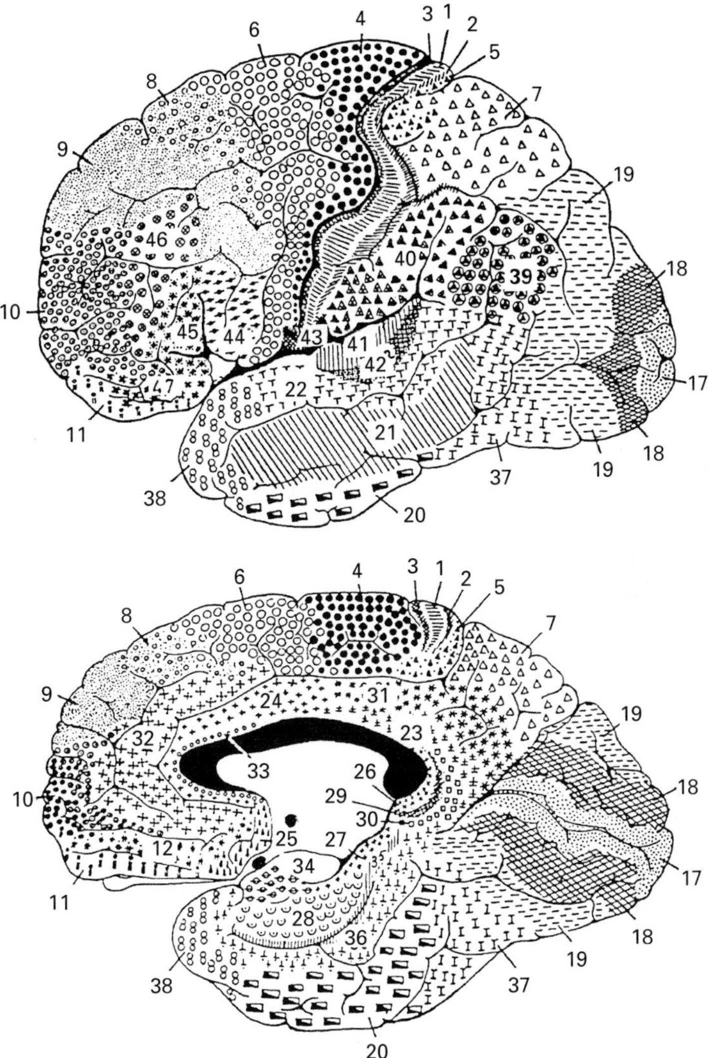

Figure 7.1. Brodmann's cytoarchitectural map of the human cortex. (Reprinted from *Progress in Brain Research, Volume 5: "The Prefrontal Cortex: Its Structure, Function and Pathology"*, Deepak N. Pandya and Edward H. Yeterian, Copyright 1990, p. 64, with permission from Elsevier Science.)

the brain's six-layered neocortex. To achieve this laminar pattern, migration progresses in an inside-out fashion and is completed by the eleventh to fifteenth weeks of human gestation in all regions of the developing cortex. However, Rakic (1995) indicates that the migratory pathway that must be traversed by developing neurons through the intermediate zone is particularly extensive in the primate's frontal lobe, spanning a length of 15mm or greater. The need for cells to negotiate such distances correctly might increase the likelihood of migratory errors. When cells root themselves in non-optimal locations, the pattern of synaptic connectivity that results is undoubtedly disruptive to information processing within cortical circuits, a process that has been theorized to underlie some of the deficits in schizophrenia (Akbarian et al., 1993). Thus, accurate migration is critical for the morphological formation of the cortex, and once it is accomplished, the aggregation of cells leads to further differentiation and areal specialization.

Differentiation involves several processes in addition to the formation of cell bodies, including selective cell death, the growth of axons and dendritic processes, and the formation of functional synaptic connections (Spreen, Risser, & Edgell, 1995). This latter process, the establishment of functional synaptic connections, implies that chemical neurotransmission is possible. Because chemical transmission indicates that information is being transferred between neurons and across neuronal networks, researchers have been intrigued by the idea that there could be a direct correspondence between synaptogenesis in the prefrontal region and the initiation of behaviours that are believed to be prefrontally guided.

In the rhesus macaque, examination of the dorsolateral PFC (specifically Brodmann's area 46) indicates that it does not reach its adult level of synaptic density until after 3 postnatal years, a time period that corresponds to young adulthood in the human (Goldman-Rakic et al., 1997). However, the presence of the first synapses is evident much earlier, at embryonic day 60 (E60), which is 3 months prior to birth after a 165-day gestation period (Bourgeois, Goldman-Rakic, & Rakic, 1994). At midgestation (from E90 to E100) corticocortical and thalamocortical afferents permeate the cortical plate and there is an overproduction of synaptic connections on the dendritic spines of pyramidal cells. This rapid and exponential increase in synaptic density continues until roughly 2 months after birth, which is the time point when the majority of corticocortical and thalamocortical afferents intersect the cortical plate (Bourgeois et al., 1994; Schwartz & Goldman-Rakic, 1991). At the time of birth, the adult pattern of sulci and gyri is generally present on the surfaces of the macaque (Goldman & Galkin, 1978) and human (Spreen et al., 1995) brains. During the perinatal period, spiny protuberances proliferate on the dendrites of pyramidal cells and are the contacts of rapidly forming synapses. Spine formation reaches a plateau approximately 2 months after birth. This plateau, representing synaptic density at higher-than-adult levels, is maintained throughout childhood until the onset of puberty (Bourgeois et al., 1994; Goldman-Rakic et al., 1997).

Intuitively, one might conjecture that, as synaptic density is increasing, behavioural development of the frontal lobe would also be increasing rapidly. One might also conjecture that when synaptic density plateaus, behavioural development would also plateau. However, what is particularly notable about this course of events is that a great deal of cognitive development occurs during this plateau period (a point that will be reconsidered in a later section), suggesting that synaptogenesis is not, in and of itself, the critical neural substrate for complete maturation of prefrontally mediated cognition. Indeed, during the transition from human childhood to adolescence, there are increases in white matter density that probably reflect age-related changes in myelination (Sowell, Thompson, Tessner, & Toga, 2001).

In the third year of monkey life, corresponding to young adulthood in the human, a slow and steady decline in the number of synapses occurs, a process that appears to have some specificity (Goldman-Rakic et al., 1997; Rakic, 1995). There are two types of synapses in the cortex, asymmetric and symmetric. The asymmetric synapses are those that regulate excitatory transmitters, such as glutamate. Symmetric synapses regulate GABA, the major monoamines, and neuropeptides, all of which have local inhibitory functions. Notably, symmetric synapses, once formed, do not appear to change over the course of neural development or the ensuing lifespan. Rather, synaptic attrition is apparently achieved through the selective elimination of asymmetric junctions on dendritic spines (Bourgeois et al., 1994), resulting in an alteration in the balance between excitatory and inhibitory neurotransmissions. This period of decline in synaptic density continues at a slight but measurable and steady rate for the remainder of the primate (macaque) lifespan. *In vivo* structural imaging studies of human brains have demonstrated reductions in cortical grey matter that likely correspond to this period of synaptic regression (Sowell et al., 2001).

Whether or not synaptogenesis and synaptic elimination are relatively prolonged processes in the frontal cortex versus other cortical regions has been a matter of some debate (Huttenlocher & Dabholkar, 1997; Rakic, 1995). It was traditionally thought that the brain developed according to a hierarchical temporal sequence with phylogenetically older regions maturing earlier than newer regions. If accurate, then brain development would proceed in a caudal-to-rostral sequence with sensory areas developing prior to motor regions, and motor regions developing prior to association regions, including the PFC. This maturational gradient would presumably be reflected in numerous aspects of neural development, including neurogenesis, synaptogenesis, and myelination. With respect to synaptogenesis, one historical expectation has been to observe concordance between a region's synaptic development and functional maturation of behaviours subserved by that region. For instance, in the primary visual cortex, synaptogenesis increases rapidly during the first 4 months of human life. Moreover, the time of maximum synaptic density is reached coincident with the development of stereoscopic vision (Huttenlocher & deCourten, 1987; Huttenlocher, deCourten, Garey, & Van Der Loos, 1982). To examine whether similar concordance between synaptic density and behavioural development holds within the frontal cortex, Huttenlocher (reviewed in Huttenlocher & Dabholkar, 1997) examined the brains of foetuses and young children who had died prematurely. He concluded that there was a protracted course of synaptic development in the frontal lobe versus posterior brain regions, notably the primary visual cortex. This finding appeared to make intuitive sense in light of the fact that behavioural development of functions attributed to the frontal lobe also appeared to be staggered, appearing late in the first year of human life and gradually maturing over the course of many years.

However, the more recent examination of non-human primate brains calls this conclusion into question. The concordant time course of neurogenesis in anterior and posterior brain regions has already been described. Additional data suggest concurrent production of synapses across multiple cortical regions (Rakic et al., 1986). Rakic and colleagues examined numerous areas of the neocortex within the brains of individual monkeys including the prefrontal, primary visual, cingulate, motor, and somatosensory cortices (see Goldman-Rakic et al., 1997, for a review). This analysis indicated that the production of synapses occurs at a similar rate in all regions examined. Similarly, the decline in synaptic density also appears to occur contemporaneously in these regions (Rakic et al., 1986). Rakic and colleagues have suggested that methodological confounds may account for the apparent discrepancy between the monkey and human data (Goldman-Rakic et al., 1997; Rakic, Bourgeois, & Goldman-Rakic, 1994). Specifically, when these authors reanalysed Huttenlocher's data, subjecting it to logarithmic transformations, plots of synaptic density in the striate and prefrontal cortices matched for both the human and monkey datasets (Rakic et al., 1994).

These neuroanatomical data have a parallel in studies of brain metabolism. Positron emission tomography (PET) was used to examine brain metabolism in human infants within the first 2 years of life (Chugani & Phelps, 1986). An adult pattern of glucose utilization in the frontal and association cortices appeared to be established in individual infants between 7.5 and 12.5 months of age. It is also evident from monkey studies that concentrations of the major monoamine neurotransmitters, including dopamine, noradrenaline (norepinephrine), and serotonin, increase rapidly from 2 to 5 months of postnatal life (Goldman-Rakic et al., 1997; Goldman-Rakic & Brown, 1982), as do corresponding transmitter receptor sites (Lidow & Rakic, 1992).

Because of these findings, Rakic's group (Goldman-Rakic et al., 1997) has rejected the notion that cortical development proceeds in a hierarchical fashion and instead adopted what they refer to as a "whole cloth" view of cortical development. They state that "The whole cloth view of the cortex as a woven tapestry in which the entire piece emerges by progressive addition of threads to all portions simultaneously derives from consideration of the comparative time course of synapse formation and synaptic density in diverse regions of the primate cortex." (Goldman-Rakic et al., 1997, pp. 33–34). Several corollaries of this theory are described, including the assumptions that the phases of cortical development occur in the same manner across all primate species, including humans, and that these phases are intrinsically programmed. Intrinsic guidance of cortical development implies that postnatal experiential differences between individuals act upon a neural architecture that is, in all likelihood, already formed or forming in a manner that is generally impervious to environmental influence. Thus, although changes in synaptic density have been observed throughout the lifespan in rodent species following environmental enrichment versus deprivation (Kolb et al., 1998), similar morphological changes are less likely to characterize the postnatal plasticity of the primate neocortex.

If we are to look for candidate processes that underlie experience-driven changes in brain and behavioural development, we need to look beyond the cyto-architectural (structural) features of the cortex and consider neural modifications that affect synaptic efficiency (Goldman-Rakic et al., 1997). Such modifications might include processes that improve synaptic conduction between networks of neurons, such as myelination, or biochemical refinements that underlie the balance of excitatory and inhibitory neurotransmission within cortical networks.

This viewpoint makes sense in light of our current understanding of the integrative nature of cortical networks that span multiple brain regions (Mesulam, 1998) as well as evidence stemming from behavioural studies indicating that prefrontally guided cognitive skills, such as successful delayed response performance, begin to emerge, but are not fully mature, at a relatively early age (Diamond, 1990a,b). Accordingly, if adult-like parameters of synaptic development are reached relatively early in life in the primate (including humans) and if these parameters are intrinsically guided and relatively impervious to environmental sources of influence as suggested by the animal data (Goldman-Rakic et al., 1997), then how are we to account for behavioural data that suggest a more protracted course of prefrontal (or prefrontal network) development? Huttenlocher (Huttenlocher & Dabholkar, 1997) favours the view that experience has the effect of incorporating existing synapses into functional circuits and that unused synapses disappear, a process referred to as functional stabilization (Changeaux & Danchin, 1976).

This concept implies that the time course of behavioural maturation should correlate more strongly with synaptic elimination versus generation, a suggestion that appears to have some merit based on existing behavioural data.

BEHAVIOURAL DEVELOPMENT OF FRONTAL LOBE FUNCTIONS

It is generally accepted that the prefrontal cortex underlies higher-order cognition, including planning and complex forms of goal-directed behaviour. Across human and animal studies, the most consistently employed measure of prefrontal function has been the spatial delayed response (DR) task. In traditional spatial DR paradigms, a research subject (animal or human) is presented with identical "wells", one of which is baited in full view of the subject with a desired object, and then occluded. Following a brief delay interval (e.g. in the range of seconds), the subject is permitted to retrieve the object without the benefit of recognition memory, using an internal representation of the object's location

(Goldman-Rakic, 1987a). Since Jacobsen (1935) demonstrated that delayed response performance was impaired in non-human primates following bilateral prefrontal excisions, DR tasks have become preferred means of examining the integrity of prefrontal function. In addition to recent memory deficits, Jacobsen's lesioned animals also demonstrated a loss of initiative, lethargy, and distractibility (see review by Jasper, 1995). Numerous studies have replicated this basic finding of recent memory deficits following dorsolateral prefrontal lesions (Fuster & Alexander, 1970; Goldman & Rosvold, 1970; Goldman-Rakic, 1987a), and numerous studies have demonstrated that cells in this region are active during the delay phase of task performance (Funahashi, Bruce, & Goldman-Rakic, 1989; Fuster & Alexander, 1971; Niki, 1974; Sawaguchi, Matsumura, & Kubota, 1988; 1990a,b).

In the monkey, lesions of the dorsolateral PFC in the region of the principal sulcus (Brodmann's area 46) impair performance, but only under delayed response conditions (Diamond & Goldman-Rakic, 1989; Goldman-Rakic, 1987a,b) That is, immediate responding to reward-salient objects is not obviously affected. There is an extensive literature replicating this basic finding that the dorsolateral prefrontal cortex is critical for spatial delayed response, a behavioural function that is currently more commonly referred to as spatial working memory.

Working memory or "working with memory" (Moscovitch, 1992) involves the use of internally represented information to guide behavioural responses toward future goals (Baddeley, 1992; Fuster, 1997; Goldman-Rakic, 1987). Given that the dorsolateral PFC appears critical for spatial working memory performance, it has often been assumed that all types of working memory are similarly dependent upon the prefrontal cortex. Indeed, one influential view is that there is regional specialization within the PFC for the processing of different stimulus attributes (Goldman-Rakic, 1988). For instance, the dorsolateral PFC in the region of the principal sulcus appears critical for the representation of spatial information, whereas the ventral region might be specialized for representing objective features of objects, such as their colours and shapes (Wilson, O'Scalaidhe, & Goldman-Rakic, 1993). The critical role of the PFC as a whole is presumably to facilitate the integration of whatever stimulus attributes are most salient to successful task performance with a soon-to-be-executed response. Hence, other empirical measures that have been used to assess the integrity of working memory functions in adult humans include temporal judgements (e.g. which item appeared more recently in a sequence; Milner, Corsi, & Leonard, 1991), self-ordered search tasks (Owen et al., 1990; Owen, Doyon, Petrides, & Evans, 1996; Petrides & Milner, 1982), look-ahead planning tasks (Shallice, 1982), and measures of set-shifting in which several different response attributes must be held simultaneously in mind and used to guide behaviour in the midst of external feedback (e.g. the Wisconsin Card Sort task; Milner, 1963). The critical importance of working memory for adult behaviour, despite the fact that it has been measured using relatively simplistic paradigms, cannot be overemphasized. It is crucial for all future-directed action, whether that action is something that is to be accomplished seconds, minutes, days, or years into the future.

Another major aspect of behaviour that has been associated with frontal lobe function is behavioural inhibition, the ability to forego immediate prepotent responding in favour of a more strategic evaluative choice. Ever since the case of Phineas Gage, it has been recognized that damage to the orbitofrontal cortex results in behavioural impulsivity and seeming imperviousness to socially appropriate behaviour (Fuster, 1997). Experimentally, one way in which the capacity for behavioural inhibition has been assessed is through variants of the go no-go task, in which the correct response to each trial is signalled by a warning stimulus that tells the subject to either "go" (make a particular response) or "not to go" (inhibit the typical response or execute an alternative response) (Diamond, 2001), with the "go" response being prominent. Other tasks that index similar functions include those that set up a competition between prepotent responses and more effortful, but not obviously correct, ones (e.g. the Stroop test; Perret, 1974). The ventromedial areas of the prefrontal cortex have also been associated with the capacity to exert emotional control in the context of socially relevant decision making (Bechara, Damasio, & Damasio, 2000).

Because the prefrontal cortex is currently viewed as a heterogeneous structure (Robbins, 1996), it is not surprising that the behaviours associated with its function are diverse. Indeed, it would be beyond the scope of this chapter to cover the developmental course of each behaviour that has been associated in adult studies with the functional integrity of the frontal lobe. However, regardless of the measures employed, studies of prefrontal function in infants, school-aged children, and adolescents converge to suggest that prefrontal development proceeds in a multi stage fashion.

EMERGENCE OF PREFRONTAL FUNCTION IN INFANCY

Because the traditional DR task is formally similar to Piaget's A-not-B task (Piaget, 1936/1954), it has been suggested that infants' development of object permanence is rooted in the maturation of prefrontal regions and associated networks (Diamond & Goldman-Rakic, 1989; Goldman-Rakic, 1987b). Piaget's A-not-B task involves hiding an object of interest, within full view of an infant, in one of two locations. After a brief delay, the infant is permitted to retrieve the object. Diamond (1990b) reported that 7- to 8-month-old infants are able to correctly retrieve objects from the first-baited location in spatial DR paradigms when delays are between 1 and 3 seconds in length. However, on some trials, they make the classic A-not-B error. This error occurs over the course of two successive trials. On the first trial, the object is hidden at location A and, typically, it is retrieved successfully by the infant. On the next trial, the object is hidden at location B, again in full view of the infant. The infant makes an error by searching at the previously rewarded location A, despite seeing that the object was hidden in a different location. This finding is quite robust. The precise reason for the infant's error is one of the most thoroughly researched phenomena in child development, and no agreement has been reached to account for the infant's performance. However, performance improves with age and, by 12–13 months, the infant can perform successfully at 10s delays before making the classic A-not-B error.

Successful spatial DR performance in human infants is dependent on the response mode employed (Diamond, 1990a,b, 2001). When accuracy of performance is measured by direction of gaze rather than by reaching behaviour, infants often appear to "know" the correct location of the hidden object. Correct performance can also be facilitated by shortening the delay interval, by allowing the infant to physically orient towards the correct location, by using landmarks to target the correct hiding location, or by using a minimal number of hiding locations. As infants are able to perform the task under simplified response demands, it has been suggested that the PFC is more functional in infancy than has been fully recognized.

A second task in which performance accelerates at the same rate as delayed response in human infants is the object retrieval task (Diamond, 1990a, 2001). In this task, a desired object is placed inside a clear-sided box that has an opening only on one side; the infant's task is simply to retrieve the object. When infants see the toy through the open side, they are able to reach correctly to retrieve it. However, if they view the toy through a clear, but occluded side, they exhibit a preferential tendency to try to reach through the occluded side to retrieve the toy. Hence, to perform the task correctly, infants must inhibit this prepotent response tendency, disengage their reaching behaviour from their looking behaviour, and reach through the open side of the box to retrieve the toy. This requires both inhibition of the prepotent response and some degree of strategic manipulation to integrate the conflicting demands of looking versus reaching behaviour (Diamond, 1990a, 2001).

Individual human infants and infant rhesus macaques develop the abilities to perform both A-not-B and the object retrieval task at the same rate over the same developmental period of time (between 6 and 12 months in the human infant and 2 and 4 months in macaques; Diamond, 1990a,b; Diamond & Goldman-Rakic, 1986). Moreover, improved performance on both tasks in human infants correlates with changes in frontal EEG activity (Bell & Fox, 1992, 1997). Diamond (1990a,b) suggested on the basis of these data that the dorsolateral PFC is engaged when both inhibitory control and delayed responding are simultaneously required and that maturation of these abilities begins during late infancy in both humans and monkeys.

To summarize, it appears that the PFC is behaviourally engaged in the monkey and human beginning in late infancy. However, it would seem erroneous to conclude that the 1-year-old human infant possesses adult-like levels of future-directed behaviour. We hardly need experimental data to recognize that this is not the case.

CONTINUITY OF DEVELOPMENT IN EARLY-TO-MIDDLE CHILDHOOD

Additional studies have employed more complex frontal lobe measures to study cognitive development in preschool and school-aged children. These measures have included set-shifting tasks, measures of behavioural conflict resolution, and attention tasks. When healthy adults perform set-shifting tasks such as the Wisconsin Card Sort, they are able to correctly sort cards that vary on at least three stimulus attributes (colour, number, and/or shape) in response to verbal feedback. On a less difficult measure of set-shifting that was analogous to the Wisconsin Card Sort, it was found that 3-year-old children could sort cards based on the first criterion that they were given (Kirkham & Diamond, 1999; Zelazo, Frye, & Rapus, 1996; Zelazo & Resnick, 1991). However, when they were required to shift set and sort the cards using a new stimulus attribute, they persisted in sorting according to the first criterion (Kirkham & Diamond, 1999; Zelazo et al., 1996). Between the ages of 3 and 6, children become progressively more adept at the task, first succeeding when they must switch between two sorting criteria (between ages of 4 and 5), and then becoming able to sort among three possible criteria by the age of 6.

Similarly, preschool-aged children have difficulties with behavioural inhibition, as exemplified by an analogue of the Stroop Colour–Word task. This task, called the Day–Night Stroop Task was first used by Levin (Levin et al., 1991) but then modified in Adele Diamond's laboratory (Gerstadt, Hong, & Diamond, 1994). In the conventional Stroop task, individuals must read words that consist of colour names (e.g. BLUE, RED, GREEN). Conflict is created by printing the words in coloured fonts that are different from the word meanings (e.g. the word "BLUE" printed in green ink). In the Day–Night Stroop task, children must respond to two cards, one of which illustrates a picture of the sun and the other that illustrates the moon. The conflict condition occurs when children are required to say "night" to a picture of the sun, and "day" when presented with a picture of the moon. This simplified task variant eliminates the reading ability that is necessary to complete the adult version. The Day–Night Stroop is difficult for 3–4-year-olds but relatively easy for 6–7-year-olds. Similarly, on measures of motor inhibition (e.g. Luria's tapping task; Luria, 1966), children perform at a similar rate as on the Day–Night Stroop, improving in their speed and accuracy between the ages of 3 and 7 years (Diamond, 2001; Diamond & Taylor, 1996; Passler, Isaac, & Hynd, 1985). Thus, through the preschool period, abilities dependent on the frontal lobe become increasingly well developed, although the task items that are used would be considered insultingly simple for a cognitively healthy adult. Those items and/or tasks that are successfully completed do not generally require a high level of multitasking ability.

MATURATION OF FRONTAL LOBE FUNCTION IN ADOLESCENCE

It is perhaps necessary at this point to interject a statement about how we might view studies in which simplified versions of traditional frontal lobe measures are utilized to study cognitive development. On the one hand, the argument could be made that we must use age-appropriate measures of frontal lobe function to study similar cognitive processes (e.g. inhibitory control) in children as well as adults. That is, a test such as the Day–Night Stroop could be viewed as functionally equivalent to the Stroop Colour–Word test, because both tests tap the capacity for behavioural inhibition. On the other hand, "similar" does not mean "identical" and, in many cases, simplified versus more difficult versions of the same test cannot be considered to be cognitively equivalent. The achievement of adult levels of performance on prefrontally mediated tasks requires mastery of a relatively high level of situational complexity through the simultaneous processing of multiple task demands. If one wishes to study when it is that the PFC is first engaged by a task, then simplified task demands can be employed. But if one wishes to determine when adult levels of proficiency are reached, then the same relatively challenging measures must be used to study behaviour in both children and adults, incorporating increasing levels of difficulty so that a dimensional assessment can be achieved.

Returning, then, to the notion of a "whole cloth view" of cortical development (Goldman-Rakic et al., 1997), whereas some measures (e.g. A-not-B at brief delays) might engage isolated threads of the overarching "cloth" or neural architecture, other tasks (Wisconsin Card Sort? Stroop Colour–Word test?) undoubtedly require that numerous components, patterns, or networks are engaged simultaneously. These are the tasks that will be most informative as to the capacity of the PFC to regulate complex behaviour. Thus, what is needed are behavioural studies of children as they progress from infancy through adolescence and into young adulthood, using tasks that incorporate ranges of difficulty and are well-validated measures of prefrontal function. Few such studies exist, and virtually none are longitudinal in nature. Most rely on cohorts of children that represent distinct age groups. These studies are consistent in suggesting that adult levels of performance on more challenging tests of frontal lobe function are not reached until adolescence or young adulthood (Levin et al., 1991; Luciana & Nelson, 1998; Passler et al., 1985; Welsh, Pennington, & Groisser, 1991).

The MacArthur Research Network on Psychopathology and Development supported a study of this type that was conducted at the University of Minnesota in which the performance of individuals between the ages of 3 and 25 years on a battery of tasks designed to reflect frontal- and temporal-lobe-mediated behavioural functions was examined (Luciana & Nelson, 1998, 2000). This battery of tests, the Cambridge Neuropsychological Testing Automated Battery (CANTAB) was developed at the University of Cambridge to examine the neural correlates of well-established neuropsychological tests that had been previously used in human and animal lesion populations (Fray, Robbins, & Sahakian, 1996). The CANTAB consists of subtasks that index three behavioural domains: working memory/planning, visual memory, and visual attention. The battery is administered through the use of a touch-screen computer but in the presence of a clinician trained in neuropsychological assessment. Subtasks measure simple reaction time, discrimination learning, recognition memory for patterns and objects, and working memory skills involving self-guided visual search and planning. As suggested by these descriptors, all CANTAB subtasks are visually guided and require no verbal responses.

Where CANTAB is unique among experimental test batteries is that in addition to a rigorous theoretical framework that was used to guide subtest selection, its developers have undertaken a comprehensive effort to validate its neural correlates in adults. This validation process has centred around several lines of inquiry, including normative studies of behavioural performance in elderly adults, studies of adults with specific brain lesions, studies of adults with specific neuropathologies, the effects of pharmacological manipulations on task performance, and assessment of brain–behaviour task correlates using both functional magnetic resonance imaging (fMRI) and PET neuroimaging techniques. These efforts strongly support the CANTAB as a valid measure for the assessment of frontal, temporal, and/or subcortical/striatal functions in adults (Downes et al., 1989; Fray et al., 1996; Lee et al., 2000; Owen, Evans, & Petrides, 1996; Robbins, 1996).

The CANTAB is particularly amenable to the study of children. The computerized format easily lends itself to rapport-building, even among atypically developing children (Hughes, Russell, & Robbins, 1994; Luciana et al., 1999). Because the method of test administration is highly standardized, performance variations due to experimenter error are negligible. The three primary measures of frontal lobe function within the CANTAB battery are: (1) a self-guided search task; (2) the Tower of London test of planning and behavioural inhibition; and (3) a set-shifting task, which measures the ability to shift cognitive response sets both within and across categories. Brain activity studies using PET and fMRI in adults have verified that the neural activity underlying performance on variations of these tasks involves frontostriatal circuits (see Lee et al., 2000, for a review). The CANTAB measures temporal lobe recognition memory functions through delayed-match-to-sample recognition memory tasks. The procedural details of each task will not be described here because of space limitations, but can be found elsewhere (Luciana & Nelson, 1998, 2000).

Our data consistently indicate that planning and working memory skills have not reached adult levels by the age of 12 years based on analyses of the self-ordered search and Tower of London tasks. Both of these tasks are relatively complex in their task demands. The self-ordered search task yields two variables of interest: one consists of "forgetting errors" and is a sum of the number of times that a subject searches a previously targeted location within a given search. The other is a strategy score that reflects the efficiency of the search process. Studies of adults with brain lesions suggest that individuals with both temporal and frontal lobe damage are likely to make forgetting errors on the task, but that deficient use of strategy is exclusively a frontal-lobe deficit (Owen et al., 1996). That is, when an efficient strategy is utilized, the mnemonic demands of the task are minimized. Accordingly, individuals with less-than-optimal functioning of the frontal lobe might be more dependent on their memory skills in organizing searches that involve a large number of items. Even in healthy adults, memory span is inversely correlated with number of errors on the task.

The Tower of London yields, as its primary variable of interest, the number of problems that can be solved in the minimum possible number of moves (Shallice, 1982). The two tasks are similar in that they both require behavioural organization or self-monitoring to complete the most difficult items with maximal efficiency.

As can be seen in Fig. 7.2, we observed that the number of total forgetting errors on the self-ordered search task is consistently high from ages 5 to 12 years. After

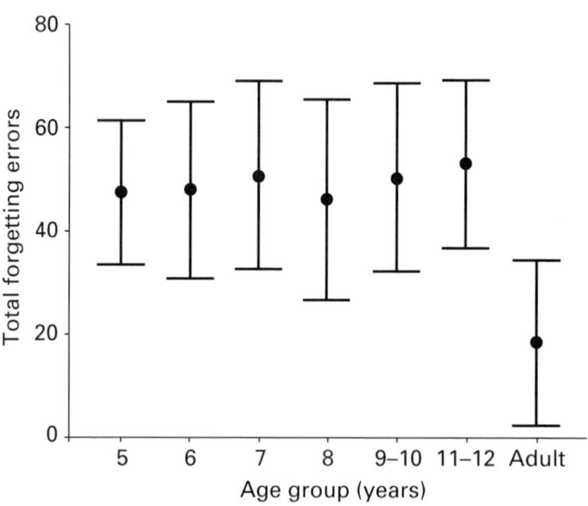

Figure 7.2. Number of total forgetting errors on CANTAB's self-ordered search task. Bars represent means and standard deviations for individuals between the ages of 5 and 25; 4-year-olds are not included here because only a very small number ($n = 8$) were able to stay on-task throughout the assessment. After the age of 12 years, the number of forgetting errors declines: main effect of age: $F(5, 300) = 3.04, p = .01$.

the age of 12 years, the number of forgetting errors declines. Moreover, a high number of forgetting errors is significantly associated with poor use of strategy within the developmental period (Pearson r ranges from .55 to .63; $p < .001$) such that individuals who utilize a search strategy that will minimize the mnemonic demands of the task make fewer errors. A similar profile characterizes efficiency of performance on the Tower of London, as indicated in Fig. 7.3. As compared with young adults, even 11–12-year-olds, as well as younger children, require a number of excess moves to solve Tower of London problems, suggesting that their ability to look ahead and plan their behavioural actions in a maximally efficient manner is not yet fully developed.

By contrast, as reported elsewhere (Luciana & Nelson, 1998, 2000), abilities that rely on posterior brain regions, such as recognition memory for patterned stimuli, appear to be stable by the age of 8. Although CANTAB's pattern recognition memory test requires a forced response to one of two choices, leading to ceiling effects in older children and adults, our findings parallel neurophysiological studies indicating early maturity of the temporal lobe hippocampally based system that supports visual recognition memory (see Nelson, 1995, for a review). Conversely, abilities that involve interactions between posterior brain regions and the frontal lobe, such as spatial memory span, show an intermediate developmental pattern, whereby there are linear increments in memory span from ages 4 to adulthood (Fig. 7.4). Improvements in memory capacity are potentially critical

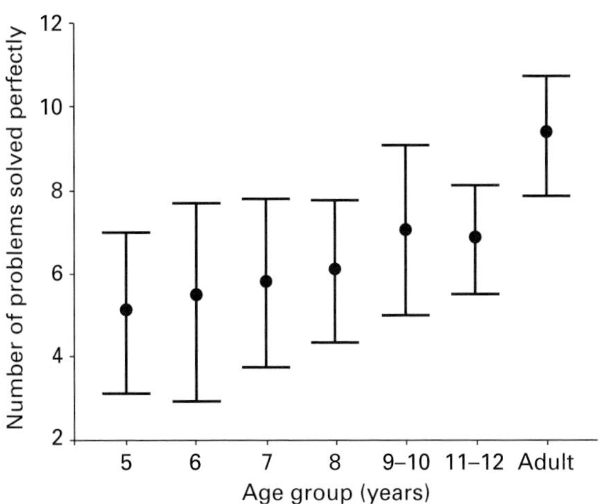

Figure 7.3. Number of perfect Tower of London solutions for individuals between the ages of 5 and 25 years. Bars represent means plus and minus one standard deviation. As with the self-ordered search task, performance levels are relatively constant throughout childhood with improvement seen after the age of 12 years. As compared to young adults, even 11–12-year-olds, as well as younger children, perform less effectively—main effect of age: $F(5, 279) = 6.78$, $p < .001$—suggesting that the ability to look ahead and plan behavioural actions is not yet fully developed.

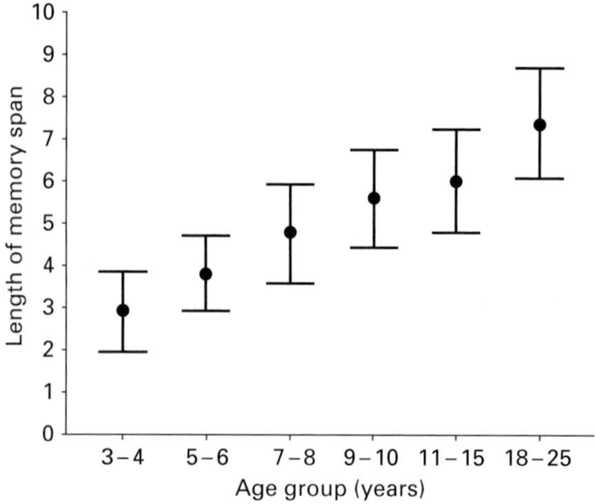

Figure 7.4. Length of spatial memory span (the number of items that could be correctly recalled in a sequence) for individuals between the ages of 4 and 25 years. Bars represent means plus or minus one standard deviation within each age group. A pronounced linear trend characterizes improvements in memory capacity throughout childhood and into young adulthood: main effect of age, $F(5, 367) = 78.22, p < .000$.

for the ability to hold multiple aspects of a situation or stimulus context simultaneously in mind.

The CANTAB is gaining in popularity as an assessment tool because of the increasing number of studies that support its utility as a measure of frontal lobe function. However, other researchers have reported a similar developmental trajectory using other "adult-level" tasks that have been applied to the study of children. For instance, Welsh et al. (1991) studied 110 children between the ages of 3 and 12 years of age using a battery of executive function measures, including visual search, verbal fluency, motor planning, the Tower of Hanoi, the Wisconsin Card Sort, and the Matching Familiar Figures test. On the more difficult tasks including the Wisconsin Card Sort and 4-disk Tower of Hanoi tasks, an adult level of performance was reached between 10 years (Wisconsin Card Sort) and adolescence (Tower of Hanoi, verbal fluency, and motor sequencing). Similarly, Levin and colleagues (1991) found that children's performance continued to improve between the ages of 13 and 15 years on measures of planning and deductive reasoning.

On the basis of these studies, it is suggested that the functional maturity of prefrontal circuitry, at a level that would permit the simultaneous processing of multiple levels of information, is not reached until postpuberty, coincident with the elimination or pruning back of synapses in the developing neocortex.

CONCLUSIONS

Several summary points are suggested based on the data reviewed here.

1. The cytoarchitectural development of the prefrontal cortex appears to be completed by the early postnatal period in both monkeys and humans. Neurogenesis and migration are largely achieved during midgestation. The formation of synapses begins during pregnancy and continues into infancy.
2. Synaptogenesis reaches a plateau during childhood that extends until post-puberty. After puberty, a gradual process of synaptic elimination ensues, largely involving asymmetric (or excitatory) synapses that might serve to functionally stabilize neural circuits that have been activated by behavioural experiences.
3. Behaviourally, the first emergence of prefrontally guided cognition, as evidenced by studies of delayed response (or A-not-B) performance in infant monkeys and human infants occurs during late infancy, around the time that independent locomotor ability is achieved. There is a gradual performance improvement throughout childhood on tasks that require the simultaneous processing of information, but adult levels of performance on complex working memory tasks are not reached until after puberty.
4. If we attempt to integrate findings from the behavioural and neurophysiological literatures, then it appears that functional maturation of the PFC occurs only when synaptic efficiency is enhanced through the elimination of extraneous connections or through chemical modifications that have yet to be fully described in development. These changes presumably bring about an optimal balance between excitatory and inhibitory neurotransmitters that modulate cellular activity within cortical networks. Myelination, not extensively discussed here, is another candidate process that could serve to enhance synaptic efficiency.

Future research that examines the nature of these synaptic processes *in vivo* through the pubertal period would seem to be crucial to refining our understanding of when maturation of the PFC is achieved. For example, Paus et al. (1999) measured the structural maturation of white matter density in fibre tracts that constitute corticocortical and frontostriatal pathways in a large sample of children and adolescents. Several age-related changes were found. In particular, the pathways subserving speech and motor functions on the left side (the side that was presumably dominant for language ability in the majority of individuals tested) were not mature until late adolescence. Similar work, using diffusion tensor magnetic resonance (MR) imaging, suggests that myelination in the frontal lobe is less well-established in prepubescent children than in adults (Klinberg et al., 1999). More recently, a correspondence between cortical grey matter density reductions and increased density of white matter tracts has been reported (Sowell et al., 2001).

Neuroimaging techniques have also been employed to examine functional activity in children as they perform working memory and behavioural inhibition tasks (Casey et al., 1995; see also Chapter 2). For example, in the context of go no-go task performance, both typically developing children and adults recruit activity in prefrontal regions. Moreover, activation of the anterior cingulate and orbitofrontal cortices is correlated with distinct aspects of task performance. However, in children with perinatal damage to the caudate nucleus, behavioural performance is disrupted and does not similarly relate to indices of anterior cingulate and orbitofrontal activity (Chapter 2).

Although structural and functional neuroimaging technologies hold a great deal of promise in delineating the nature of cortical networks that underlie executive functioning in children, we are still left with the task of describing how patterns of synaptic efficiency can be altered through experiential means. One promising area of work that addresses this issue concerns the behavioural pharmacology of working memory and other complex cognitive functions. For example, it has been recognized for decades that spatial working memory functions subserved by the dorsolateral PFC are modulated by alterations in ascending dopamine pathways (Goldman-Rakic, 1987a). When dopamine activity is manipulated in healthy adults, working memory functions are impacted (Luciana & Collins, 1997). Recently, there have been attempts to associate individual differences in dopamine receptor activity with variations in behaviour. For instance, a variant of the dopamine D4 receptor gene (DRD4) has been associated with attention deficit hyperactivity disorder (ADHD) in several studies (McCracken et al., 2000; Swanson et al., 2000). This literature is complicated, and findings have not always been replicated across studies (Faraone, Doyle, Mick, & Biederman, 2001). ADHD has been conceptualized as a disorder of executive function (Barkley, 1997). It might be that vulnerability to it and other clinical disorders could be measurable at some point in the future through the analysis of individual genotypes.

To conclude, research strategies that apply structural and functional neuroimaging, molecular genetics, and behavioural pharmacology to the study of frontal lobe maturation hold a great deal of promise in describing both typical and atypical aspects of development. To the extent that these approaches can be further refined, perhaps to the point of indexing patterns of activity within specific neurotransmitter systems as they develop, we can further our understanding of when the developing brain becomes capable of engaging multiple distributed prefrontally guided networks in the service of complex behavioural functions.

REFERENCES

Akbarian, S., Bunney, W.E., Potkin, S.G., Wigal, S.B., Hagman, J.O., Sandman, C.A. et al. (1993). Altered distribution of nicotinamide-adenine dinucleotide phosphate-diaphorase cells in frontal lobe of schizophrenics implies disturbances of cortical development. *Archives of General Psychiatry, 50*, 227–230.

Baddeley, A. (1992). Working memory. *Science, 255*, 556–559.

Barkley, R.A. (1997). Behavioral inhibition, sustained attention, and executive functions: Constructing a unifying theory of ADHD. *Psychological Bulletin, 121*, 65–94.

Bechara, A., Damasio, H., & Damasio, A.R. (2000). Emotion, decision-making, and the orbitofrontal cortex. *Cerebral Cortex, 10*, 295–307.

Bell, M.A., & Fox, N.A. (1992). The relations between frontal brain electrical activity and cognitive development during infancy. *Child Development, 63*, 1142–1163.

Bell, M.A., & Fox, N.A. (1997). Individual differences in object permanence performance at 8 months: Locomotor experience and brain electrical activity. *Developmental Psychobiology, 31*, 287–297.

Bourgeois, J.P., Goldman-Rakic, P.S., & Rakic, P. (1994). Synaptogenesis in the prefrontal cortex of rhesus monkeys. *Cerebral Cortex, 4*, 78–96.

Casey, B.J., Cohen, J.D., Jezzard, P., Turner, R., Noll, D.C. et al. (1995). Activation of prefrontal cortex in children using a nonspatial working memory task with functional MRI. *Neuroimage, 2*(3), 221–229.

Cavada, C., & Goldman-Rakic, P.S. (1989). Posterior parietal cortex in rhesus monkey: II: Evidence for segregated corticocortical networks linking sensory and limbic areas with the frontal lobe. *Journal of Comparative Neurology, 287*, 422–445.

Changeaux, J-P., & Danchin, A. (1976). Selective stabilization of developing synapses as a mechanism for the specification of neural networks. *Nature, 264*, 705–712.

Chugani, H.T., & Phelps, M.E. (1986). Maturational changes in cerebral function in infants determined by FDG positron emission tomography. *Science, 231*, 840–843.

Diamond, A. (1990a). Developmental time course in human infants and infant monkeys and the neural basis of inhibitory control in reaching. In A. Diamond (Ed.), *The development and neural basis of higher cognitive functions* (pp. 637–676). New York: New York Academy of Science Press.

Diamond, A. (1990b). The development and neural bases of memory functions as indexed by the AB and delayed response tasks in human infants and infant monkeys. *Annals of the New York Academy of Sciences, 608*, 267–317.

Diamond, A. (2001). A model system for studying the role of dopamine in prefrontal cortex during early development in humans: early and continuously treated phenylketonuria (PKU). In C.A. Nelson & M. Luciana (Eds.), *Handbook of developmental cognitive neuroscience*, Cambridge, MA: MIT Press.

Diamond, A., & Goldman-Rakic, P.S. (1986). Comparative development in human infants and infant rhesus monkeys of cognitive functions that depend on prefrontal cortex. *Society for Neuroscience Abstracts, 12*, 742.

Diamond, A., & Goldman-Rakic, P.S. (1989). Comparison of human infants and rhesus monkeys on Piaget's AB task: Evidence for dependence on dorsolateral prefrontal cortex. *Experimental Brain Research, 74*, 24–40.

Diamond, A., & Taylor, C. (1996). Development of an aspect of executive control: Development of the abilities to remember what I said and to "do as I say, not as I do". *Developmental Psychobiology, 29*, 315–334.

Downes, J.J., Roberts, A.C., Sahakian, B.J., Evenden, J.L., Morris, R.G., & Robbins, T.W. (1989). Impaired extra-dimensional shift performance in medicated and unmedicated Parkinson's disease: Evidence for a specific attentional dysfunction. *Neuropsychologia, 27*, 1329–1343.

Faraone, S.V., Doyle, A.E., Mick, E., & Biederman, J. (2001). Meta-analysis of the association between the 7-repeat allele of the dopamine D(4) receptor gene and attention deficit hyperactivity disorder. *American Journal of Psychiatry, 158*(7), 1052–1057.

Fray, P.J., Robbins, T.W., & Sahakian, B.J. (1996). Neuropsychiatric applications of CANTAB. *International Journal of Geriatric Psychiatry, 11*, 329–336.

Funahashi, S., Bruce, C.J., & Goldman-Rakic, P.S. (1989). Mnemonic coding of visual space in the monkey's dorsolateral prefrontal cortex. *Journal of Neurophysiology, 61*, 1–19.

Fuster, J.M. (1997). *The prefrontal cortex: Anatomy, physiology, and neuropsychology of the frontal lobe* (3rd ed.) Philadelphia: Lippincott-Raven Press.

Fuster, J.M., & Alexander, G.E. (1970). Delayed response deficit by cryogenic depression of frontal cortex. *Brain Research, 61*, 79–91.

Fuster, J.M., & Alexander, G.E. (1971). Neuronal activity related to short-term memory. *Science, 173*, 652–654.

Gerstadt, C., Hong, Y., & Diamond, A. (1994). The relationship between cognition and action: Performance of 3.5–7-year-old children on a Stroop-like day-night test. *Cognition, 53*, 129–153.

Goldman, P.S., & Galkin, T.W. (1978). Prenatal removal of frontal association cortex in the fetal rhesus monkey: Anatomical and functional consequences in postnatal life. *Brain Research, 152*(3), 451–485.

Goldman, P.S., & Rosvold, H.E. (1970). Localization of function within the dorsolateral prefrontal cortex of the rhesus monkey. *Experimental Neurology, 29*, 291–304.

Goldman-Rakic, P.S. (1987a). Circuitry of primate prefrontal cortex and regulation of behavior by representational memory. In F. Plum (Ed.), *Handbook of physiology, the nervous system, higher functions of the brain* (Vol. V, pp. 373–417). Bethesda, MD: American Physiological Society.

Goldman-Rakic, P.S. (1987b). Development of cortical circuitry and cognitive function. *Child Development, 58*, 601–22.

Goldman-Rakic, P.S. (1988). Topography of cognition: Parallel distributed networks in primate association cortex. *Annual Review of Neuroscience, 11*, 137–156.

Goldman-Rakic, P.S., Bourgeois, J.P., & Rakic, P. (1997). Synaptic substrate of cognitive development: Lifespan analysis of synaptogenesis in the prefrontal cortex of the nonhuman primate. In N.A. Krasnegor, G.R. Lyon, & P.S. Goldman-Rakic (Eds.), *Development of the prefrontal cortex: Evolution, neurobiology, and behavior* (pp. 27–48). Baltimore, MD: Paul H. Brooks.

Goldman-Rakic, P.S., & Brown, R.M. (1982). Postnatal development of monoamine content and synthesis in the cerebral cortex of rhesus monkeys. *Brain Research, 256*(3), 339–349.

Goldman-Rakic, P.S., & Porrino, L.J. (1985). The primate mediodorsal (MD) nucleus and its projection to the frontal lobe. *Journal of Comparative Neurology, 242*, 535–560.

Harlow, J.M. (1868). Recovery from the passage of an iron bar through the head. *Proceeding of the Massachusetts Medical Society, 2*, 327–346. (Original report published in 1848 in a letter to the *Boston Medical and Surgical Journal*, later to become the *New England Journal of Medicine 39*, 389–392.)

Hughes, C., Russell, J., & Robbins, T.W. (1994). Evidence for executive dysfunction in autism. *Neuropsychologia, 32*, 477–492.

Huttenlocher, P.R., & de Courten, C. (1987). The development of synapses in striate cortex of man. *Human Neurobiology, 6*(1), 1–9.

Huttenlocher, P.R., deCourten, C., Garey, L.J., & Van Der Loos, H. (1982). Synaptic development in human cerebral cortex. *International Journal of Neurology, 16–17*, 144–154.

Huttenlocher, P.R., & Dabholkar, A.S. (1997). Development and anatomy of prefrontal cortex. In N.A. Krasnegor, G.R. Lyon, & P.S. Goldman-Rakic (Eds.), *Development of the prefrontal cortex: Evolution, neurobiology, and behavior* (pp. 69–84). Baltimore, MD: Paul H. Brooks.

Jacobsen, C.F. (1935). Functions of the frontal association areas in primates. *Archives of Neurology & Psychiatry, 33*, 558–560.

Jasper, H.H. (1995). A historical perspective: The rise and fall of prefrontal lobotomy. In H.H. Jasper, S. Riggio, & P.S. Goldman-Rakic (Eds.), *Advances in neurology, volume 66: Epilepsy and the functional anatomy of the frontal lobe*. (pp. 97–114). New York: Raven Press.

Kirkham, N.Z., & Diamond, A. (1999). *Integrating competing ideas in word and action*. Paper presented at the Biennial Meeting of the Society for Research in Child Development, Albuquerque, NM, April 1999.

Klinberg, T., Vaidya, C.J., Gabrieli, J.D., Moseley, M.E., & Hedehus, M. (1999). Myelination and organization of the frontal white matter in children: A diffusion tensor MRI study. *Neuroreport, 10*(13), 2817–2821.

Kolb, B., Forgie, M., Gibb, R., Gorny, G., & Rowntree, S. (1998). Age, experience and the changing brain. *Neuroscience and Biobehavioral Reviews, 22*(2), 143–459.

Kostovic, I., & Rakic, P. (1980). Cytology and time of origin of interstitial neurons in the white matter in infant and adult human and monkey telencephalon. *Journal of Neurocytology, 9*, 219–242.

Kostovic, I., & Rakic, P. (1990). Developmental history of transient subplate zone in the visual and somatosensory cortex of the macaque monkey and human brain. *Journal of Comparative Neurology, 297*, 441–470.

Lee, A.C., Owen, A.M., Rogers, R.D., Sahakian, B.J., & Robbins, T.W. (2000). Utility of CANTAB in functional neuroimaging. In M. Ernst & J.M. Rumsey (Eds.), *Functional neuroimaging in child psychiatry*. Cambridge: Cambridge University Press.

Levin, H.S., Culhane, K.A., Hartman, J., Evankovich, K., Mattson, A.J., Harward, H. et al. (1991). Developmental changes in performance on tests of purported frontal lobe functioning. *Developmental Neuropsychology, 7*(3), 377–395.

Lidow, M.S., & Rakic, P. (1992). Scheduling of monoaminergic neurotransmitter receptor expression in the primate neocortex during postnatal development. *Cerebral Cortex, 2*, 401–416.

Luciana, M., & Collins, P.F. (1997). Dopaminergic modulation of working memory for spatial but not object cues in normal humans. *Journal of Cognitive Neuroscience, 9*(3), 330–347.

Luciana, M., Lindeke, L., Georgieff, M., Mills, M., & Nelson, C.A. (1999). Neurobehavioral evidence for working-memory deficits in school-aged children with histories of prematurity. *Developmental Medicine & Child Neurology, 41*(8), 521–533.

Luciana, M., & Nelson, C.A. (1998). The functional emergence of prefrontally-guided working memory systems in four-to-eight year-old children. *Neuropsychologia, 36*(3), 273–293.

Luciana, M., & Nelson, C.A. (2000). Neurodevelopmental assessment of cognitive function using the Cambridge Neuropsychological Testing Automated Battery (CANTAB): Validation and future goals. In M. Ernst & J.M. Rumsey (Eds.), *Functional neuroimaging in child psychiatry*. Cambridge: Cambridge University Press.

Luria, A.R. (1966). *The higher cortical functions in man*. New York: Basic Books.

McCracken, J.T., Smalley, S.L., McGough, J.J., Crawford, L., Del'Homme, M., Cantor, R.M. et al. (2000). Evidence for linkage of a tandem duplication polymorphism upstream of the dopamine D4 receptor gene (DRD4) with attention deficit hyperactivity disorder (ADHD). *Molecular Psychiatry, 5*(5), 531–536.

Mesulam, M.M. (1998). From sensation to cognition. *Brain, 121*, 1013–1052.

Milner, B. (1963). Effects of different brain lesions on card sorting: The role of the frontal lobe. *Archives of Neurology, 9*, 90–100.

Milner, B., Corsi, P., & Leonard, G. (1991). Frontal lobe contribution to recency judgements. *Neuropsychologia, 29*, 601–618.

Moscovitch, M. (1992). Memory and working-with-memory: A component process model based on modules and central systems. *Journal of Cognitive Neuroscience, 4*(3), 257–267.

Nelson, C.A. (1995). The ontogeny of human memory: A cognitive neuroscience perspective. *Developmental Psychology, 31*, 723–738.

Niki, H. (1974). Differential activity of prefrontal units during right and left delayed response trials. *Brain Research, 70*(2), 346–349.

Owen, A.M., Evans, A.C., & Petrides, M. (1996). Evidence for a two-stage model of spatial working memory processing within the lateral frontal cortex: A positron emission tomography study. *Cerebral Cortex, 6*, 31–38.

Owen, A.M., Morris, R.G., Sahakian, B.J., Polkey, C.E., & Robbins, T.W. (1996). Double dissociations of memory and executive functions in a self-ordered working memory task following frontal lobe excision, temporal lobe excision, or amygdalahippocampectomy in man. *Brain, 119*, 1597–1615.

Owen, A.M., Downes, J.J., Sahakian, B.J., Polkey, C.E., & Robbins, T.W. (1990). Planning and spatial working memory deficits following frontal lobe lesions in man. *Neuropsychologia, 28*, 1021–1034.

Owen, A.M., Doyon, J., Petrides, M., & Evans, A.C. (1996). Planning and spatial working memory: a positron emission tomography study in humans. *European Journal of Neuroscience, 8*, 353–364.

Pandya, D.N., & Yeterian, E.H. (1990). Prefrontal cortex in relation to other cortical areas in rhesus monkey: Architecture and connections. In H.H.M. Uylings, C.G. van Eden, J.P.C. de Bruin, M.A. Corner, & M.G.P. Feenstra (Eds.), *The prefrontal cortex: Its structure, function, and pathology. Progress in brain research* (Vol. 85, pp. 63–94). Amsterdam: Elsevier Science.

Passler, P.A., Isaac, W., & Hynd, G.W. (1985). Neuropsychological development of behavior attributed to frontal lobe functioning in children. *Developmental Neuropsychology, 4*, 349–370.

Paus, T., Azjdenbos, A., Worsley, K., Collins, D.L., Blumenthal, J., Giedd, J.H. et al. (1999). Structural maturation of neural pathways in children and adolescents: An *in vivo* study. *Science, 283*(5409), 1908–1911.

Perret, E. (1974). The left frontal lobe of man and the suppression of habitual responses in verbal categorical behaviour. *Neuropsychologia, 12*, 527–537.

Petrides, M., & Milner, B. (1982). Deficits in subject-ordered tasks after frontal and temporal-lobe lesions in man. *Neuropsychologia, 20*, 249–262.

Piaget, J. (1936/1954). *The construction of reality in the child.* (M. Cook, Trans.). New York: Basic Books. (Original work published, 1936.)

Rakic, P. (1974). Neurons in the monkey visual cortex: Systematic relation between time of origin and eventual disposition. *Science, 183*, 425–7.

Rakic, P. (1977). Prenatal development of the visual system in the rhesus monkey. *Philosophical Transactions of the Royal Society of London B, 278*, 245–60.

Rakic, P. (1995). The development of the frontal lobe: A view from the rear of the brain. In H.H. Jasper, S. Riggio, & P.S. Goldman-Rakic (Eds.), *Advances in neurology, volume 66: Epilepsy and the functional anatomy of the frontal lobe* (pp. 1–8), New York: Raven Press.

Rakic, P., Bourgeois, J.P., Eckenhoff, M.F., Zecevic, N., & Goldman-Rakic, P.S. (1986). Concurrent overproduction of synapses in diverse regions of the primate cerebral cortex. *Science, 232*(4747), 232–235.

Rakic, P., Bourgeois, J.P., & Goldman-Rakic, P.S. (1994) Synaptic development of the cerebral cortex: Implications for learning, memory, and mental illness. *Progress in Brain Research, 102*, 227–243.

Robbins, T.W. (1996). Dissociating executive functions of the prefrontal cortex. *Philosophical Transactions of the Royal Society of London, B: Biological Sciences, 351*(1346), 1463–1470.

Rose, J.E., & Woolsey, C.N. (1948). The orbitofrontal cortex and its connections with the mediodorsal thalamus in rabbit, sheep, and cat. *Research Publications of the Association for Research on Nervous and Mental Disorders, 27*, 210–232.

Sawaguchi, T., Matsumura, M., & Kubota, K. (1988). Dopamine enhances the neuronal activity of spatial short-term memory task in the primate prefrontal cortex. *Neuroscience Research, 5*, 465–473.

Sawaguchi, T., Matsumura, M., & Kubota, K. (1990a). Catecholamine effects on neuronal activity related to a delayed response task in monkey prefrontal cortex. *Journal of Neurophysiology, 63*(6), 1385–1400.

Sawaguchi, T., Matsumura, M., & Kubota, K. (1990b). Effects of dopamine antagonists on neuronal activity related to a delayed response task in monkey prefrontal cortex. *Journal of Neurophysiology, 63*(6), 1401–1412.

Schwartz, M.L., & Goldman-Rakic, P.S. (1991). Callosal and intrahemispheric connectivity of the prefrontal association cortex in rhesus monkey: Relation between intraparietal and principal sulcal cortex. *Journal of Comparative Neurology, 226*, 403–420.

Selemon, L.D., & Goldman-Rakic, P.S. (1988). Common cortical and subcortical targets of the dorsolateral prefrontal and posterior parietal cortices in the rhesus monkey: Evidence for a distributed neural network subserving spatially-guided behavior. *Journal of Neuroscience, 8*, 4049–4068.

Shallice, T. (1982). Specific impairments in planning. *Philosophical Transactions of the Royal Society of London, B, 298*, 199–209.

Sowell, E.R., Thompson, P.M., Tessner, K.D., & Toga, A.W. (2001). Mapping continued brain growth and gray matter density reduction in dorsal frontal cortex: Inverse relationships during postadolescent brain maturation. *Journal of Neuroscience, 21*(22), 8819–8829.

Spreen, O., Risser, A.T., & Edgell, D. (1995). *Developmental neuropsychology*. New York: Oxford University Press.

Swanson, J.M., Flodman, P., Kennedy, J., Spence, M.A., Moyzis, R., Schuck, S. et al. (2000). Dopamine genes and ADHD. *Neuroscience & Biobehavioral Reviews, 24*(1) 21–25.

Walker, A.E. (1940). A cytoarchitectural study of the prefrontal area of the macaque monkey. *Journal of Comparative Neurology, 73*, 59–86.

Welsh, M.C., Pennington, B.F., & Groisser, D.B. (1991). A normative-developmental study of executive function: A window on prefrontal function in children. *Developmental Neuropsychology, 7*(2), 131–149.

Wilson, F.A., O'Scalaidhe, S.P., & Goldman-Rakic, P.S. (1993). Dissociation of object and spatial processing in primate prefrontal cortex. *Science, 260*, 1955–1958.

Zelazo, P.D., Frye, D., & Rapus, T. (1996). An age-related dissociation between knowing rules and using them. *Cognitive Development, 11*, 37–63.

Zelazo, P.D., & Reznick, J.S. (1991). Age-related asynchrony of knowledge and action. *Child Development, 62*, 719–735.

CHAPTER EIGHT

Emotion, cognition, and the hypothalamic–pituitary–adrenocortical axis: a developmental perspective

Elysia Poggi Davis*, Susan Whitmore Parker*, Nim Tottenham* and Megan R. Gunnar
Institute of Child Development, University of Minnesota, USA

INTRODUCTION

Living organisms must both adapt to change and maintain their integrity in order to survive. Young organisms must do this while engaging in ontological change and development. Changing to maintain integrity in the face of stressors, or threats to homeostasis, involves systems capable of orchestrating whole-body reactions to events, shifting energy and resources in ways that promote immediate survival, often at the expense of growth and repair. Thus, the systems that support adaptation to stressors are intertwined with those that support growth and development. Understanding these systems and their functioning is crucial to our understanding of developmental processes.

The hypothalamic–pituitary–adrenocortical (HPA) system has often been conceptualized as a stress system (Sapolsky, 1996). Although the HPA system is typically involved in the stress response, its effects are much broader. Under non-stress conditions, when the system is functioning in its basal state, its pro-active functions support growth and development (de Kloet, Vreugdenhil, Oitzl, & Joels, 1998). Under conditions of challenge, the activity of the HPA system increases, resulting in the release of hormones and peptides that are involved in suppressing growth and repair, and supporting functions necessary for immediate survival.

Challenges that threaten survival can produce increases in HPA activity. There are two categories of stressor: physiological and psychological. Physiological stressors, like ether exposure or hypoxia, involve brainstem circuits, bypassing the need for cognitive processing. Psychological stressors, such as restraint, fear conditioning, or exposure to novel environments, require higher-order processing. Unlike

* Order of authorship was determined alphabetically.

physiological stressors, this latter type of stressor does not involve immediate threat to physiological homeostasis (Herman & Cullinan, 1997). Psychological stressors make connections with limbic circuits crucial for reacting to this type of stressor. Recognizing this distinction between physiological and psychological stress is vital, because they involve different neural pathways (Herman & Cullinan, 1997). The aim of this chapter is to understand the relationship between cognitive and emotional processing and the HPA axis. Thus, we will focus on the role of psychologically mediated processes in the regulation of the HPA axis as well as with the effects of the HPA system in affecting the development of cognition and emotion. Although there is clearly a dynamic interplay between environmental and genetic influences that create the individual differences we see in reactivity (Francis, Diorio, Liu, & Meaney, 1999), this chapter discusses how experience shapes the activity of the HPA axis.

THE NEUROBIOLOGY OF THE HPA SYSTEM

The endocrine response to threat or challenge is coordinated in the central nervous system. In discussing this coordination we will first describe the HPA axis, and then the limbic inputs to this axis that allow cognitive-emotional challenges to activate the axis. Signals arriving at the parvocellular cells in the paraventricular nucleus (PVN) in the medial hypothalamus stimulate the release of corticotrophin-releasing hormone (CRH) (Fig. 8.1). CRH, along with other secretagogues such as vasopressin, stimulate the production and release of adrenocorticotrophic hormone (ACTH) by the pituitary gland (de Kloet et al., 1998; Johnson, Kamilaris, Chrousos, & Gold, 1992), which is then transported via the systemic circulation to the adrenal glands that lie on the top of the kidneys. Whereas the adrenal medulla is stimulated directly by the sympathetic nervous system and produces a stress hormone, adrenaline (Chrousos & Gold, 1992), the cortex of the adrenal gland responds to adrenocorticotrophic hormone with the production of glucocorticoids. In primates, cortisol is the predominant glucocorticoid produced in response to adrenocorticotrophic hormone (Johnson et al., 1992). Approximately 95 per cent of circulating cortisol is bound to cortisol-binding globulins. This bound portion of cortisol is physiologically inactive, but might serve as a store that can be mobilized rapidly (Rosner, 1990). Only the unbound cortisol exert effects on target tissue throughout the body.

For this chapter the end product of the HPA system will be referred to as glucocorticoids—this is for simplicity as in rodents this hormone is corticosterone (Sippell, Dorr, Bidlingmaier, & Knorr, 1980), while in primates, including humans, it is cortisol.

Glucocorticoids are synthesized and released from the adrenal gland into the general circulation and have effects on nearly every organ and tissue in the body (Munk, Guyre, & Holbrook, 1984), including energy mobilization and immunosuppressive effects (Chrousos & Gold, 1992). Glucocorticoids pass easily through

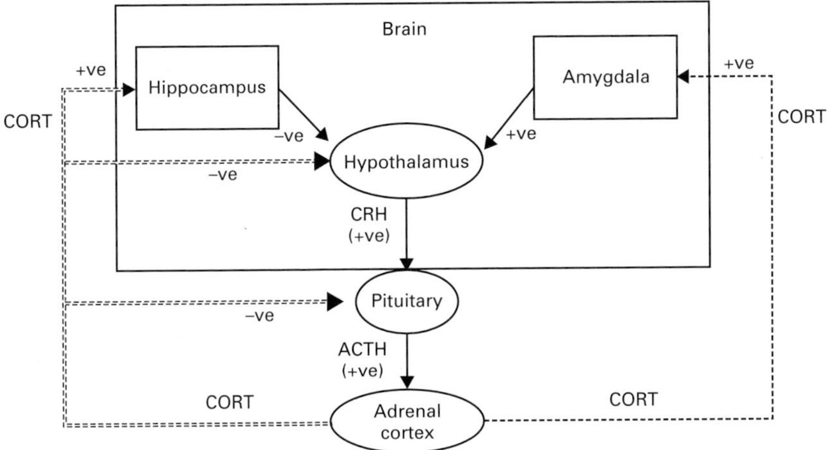

Figure 8.1. Schematic representation of the HPA axis including limbic inputs. Note the excitatory and inhibitory relationships between levels of the axis and limbic circuits. Limbic inputs include interactions with cortical circuits. −ve indicates a negative feedback mechanism; +ve indicates a positive feedback mechanism. However, positive feedback from the amygdala typically requires high levels of circulating glucocorticoids (CORT) over prolonged periods. Other secretogogues (e.g. vasopressin) have been omitted for the sake of clarity. ACTH, adrenocorticotrophic hormone; CRH, corticotrophin-releasing hormone.

the blood–brain barrier (Zarrow, Philpott, & Denenberg, 1970). There are receptors for glucocorticoids throughout the central nervous system (de Kloet et al., 1998; Sanchez, Young, Plotsky, & Insel, 2000).

Activation of the HPA system

Multiple sensory inputs contribute to the coordination of the HPA system. The response of the HPA system to psychological stressors is mediated largely by the limbic regions (Herman & Cullinan, 1997), including the amygdala and the extended amygdala, the bed nucleus of the stria terminalis (Davis, 1992). Lesions to these regions prevent elevations in the level of glucocorticoids in response to events such as restraint in rats, but do not prevent elevations in response to physiological stressors such as illness or injury (Feldman, Conforti, Itzik, & Weidenfeld, 1994; Herman & Cullinan, 1997). Because of the importance of limbic regulation of the HPA axis, this system is frequently referred to as the limbic–HPA (LHPA) axis. In addition to the hypothalamus, CRH is produced in other regions of the brain. There are a large number of CRH-producing neurons in the amygdala, and infusion of CRH to this area produces large increases in levels of glucocorticoids, along with behaviours indicative of fear and anxiety (Rosen & Schulkin, 1998).

Regulation of glucocorticoids: the role of receptors

Levels of glucocorticoids are regulated via negative feedback loops at several levels of the axis. In rodents, glucocorticoid feedback sites include the pituitary gland, hypothalamus, hippocampus, and frontal cortex (Diorio, Viau, & Meaney, 1993; Jacobson & Sapolsky, 1991). Increases in glucocorticoids result in inhibition of CRH production from the paraventricular nucleus (Keller-Wood & Dallman, 1984). Low levels of glucocorticoids, produced by adrenalectomy, result in elevated levels of CRH and adrenocorticotrophic hormone (Dallman et al., 1991).

Two receptors allow glucocorticoids to regulate negative feedback under both basal and stress conditions (de Kloet et al., 1998): mineralocorticoid receptors and glucocorticoid receptors. Mineralocorticoid receptors have a higher affinity for glucocorticoids than glucocorticoid receptors (Jacobson & Sapolsky, 1991); yet both are involved in the stress response and are necessary for a well-regulated system (Bradbury, Akana, & Dallman, 1994). In the rat, glucocorticoid receptors exist ubiquitously in the brain and mineralocorticoid receptors are expressed primarily in the hippocampus (de Kloet et al., 1998; Meaney et al., 1996). However, there is now evidence that the distribution of mineralocorticoid and glucocorticoid receptors differs in the primate brain. In comparison to the rat brain, glucocorticoid receptors are expressed in the rhesus monkey prefrontal cortex at greater frequency than in the hippocampus (Sanchez et al., 2000). The implications for human receptor distribution remain unknown. However, if verified in subsequent studies, it might indicate that the frontal cortex is more relevant for negative feedback containment of the glucocorticoid response to stressors than is the case in the rodent. Even in the rodent, however, there is evidence that lesions to the cingulate cortex result in prolonged elevations in glucocorticoids in response to psychological stressors (Diorio et al., 1993).

The baseline activity of the LHPA axis

In addition to being responsive to stress, the LHPA system also displays circadian variation. Peak basal glucocorticoid production occurs shortly after waking and the trough occurs around the onset of sleep. This occurrence is probably related to the need to mobilize energy stores at the start of a day (Sapolsky, 1992). A normal circadian rhythm appears to be necessary, at least in rodents, for an appropriate stress response (Dallman et al., 1991).

Development of the LHPA axis

Unlike an adult system, a newborn's basal glucocorticoid levels do not follow a circadian rhythm (Zurbrugg, 1976). Circadian patterns of glucocorticoid production become apparent 2–3 months after birth (Larson, White, Cochran, Donzella, & Gunnar, 1998; Price, Close, & Fielding, 1983). Development of the 24-hour sleep–wake cycle coincides with the emerging circadian pattern of glucocorticoid production (Spangler, 1991). However, patterns of basal glucocorticoid production during the day do not approach the fully adult-like pattern until about the time children give up their daytime nap (at around 4 or 5 years of age). Until then, average levels in the afternoon are similar to, not lower than, average levels in the mid-morning (Lane & Donzella, 1999).

The fullterm neonate exhibits robust, graded elevations in levels of glucocorticoids to pain-eliciting events (e.g. heel stick) and other stressors (e.g. physical examination) (Gunnar, 1992). However, responsiveness to stressors, such as handling, appears to decrease between 2 and 4 months of age, after which stressors like physical examinations fail to provoke elevations in glucocorticoid levels for most infants (Gunnar, Brodersen, Krueger, & Rigatuso, 1996a). Another marked decrease in glucocorticoid responsivity is observed between 6 and 12 months, when it becomes difficult to produce elevations in glucocorticoid levels to many mild stressors when parents are present (Gunnar et al., 1996a).

EARLY EXPERIENCE AND THE LHPA AXIS

Development involves interplay between the organism and a complex and changing environment. Neurobiological systems underlying emotion processing are plastic and thus can be altered by experience. These systems can be especially malleable early in life, when connections between limbic structures are still developing. In rat pups, manipulations such as daily handling or maternal deprivation produce lifelong changes in stress reactivity, fearful behaviour, and cognitive functioning (Liu et al., 1997; Meaney, Aitken, Bhatnagar, Van Berkel, & Sapolsky, 1988). These effects of early experience are mediated in part through alteration to the negative feedback process, which is regulated by changes in the number of glucocorticoid receptors (Meaney et al., 1996).

After decades of research on early experience, investigators have found that the mother–infant interaction is an important mediator of the development of the LHPA axis (Levine, 1957; see Denenberg, 1999, for a counterargument). Manipulations that enhance the vigour and organization of maternal care result in adult offspring who are less reactive (as demonstrated by lowered levels of glucocorticoids and adrenocorticotrophic hormone) to psychological stressors (Liu et al., 1997). These animals did not demonstrate differences in basal levels of glucocorticoids or adrenocorticotrophic hormone. However, they exhibited attenuated fearfulness in novel environments and decreased LHPA activity to a wide variety of stressors, accompanied by a quick termination of the glucocorticoids response, indicative of a highly effective negative feedback system (Liu et al., 1997; Meaney et al., 1988, 1996). In fact, animals with this type of experience had increased numbers of glucocorticoid receptors in the hippocampus and frontal cortex (Bhatnagar & Meaney, 1995; Meaney et al., 1996). In contrast, manipulations that disrupt maternal responsiveness have the opposite effect, namely more reactive offspring who display lower levels of glucocorticoid receptors (Plotsky & Meaney, 1993). These animals demonstrate a dysregulated system.[1]

Early deprivation studies have also been conducted with non-human primates. With regard to the LHPA axis, results of these studies have been quite mixed. Baby monkeys who are reared under conditions of social deprivation often display increases in fearful behaviour; however, altered baseline and stress response glucocorticoid levels are not consistently noted (see review by Sanchez, Ladd, & Plotsky, 2001). At minimum, peer-rearing provides the infant with animate, albeit inconsistent and less responsive, attachment figures. Peer-reared monkeys are typically shy, low in dominance, and fearful of novelty compared with same-aged mother-reared monkeys. They also show greater LHPA reactions to stress (Suomi, 1997). Less severe disruptions of the mother–infant relationship can impact the LHPA system. In macaque monkeys, forcing the mother to forage for food on an unpredictable schedule is stressful and thus disturbs maternal behaviour, resulting in offspring with similar behavioural profiles as peer-reared monkeys. As adults these animals also have higher CRH levels (Coplin et al., 1996).

Studies of early experience and LHPA axis activity in humans are extremely rare. Children reared in a Romanian orphanage demonstrated no evidence of the circadian pattern of daytime glucocorticoid production that are found in typically developing children (Carlson & Earls, 1997). A second study examined a group of children adopted from Romanian orphanages into Canadian families in British Columbia. Children who were adopted after 8 months of age exhibited higher levels of glucocorticoids through the day than children adopted before 4 months of age or than Canadian children raised in their families of origin. For those with 8 months or more of orphanage care, the duration of time in the orphanage correlated highly with elevated glucocorticoid levels (Gunnar, Morison, Chisholm, & Schuder, 2001). Similar long-term effects on glucocorticoid levels have been noted for children who develop post-traumatic stress disorder (PTSD) after many years of abuse (De Bellis et al., 1999a). These children displayed dysregulation at multiple levels of the LHPA axis, including elevated baseline glucocorticoid levels. In adulthood, women who had been sexually abused as children exhibited larger elevations in adrenocorticotrophic hormone in response to a stressor (Heim et al., 2000). These results should be interpreted with caution because they might not tell us much about development within the normal range of experiences. None the less, this line of research adds to a growing body of knowledge about the ways in which early experience can act to shape the developing LHPA axis.

To study the effects of less extreme rearing conditions, researchers have examined natural variations in parenting, commonly employing attachment paradigms.

---

[1] Dysregulation of the HPA system can be characterized by alterations to circadian rhythms and/or the stress response, due to impairments at any or all levels of the axis. While rodent research typically finds that early experiences impact stress, rather than basal levels, primate work has identified both types of disruptions.

Insecure attachment relationships are characterized by insensitive and inconsistent caregiving (Ainsworth & Bell, 1970). Children who develop an insecure relationship with their primary caregiver were more likely than children with secure attachment relationships to show glucocorticoid elevations in response to a variety of potentially threatening stimuli, including inoculations, maternal separation, and novel events (Gunnar, Brodersen, Nachmias, Buss, & Rigatuso, 1996b; Nachmias, Gunnar, Mangelsdorf, Hornik-Parritz, & Buss, 1996; Spangler & Schieche, 1998). These data suggest that the activity of the LHPA system can be impacted by maternal care (Gunnar et al., 1996b; Nachmias et al., 1996). We should be cautious in interpreting this as solely a parenting effect, however, as characteristics of the child might also contribute to the development of a secure relationship.

In this section, we have presented evidence for the effects of early experience in multiple species. Such discussion could lead to the potentially incorrect assumption that identical mechanisms operate across these species. In fact, research has found differences in the regulators of the LHPA axis for monkeys and rats (e.g. differences in receptor distribution; Sanchez et al., 2000). In rodents, glucocorticoid levels do not appear to play a role in producing effects on the LHPA system caused by manipulating mother–infant interactions (van Oers, de Kloet, Whelen, & Levine, 1998). The handling effect on hippocampal glucocorticoid receptor expression appears to be dependent on peripheral thyroid hormone release and the activation of ascending serotonergic pathways (Meaney et al., 2000). In non-human and human primates we are even less clear about how experience could alter later LHPA axis activity. We do not have evidence to determine how early experiences shape these circuits in humans. However, possibilities include mechanisms such as modifications to limbic circuits involved in the regulation of the LHPA axis and changes in mineralocorticoid/glucocorticoid receptor number.

As these caveats indicate, we are a long way from understanding whether and how experiences during development influence the primate, including the human, LHPA system. The available evidence, however, suggests that regulation of the LHPA system in humans will be intimately intertwined with cognitive and emotional processes in early development. Thus, understanding the role of experience in LHPA axis reactivity and regulation will require a better understanding of the bidirectional flow of influence between the LHPA system and cognitive–emotional processes.

COGNITION AND THE LHPA AXIS

Effect of glucocorticoids on information processing in the hippocampus

As discussed earlier, except at the peak of circadian cycle, baseline levels of glucocorticoids primarily activate mineralocorticoid receptors, whereas glucocorticoid receptors are occupied in the presence of higher levels of glucocorticoids, such as those that occur in response to stress. The reader should be aware that although most of the data presented in this section are from studies of rodents, there are major implications for similar mechanisms working in humans. Both mineralocorticoid and glucocorticoid receptors have an effect on neural transmission in the hippocampus (de Kloet et al., 1998). Mineralocorticoid receptor binding enhances cellular excitability in the hippocampus, whereas glucocorticoid receptor activation suppresses activity, indicating that both receptors contribute uniquely to homeostatic control of cellular activity in the hippocampus. Optimal hippocampal performance occurs when most mineralocorticoid receptors and an intermediate level of glucocorticoid receptors are bound, thus suggesting that the relationship between glucocorticoids and hippocampal performance follows an inverted U-shape rather than a linear relation (Conrad, Lupien, & McEwen, 1999; de Kloet, Oitzl, & Joels, 1999).

Modulating the activity of hippocampal neurons affects long-term potentiation. Long-term potentiation is a long-lasting enhancement in synaptic efficacy that occurs in response to high-frequency electrical stimulation, a process often viewed as essential for learning (Teyler & DiScenna, 1987). Evidence suggests that long-term potentiation is moderated by glucocorticoids in a similar fashion, with impairments in long-term potentiation typically occurring during exposure to extremely low and high levels of glucocorticoids, whereas moderate levels appear to enhance long-term potentiation (de Kloet et al., 1999). Not only do glucocorticoids affect neural activity, there is also evidence that prolonged or extreme elevation of glucocorticoid levels leads to neurodegeneration in the hippocampus. Exposure to 3 weeks of restraint stress or injection of high levels of glucocorticoids causes regression of apical dendrites of hippocampal neurons in rats (Magarinos & McEwen, 1995). Furthermore, chronic, high levels of glucocorticoids appear not only to damage the neurons outright but also to hamper their ability to survive other coincident challenges, such as epileptic seizures and hypoglycaemia (McIntosh & Sapolsky, 1996).

Evidence suggests that a high level of excitatory amino acids (e.g. glutamate), acting on *N*-methyl-D-aspartate (NMDA) receptors, is the primary cause of dendritic atrophy. The release of excitatory amino acids is modulated, in part, by glucocorticoids (Magarinos & McEwen, 1995). Elevations in levels of glucocorticoids, because of chronic stress, lead to prolonged and increased levels of glutamate (Abraham, Juhasz, Kekesi, & Kovacs, 1998; Magarinos & McEwen, 1995), resulting in persistent activation of NMDA receptors and the increased potential for cell death (Kandel, Schwartz, & Jessel, 1991).

The negative impact of excitatory amino acids can be further compounded by the glucocorticoid-induced reduction of the cell's ability to meet energy demands. Glucocorticoids inhibit cerebral glucose transport, resulting in an energy deficit and making it more difficult for the hippocampus to carry-out maintenance processes. This energy deficit might be a primary mechanism by which glucocorticoids induce damage in the hippocampus, and explains the way that glucocorticoids might exacerbate neurological insults (McEwen & Sapolsky, 1995; Sapolsky & Meaney, 1986).

The hippocampus serves a critical role in numerous cognitive processes, including learning and memory (Squire, Haist, & Shimamura, 1989). Thus, alterations of hippocampal activity by prolonged exposure to elevated levels of glucocorticoids, as discussed above, can lead to deficits in cognition (Sapolsky, 1992). It should be noted that most of the data presented in this section are from work with adult, non-human populations. In rodent work, researchers have reported both adverse (Kirschbaum, Wolf, May, Wippich, & Hellhammer, 1996; Newcomer, Craft, Hershey, Askins, & Bardgett, 1994) and facilitating (Luine, Martinez, Villegas, Magarinos, & McEwen, 1996; Sandi, Loscertales, & Guaza, 1997) effects of glucocorticoid exposure on cognitive functions associated with the hippocampus. Like the relationship between glucocorticoids and long-term potentiation, these results can be considered in terms of an inverted U-shaped dose–response curve (Bennett, Diamond, Fleshner, & Rose, 1991; Lupien & McEwen, 1997).

Hippocampal atrophy, caused by chronic elevations in glucocorticoid levels, has been associated with deficits in memory function (Luine, Villegas, Martinez, & McEwen, 1994). Alternatively, in rats, adrenalectomy (which results in a lack of glucocorticoid production) induces memory deficits, and restoration of glucocorticoids to normal levels reinstates such abilities (McCormick, McNamara, Kelsey, & Kleckner, 1995). This U-shaped dose–response might in fact be a product of shifts in the ratio of mineralocorticoid and glucocorticoid receptor occupation (de Kloet et al., 1999; Lupien & McEwen, 1997).

Despite this evidence from animal work, less work has been done in humans to examine the effects of glucocorticoid levels on cognition. There is, however, some evidence to suggest that glucocorticoids might impair human cognition. Acute administration of glucocorticoids is associated with impairments to memory systems that rely on the hippocampus (Monk & Nelson, 2002; Newcomer et al., 1994; Wolkowitz et al., 1990), but does not appear to affect memory systems that do not rely on the hippocampus (Kirschbaum et al., 1996). Furthermore, glucocorticoids administered over the course of several days, at doses associated with physical and psychological stress in humans, can reversibly decrease verbal declarative memory function in healthy adults (Newcomer et al., 1999). These data suggest that impairment in human memory performance can occur during an acute or an extended period of moderate to severe stress.

Effect of glucocorticoids on the prefrontal cortex

As discussed earlier, glucocorticoid and mineralocorticoid receptors are distributed widely throughout the primate cortex (Sanchez et al., 2000). In fact, there is evidence for an association between glucocorticoids and prefrontally mediated, executive functions in adult (Bohnen, Houx, Nicholson, & Jolles, 1990; Lupien et al., 1994) and child populations (Davis, Bruce, & Gunnar, 2002; Kruesi, Schmidt, Donnelly, Hibbs, & Hamburger, 1989).

Because of the correlational nature of the evidence for associations between glucocorticoids and the prefrontal cortex, directionality cannot be determined. However, it is possible that elevated glucocorticoid levels affect the neural systems that mediate attention. In fact, studies of patients with Cushing's disease and patients treated with glucocorticoids have found that increased glucocorticoid levels are associated with difficulties with frontal functions, such as attention (Varney, Alexander, & MacIndoe, 1984; however, see Monk & Nelson, 2002, for counter-evidence). To determine whether there is a direct effect of glucocorticoids on the prefrontal cortex, experimenters have administered exogenous glucocorticoids. Such work indicates that increasing levels of glucocorticoids interfere with frontal processes such as planning, attention regulation, and working memory (Kopell, Wittner, Lunde, Warrick, & Edwards, 1970; Lupien, Gillin, & Hauger, 1999; Young, Sahakian, Robbins, & Cowen, 1999). Although the neural mechanism underlying this effect has not been identified in humans, work conducted with rats indicates that chronic elevation of glucocorticoids might result in neural degeneration in the frontal cortex (Lowy, 1994). High levels of glucocorticoids could result in potentially damaging increases in extracellular excitatory amino acids (Bagley & Moghaddam, 1997; Karreman, 1996; Moghaddam, 1993), similar to the mechanisms acting in the hippocampus. In studies involving exogenous glucocorticoids, typically high levels are administered; thus, it seems unlikely that modest increases, such as those noted in studies of children facing new challenges, would have these kinds of deleterious effects.

Although there is evidence that elevations in glucocorticoids impact the functioning of the prefrontal cortex, it is also possible that individual differences in the prefrontal cortex could affect the activation of the LHPA axis. For example, children who have difficulty planning or regulating their behaviour might create situations for themselves that activate the LHPA system. From existing data, researchers can begin to piece together the story of how glucocorticoids act on the prefrontal cortex. This story is far from complete, however. The data linking the prefrontal cortex and the LHPA axis remain sparse. However, the consistent and converging pieces of evidence from rat and primate studies seem to suggest links between prefrontal cortex functioning and regulation of the LHPA axis.

Much of the research examining the effects of glucocorticoids on cognition involves acute administration of glucocorticoids to adults. Just as we encounter problems when attempting to extrapolate from rat to primate research, similar problems arise when generalizing from adults to children. For example, it is not known whether adults and children rely on identical brain circuits to perform the same cognitive tasks. Moreover, the receptor distribution for glucocorticoids might differ between adults and children, leading to distinct effects on cognitive performance. It is important to examine cognition and the LHPA axis from a developmental perspective, because such work can inform researchers of the potential impact of early adverse circumstances on the development of learning and memory. Although some of these effects on cognition might be subtle at young ages, even a subtle difference could place a child on a trajectory that could develop into significant difficulties later in life.

THE LHPA AXIS AND EMOTION

Investigators of emotion have long used glucocorticoids as a biological marker of the individual differences in negative emotional reactivity, such as fear (see Mason, 1968, for a review). Because of the association between activation of the LHPA axis and the fear system, it has been assumed that the individuals who show the largest increases in glucocorticoids in response to a threatening event are the most frightened or anxious.[2] However, numerous examples of contradictory findings permeate the literature. For example, parents of children dying of leukaemia who displayed the most emotional distress exhibited less LHPA axis activation than parents who displayed less emotional distress (Friedman, Mason, & Hamburg, 1963). Also, front-line soldiers have been found to display smaller increases in glucocorticoids than their commander, despite the fact that the commander was, in reality, safer from attack (Bourne, Rose, & Mason, 1968). Such findings have led researchers to argue that glucocorticoids are not just "emotion juice" (Levine & Wiener, 1989).

Studies of children and animals pose similar problems of relating glucocorticoid activity directly to negative emotionality. There is a problem in attempting to view elevations in glucocorticoids as maladaptive. Our discussion will attempt to elucidate the necessity of viewing the LHPA axis in the context of its dynamic relationships with the neural systems involved in affective processing. In particular, we will focus on the bidirectional interactions between the LHPA axis and the amygdala.

The amygdala and LHPA axis

Limbic regions modulate the activity of the LHPA axis in response to psychological stressors. Moreover, the LHPA axis modulates the emotional processing in limbic regions. We will focus on the interplay between the LHPA system and the amygdala, which assumes a critical role in fear processing (Davis, Walker, & Lee, 1997).

---

[2] The reader might be curious about the concomitant discussion of fear and stress. It should be noted here that the authors take the position that, although the two systems are separate from each other, fear is one system that can activate the HPA system; therefore, it is appropriate to discuss them conjointly.

The amygdala is considered to be the structure where fear-inducing sensory and autonomic input and behavioural output converge. CRH in the amygdala plays a role in increasing activity in the LHPA axis and mediating amygdalar responses to fear (Davis, 1992). Stimulation of the amygdala results in increased production of glucocorticoids in rats (Mason, 1959). Negative life events that increase glucocorticoids have been found to impact levels of CRH in the hypothalamus and amygdala (Makino, Gold, & Schulkin, 1994). Indeed, glucocorticoid receptors have been identified within CRH-producing cell bodies in the amygdala (Honkaniemi et al., 1992).

Multiple subtypes of CRH receptors have been identified in the central nervous system (Steckler & Holsboer, 1999). One of these—CRH1—has been characterized as the main target for CRH in mediating anxiogenesis. Like mineralocorticoid and glucocorticoid receptor distribution, there are marked differences between CRH receptor distribution in the rat and monkey brain. CRH1 receptors are found more widely throughout the monkey brain, particularly in limbic regions (Sanchez, Young, Plotsky, & Insel, 1999). Furthermore, the expression of CRH receptors has demonstrated a considerable level of plasticity. A variety of stressors (Bonaz & Rivest, 1998), as well as administration of high levels of glucocorticoids, result in increased mRNA for CRH1 receptors in the rat brain, including the amygdala (Makino et al., 1994). Additionally, maternally deprived rhesus monkeys expressed significantly more CRH1 receptors in the hippocampus and prefrontal cortex (Sanchez et al., 1999). This upregulation can theoretically lead to an increased fear response, or a lowered threshold for the fear response to occur. Thus, the interplay between the glucocorticoid and CRH systems is a potential mechanism through which a stressful environment might influence the individual's reactivity to future stressors (Makino et al., 1994, 1999).

To determine whether the changes seen with high elevations of glucocorticoids and CRH in the amygdala are reflected in actual behaviour, investigators have employed the technique known as fear-potentiated startle. The amplification of the startle reflex in the presence of fear-eliciting stimuli is dependent on amygdalar input (Lang, Bradley, & Cuthbert, 1990). Additionally, CRH infusion into the amygdala also results in a enhancement of the fear-potentiated startle reflex, whereas CRH antagonists block this potentiation (Swerdlow, Britton, & Koob, 1989). Similarly, lesions of the amygdala attenuate the excitatory effects that CRH has on the startle reflex (Liang et al., 1992). These data lend support to the notion that amygdalar CRH is involved in fear potentiation. Circulating glucocorticoids can also affect this potentiation. Indeed, chronic glucocorticoid administration acts to augment the CRH-enhanced startle response in rats (Lee, Schulkin, & Davis, 1994).

Investigators have postulated that activation of these systems might contribute to the development of pathological anxiety (Rosen & Schulkin, 1998). Individual variation in general levels of fear or anxiety might be related to differences in the excitability of the amygdala and/or the bed nucleus of the stria terminalis;

differences that can result in part from differing levels of CRH (Davis, 1997; Rosen & Schulkin, 1998). Experience with chronic, repeated stress may impact fear circuits to produce long-term changes in these circuits. These changes would then lower the threshold for fear-eliciting stimuli, potentially resulting in anxiety. We have discussed evidence for the role of CRH in this process. Moreover, patients with post-traumatic stress disorder exhibit increased basal levels of CRH as compared to controls (Bremner et al., 1997). Such research lends support for sensitization processes involving the amygdala and the LHPA axis. Therefore, many of the theories that relate negative emotionality to the LHPA axis might be better understood through consideration of CRH–amygdala relations.

THE LHPA AXIS AND DEVELOPMENT

One way that researchers have attempted to investigate the associations between LHPA activity and fear/anxiety in the developing organism is by examining individual differences in response to the same event. On a group level, elevations in glucocorticoids are typically noted when events are threatening. Rosen and Schulkin (1998) have argued that this reflects a normal "fear" response to threat. Similarly, the situations that elevate glucocorticoids in infants are typically ones that also elicit crying and other signs of behavioural distress and withdrawal (see Gunnar & Donzella, 1999, for a review). Thus, when approached on a group level, there are few instances of fear/anxiety that are not accompanied by activation of the LHPA axis. The problems arise in moving from the group level to that of the individual.

To examine whether individuals who appear the most frightened and anxious are the ones showing the largest increases in glucocorticoids, researchers have considered associations between temperament and glucocorticoid reactivity. Many of these studies have involved rhesus monkeys (Suomi, 1997). Researchers have found that infant monkeys who exhibit higher levels of freezing behaviour during a challenge (one index of fear) display elevated basal glucocorticoid levels (Kalin, Shelton, Rickman, & Davidson, 1998). In addition, monkeys identified as more reactive and having a more negative temperament were found to produce higher levels of glucocorticoids in response to a psychological challenge (Higley et al., 1994). Parallel findings associating anxious behaviour and glucocorticoids have been found in human children. Kagan and colleagues have found that elevated basal glucocorticoid levels in 5-year-old children were associated with increased behavioural inhibition in a strange laboratory setting (Kagan, Reznick, & Snidman, 1987).

Despite this evidence, it is also remarkably easy to demonstrate the lack of association between fearful/anxious temperament and glucocorticoid activity. For instance, the extremely inhibited children in Kagan's sample who displayed elevated glucocorticoid levels at 5 years of age were indistinguishable, in terms of glucocorticoids, from uninhibited children at 7 years (Kagan, Reznick, Snidman,

Gibbons, & Johnson, 1988; see also Schmidt et al., 1997). Similarly, multiple studies have shown that trait-anxious individuals have not been the ones to exhibit the most marked glucocorticoid response to a threatening situation (for a review, see Gunnar, 2001). Thus, the link between differences in glucocorticoids and individual differences in temperament remains tenuous.

In fact, researchers have consistently found an association between extroverted/outgoing behaviour and greater glucocorticoid reactivity in response to challenge. Our laboratory has performed studies with 2-year-olds entering group care (de Haan, Gunnar, Tout, Hart, & Stansbury, 1998), 3- and 4-year-olds starting a new year at nursery school (Gunnar, Tout, de Haan, Pierce, & Stansbury, 1997), and primary school children during their first week of school (Bruce, Davis, & Gunnar, 2002; Davis, Donzella, Krueger, & Gunnar, 1999). In all three age groups, shy/anxious children were not the ones exhibiting the highest elevations in glucocorticoids compared with their home baseline levels. Instead, it was typically the most surgent/extroverted children who exhibited the highest responses to the challenging situations. At first, findings like these seem contradictory. One potential explanation is that elevations in glucocorticoids in challenging situations are actually appropriate and could be beneficial in enabling extroverted children to gear up in the face of challenge. Alternatively, shy/anxious children might develop coping strategies, such as watching others from afar, when entering a strange situation that help them maintain lower glucocorticoid levels during the challenge of group entry (Kagan et al., 1987).

The way a child processes an event can also mediate the association between glucocorticoid production and fear/anxiety. For example, the information to which the child attends will determine his or her emotional and behavioural response to the situation. Children who are able to divert their attention from threatening stimuli and inhibit impulsive responses might be more successful in using such strategies to allay their anxiety (Derryberry & Rothbart, 1988). This individual difference, sometimes referred to as effortful control, represents a form of attention that allows the children voluntarily to regulate their behaviour (Ahadi, Rothbart, & Ye, 1993).

Temperament researchers have long suspected that children who are better able to regulate their attention are also less susceptible to fear-provoking stimuli (Rothbart, Derryberry, & Posner, 1994). In fact, researchers have found that effortful control is associated with activity of the LHPA axis when cortisol is assessed while children are in socially demanding, peer group settings (Dettling, Parker, Lane, Sebanc, & Gunnar, 2000; Gunnar et al., 1997; Gunnar et al., 1996b).

In addition to regulation of attention, context is also a mediator of fear/anxiety and glucocorticoids. For example, in the aforementioned research conducted by Gunnar and colleagues, it was found that surgent/extroverted children displayed elevated levels of glucocorticoids at the start of a new school year. However, when examined later in the year, once the classroom had become familiar, these children had lower indices of glucocorticoid reactivity (Gunnar et al., 1997).

Indeed, later in the school year the children who were poorly integrated in the playgroup and exhibited negative affect displayed the higher levels of glucocorticoid reactivity (Gunnar et al., 1997). Similarly, in studies that examine group entry, it is often the case that during the transition the subordinate individual, who is presumably more fearful, is found to show smaller or even blunted glucocorticoid increases to group entry when compared with the dominant individual (Hellhammer, Buchtal, Gutberlet, & Kirschbaum, 1997).

Evidence suggests that different characteristics are associated with glucocorticoid elevation in novel versus familiar situations. Novel encounters with threat have often been associated with increases in LHPA activity. Glucocorticoid response to an initial encounter with a challenge might be supporting necessary functions. For example, whereas human newborns elevated glucocorticoid levels in response to a physical examination, they did not show this elevation in response to the same examination 24h later (Gunnar, Hertsgaard, Larson, & Rigatuso, 1992). Similarly, adults giving a speech to an audience exhibited marked increases in glucocorticoids during the first presentation (Pruessner et al., 1997). However, with repeated presentations, only those individuals displaying negative emotionality continued to respond (i.e. failed to adapt).

Although repeated exposure typically results in a decrease in the glucocorticoid response, there are situations when this adaptation does not occur. Some individuals are subjected to environments marked by prolonged stress. Over time, these individuals do not show a typical reduction in glucocorticoid production in response to the stress. Instead, their LHPA systems sensitize to this environment. Although these alterations in LHPA function might appear pathological out of context, within context they could actually be adaptive responses. However, they could increase vulnerability for developing affective disorders.

A dysregulated system, resulting from such adverse environments, can lead to an excess of circulating glucocorticoid, potentially altering the brain circuitry involved in fear/anxiety. One proposed mechanism for this process involves high levels of glucocorticoids feeding back onto glucocorticoid receptors on the surface of CRH-producing neurons in the amygdala and extended amygdala. The resulting elevations in CRH could foster an oversensitive amygdala, and thus vulnerability for an anxiety disorder. In a regulated system, these high levels of glucocorticoids, through the negative feedback system, would normally decrease release of glucocorticoids to basal levels. However, in a dysregulated system, chronic high levels might down-regulate receptors involved in this feedback process. This would impair the system's ability to shut itself off, resulting in continued high levels of circulating glucocorticoid. The perpetuation of this process could lead to glucocorticoid-related pathology. Adult work has provided evidence for these speculations (Plotsky, Owens, & Nemeroff, 1998; Wolkowitz et al., 1990).

Although evidence is sparse, there has been some work on affective disorders with developmental populations. Researchers have found that sexually abused girls exhibit lower levels of adrenocorticotrophic hormone but increased basal levels of glucocorticoids (De Bellis et al., 1994). The authors speculate that developing systems work to compensate for the apparent hyporesponsiveness of the pituitary gland to CRH. These results are also in line with findings that depressed adults (Plotsky et al., 1998) and children (De Bellis et al., 1999a) have elevated basal levels of glucocorticoids, perhaps because of impaired feedback mechanisms.

Thus, because of the dynamic nature of the LHPA axis, study of the system must include examination at multiple levels. Fear-potentiated startle paradigms examine the role of the amygdala, plasma assays are used to assess levels of adrenocorticotrophic hormone, and plasma and salivary assays[3] are employed to assess levels of glucocorticoids. In some cases, it is also possible to obtain CRH levels in cerebral spinal fluid (Bremner et al., 1997). The lack of assessment at any level may potentially result in an erroneous conclusion. For example, a decrease in glucocorticoids might reflect either an excessive feedback mechanism or a hyporesponsive pituitary. Our goal should be to develop a more thorough understanding of the LHPA system and to be able to predict when elevations are and are not associated with negative emotions. Thus far, we have been more adept at forming post hoc explanations than at generating a priori predictions.

CONCLUSIONS

1. The HPA response to stress involves a cascade of hormones that leads to the release of glucocorticoids (CRH → adrenocorticotrophic hormone → glucocorticoids).
2. Limbic inputs into the HPA system allow cognitive and emotional challenges to activate the axis.
3. In addition to their role in the stress response, glucocorticoids also have proactive functions in the body.
4. There is evidence that early experience affects the development of the HPA system, although the evidence is limited in human populations.
5. Dysregulation of the HPA system is associated with alterations in cognitive and emotional function. Evidence suggests that the effect of glucocorticoids on cognitive and emotional functions typically follows an inverted U-shaped dose–response relationship.
6. Further research is needed to elucidate the role of HPA activation in human and developing populations.

---

[3] Collecting saliva from children is not difficult. Children old enough to chew gum (5 years and above) can be given Trident Original™ gum to stimulate salivation. The child is then asked to expel the saliva through a straw into a small plastic vial. Younger children can be given a few grains ($\frac{1}{8}$ of a teaspoon) of sugar-sweetened Kool-Aid™. The child then mouths a 2-inch cotton dental roll until the cotton is saturated. The saliva is then expressed into a plastic vial. With infants, the cotton roll method can be used without Kool-Aid™.

This chapter provides a sketch of the role of the LHPA axis in the developing human. As well as playing a role in the stress response, glucocorticoids have proactive functions in the body. Glucocorticoids clearly have beneficial, as well as harmful, functions; thus, a non-linear dose–response relationship should be considered, with moderate doses benefiting the organism.

At moderate levels, glucocorticoids can have positive effects on mood and cognition (Zorrilla, DeRubeis, & Redei, 1995). However, with chronic administration of glucocorticoids, at levels representative of high stress, mood becomes more negative and cognitive abilities worsen (Schmidt, Fox, Goldberg, Smith, & Schulkin, 1999; Wolkowitz et al., 1990). Negative effects are also observed when levels of glucocorticoids are too low. For example, adrenalectomized rats have shown impairments in context fear conditioning (Pugh, Fleshner, Fleshner, Tremblay, & Rudy, 1997). Although there is limited research involving exogenous administration of glucocorticoids to developmental populations, there is some evidence that children treated with higher levels of glucocorticoids for medical purposes report more anxious and depressive symptoms than children receiving lower doses (Bender, Lerner, & Kollasch, 1988).

Many of the findings discussed raise the question of whether elevated glucocorticoid levels should be viewed as maladaptive, associated with behaviours and emotions that reflect failures in managing threat, or as adaptive, associated with behaviours and emotions that support the individual's attempts to manage threatening events (de Kloet et al., 1999; Zorrilla et al., 1995). At different times, both elevations and suppressions are functional. Instead of focusing on specific levels of glucocorticoids as an index of LHPA functioning, it might be more appropriate to focus on the system's ability to shut itself off and turn itself on when necessary. Thus, as discussed, the context of the organism cannot be ignored. High levels of glucocorticoids during a challenging situation are indicative of something very different than high baseline levels. Furthermore, focusing on levels of glucocorticoids can lead to incorrect conclusions if other levels of the axis are ignored. The axis often compensates to adjust itself when one or more levels are altered. For example, an underproduction of adrenocorticotrophic hormone can result in an overproduction of glucocorticoids. Thus, measuring only glucocorticoids could give an inaccurate picture of the regulation of the axis. We have listed different levels at which the axis would ideally be assessed (i.e. blood samples, cerebrospinal fluid). However, obtaining such measures in typically developing children is often unrealistic. Therefore, we will have to become creative in the methods we choose to utilize. For example, options might include taking advantage of naturally occurring events, such as when blood samples are obtained for medical reasons.

Although we have discussed correlations between LHPA axis activity and behaviour, directionality of effects remains unknown. There are at least two levels of directionality to be considered. The first involves the coupling of behaviour and the HPA axis. It is not known whether it is behaviour that gives rise to a certain profile of HPA functioning, or vice versa. It is likely that it is a bidirectional relationship, which could be influenced by other factors. The second level requires consideration of developmental pathways and the ways that the organism seeks out and affects the environment in which it lives. For example, does developing in an unstable/stressful environment "produce" a reactive organism? Or alternatively, could an organism, genetically predisposed towards reactivity, create an increasingly stressful environment for itself, which would feedback onto the reactive organism? Hopefully, subsequent evidence will help elucidate such questions.

Many theories about LHPA function have been conceived at the crossroads of primate and rat work, and adult and child work. Such theories have enabled us to study the axis in a more holistic fashion. However, we must proceed with caution. Because our understanding of the mechanism has come primarily from rodent studies, our ability to extrapolate from these data is limited. This point is illustrated by the gap in our knowledge concerning the distribution of mineralocorticoid and glucocorticoid receptors in the developing child. Although developmental work has been performed with monkeys and rats, this type of research begs the question of whether the developmental time-course of these animals coincides with that of the human.

Because there are individuals living with elevated levels of glucocorticoids resulting from illness, medication, or stressful environments, continued research in this area remains important. Within such populations, including patients with Cushing's syndrome (Starkman, Gebarski, Berent, & Schteingart, 1992), it has been noted that these elevations are associated with memory deficits and increases in negative emotion. Furthermore, although we have focused on the impact of endogenous glucocorticoids, it is also important to understand the effect of glucocorticoids because they are often administered for medical purposes. In fact, children with medical conditions, such as prematurity and asthma, frequently receive synthetic glucocorticoids; however, the effect of this treatment on their development is poorly understood. Limited evidence indicates that synthetic glucocorticoids do in fact have a negative impact on development. For example, asthmatic children who use larger doses of steroid treatments are reported to have more negative mood than children receiving smaller doses (Bender et al., 1988). Because of the large number of children receiving hormone treatment, it is particularly important to study the mechanisms by which HPA axis activity affects the developing brain. Data indicating that psychological trauma can have different effects on adults and children (Bremner & Narayan, 1998; De Bellis et al., 1999b) lend support for the importance of studying the effects of glucocorticoids on the developing brain.

Furthermore, whereas the bulk of human research has focused on extreme or acute elevations of glucocorticoids, moderate daily elevations could also have long-term effects on the system. Rodent research has already pointed to the fact that small variations in social experiences (i.e. licking and grooming) affect the

HPA axis, and the same could be true in humans. By studying only extreme or acute elevations, we might miss some of the mechanisms by which early experience affects the system.

REFERENCES

Abraham, I., Juhasz, G., Kekesi, K.A., & Kovacs, K.J. (1998). Corticosterone peak is responsible for stress-induced elevation of glutamate in the hippocampus. *Stress, 2*, 171–181.

Ahadi, S., Rothbart, M.K., & Ye, R. (1993). Children's temperament in the US and China: Similarities and differences. *European Journal of Personality, 7*, 359–377.

Ainsworth, M., & Bell, S.M. (1970). Attachment, exploration, and separation: Illustrated by the behavior of one-year-olds in a strange situation. *Child Development, 41*(1), 49–67.

Bagley, J., & Moghaddam, B. (1997). Temporal dynamics of glutamate efflux in the prefrontal cortex and in the hippocampus following repeated stress: Effects of pretreatment with saline or diazepam. *Neuroscience, 77*(1), 65–73.

Bender, B.J., Lerner, J.A., & Kollasch, E. (1988). Mood and memory changes in asthmatic children receiving corticosteroids. *American Academy of Child and Adolescent Psychiatry, 27*(6), 720–725.

Bennett, M.C., Diamond, D.M., Fleshner, M., & Rose, G.M. (1991). Serum corticosterone level predicts the magnitude of hippocampal primed burst potentiation and depression in urethane-anesthetised rats. *Psychobiology, 19*, 301–307.

Bhatnagar, S., & Meaney, M.J. (1995). Hypothalamic-pituitary-adrenal function in chronic intermittently cold-stressed neonatal handled and non handled rats. *Journal of Neuroendocrinology, 7*, 97–108.

Bohnen, N., Houx, P., Nicholson, N., & Jolles, J. (1990). Cortisol reactivity and cognitive performance on a continuous mental task paradigm. *Biological Psychiatry, 31*, 107–116.

Bonaz, B., & Rivest, S. (1998). Effect of a chronic stress on CRF neuronal activity and expression of its type 1 receptor in the rat brain. *American Journal of Physiology, 275*(5 Part 2), R1438–1449.

Bourne, P.G., Rose, R.M., & Mason, J.W. (1968). 17-OHCS levels in combat: Special forces "A" team under threat of attack. *Archives of General Psychiatry, 19*, 135–140.

Bradbury, M.J., Akana, S.F., & Dallman, M.F. (1994). Roles of Type I and Type II corticosteroid receptors in basal activity in the hypothalamo pituitary adrenal axis during the diurnal trough and the peak: Evidence for a nonadditive effect of combined receptor occupation. *Endocrinology, 134*, 1286–1296.

Bremner, J.D., Licinio, J., Darnell, A., Krystal, J.H., Owens, M.J., Southwick, S.M. et al. (1997). Elevated CSF corticotropin-releasing factor concentrations in post-traumatic stress disorder. *American Journal of Psychiatry, 154*, 624–629.

Bremner, J.D., & Narayan, M. (1998). The effects of stress on memory and the hippocampus throughout the life cycle: Implications for childhood development and aging. *Development and Psychopathology, 10*, 871–885.

Bruce, J., Davis, E.P., & Gunnar, M.R. (2002). Individual differences in children's cortisol response to the beginning of a new school year. *Psychoneuroendocrinology, 27*, 635–650.

Carlson, M., & Earls, F. (1997). Psychological and neuroendocrinological sequelae of early social deprivation in institutionalised children in Romania. *Annals of the New York Academy of Sciences, 807*, 419–428.

Chrousos, G.P., & Gold, P.W. (1992). The concept of stress and stress system disorders. *Journal of the American Medical Association, 267*(9), 1244–1252.

Conrad, C.D., Lupien, S.J., & McEwen, B.S. (1999). Support for a bimodal role for Type II adrenal steroid receptors in spatial memory. *Neurobiology of Learning and Memory, 72*, 39–46.

Coplin, J.D., Andrews, M.W., Rosenbaum, L.A., Owens, M.J., Friedman, S., Orman, J.M. et al. (1996). Persistent elevations of cerebral spinal fluid concentrations of corticotropin releasing factor in adult nonhuman primate exposed to early life stressors: Implications for the pathophysiology of mood and anxiety disorders. *Proclamations of the National Academy of Sciences, 93*, 1619–1623.

Dallman, M.F., Akana, S.F., Scribner, K.A., Bradbury, M.J., Walker, C.D., Strack, A.M. et al. (1991). Stress, feedback and facilitation in the hypothalamo–pituitary– adrenal axis. *Journal of Neuroendocrinology, 4*(5), 518–526.

Davis, E.P., Bruce, J., & Gunnar, M.R. (2002). The anterior attention network: Associations with temperament and neuroendocrine activity in 6-year-old children. *Developmental Psychobiology, 40*, 43–56.

Davis, E., Donzella, B., Krueger, W.K., & Gunnar, M.R. (1999). The start of a new year: Individual differences in salivary cortisol response in relation to child temperament. *Developmental Psychobiology, 35*, 188–196.

Davis, M. (1992). The role of the amygdala in conditioned fear. In J. Aggleton (Ed.), *The amygdala: Neurobiological aspects of emotion, memory, and mental dysfunction* (pp. 255–305). New York: Wiley-Liss.

Davis, M. (1997). Neurobiology of fear responses: The role of the amygdala. *Journal of Neuropsychiatry, 9*(3), 382–402.

Davis, M., Walker, D.L., & Lee, Y. (1997). Roles of the amygdala and bed nucleus of the stria terminalis in fear and anxiety as measured with the acoustic startle reflex. *Annals of the New York Academy of Sciences, 821*, 305–331.

De Bellis, M.D., Baum, A.S., Birmaher, B., Keshavan, M.S., Eccard, C.H., Boring, A.M. et al. (1999a). Developmental traumatology. Part I: Biological stress systems. *Biological Psychiatry, 45*, 1259–1270.

De Bellis, M.D., Chrousos, G.P., Dorn, L.D., Burke, L., Helmers, K., Kling, M.A. et al. (1994). Hypothalamic–pituitary–adrenal axis dysregulation in sexually abused girls. *Journal of Clinical Endocrinology and Metabolism, 78*(2), 249–255.

De Bellis, M.D., Keshavan, M.S., Clark, D.B., Casey, B.J., Giedd, J.N., Boring, A.M. et al. (1999b). Developmental traumatology. Part II: Brain development. *Biological Psychiatry, 45*, 1271–1284.

de Haan, M., Gunnar, M.R., Tout, K., Hart, J., & Stansbury, K. (1998). Familiar and novel contexts yield different associations between cortisol and behavior among 2-year-old children. *Developmental Psychobiology, 33*(1), 93–101.

de Kloet, E.R., Oitzl, M.S., & Joels, M. (1999). Stress and cognition: Are corticosteroids good or bad guys? *Trends in Neuroscience, 22*, 422–426.

de Kloet, R., Vreugdenhil, E., Oitzl, M.S., & Joels, A. (1998). Brain corticosteroid receptor balance in health and disease. *Endocrine Reviews, 19*(3), 269–301.

Denenberg, V.H. (1999). Commentary: Is maternal stimulation the mediator of the handling effect in infancy? *Developmental Psychobiology, 34*(1), 1–3.

Derryberry, D., & Rothbart, M.K. (1988). Arousal, affect, and attention as components of temperament. *Journal of Personality and Social Psychology, 55*(6), 958–966.

Dettling, A.C., Parker, S.W., Lane, S., Sebanc, A., & Gunnar, M.R. (2000). Quality of care and temperament determine changes in cortisol concentrations over the day in young children in childcare. *Psychoneuroendocrinology, 25*, 819–836.

Diorio, D., Viau, V., & Meaney, M.J. (1993). The role of the medial prefrontal cortex (cingulate gyrus) in the regulation of hypothalamic–pituitary–adrenal responses to stress. *The Journal of Neuroscience, 13*(9), 3839–3847.

Feldman, S., Conforti, N., Itzik, A., & Weidenfeld, J. (1994). Differential effect of amygdaloid lesion on CRF-41, ACTH and corticosterone following neural stimuli. *Brain Research, 658*, 21–26.

Francis, D., Diorio, J., Liu, D., & Meaney, M.J. (1999). Nongenomic transmission across generations of maternal behavior and stress responses in the rat. *Science, 286*(5442), 1155–1163.

Friedman, S.B., Mason, J.W., & Hamburg, D.A. (1963). Urinary 17-hydroxycorticosteroids levels in parents of children with neoplastic disease. *Psychosomatic Medicine, 25*, 364.

Gunnar, M. (1992). Reactivity of the hypothalamic–pituitary–adrenocortical system to stressors in normal infants and children. *Pediatrics, 90*(3 Part 2), 491–497.

Gunnar, M. (2001). The role of glucocorticoids in anxiety disorders: A critical analysis. In M.W. Vasey & M.R. Dadds (Eds.), *The developmental psychopathology of anxiety* (pp. 143–159). Oxford: Oxford University Press.

Gunnar, M., & Donzella, B. (1999). "Looking for the Rosetta Stone": An essay on crying, soothing, and stress. In M. Lewis & D. Ramsay (Eds.), *Soothing and stress* (pp. 39–56). Mahwah, NJ: Lawrence Erlbaum Associates Inc.

Gunnar, M.R., Brodersen, L., Krueger, K., & Rigatuso, J. (1996a). Dampening of adrenocortical responses during infancy: Normative changes and individual differences. *Child Development, 67*, 877–889.

Gunnar, M.R., Brodersen, L., Nachmias, M., Buss, K., & Rigatuso, J. (1996b). Stress reactivity and attachment security. *Developmental Psychobiology, 29*(3), 191–204.

Gunnar, M.R., Hertsgaard, L., Larson, M., & Rigatuso, J. (1992). Cortisol and behavioral responses to repeated stressors in the human newborn. *Developmental Psychobiology, 24*(7), 487–505.

Gunnar, M.R., Morison, S.J., Chisholm, K., & Schuder, M. (2001). Salivary cortisol levels in children adopted from Romanian orphanages. *Development and Psychopathology, 13*, 611–628.

Gunnar, M.R., Tout, K., de Haan, M., Pierce, S., & Stansbury, K. (1997). Temperament, social competence, and adrenocortical activity in preschoolers. *Developmental Psychobiology, 31*(1), 65–85.

Heim, C., Newport, D.J., Heit, S., Graham, Y.P., Wilcox, M., Bonsall, R. et al. (2000). Pituitary–adrenal and autonomic responses to stress in women after sexual and physical abuse in childhood. *Journal of the American Medical Association, 284*, 592–597.

Hellhammer, D.H., Buchtal, J., Gutberlet, I., & Kirschbaum, C. (1997). Social hierarchy and adrenocortical stress reactivity in men. *Psychoneuroendocrinology, 22*(8), 643–650.

Herman, J.P., & Cullinan, W.E. (1997). Neurocircuitry of stress: Central control of the hypothalamic–pituitary–adrenocortical axis. *Trends in Neuroscience, 20*(2), 78–84.

Higley, J.D., Mehlman, P.T., Taub, D.M., Higley, S.B., Suomi, S.J., Vickers, J.H. et al. (1994). Cerebrospinal fluid monoamine and adrenal correlates of aggression in free-ranging rhesus monkeys. *Archives of General Psychiatry, 49*(6), 436–441.

Honkaniemi, J., Pelto-Huikko, M., Rechardt, L., Isola, J., Lammi, A., Fuxe, K. et al. (1992). Colocalization of peptide and glucocorticoid receptor immunoreactivities in rat central amygdaloid nucleus. *Neuroendocrinology, 55*(4), 451–459.

Jacobson, J., & Sapolsky, R. (1991). The role of the hippocampus in feedback regulation of the hypothalamic pituitary adrenocortical axis. *Endocrine Reviews, 12*(2), 118–134.

Johnson, E.O., Kamilaris, T.C., Chrousos, G.P., & Gold, P.W. (1992). Mechanisms of stress: A dynamic overview of hormonal and behavioral homeostasis. *Neuroscience and Biobehavioral Reviews, 16*, 115–130.

Kagan, J., Reznick, J.S., & Snidman, N. (1987). The physiology and psychology of behavioral inhibition in children. *Child Development, 58*(6), 1459–1473.

Kagan, J., Reznick, J.S., Snidman, N., Gibbons, J., & Johnson, M.O. (1988). Childhood derivatives of inhibition and lack of inhibition to the unfamiliar. *Child Development, 59*(6), 1580–1589.

Kalin, N.H., Shelton, S.E., Rickman, M., & Davidson, R.J. (1998). Individual differences in freezing and cortisol in infant and mother rhesus monkeys. *Behavioral Neuroscience, 112*(1), 251–254.

Kandel, E.R., Schwartz, J.H., & Jessel, T.M. (Eds.). (1991). *Principles of neuroscience*. New York: Elsevier.

Karreman, M.M.B. (1996). Effect of a pharmacological stressor on glutamate efflux in the prefrontal cortex. *Brain Research, 716*(1–2), 180–182.

Keller-Wood, M., & Dallman, M. (1984). Corticosteroid inhibition of ACTH secretion. *Endocrine Reviews, 5*, 1–24.

Kirschbaum, C., Wolf, O.T., May, M., Wippich, W., & Hellhammer, D.H. (1996). Stress- and treatment-induced elevations of cortisol levels associated with impaired declarative memory in healthy adults. *Life Science, 58*, 1475–1483.

Kopell, B.S., Wittner, W., Lunde, D., Warrick, G., & Edwards, D. (1970). Cortisol effects on averaged evoked potential, alpha rhythm, time estimation and two flash fusion threshold. *Psychosomatic Medicine, 32*, 39–49.

Kruesi, M.J.P., Schmidt, M.E., Donnelly, M., Hibbs, E.D., & Hamburger, S.D. (1989). Urinary free cortisol output and disruptive behavior in children. *Journal of the American Academy of Child and Adolescent Psychiatry, 28*(3), 441–443.

Lane, S.K., & Donzella, B. (1999). *Relationship between cortisol levels across the day, sleep/wake patterns, and temperament in 24- and 36-month-olds*. Paper presented at the Society for Research in Child Development, Albuquerque, NM.

Lang, P.J., Bradley, M.M., & Cuthbert, B.N. (1990). Emotion, attention, and the startle reflex. *Psychological Review, 97*(3), 377–395.

Larson, M., White, B.P., Cochran, A., Donzella, B., & Gunnar, M.R. (1998). Dampening of the cortisol response to handling at 3-months in human infants and its relation to sleep, circadian cortisol activity, and behavioral distress. *Developmental Psychobiology, 33*(4), 327–337.

Lee, Y., Schulkin, J., & Davis, M. (1994). Effect of corticosterone on the enhancement of the acoustic startle reflex by corticotropin releasing factor (CRF). *Brain Research, 666*(1), 93–98.

Levine, S. (1957). Infantile experience and resistance to physiological stress. *Science, 126*, 405–406.

Levine, S., & Wiener, S.G. (1989). Coping with uncertainty: A paradox. In D.S. Palermo (Ed.), *Coping with uncertainty: Behavioral and developmental perspectives*. Hillsdale, NJ: Lawrence Erlbaum Associates Inc.

Liang, K.C., Melia, K.R., Campeau, S., Falls, W.A., Miserendino, M.J.D., & Davis, M. (1992). Lesions of the central nucleus of the amygdala, but not the paraventricular nucleus of the hypothalamus, block the excitatory effects of corticotropin-releasing factor on the acoustic startle reflex. *Journal of Neuroscience, 12*(6), 2313–2320.

Liu, D., Tannenbaum, B., Caldji, C., Francis, D., Freedman, A., Sharma, S. et al. (1997). Maternal care, hippocampal glucocorticoid receptors, and hypothalamic–pituitary–adrenal responses to stress. *Science, 277*, 1659–1662.

Lowy, M.T. (1994). Adrenalectomy attenuates kainic acid induced spectrin proteolysis and heat shock protein 70 in the hippocampus and cortex. *Neurochemistry, 63*, 886–894.

Luine, V., Martinez, C., Villegas, M., Magarinos, A.M., & McEwen, B.S. (1996). Restraint stress reversibly enhances spatial memory performance. *Physiology & Behavior, 59*, 27–32.

Luine, V., Villegas, M., Martinez, C., & McEwen, B.S. (1994). Repeated stress causes reversible impairments of spatial memory performance. *Brain Research, 639*(1), 167–170.

Lupien, S.J., Gillin, C.J., & Hauger, R.L. (1999). Working memory is more sensitive than declarative memory to the acute effects of corticosteroids: A dose–response study in humans. *Behavioral Neuroscience, 113*(3), 420–430.

Lupien, S.J., & McEwen, B.S. (1997). The acute effects of corticosteroids on cognition: Integration of animal and human model studies. *Brain Research Reviews, 24*, 1–27.

Magarinos, A.M., & McEwen, B.S. (1995). Stress-induced atrophy of apical dendrites of hippocampal CA3c neurons: Involvement of glucocorticoid secretion and excitatory amino axid receptors. *Neuroscience, 69*(1), 89–98.

Makino, S., Gold, P.W., & Schulkin, J. (1994). Corticosterone effects on corticotropin-releasing hormone mRNA in the central nucleus of the amydgala and the parvocellular region of the paraventricular nucleus of the hypothalamus. *Brain Research, 640*(1–2), 105–112.

Makino, S., Shibasaki, T., Yamauchi, N., Nishioka, T., Mimoto, T., Wakabayashi, I. et al. (1999). Psychological stress increased corticotropin-releasing hormone mRNA and content in the central nucleus of the amygdala but not in the hypothalamic paraventricular nucleus in the rat. *Brain Research, 850*, 136–143.

Mason, J.W. (1968). A review of psychoendocrine research on the pituitary adrenal cortical system. *Psychosomatic Medicine, 30*(5), 576–605.

McCormick, C.M., McNamara, M., Kelsey, J.F., & Kleckner, N.W. (1995). Acute corticosterone replacement three-months after adrenalectomy improves performance in a morris water maze despite degeneration in the dentate gyrus. *Society for Neuroscience Abstracts, 21*, 1944.

McEwen, B.S., & Sapolsky, R.M. (1995). Stress and cognitive function. *Current Opinion in Neurobiology, 5*, 205–215.

McIntosh, L.J., & Sapolsky, R.M. (1996). Glucocorticoids may enhance oxygen mediated neurotoxicity. *Neurotoxicology, 17*(3–4), 873–882.

Meaney, M.J., Aitken, D.H., Bhatnagar, S., Van Berkel, C., & Sapolsky, R.M. (1988). Effect of neonatal handling on age-related impairments associated with the hippocampus. *Science, 239*, 766–768.

Meaney, M.J., Diorio, J., Francis, D., Weaver, S., Yau, J., Chapman, K. et al. (2000). Postnatal handling increases the expression of cAMP-inducible transcription factors in the rat hippocampus: the effects of thyroid hormones and serotonin. *Journal of Neuroscience, 20*(10), 3926–3935.

Meaney, M.J., Diorio, J., Francis, D., Widdowson, J., La Plante, P., Caldui, C. et al. (1996). Early environmental regulation of forebrain glucocorticoid gene expression: Implications for adrenocortical response to stress. *Developmental Neuroscience, 18*, 49–72.

Mishkin, M., Malamut, B., & Bachevalier, J. (1984). Memories and habits: Two neural systems. In G. Lynch, J.L. McGaugh, & N.M. Weinberger (Eds.), *Neurobiology of learning and memory* (pp. 65–77). New York: Guilford Press.

Moghaddam, B. (1993). Stress preferentially increases extraneuronal levels of excitatory amino acids in the prefrontal cortex: Comparison to hippocampus and basal ganglia. *Journal of Neurochemistry, 60*, 1650–1657.

Monk, C.S., & Nelson, C.A. (2002). The effects of hydrocortisone on cognitive and neural function: A behavioral and event-related potential investigation. *Neuropsychopharmacology, 26*, 505–519.

Munk, A., Guyre, P.M., & Holbrook, N.J. (1984). Physiological functions of glucocorticoids in stress and their relation to pharmacological actions. *Endocrine Reviews, 5*(1), 25–44.

Nachmias, M., Gunnar, M.R., Mangelsdorf, S., Hornik-Parritz, R., & Buss, K. (1996). Behavioral inhibition and stress reactivity: The moderating role of attachment security. *Child Development, 67*, 508–522.

Newcomer, J.W., Craft, S., Hershey, T., Askins, K., & Bardgett, M.E. (1994). Glucocorticoid-induced impairment in declarative memory performance in adult humans. *Journal of Neuroscience, 14*, 2047–2053.

Newcomer, J.W., Selke, G., Melson, A.K., Hershey, T., Craft, S., Richards, K. et al. (1999). Decreased memory performance in healthy humans induced by stress-level cortisol treatment. *Archives of General Psychiatry, 56*, 527–533.

Plotsky, P.M., & Meaney, M.J. (1993). Early postnatal experience alters hypothalamic corticotropin-releasing factor (CRF) mRNA, median eminence CRF content and stress-induced release in adult rats. *Molecular Brain Research, 18*, 195–200.

Plotsky, P.M., Owens, M.J., & Nemeroff, C.B. (1998). Psychoneuroendocrinology of depression. Hypothalamic–pituitary–adrenal axis. *Psychiatric Clinics of North America, 21*(2), 293–307.

Price, D.A., Close, G.C., & Fielding, B.A. (1983). Age of appearance of circadian rhythm in salivary cortisol values in infancy. *Archives of Disease in Childhood, 58*, 454–456.

Pruessner, J.C., Gaab, J., Hellhammer, D.H., Lintz, D., Schommer, N., & Kirschbaum, C. (1997). Increasing correlations between personality traits and cortisol stress responses obtained by data aggregation. *Psychoneuroendocrinology, 22*(8), 615–625.

Pugh, C.R., Fleshner, M., Fleshner, D., Tremblay, D., & Rudy, J.W. (1997). A selective role for corticosterone in fear conditioning. *Behavioral Neuroscience, 111*, 303–311.

Rosen, J.B., & Schulkin, J. (1998). From normal fear to pathological anxiety. *Psychological Review, 105*(2), 325–350.

Rosner, W. (1990). The functioning of corticosteroid-binding globulin and sex hormone-binding globulin: Recent advances. *Endocrine Reviews, 11*(1), 80–91.

Rothbart, M.K., Derryberry, D., & Posner, M.I. (1994). A psychobiological approach to the development of temperament. In J.E. Bates & T.D. Wachs (Eds.), *Temperament: Individual differences in biology and behavior* (pp. 83–116). Washington, DC: American Psychological Association.

Sanchez, M.M., Ladd, C.O., & Plotsky, P.M. (2001). Early adverse experience as a developmental risk factor for later psychopathology: Evidence from rodent and primate models. *Development & Psychopathology, 13*, 419–450.

Sanchez, M.M., Young, L.J., Plotsky, P.M., & Insel, T.R. (1999). *Different rearing conditions affect the development of corticotropin releasing factor (CRF) and vasopressin (AVP) systems in non-human primates.* Poster presented at the Society for Neuroscience, Miami, FL.

Sanchez, M.M., Young, L.J., Plotsky, P.M., & Insel, T.R. (2000). Distribution of corticosteroid receptors in the rhesus brain: Relative absence of glucocorticoid receptors in the hippocampal formation. *The Journal of Neuroscience, 20*(12), 4657–4668.

Sandi, C., Loscertales, M., & Guaza, C. (1997). Expression-dependent facilitating effect of corticosterone on spatial memory formation in the water maze. *European Journal of Neuroscience, 9*, 637–642.

Sapolsky, R. (1992). *Stress, the aging brain, and the mechanisms of neuron death.* Cambridge, MA: MIT Press.

Sapolsky, R.M. (1996). Why stress is bad for the brain. *Science, 273*(5276), 749–750.

Sapolsky, R.M., & Meaney, M.J. (1986). Maturation of the adrenocortical stress response: Neuroendocrine control mechanisms and the stress hyporesponsive period. *Brain Research Reviews, 11*, 65–76.

Schmidt, L.A., Fox, N.A., Goldberg, M.C., Smith, C.C., & Schulkin, J. (1999). Effects of acute prednisone administration on memory, attention and emotion in healthy human adults. *Psychoneuroendocrinology, 24*(4), 461–483.

Schmidt, L.A., Fox, N.A., Rubin, K.H., Sternberg, E.M., Gold, P.W., Smith, C.C. et al. (1997). Behavioral and neuroendocrine responses in shy children. *Developmental Psychobiology, 30*, 127–140.

Schmidt, L.A., Fox, N.A., Schulkin, J., & Gold, P.W. (1999). Behavioral and physiological correlates of self-presentation in temperamentally shy children. *Developmental Psychobiology, 35*, 119–135.

Sippell, W.G., Dorr, H.G., Bidlingmaier, F., & Knorr, D. (1980). Plasma levels of aldosterone, corticosterone, 11-deoxycorticosterone, progesterone, 17-hydroxyprogesterone, cortisol, and cortisone during infancy and childhood. *Pediatric Research, 14*, 39–46.

Spangler, G. (1991). The emergence of adrenocortical circadian function in newborns and infants and its relationship to sleep, feeding, and maternal adrenocortical activity. *Early Human Development, 25*, 197–208.

Spangler, G., & Schieche, M. (1998). Emotional and adrenocortical responses of infants to the strange situation: The differential function of emotional expression. *International Journal of Behavioral Development, 22*(4), 681–706.

Squire, L.R., Haist, F., & Shimamura, A.P. (1989). The neurology of memory: Quantitative assessment of retrograde amnesia in two groups of amnesiac patients. *Journal of Neuroscience, 9*, 828–839.

Starkman, M.N., Gebarski, S.S., Berent, S., & Schteingart, D.E. (1992). Hippocampal formation volume, memory dysfunction, and cortisol levels in patients with Cushing's syndrome. *Biological Psychiatry, 32*, 756–765.

Steckler, T., & Holsboer, F. (1999). Corticotropin-releasing hormone receptor subtypes and emotion. *Biological Psychiatry, 46*, 1480–1508.

Suomi, S.J. (1997). Early determinants of behavior: Evidence from primate studies. *British Medical Bulletin, 53*(1), 170–184.

Swerdlow, N.R., Britton, K.T., & Koob, G.F. (1989). Potentiation of acoustic startle by corticotropin-releasing factor (CRF) and by fear are both reversed by alpha-helical CRF (9–41). *Neuropsychopharmacology, 2*, 285–292.

Teyler, T.J., & DiScenna, P. (1987). Long-term potentiation. *Annual Review of Neuroscience, 10*, 131–161.

van Oers, H.J.J., de Kloet, E.R., Whelen, T., & Levine, S. (1998). Maternal deprivation effect on the infant's neural stress markers is reversed by tactile stimulation and feeding, but not by suppressing corticosterone. *The Journal of Neuroscience, 18*(23), 10171–10179.

Varney, N.R., Alexander, B., & MacIndoe, J.H. (1984). Reversible steroid dementia in patients without steroid psychosis. *Journal of Psychiatry, 141*(3), 369–372.

Wolkowitz, O.M., Reus, V.I., Weingartner, H., Thompson, K., Breier, A., Doran, A. et al. (1990). Cognitive effects of corticosteroids. *American Journal of Psychiatry, 147*(10), 1297–1303.

Young, A.H., Sahakian, B.J., Robbins, T.W., & Cowen, P.J. (1999). The effects of chronic administration of hydrocortisone on cognitive function in normal male volunteers. *Psychopharmacology, 145*(145), 260–266.

Zarrow, M.X., Philpott, J.E., & Denenberg, V.H. (1970). Passage of 14C-4 corticosterone from the rat mother to the fetus and neonate. *Nature, 226*, 1058–1059.

Zorrilla, E.P., DeRubeis, R.J., & Redei, E. (1995). High self-esteem, hardiness and affective stability are associated with higher basal pituitary-adrenal hormone levels. *Psychoneuroendocrinology, 20*(6), 591–601.

Zurbrugg, R. (1976). Hypothalamic–pituitary–adrenocortical regulation. *Monographs in Pediatrics, 7*, 12–21.

CHAPTER NINE

Neuroendocrinology: Cognitive effects of sex hormones

Sheri A. Berenbaum
Department of Psychology, The Pennsylvania State University, USA

Scott Moffat
National Institute on Aging, Baltimore, USA

Amy Wisniewski
Johns Hopkins University, Baltimore, USA

Susan Resnick
National Institute on Aging, Baltimore, USA

INTRODUCTION

Cognition is influenced in many ways by sex hormones acting at different points in development. Understanding hormone effects on cognition can lead to increased understanding of the neural substrates of cognition and cognitive development more generally. This chapter summarizes the evidence that sex hormones influence cognitions, considers issues in studying this topic, and highlights some of the exciting developments in this area.

WHY AND HOW MIGHT HORMONES AFFECT COGNITION?

Cognition is just one aspect of psychological development that is affected by sex hormones. In many species, including human beings, sex hormones are involved in many aspects of behavioural development, paralleling their effects on the body (Becker, Breedlove, & Crews, 1992; Berenbaum, 1998; Collaer & Hines, 1995; Goy, 1996; Goy & McEwen, 1980; Hampson & Kimura, 1992).

The main sex hormones involved in behaviour are androgens (including testosterone) and oestrogens. Both males and females produce both hormones, but in dramatically different amounts. These hormones affect behaviour in two primary ways. First, during sensitive periods early in development, hormones produce permanent changes in the organization of the brain, and these changes have long-lasting effects on behaviour throughout the organism's life. Second, sex hormones continue to act on the brain throughout life, by activating neural systems that were organized earlier in development. These activational effects are partly responsible for the plasticity shown by the mature brain. The main differences between organizational and activational effects are permanence (organizational effects persist after the hormones are no longer present) and timing (organizational effects generally occur early in development), but sex hormones may continue to produce permanent changes to the brain later in development (Arnold & Breedlove, 1985).

Cognition is affected by hormones acting both early in development and later in life, but different aspects of cognition appear to be affected by different hormones at different times. Spatial abilities are enhanced by moderately high levels of androgens present in prenatal development and then again throughout adulthood, whereas verbal abilities, especially fluency and memory, and fine motor skills are enhanced by high levels of oestrogens, especially in adulthood.

Cognitive effects of sex hormones in non-human species

Many studies in a variety of non-human mammalian species show that sex hormones are major contributors to behavioural sex differences (for reviews see Arnold & Gorski, 1984; Beatty, 1992; Becker et al., 1992; Breedlove, 1994; Goy & McEwen, 1980; MacLusky & Naftolin, 1981). Early studies focusing on reproductive behaviours established that male-typical adult behaviour is produced by the presence of high levels of androgen during early sensitive periods of development. For example, female rodents and primates exposed to high levels of androgen in the prenatal and neonatal periods are more likely than unexposed females to mount other females as sex partners, and less likely to be sexually receptive to males, whereas male rodents deprived of androgen during these sensitive periods show the opposite pattern of sexual behaviour. These behavioural effects are mediated by brain regions, particularly the hypothalamus, that show sex differences and are affected by changing androgen levels early in development.

Sex hormones also have profound effects on non-reproductive behaviours, including aspects of learning and memory. These effects occur both through permanent changes to the brain produced by hormones that are present early in development and through transient changes caused by hormones that are present for short periods later in life. With respect to the former organizational effects, for example, female rats given masculinizing hormones during critical periods of development learn the radial-arm maze as well as normal males, and better than normal females and male rats castrated neonatally; the superior performance of males and hormone-exposed females might be related to their use of geometric, rather than landmark, cues (Williams & Meck, 1991; Williams, Barnett, & Meck, 1990). Regions of the rat brain thought to subserve aspects of spatial learning, including the hippocampus, have also been shown to be affected by sex hormones (Juraska, 1991; Roof & Havens, 1992; Williams & Meck, 1991). In rhesus monkeys, androgens present in the prenatal or postnatal periods affect learning abilities that show sex differences as well as the maturation of the cortical regions subserving these abilities (Bachevalier & Hagger, 1991; Clark & Goldman-Rakic, 1989).

With respect to activational effects in other species, there is now a large literature showing that learning in female rodents varies in association with changes in hormones caused by: (1) normal cycling; (2) declines due to ageing; and (3) experimental manipulations in young and old adulthood. For example, long-term administration of oestrogen and progesterone has been found to improve performance on a spatial memory task in aged ovariectomized rats (Gibbs, 2000), whereas acute administration of oestrogen and progesterone has been found to impair performance on the Morris water maze in young rats (Chesler & Juraska, 2000). Some of these cognitive changes reflect hormonally induced synaptic changes in the brain, especially the hippocampus (Woolley & McEwen, 1994). Similar effects have been observed in primates. For example, peri- and post-menopausal monkeys were found to be significantly impaired on a delayed response task compared to both age-matched premenopausal and young females, and higher oestrogen metabolite levels were associated with better performance, as reflected in fewer trials to reach criterion and increased accuracy (Roberts, Gilardi, Lasley, & Rapp, 1997).

Thus, studies in other species provide compelling evidence that sex hormones affect various aspects of behaviour, including learning and memory. It is, therefore, reasonable to expect that such effects would be present in humans too.

Methods for studying human cognitive effects of sex hormones

It is obviously not possible to manipulate hormones in people, but several excellent methods are available to study the cognitive effects of sex hormones in human beings. In this area, as in all areas of science, each method has its limitations, and conclusions depend on convergence of evidence across methods.

In humans, much of the evidence for the behavioural effects of early (organizing) hormones comes from individuals exposed to unusually high or low sex hormones as a result of genetic disease (such as congenital adrenal hyperplasia and Turner's syndrome) or maternal ingestion of drugs (such as diethylstilboestrol, DES). In recent years, studies of variations in prenatal hormones within the typical range have provided important converging evidence for studies in clinical populations. These paradigms include studies of females with a male co-twin, who are thought to be exposed to high average levels of testosterone by virtue of sharing a uterine environment with a male, and studies of children for whom prenatal testosterone levels were known because they were assessed in amniotic fluid at 14–16 weeks of gestation.

Evidence for the behavioural effects of activational hormones in adolescence and adulthood comes primarily from normal populations, taking advantage of naturally occurring variations in hormones to study their behavioural effects. These variations occur within individuals, such as across the menstrual cycle and with menopause, and across individuals, such as men and women taking hormone replacement therapy compared with those who are not.

Which aspects of cognition?

Studies in other species indicate that sex hormones are most likely to affect behaviours that show sex differences. Therefore, most studies of cognitive effects of sex hormones have focused on aspects of cognitive function that show sex differences. On average, males are better than females at spatial orientation and visualization, throwing accuracy (targeting), mechanical knowledge, and mathematical reasoning, whereas females are better than males at verbal fluency, verbal learning and memory, emotional perception, fine motor skills, and perceptual speed (Bleecker, Bolla-Wilson, Agnew, & Meyers, 1988; Halpern, 2000; Kimura, 1999; Maccoby & Jacklin, 1974; Plomin & Foch, 1981). The largest cognitive sex differences (0.75 to 1.0 standard deviations) are seen on measures of three-dimensional spatial rotational ability (e.g. Linn & Petersen, 1985; Vandenberg & Kuse, 1978), with small to moderate-sized differences in other aspects of cognition (see Halpern, 2000; Kimura, 1999, for reviews). Studies that demonstrate cognitive effects of sex hormones have usually measured these abilities.

There has been much interest in delineating the neural substrates of these cognitive sex differences. Initial studies have been directed towards documenting sex differences in the brain, and it is likely that future studies will attempt to determine how these brain differences underlie behavioural sex differences, and how they are affected by sex steroid hormones. This work follows logically from studies in other species, in which a substantial number of brain sex differences have been described and related to behaviour and to exposure to sex steroid hormones, as mentioned above. Various sex differences have been reported in human brain structure and function, although this area is not without controversy (for a review, see Resnick & Maki, 1999). In terms of structure, for example, the splenium of the corpus callosum has been reported to be wider and more bulbous in females than in males (de Lacoste-Utamsing & Holloway, 1982), the relative size of the language areas has been reported to be larger in females than in males (Harasty, Double, Halliday, Kril, & McRitchie, 1997), and females have been reported to have greater neuronal density than males in regions of the temporal lobe known to subserve language functions (Witelson, Glezer, & Kigar, 1995). Functional sex differences have been observed with brain imaging techniques while subjects are performing simple cognitive tasks. For example, during the processing of rhymes, females have been reported to activate both left and right inferior frontal gyrus regions, whereas males activate only the left (Shaywitz et al., 1995).

Sex differences in cerebral hemispheric specialization (lateralization) have also been suggested to underlie sex differences in cognition. There are sex differences in perceptual asymmetries, although they are small and there is some controversy about their exact nature (Bryden, 1982; Wisniewski, 1998). For example, males are more likely than are females to demonstrate a right-ear advantage on verbal dichotic listening tests and a right visual-field bias on language tasks. Left-handedness, which is generally associated with reduced lateralization for language, is slightly more common in males than in females (Bryden, 1982).

Sex differences in cognition will eventually be tied to sex differences in the brain, and many of these will be found to be organized and activated by sex hormones. Therefore, some investigations of hormonal influences on cognition have included assessments of brain regions that have shown sex differences (such as the corpus callosum) or that subserve abilities that show sex differences (such as the parietal lobe, because of its role in spatial ability), or assessments of lateralization.

EVIDENCE FOR COGNITIVE EFFECTS OF ORGANIZATIONAL HORMONES: STUDIES IN CLINICAL CONDITIONS AND NORMAL SAMPLES

Some aspects of cognition in childhood, adolescence, and adulthood are affected by sex hormones present very early in development, in prenatal life. The evidence is clearest for spatial ability, which appears to be facilitated by moderate levels of prenatal androgens. The evidence for cognitive effects of early oestrogens is not as clear.

Prenatal androgens

Evidence from endocrine disorders. Evidence that prenatal androgens act to organize the brain to subserve later cognition comes from several sources. The primary evidence is from females with congenital adrenal hyperplasia (CAH) who, because of a genetic disease, produce high levels of adrenal androgens beginning early in gestation and continuing throughout gestation. Diagnosis is usually made neonatally, and treatment with corticosteroids normalizes androgen levels (for reviews, see Pang, 1997; Speiser, 2001). Because females with CAH are exposed to high levels of androgens during early development, but relatively normal androgen levels postnatally with good treatment, they provide a valuable opportunity to study the human behavioural effects of prenatal androgens. If cognitive sex differences in the general population are affected by the concentration of prenatal androgen present during early development, then females with CAH would be expected to have differential cognitive enhancements and reductions. Compared with comparison females, they should have better spatial, mechanical, and mathematical abilities and worse memory, perceptual speed, and verbal fluency. (The best comparison group is their sisters, who provide a control for general genetic and environmental background.)

Hypothesized cognitive effects of prenatal androgens have been confirmed in two studies. Females with CAH scored higher than their unaffected female relatives on tests of spatial ability in adolescence and young adulthood (Resnick, Berenbaum, Gottesman, & Bouchard, 1986) and in childhood (ages 8 to 12) (Hampson, Rovet, & Altmann, 1998). The cognitive advantage was unique to spatial ability: female patients and controls had similar overall intelligence and similar (or lower) scores on other cognitive abilities. Other studies failing to find enhanced spatial ability in females with CAH relative to control females used tests that do not show sex differences and had limited statistical power (for review, see Berenbaum, 2001). It is not clear whether prenatal androgens also inhibit female-typical abilities. The single finding of reduced perceptual speed in girls with CAH (Hampson et al., 1998) requires replication, especially because the reduction was also observed in boys with CAH and there was not the expected sex difference (female superiority) in control children. In addition, no such differences in perceptual speed were observed across multiple measures in the adolescents and adults studied by Resnick et al. (Resnick et al., 1986).

There is very little information about the effects of early androgens on other aspects of cognitive abilities. It will be interesting to study whether females with CAH have abilities that are male-typical in other ways, for example, whether, compared with unaffected females, they have lower verbal memory and fine motor skills, and higher mathematical reasoning ability. These studies will be challenging, however, because sex differences in some of these abilities are smaller than those in spatial ability, so that large samples will be necessary to detect any effects of early hormones.

CAH does not provide a perfect test of the behavioural effects of prenatal androgens, because the disease affects other hormones and because the girls have virilized genitalia that might elicit social responses affecting behaviour. Indirect evidence suggests that these factors do not account for behavioural differences between CAH females and their relatives (see Berenbaum, 2000; Resnick, 1982 for detailed discussion), but it is important to seek confirmation of the findings in females with CAH in other research samples.

One such confirmation comes from another endocrine population. Spatial ability is lower in males with low levels of androgens due to idiopathic hypogonadotrophic hypogonadism (IHH) than in control males (Hier & Crowley, 1982). Interpretation of these results is somewhat complicated by lack of information about the precise timing of the androgen reduction in males with IHH. Nevertheless, three pieces of evidence suggest that the decrease in spatial ability results from reduced androgens early in development: (1) spatial ability has been reported to correlate with testicular volume; (2) spatial ability does not improve with androgen replacement in males with IHH; and (3) spatial ability is not reduced in males with acquired (late-onset) hypogonadism (Hier & Crowley, 1982).

Evidence from non-clinical samples. Given the limitations of studies in clinical populations, it is important to note that results from CAH and IHH have been confirmed in two groups of individuals without hormone abnormalities. First, females with a male co-twin were reported to have higher spatial ability than females with a female co-twin (Cole-Harding, Morstad, & Wilson, 1988). This finding has been interpreted to reflect the effects of prenatal testosterone exposure from the male co-twin, following studies in rodents showing that females whose uterine position is between two males are behaviourally masculinized compared to females who are between two females (Clark & Galef, 1998; vom Saal, Clark, Galef, Drickamer, & Vandenbergh, 1998). Nevertheless, it is not possible to exclude the alternative explanation that enhanced spatial ability might result from sharing the postnatal social and physical environment with a brother. Second, speed of mental rotation in 7-year-old girls was positively associated with their prenatal testosterone levels, assessed in amniotic fluid at 14–16 weeks of gestation (Grimshaw, Sitarenios, & Finegan, 1995).

Neural substrates of cognitive effects of prenatal androgens. It is currently unclear what neural substrates mediate androgen effects on spatial ability, although this is an area of active investigation. Two preliminary studies of brain structure in patients with CAH have not shown them to be different from controls (D. Merke, personal communication; Plante, Bollek, Binkiewicz, & Erly, 1996).

There are several studies of lateralization in patients with CAH. Consistent with an androgen effect on handedness, females with CAH have been reported to be more "left-biased" than their sisters (Nass et al., 1987). It is unclear whether females with CAH are actually more likely than their sisters to be left-handed, or to have weaker right-hand preference, given the way that handedness was assessed. It has been difficult to replicate this finding (Helleday, Siwers, Ritzen, & Hugdahl, 1994; Resnick, 1982), perhaps because expected group differences are likely to be small and most studies do not have large samples. Even apparent replications are difficult to interpret (Kelso, Nicholls, Warne, & Zacharin, 2000; Tirosh, Rod, Cohen, & Hochberg, 1993), because males and females were not considered separately.

Lateralization in patients with CAH has also been studied with measures of perceptual asymmetries. Results have been inconsistent, probably because studies do not have sufficient statistical power to detect what are likely to be small effects (Helleday et al., 1994; Kelso et al., 2000; for a review, see Wisniewski, 1998). Further, given that lateralization differences (sex differences and CAH-control female differences) are quite small, it is clear that differences in lateralization cannot account for differences in patterns of cognitive abilities. It is also important to note that the two different aspects of lateralization studied—handedness and cerebral hemispheric specialization—show opposite patterns of sex differences. Males are less lateralized in their handedness, but more lateralized in their hemispheric specialization (Bryden, 1982). This means that any relations between androgens, handedness, and brain asymmetry are complex.

Effects through aromatization? Studies in rodents suggest that androgens exert some of their masculinizing effects through conversion ("aromatization") to oestrogens in the brain. Interestingly, however, human behavioural masculinization does not appear to proceed that way. Two groups of individuals exposed to very high levels of oestrogens in the absence of high levels of androgens do not differ from typical individuals in cognition or other aspects of behaviour. The first group includes women whose mothers took DES to prevent miscarriage. DES is a synthetic oestrogen that has been shown to masculinize behaviour in rodents. In two studies, women with prenatal exposure to DES obtained scores that were not significantly different than those of their unexposed sisters on any aspect of cognition, including spatial orientation and visualization, and verbal fluency (Hines & Sandberg, 1996; Hines & Shipley, 1984). The second group with exposure to oestrogens includes individuals with complete androgen-insensitivity syndrome (AIS), who have a 46,XY (typical male) karyotype but, because of receptor defects, are unable to respond to the high (male-typical) levels of androgens they produce. Because androgens are necessary for sexual differentiation to proceed in a male direction, these individuals appear female and are reared as females. Nevertheless, because they have a Y chromosome and levels of androgens that are male-typical, they also have levels of oestrogens that are male-typical, as they are converted from androgens. Individuals with AIS, therefore, provide the best evidence about the role of aromatized oestrogens in human behaviour. The little data that exist suggest that they have a female-typical pattern of cognitive abilities (Imperato-McGinley, Pichardo, Gautier, Voyer, & Bryden, 1991). This is consistent with their insensitivity to androgen and female rearing and suggests that aromatized oestrogens do not affect human cognitive abilities, but there have been no studies using measures that show large sex differences, such as measures of three-dimensional spatial orientation.

Ovarian oestrogens early in development

Much of the development of female-typical characteristics does not require the presence of high levels of feminizing hormones (especially oestrogen from the ovaries), but occurs in the absence of high levels of masculinizing hormones (androgens). The limited role for ovarian oestrogen in early development probably relates to the need to protect the foetus from the high levels of oestrogens transmitted from the mother. Nevertheless, there has been increasing speculation about the importance of these oestrogens for complete female-typical brain and behavioural development, with suggestions that the organizational period for behavioural effects of oestrogens is later than that for androgens (Fitch & Denenberg, 1998).

Turner's syndrome. The cognitive effects of reduced oestrogens early in development can be assessed in females with Turner's syndrome, who have an abnormal sex chromosome complement and consequently abnormal sex hormones. Whereas typical females have a 46,XX karyotype, females with Turner's syndrome do not. Some females with Turner's syndrome have only one X-chromosome in all of their cells (45,X karyotype), some have one X chromosome in some cells and two X chromosomes in other cells (mosaic karyotype such as 45,X/46,XX), and still others have both X chromosomes, but one of them is abnormal. Although Turner's syndrome foetuses develop ovaries containing germ cells, they quickly lose those cells, so that by birth they often possess "streak gonads" incapable of ovarian hormone production (for a review, see Migeon, Berkovitz, & Brown, 1994). In the overwhelming majority of Turner's syndrome patients, oestrogen production is very low or absent, and life-long oestrogen replacement therapy is initiated in adolescence. Turner's syndrome has historically been used as an opportunity to study behavioural effects of reduced ovarian hormones early in development (organizational effects), but recent studies have also addressed behavioural effects of increasing oestrogens with treatment (activational effects).

Early reports of cognitive performance in Turner's syndrome erroneously concluded that patients were mentally retarded. It is now clear that they have specific cognitive deficits, particularly in visual spatial ability and executive function (see also Chapter 10). With respect to the former, females with Turner's syndrome on average exhibit verbal IQ considerably higher than non-verbal IQ (Money, 1964), and perform poorly on tasks of direction sense (Alexander, Walker, & Money, 1964), mental rotation (Money & Alexander, 1966; Rovet & Netley, 1980), drawing and object assembly (Alexander, Ehrhardt, & Money, 1966; McCauley, Kay, Ito, & Treder, 1987; Temple & Carney, 1995), spatially mediated motor tasks (Ross, Roeltgen, Feuillan, Kushner, & Cutler, 1998), and mathematics performance (Mazzocco, 1998) (for a review, see Rovet, 1990). Some spatial deficits have been related to the extent of X-chromosome mosaicism (Temple & Carney, 1995). The visuospatial deficits observed in Turner's syndrome have recently been mapped to a specific region of the X chromosome (Ross, Roeltgen, Kushner, Wei, & Zinn, 2000a). Indications of executive function deficits in females with Turner's syndrome include problems in attention and organization (Reiss, Mazzocco, Greenlaw, Freund, & Ross, 1995; Waber, 1979), adherence to rules (Money, 1973), behavioural inhibition (Skuse et al., 1997), and working memory (Berch, 1996; Buchanan, Pavlovic, & Rovet, 1998).

Some of the deficits in females with Turner's syndrome have been related to specific brain changes, both structural (as revealed through magnetic resonance imaging, MRI) and functional (as revealed through positron emission tomography, PET). In childhood and adolescence, girls with Turner's syndrome were found to have proportionately smaller parietal regions bilaterally, and a proportionately larger right parietal–occipital region than unrelated control girls

(Reiss et al., 1995). In young adulthood, females with Turner's syndrome were found to have smaller cerebral hemispheres, regions of the parietal–occipital area, diencephalon, and basal ganglia than unrelated control females (Murphy et al., 1993). Women with Turner's syndrome compared with controls were also found to have absolute values of brain glucose metabolism that were hypermetabolic in most brain regions, with the differences related to degree of chromosomal mosaicism (Murphy et al., 1997). Given some inconsistencies across studies, these results clearly require replication and elaboration, but the abnormalities in the right parietal region are consistent with the role of this region in visual spatial abilities, and the poor visual spatial performance of females with Turner's syndrome.

The cognitive deficits and brain changes found in females with Turner's syndrome have generally been interpreted to reflect decreased or absent ovarian hormone production early in development. However, few studies have documented the specific karyotype or endocrine history of the participants, and none has measured hormone levels at the time of testing. Further, there is evidence that some of the cognitive deficits in Turner's syndrome might also reflect the effects of continuing reductions in oestrogen levels later in development (activational effects). Treatment with oestrogen has been shown to improve several aspects of cognition in girls with Turner's syndrome, including non-verbal processing speed, motor function, and verbal and non-verbal memory (Ross et al., 1998; Ross, Roeltgen, Feuillan, Kushner, & Cutler, 2000b), but there is little evidence about oestrogen effects on spatial ability.

The fact that females with Turner's syndrome have a major chromosomal anomaly limits inferences about oestrogen contributions to the cognitive changes. Because the amount of the X-chromosome present correlates with production of ovarian hormones (Migeon et al., 1994), it is difficult to know whether cognition is affected directly by genes on the X chromosome or by ovarian hormones. Evidence for a direct genetic effect on spatial ability comes from a recent study showing that deletions in distal regions of the short arm of the X chromosome account for visuospatial deficits regardless of ovarian hormone status (Ross et al., 2000a). Further evidence for direct genetic effects on at least some of the cognitive deficits in Turner's syndrome comes from studies examining cognition in relation to the parental origin of the intact X chromosome. Girls with Turner's syndrome who inherited the single X chromosome from the mother ($45,X^m$) performed worse than those who inherited the X chromosome from the father ($45,X^p$) on tasks of social cognition, planning, behavioural inhibition (Skuse et al., 1997), and selected aspects of verbal memory (Bishop et al., 2000), but these intriguing results await replication. Because the endocrine milieu is presumed to be similar in $45,X^m$ and $45,X^p$ females, differences between them must reflect direct genetic effects.

In addition to decreased ovarian hormone production and an atypical karyotype, many patients with Turner's syndrome also have other physical abnormalities, such as problems with vision and hearing, kidney problems, cardiac problems, and hypertension. Some of these can limit physical activity in patients, which could inhibit development of visual spatial skills. This seems an unlikely explanation for cognitive deficits in Turner's syndrome, however, because other abilities not dependent on physical activity are also deficient in Turner's syndrome, and there is not good evidence from other clinical conditions or from normal individuals that spatial ability depends on physical ability.

Overall, the cognitive data from females with Turner's syndrome provide little direct support for organizational effects of ovarian hormones early in development, although additional cognitive studies in young girls with Turner's syndrome would be informative if they included measures of hormone status. Instead, it appears that at least some of the deficits in spatial ability and executive function in Turner's syndrome may relate directly to genes on the X chromosome, and that deficits in motor and memory functions are related directly to circulating ovarian oestrogens in young girls. Because the cognitive effects of oestrogen treatment have been studied in young girls (preadolescence and adolescence) treated for only short periods of time, it is unclear whether the cognitive changes represent temporary brain changes associated with circulating oestrogen or whether they reflect permanent changes to the brain during a sensitive period. It remains to be determined whether oestrogen treatment also reverses deficits in adult women with Turner's syndrome, and whether the changes occur only during active treatment.

EVIDENCE FOR COGNITIVE EFFECTS OF ACTIVATIONAL HORMONES: COGNITION IS ASSOCIATED WITH HORMONAL VARIATIONS IN ADULTS

As already described, organizational effects of sex steroid hormones on later behaviour have been documented in a variety of mammalian species, including human beings. In addition to these organizational effects, hormones also have activational effects on behaviour during adolescence and adulthood. Activational effects most often result in relatively transient changes in behaviour and neurophysiology, which occur only when the steroids are at a particular concentration. As the steroid concentration returns to its prior level, the behavioural and physiological effects subside (Arnold & Breedlove, 1985; Breedlove, 1992; McEwen, 1981). Activational effects of hormones are often dependent upon earlier exposure to organizational effects of sex steroids (Breedlove, 1992). Whereas some organizational effects of hormones are thought to act through permanent modification of brain structure and neural circuitry, activational effects of hormones can involve temporary modulation of neurotransmitter concentrations and receptors (Arnold & Breedlove, 1985; McEwen, 1981), neuronal microstructure (Gould, Woolley, Frankfurt, & McEwen, 1990; Woolley, Gould, Frankfurt, & McEwen, 1990), or characteristics of the cell membrane (McEwen, 1991).

Several paradigms have been used to investigate the activational effects of sex hormones on human cognition. These include studies of cyclic variation, such as menstrual cycle variation in ovarian steroids in women and seasonal fluctuations in testosterone in men, investigations of the correlations between circulating concentrations of hormones and patterns of cognitive abilities, and cognitive changes in response to exogenous administration of steroid hormones, such as oestrogen replacement therapy in postmenopausal women and treatment with testosterone or dehydroepiandrosterone (DHEA) in older men. Most of these studies emphasize cognitive abilities for which sex differences have been reported.

Oestrogens in women

Cognitive changes associated with menstrual cycle variation in premenopausal women. Oestrogen and progesterone concentrations fluctuate systematically during the normal menstrual cycle. During menses or the early follicular phase, both oestrogen and progesterone concentrations are low. Oestrogen increases and peaks in the preovulatory phase, when progesterone levels remain low. By contrast, both oestrogen and progesterone concentrations are high during the midluteal phase of the cycle. Early studies (Broverman et al., 1981) showed increased performance on simple repetitive or "automatized" tasks, such as speed of colour naming, and decreased performance on tasks requiring perceptual restructuring, such as embedded figures, during the preovulatory phase (oestrogen peak) compared with the luteal phase (progesterone peak). Recent studies of menstrual-cycle-related cognitive variation have emphasized cognitive tasks for which sex differences have been reported. For example, Hampson and Kimura (1988) demonstrated relative increases in speeded motor coordination and decreases in spatial ability during the midluteal high oestrogen (and progesterone) phase compared with the menses, when oestrogen and progesterone are low. A second study (Hampson, 1990a), using a comprehensive battery of cognitive tests, yielded a similar pattern of findings, although some comparisons for individual tests did not reach conventional levels of statistical significance. Performance on tests typically favouring females, such as articulatory skills, verbal fluency, speeded manual coordination, and perceptual speed, was higher during the midluteal phase than during the menses. By contrast, performance on tests favouring males, such as spatial ability and some types of deductive reasoning, was higher during the menses than during the midluteal phase.

Other studies have provided results consistent with effects reported by Hampson. Three-dimensional spatial rotational ability has been reported to be lower during the luteal phase than during the menses (Silverman & Phillips, 1993). Delayed visual memory performance was found to be better during the luteal phase than during the menses, but no significant menstrual cycle effects were found on verbal memory, measured by paragraph recall and paired associate learning (Phillips & Sherwin, 1992).

Interpretation of these findings is limited by the fact both oestrogen and progesterone are high during the luteal phase when assessments were done. Hampson (1990b) addressed this limitation by comparing performance during the menses with performance during the preovulatory phase when oestrogen is high but progesterone is low. Consistent with her prior results, performance on tests of articulatory and fine motor skills was enhanced and spatial ability was reduced during the high oestrogen preovulatory phase compared with the low oestrogen menstrual phase. These findings provide support for an oestrogen effect on menstrual-cycle-related cognitive variation. Moreover, oestrogen-related effects on the neural circuitry associated with some cognitive tasks were suggested by Hampson's observation of a greater right ear (left hemisphere) advantage on a dichotic listening test during the preovulatory versus menstrual phase. Although men typically show greater asymmetry on these tasks than women, Hampson speculated that high levels of oestrogen might inhibit specific regions of the right hemisphere, resulting in the increased left hemispheric advantage.

Menstrual-cycle-related fluctuations in cognitive ability, including spatial memory (Postma, Winkel, Tuiten, & van Honk, 1999) and cerebral asymmetry for verbal (Altemus, Wexler, & Boulis, 1989; Chiarello, McMahon, & Schaefer, 1989; Heister, Landis, Regard, & Schroeder-Heister, 1989; Sanders & Wenmoth, 1998) and musical tasks (Sanders & Wenmoth, 1998), have also been reported by other investigators, but most of the latter studies relied on self-reported staging of menstrual phase rather than direct assessment of hormone levels as performed in the majority of the studies detailed above. Nevertheless, the results of these studies are generally consistent with the findings described above and indicate menstrual-cycle-related variability in cognitive performance and the neural circuitry associated with performance on specific cognitive tasks.

Circulating oestrogens and cognition in young women. There is only limited evidence for associations between circulating concentrations of oestrogens and cognitive functioning in adult women. Nyborg (1983) hypothesized that the association between oestradiol concentration and spatial ability would show an inverted U relationship, with intermediate levels of oestrogen associated with optimal levels of performance across men and women. Consistent with this hypothesis, scores on the Space Relations test have been found to be highest for women with moderate serum oestradiol concentrations, measured during the early follicular phase (menses), whereas lower scores were found in women with both relatively low and high oestradiol levels (Hampson, 1990b).

Circulating oestrogens and cognition in older women. There have also been several attempts to examine associations between circulating oestrogens and cognition in postmenopausal women, with mixed results. Difficulties in these studies include low levels of endogenous oestradiol, often at the limits of the sensitivity of the assay, assessment of total versus bioavailable hormone, possible confounds of prior and current hormone replacement therapy, and inclusion of cognitively impaired individuals in some samples. For example, high oestradiol levels were associated with better delayed verbal memory and retrieval efficiency, whereas low levels were associated with better immediate and delayed visual memory in a sample of 39 normal elderly women, including past and current users of hormone therapy (Drake et al., 2000), but no significant associations were found between oestradiol or oestrone and scores on 12 neuropsychological measures in 393 older women who were not receiving hormone therapy, although the sample included women who were cognitively impaired (Barrett-Connor & Kritz-Silverstein, 1993).

Cognitive effects of oestrogen replacement therapy. Hormone replacement therapy, including oestrogen replacement (ERT) and combination oestrogen and progestin replacement (HRT) are increasingly prescribed during menopause for the relief of vasomotor and urogenital symptoms, such as hot flushes and vaginal dryness, and for the prevention of osteoporosis in postmenopausal women. Recent reports that ERT/HRT might decrease the risk for Alzheimer's disease and protect against age-associated memory loss have led to a surge in research on the effects of oestrogen on cognitive and brain aging in postmenopausal women.

Results of a meta-analysis of studies conducted through 1997 (Yaffe, Sawaya, Lieberburg, & Grady, 1998) indicated that ERT/HRT was associated with a 29 per cent reduction in the risk for Alzheimer's disease across studies. Moreover, the two studies involving *prospective* assessment of ERT and dementia status revealed more than a 50 per cent reduction in the risk for Alzheimer's disease (Kawas et al., 1997; Tang et al., 1996). In one of these studies, there was evidence of a dose–response effect, with longer duration of use associated with greater risk reduction (Tang et al., 1996). Thus, these observational studies, where women choose themselves whether to take hormone therapy, provide evidence that ERT and HRT can offer some protection against a diagnosis of Alzheimer's disease. However, the results of recent randomized clinical trials (Henderson et al., 2000; Mulnard et al., 2000; Wang et al., 2000) examining oestrogen therapy as a treatment for women who already have Alzheimer's disease do not support a beneficial effect in women who have already been diagnosed with the disease.

There is a growing body of scientific literature on the effects of oestrogen on memory and other cognitive functions in postmenopausal women who are free of dementia. A number of small, randomized clinical trials (Sherwin, 1988, 1997) provide evidence that ERT protects against cognitive decline, most consistently in verbal memory, following surgical menopause (hysterectomy and bilateral oophorectomy). A recent intervention trial in 37 elderly women suggests that ERT effects on memory might also hold in women after natural menopause (Duka, Tasker, & McGowan, 2000). Administration of transdermal oestradiol enhanced visual memory, but not executive functioning, after a 3-week treatment period.

Observational studies including larger numbers of women also support the role of oestrogen in protecting against age-associated cognitive decline. Compared with women not receiving hormone replacement, those on ERT/HRT show better memory, with respect to paragraph recall (Kampen & Sherwin, 1994), encoding and retrieval of a word list (Maki, Zonderman, & Resnick, 2000; Verghese et al., 2000), recall of proper names from visual face cues (Robinson, Friedman, Marcus, Tinklenberg, & Yesavage, 1994), and figural memory (Resnick, Metter, & Zonderman, 1997). In two longitudinal within-subject studies, ERT/HRT was found to protect against age-associated declines in figural (Resnick et al., 1997) and verbal memory (Jacobs et al., 1998). In contrast to the positive findings from a number of observational studies, results of two large-scale observational studies reported no cross-sectional differences between ERT users and non-users (Barrett-Connor & Kritz-Silverstein, 1993; Szklo et al., 1996). It is notable, however, that the verbal memory tasks in both of these studies required subjects to reach a criterion of performance prior to recall testing, which eliminates differences in initial encoding and might mask potentially important differences between groups. In a third large-scale observational study (Grodstein et al., 2000), differences between ERT/HRT users and non-users were observed on a measure of semantic memory (category fluency), but not on paragraph recall or word list memory. However, cognitive assessments in this study were conducted by telephone, and hormone status was ascertained through biennial reports rather than concurrently with cognitive testing.

The results of several neuroimaging studies provide additional support for an effect of ERT/HRT on memory in postmenopausal women. Women who received hormone therapy showed different patterns of brain activation during performance of tasks assessing verbal and figural delayed recognition memory (Resnick, Maki, Golski, Kraut, & Zonderman, 1998) and working memory (Shaywitz et al., 1999). Furthermore, ERT/HRT users compared with non-users showed greater longitudinal increases over a 2-year interval in relative cerebral blood flow in the hippocampus and other mesial temporal lobe regions important in memory functioning (Maki & Resnick, 2000).

Although the results just described suggest that ERT/HRT protects against Alzheimer's disease and age-associated memory decline, the available data suffer from several limitations. All studies examining ERT/HRT in prevention of Alzheimer's disease and the data from larger scale studies of age-associated memory change in non-demented postmenopausal women derive from observational studies, which compare women who choose themselves whether or not to take hormone therapy. These results are limited by the "healthy user" bias, because HRT users tend to be healthier overall and have higher levels of education. Although there have been a number of placebo-controlled randomized trials of ERT/HRT and cognition in non-demented women, these have included only small numbers of subjects and most involve women undergoing surgical menopause. There are several ongoing large-scale randomized trials examining the cognitive effects of ERT/HRT and more definitive conclusions await the completion of these trials. For example, the role of ERT/HRT in the prevention of Alzheimer's disease is being examined in the Women's Health Initiative Memory Study (WHIMS; Shumaker et al., 1998), and the role of ERT/HRT in the reduction of age-associated memory change is being assessed in the Women's Health Initiative Study of Cognitive Aging (WHISCA).

Androgens in Men and Women

Circulating androgens and cognition in young adults. A common approach to investigating possible testosterone effects on adult cognitive performance has been to relate circulating hormone levels measured in blood or saliva to scores on standardized neuropsychological or cognitive tests. Although there have been conflicting findings among studies using this approach, several studies have reported that an optimal level of testosterone might facilitate spatial cognitive processing. For example, males with lower testosterone were reported to perform better on measures of spatial/mathematical abilities than males with high testosterone, whereas females with higher testosterone were reported to outperform lower-testosterone females on the same measures (Gouchie & Kimura, 1991). Subsequent studies (Moffat & Hampson, 1996; Neave, Menaged, & Weightman, 1999) reported a similar inverted U-shaped relationship between testosterone and spatial cognition in samples of young adult males and females. It is important to note that inverted quadratic relationships between testosterone and spatial cognition were observed only when males and females were included in the same analysis. This suggests an optimum level of testosterone for spatial processing, which might be near the low end of the normal adult male distribution.

Not all studies investigating the relationship between circulating testosterone and spatial ability have observed non-linear relationships (Christiansen & Knussmann, 1987; Silverman, Kastuk, Choi, & Phillips, 1999). It seems likely that some of the inconsistencies across studies result from different operational definitions of spatial ability. Spatial tests can differ considerably in their processing demands and factor analytic studies demonstrate that different tests of spatial ability load on separate spatial factors (Borich & Bauman, 1972; Ekstrom, French, & Harman, 1976). It is possible that testosterone or other steroids are selectively related to different aspects of visuospatial processing.

Although males do not show monthly hormonal cyclicity characteristic of females, testosterone concentrations do vary throughout the day and over the course of the year, allowing an assessment of cognitive changes associated with cyclicity in males. Male testosterone concentrations show a marked circadian rhythm, with testosterone concentration peaking in the early morning hours and declining sharply thereafter, with a trough approximately 12h later (Dabbs, 1990; Nieschlag, 1974). Taking advantage of this diurnal variation, Moffat and Hampson (1996) studied cognition in adult males and females assigned to either early morning or late morning sessions. The diurnal change in testosterone concentrations was verified by radioimmunoassay. Males tested in early morning when testo-sterone concentrations were high performed more poorly on the spatial tests than males tested later, when testosterone concentrations were lower; females showed the reverse pattern. These findings were specific to the spatial cognitive tests; verbal performance showed no diurnal fluctuation. Although these findings require replication, they suggest that spatial performance changes dynamically over a relatively short time span, in concert with the diurnal fluctuation in testosterone.

Testosterone concentrations in men also exhibit circannual variability, with testosterone levels higher in autumn than in spring (Bellastella et al., 1986; Meriggiola, Noonan, Paulsen, & Bremner, 1996). Consistent with other work on relations between testosterone and spatial ability described above, spatial performance in men was found to be better in the spring, when testosterone concentrations were lower than in the autumn, when testosterone levels were higher (Kimura & Hampson, 1994). Once again, this effect was specific to the spatial tasks, with other cognitive measures showing no seasonal fluctuations. In contrast to the significant seasonal variation observed in men, women showed no seasonal fluctuation in cognitive scores. Although a number of other hormonal and non-hormonal factors change as a function of time of day and season, they are unlikely to account for the findings, given the specificity to the spatial cognitive tests, the divergence of the pattern of results in male and female subjects, and the consistency of results across designs.

Cognitive effects of age-related androgen loss in men and women. Age-associated declines in testosterone concentrations are well established, with testosterone decreasing by as much as 50 per cent from age 30 to age 80 (Lamberts, van den Beld, & van der Lely, 1997). This suggests that the cumulative loss of androgens with age might be partially responsible for the well-established decline in certain cognitive abilities with age. Conversely, replacement of testosterone might result in recovery of cognitive function. Two recent population-based epidemiological studies suggest that endogenous testosterone might continue to influence cognitive function in elderly subjects. In one study (Barrett-Connor, Goodman-Gruen, & Patay, 1999), androgen levels and neuropsychological performance were measured in 547 men between the ages of 59 and 89 years. Higher testosterone concentrations predicted better performance on measures of short-term memory and concentration; spatial abilities were not measured. Non-linear relationships were also found in which moderately high testosterone levels were associated with better mental control and improved long-term verbal memory among men. In thc second study, the relationship between endogenous steroid levels and cognitive performance was investigated in 383 women, aged 55–89 years (Barrett-Connor & Goodman-Gruen, 1999). Women with higher scores on measures of mental status had significantly higher total and bioavailable testosterone levels. These data suggest that testosterone levels might modulate neuropsychological performance in elderly women and underscore the importance of undertaking androgen intervention studies in women as well as men. It is unclear whether androgen has a more general cognitive effect in the elderly than in young individuals, because the relevant studies have not been done, that is, assessing memory in young adults and spatial ability in older adults, with one exception (Janowsky, Oviatt, & Orwoll, 1994). Thus, differences across studies might reflect age differences in the action of testosterone or a methodological artifact.

In addition to androgen loss as a result of testosterone depletion, both males and females show a marked age-related decline in DHEA. This steroid, secreted by the adrenal cortex, can be converted to oestradiol and testosterone, and it thus might serve as an important storehouse of both androgens and oestrogens. DHEA has recently received considerable scientific attention due in part to its availability as an over-the-counter food supplement. Elderly individuals currently self-administer DHEA because of its reputed anti-ageing physiological and psychological effects. Empirical support for possible cognitive effects of DHEA comes primarily from animal studies in which DHEA enhanced long-term memory (Roberts, Bologa, Flood, & Smith, 1987), increased hippocampal long-term potentiation (Yoo, Harris, & Dubrovsky, 1996), and reduced neuronal death in mouse embryo brain cells (Bologa, Sharma, & Roberts, 1987).

Nevertheless, epidemiological studies of the association between DHEA concentrations and cognitive status in elderly people have been largely negative. DHEA levels have not been found to relate to various indicators of memory, fluency, or motor functioning in men or women (Barrett-Connor & Edelstein, 1994; Yaffe et al., 1998), nor to cognitive change across time (Yaffe et al., 1998). In the most comprehensive study to date, 883 men were studied longitudinally for an average of 12 years, with assessment of both serum DHEA and cognitive abilities every 2 years (Moffat et al., 2000). This design allowed the quantification of long-term change in DHEA concentrations in direct temporal association with change in a wide variety of neuropsychological outcome measures, including verbal and visual memory, mental status, and visuomotor scanning and attention. Cognition was unrelated to DHEA: neither long-term mean DHEA concentration nor rate of change of DHEA predicted cognitive status or cognitive decline; there were no cognitive differences between men with the highest and lowest DHEA quartiles (which differed in DHEA concentration by more than a factor of 4 for a mean duration of 12 years). Current evidence from epidemiological studies suggests that although both DHEA concentrations and neuropsychological performance clearly decline with age, these changes appear to be independent.

Cognitive effects of androgen replacement in men and women. A drawback of correlational studies is the difficulty in confirming that testosterone concentration *per se* causes observed cognitive effects. Testosterone replacement therapy (TRT), although still much less common that the corollary ERT/HRT in women, is becoming more common and testosterone replacement trials examining cognitive performance in older men are currently underway. In a double-blind, placebo-controlled study, the effect of TRT on cognitive performance was examined in older androgen-depleted men (Janowsky et al., 1994). Men who received testosterone had selectively enhanced WAIS-R block design scores compared with men who had received placebo, demonstrating that TRT in older men might enhance spatial/constructional skills. Testosterone supplementation was reported not to affect verbal or visual memory in a small sample of elderly men; unfortunately, spatial measures were not included (Sih et al., 1997). In a study of working memory performance in men randomly assigned to receive either placebo or a month-long regimen of testosterone supplementation (Janowsky, Chavez, & Orwoll, 2000), men who received testosterone supplementation showed a marked reduction in working memory errors following testosterone treatment compared with placebo-treated men. Most recently, Cherrier et al. (2001) investigated cognitive performance in 25 healthy older men (aged 50–80) who were randomized to receive either weekly intramuscular injections of testosterone or placebo. Relative to baseline performance and to placebo, testosterone injection improved spatial memory (route learning), spatial ability (block construction) and verbal memory. To understand more clearly the cognitive effects of testosterone, additional TRT studies are required in both men and women, preferably using randomized, placebo-controlled experimental designs.

There have also been some intervention studies examining possible cognitive effects of DHEA supplementation. Confirming the correlational studies, these intervention trials have not provided strong evidence that DHEA enhances cognition. In two double-blind cross-over, placebo-controlled clinical trials examining the cognitive effects of DHEA replacement therapy (Wolf, Naumann, Hellhammer, & Kirschbaum, 1998a; Wolf et al., 1997), supplementation of 50mg/day for 2 weeks failed to have any cognitive-enhancing effects in either men or women. Because DHEA might have antiglucocorticoid actions, and hence its beneficial effects might be observed only under conditions of stress, there has been assessment of DHEA supplementation on cognitive function following the application of a stressor (Wolf, Kudielka, Hellhammer, Hellhammer, & Kirschbaum, 1998b). Under stress, attention/concentration was found to be enhanced, and recall of previously learned material to be impaired, with DHEA compared with placebo (Wolf et al., 1998b). Although current evidence from placebo-controlled trials of DHEA supplementation does not support its cognition-enhancing role, it should be noted that these clinical trials sampled only a limited range of cognitive abilities in relatively small samples of subjects over short durations, so a large placebo-controlled clinical trial will be needed to evaluate conclusively the efficacy of exogenous DHEA supplementation on preventing cognitive decline with ageing.

The results from various studies, using different methodologies provide evidence that circulating androgens exert a detectable effect on cognition in both men and women. Cumulatively, these studies suggest that, in young adults, moderate levels of testosterone are optimal for the performance of some visuospatial cognitive tests. Among elderly men, who have already experienced age-related testosterone depletion, testosterone loss can be associated with cognitive decline, and testosterone replacement can be beneficial to spatial performance and working memory. Although earlier studies suggested that testosterone effects might be limited to spatial cognition (Gouchie & Kimura, 1991; Janowsky et al., 1994; Moffat & Hampson, 1996), recent epidemiological studies and clinical trials in both men and women demonstrate that non-spatial cognitive performance might also be associated with endogenous or exogenous testosterone, at least among elderly subjects. However, neither high endogenous DHEA concentrations among the elderly, nor DHEA replacement, has been associated with improved cognitive function. It is not clear why DHEA has not been shown to affect cognition, whereas both testosterone and oestrogen have, although some speculations can be made. No studies have measured or administered DHEA and testosterone in the same individuals, so direct comparisons are not possible. It has also been suggested that the DHEA/cortisol ratio might be a more critical measure than DHEA levels alone (Hechter, Grossman, & Chatterton, 1997), considering the antiglucocorticoid effect of DHEA observed in rodents (Kalimi, Shafagoj, Loria, Padgett, & Regelson, 1994). Moreover, although a DHEA-activated receptor has been identified in the rodent liver, to our knowledge no DHEA receptor has been identified in the brain of any mammal (Wolf & Kirschbaum, 1999). This suggests that DHEA could exert cognitive effects only through conversion to other substances, or via interactions with specific neurotransmitter systems (Wolf & Kirschbaum, 1999), and might, therefore, be a less direct measure of active steroid levels than either testosterone or oestradiol. The understanding of the physiological mechanisms of DHEA action in the human CNS remains preliminary.

SUMMARY

The evidence reviewed above makes it clear that sex hormones have important effects on cognition throughout the lifespan. Future work in this area is likely to reveal important information about neural mechanisms underlying cognitive development and cognitive decline.

1. Spatial ability is enhanced by moderate levels of androgens at several points in development. The importance of androgen during prenatal development is suggested by studies in both endocrine and normal populations. The continuing importance of androgens to spatial ability in adulthood is suggested by studies of normal variations both within and across individuals.
2. There is some suggestion that androgens facilitate additional aspects of cognition later in life, including working memory, but additional experimental studies are necessary.

3. Memory and verbal fluency are enhanced by circulating oestrogens, beginning at least in adolescence and probably earlier. The importance of oestrogen during adulthood is documented in studies of normal variations, especially menstrual cycle variations, and hormone replacement in menopausal women. Studies of oestrogen treatment in females with Turner's syndrome suggest that oestrogen is important for cognition even in childhood, but it is unclear whether that reflects temporary or permanent changes to the brain. Oestrogens also appear to facilitate cognition late in life, although additional experimental work is necessary to document the details and magnitude of these effects.
4. Studies of the cognitive effects of sex hormones can also provide opportunities for understanding the development of cognition *per se*. For example, cognitive developmentalists might differentiate aspects of spatial ability that are facilitated primarily by androgen-induced brain organization early in development from those that reflect ongoing androgen modulation of neural circuitry in adulthood.
5. The investigation of the effects of organizational and activational influences of sex hormones on cognition has advanced rapidly in the last decade and is likely to continue to do so in the near future. The nature, variety, and neural circuitry underlying the cognitive effects of sex hormones will undoubtedly be understood more fully in the coming decade with advances in cognitive psychology, neuropsychology and neuroimaging.

ACKNOWLEDGEMENTS

Preparation of this chapter was supported in part by National Institutes of Health grants HD19644 (SAB) and HD08544 (AW).

REFERENCES

Alexander, D., Walker, H.T., & Money, J. (1964). Studies in direction sense. I. Turner's syndrome. *Archives of General Psychiatry, 10*, 337–339.

Alexander, D., Ehrhardt, A.A., & Money, J. (1966). Defective figure drawing, geometric and human, in Turner's syndrome. *Journal of Nervous and Mental Disease, 142*, 161–167.

Altemus, M., Wexler, B.E., & Boulis, N. (1989). Changes in perceptual asymmetry with the menstrual cycle. *Neuropsychologia, 27*, 233–240.

Arnold, A.P., & Breedlove, S.M. (1985). Organizational and activational effects of sex steroids on brain and behavior: A reanalysis. *Hormones and Behavior, 19*, 469–498.

Arnold, A.P., & Gorski, R.A. (1984). Gonadal steroid induction of structural sex differences in the central nervous system. *Annual Review of Neuroscience, 7*, 413–442.

Bachevalier, J., & Hagger, C. (1991). Sex differences in the development of learning abilities in primates. *Psychoneuroendocrinology, 16*, 177–188.

Barrett-Connor, E., & Edelstein, S.L. (1994). A prospective study of dehydroepiandrosterone sulfate and cognitive function in an older population: The Rancho Bernardo Study. *Journal of the American Geriatric Society, 42*(4), 420–423.

Barrett-Connor, E., & Goodman-Gruen, D. (1999). Cognitive function and endogenous sex hormones in older women. *Journal of the American Geriatric Society, 47*(11), 1289–1293.

Barrett-Connor, E., Goodman-Gruen, D., & Patay, B. (1999). Endogenous sex hormones and cognitive function in older men. *Journal of Clinical Endocrinology and Metabolism, 84*(10), 3681–3685.

Barrett-Connor, E., & Kritz-Silverstein, D. (1993). Estrogen replacement therapy and cognitive function in older women. *Journal of the American Medical Association, 269*(20), 2637–2641.

Beatty, W.W. (1992). Gonadal hormones and sex differences in nonreproductive behaviors. In A.A. Gerall, H. Moltz, & I.L. Ward (Eds.), *Handbook of behavioral neurobiology, Vol 11, Sexual differentiation* (pp. 85–128). New York: Plenum.

Becker, J.B., Breedlove, S.M., & Crews, D. (Eds.) (1992). *Behavioral endocrinology*. Cambridge, MA: MIT Press.

Bellastella, A., Criscuolo, T., Sinisi, A.A., Iorio, S., Sinisi, A.M., Rinaldi, A. et al. (1986). Circannual variations of plasma testosterone, luteinizing hormone, follicle-stimulating hormone and prolactin in Klinefelter's syndrome. *Neuroendocrinology, 42*(2), 153–157.

Berch, D. (1996). Memory. In J. Rovet (Ed.), *Turner syndrome across the life span*. Toronto: Klein Graphics.

Berenbaum, S.A. (Ed.). (1998). Gonadal hormones and sex differences in behavior. *Developmental Neuropsychology, 14*, 175–441.

Berenbaum, S.A. (2000). Psychological outcome in congenital adrenal hyperplasia. In B. Stabler & B.B. Bercu (Eds.), *Therapeutic outcome of endocrine disorders: efficacy, innovation, and quality of life* (pp. 186–199). New York: Springer.

Berenbaum, S.A. (2001). Cognitive function in congenital adrenal hyperplasia. *Endocrinology and Metabolism Clinics of North America, 30*, 173–192.

Bishop, D.V.M., Canning, E., Elgar, K., Morris, E., Jacobs, P.A., & Skuse, D.H. (2000). Distinctive patterns of memory function in subgroups of females with Turner syndrome: Evidence for imprinted loci on the X-chromosome affecting neurodevelopment. *Neuropsychologia, 38*, 712–721.

Bleecker, M.L., Bolla-Wilson, K., Agnew, J., & Meyers, D.A. (1988). Age-related sex differences in verbal memory. *Journal of Clinical Psychology, 44*, 403–411.

Bologa, L., Sharma, J., & Roberts, E. (1987). Dehydroepiandrosterone and its sulfated derivative reduce neuronal death and enhance astrocytic differentiation in brain cell cultures. *Journal of Neuroscience Research, 17*(3), 225–234.

Borich, G., & Bauman, P. (1972). Convergent and discriminant validation of the French and Guilford and Zimmerman spatial orientation and spatial visualization factors. *Educational and Psychological Measurement, 32*, 1029–1033.

Breedlove, S. (1992). Sexual dimorphism in the vertebrate nervous system. *The Journal of Neuroscience, 12*, 4133–4142.

Breedlove, S.M. (1994). Sexual differentiation of the human nervous system. *Annual Review of Psychology, 45*, 389–418.

Broverman, D.M., Vogel, W., Klaiber, E.L., Majcher, D., Shea, D., & Paul, V. (1981). Changes in cognitive task performance across the menstrual cycle. *Journal of Comparative and Physiological Psychology, 95*(4), 646–654.

Bryden, M. (1982). *Laterality: Functional asymmetry in the intact brain.* New York: Academic Press.

Buchanan, L., Pavlovic, J., & Rovet, J. (1998). A reexamination of the visuospatial deficit in Turner syndrome: Contributions of working memory. *Developmental Neuropsychology, 14*, 341–367.

Cherrier, M.M., Asthana, S., Plymate, S., Bakes, L., Matsumoto, A.M., Peskind, E., et al. (2001). Testosterone supplementation improves spatial and verbal memory in healthy older men. *Neurology, 57*, 80–88.

Chesler, E.J., & Juraska, J.M. (2000). Acute administration of estrogen and progesterone impairs the acquisition of the spatial morris water maze in ovariectomized rats. *Hormones and Behavior, 38*, 234–242.

Chiarello, C., McMahon, M.A., & Schaefer, K. (1989). Visual cerebral lateralization over phases of the menstrual cycle: A preliminary investigation. *Brain and Cognition, 11*, 18–36.

Christiansen, K., & Knussmann, R. (1987). Sex hormones and cognitive functioning in men. *Neuropsychobiology, 18*(1), 27–36.

Clark, A.S., & Goldman-Rakic, P.S. (1989). Gonadal hormones influence the emergence of cortical function in nonhuman primates. *Behavioral Neuroscience, 103*, 1287–1295.

Clark, M.M., & Galef, B.G. (1998). Effects of intrauterine position on the behavior and genital morphology of litter-bearing rodents. *Developmental Neuropsychology, 14*, 197–211.

Cole-Harding, S., Morstad, A.L., & Wilson, J.R. (1988). Spatial ability in members of opposite-sex twin pairs (Abstract). *Behavior Genetics, 18*, 710.

Collaer, M., & Hines, M. (1995). Human behavioral sex differences: A role for gonadal hormones during early development? *Psychology Bulletin, 11*(8), 55–107.

Dabbs, J.M. (1990). Salivary testosterone measurements: reliability across hours, days, and weeks. *Physiology and Behavior, 48*(1), 83–86.

de Lacoste-Utamsing, C., & Holloway, R.L. (1982). Sexual dimorphism in the corpus callosum. *Science, 216*, 1431–1432.

Drake, E.B., Henderson, V.W., Stanczyk, F.Z., McCleary, C.A., Brown, W.S., Smith, C.A. et al. (2000). Associations between circulating sex steroid hormones and cognition in normal elderly women. *Neurology, 54*(3), 599–603.

Duka, T., Tasker, R., & McGowan, J.F. (2000). The effects of 3-week estrogen hormone replacement on cognition in elderly healthy females. *Psychopharmacology (Berl), 149*(2), 129–139.

Ekstrom, R., French, J., & Harman, H. (1976). *Manual for kit of factor-referenced cognitive tests.* Princeton, NJ: Educational Testing Service.

Fitch, R., & Denenberg, V. (1998). A role for ovarian hormones in sexual differentiation of the brain. *Behavioral and Brain Sciences, 21*, 311–352.

Gibbs, R.B. (2000). Long-term treatment with estrogen and progesterone enhances acquisition of a spatial memory task by ovariectomized aged rats. *Neurobiology of Aging, 21*, 107–116.

Gouchie, C., & Kimura, D. (1991). The relationship between testosterone levels and cognitive ability patterns. *Psychoneuroendocrinology, 16*, 323–334.

Gould, E., Woolley, C.S., Frankfurt, M., & McEwen, B.S. (1990). Gonadal steroids regulate dendritic spine density in hippocampal pyramidal cells in adulthood. *Journal of Neuroscience, 10*(4), 1286–1291.

Goy, R. (1996). Sexual differences in behavior. *Hormones and Behavior, 30*, 299–691.

Goy, R.W., & McEwen, B.S. (1980). *Sexual differentiation of the brain.* London: Oxford University Press.

Grimshaw, G.M., Sitarenios, G., & Finegan, J.K. (1995). Mental rotation at 7 years: Relations with prenatal testosterone levels and spatial play experience. *Brain and Cognition, 29*, 85–100.

Grodstein, F., Chen, J., Pollen, D., Albert, M., Wilson, R., Folstein, M. et al. (2000). Postmenopausal hormone therapy and cognitive function in healthy older women. *Journal of the American Geriatrics Society, 48*, 746–752.

Halpern, D. (2000). *Sex differences in cognitive abilities* (3rd ed.). Mahwah, NJ: Lawrence Erlbaum Associates Inc.

Hampson, E. (1990a). Variations in sex-related cognitive abilities across the menstrual cycle. *Brain and Cognition, 14*, 26–43.

Hampson, E. (1990b). Estrogen-related variations in human spatial and articulatory–motor skills. *Psychoneuroendocrinology, 15*, 97–111.

Hampson, E., & Kimura, D. (1988). Reciprocal effects of hormonal fluctuations on human motor and perceptual–spatial skills. *Behavioral Neuroscience, 102*, 456–459.

Hampson, E., & Kimura, D. (1992). Sex differences and hormonal influences on cognitive function in humans. In J.B. Becker, S.M. Breedlove, & D. Crews (Eds.), *Behavioral endocrinology* (pp. 357–397). Cambridge, MA: MIT Press.

Hampson, E., Rovet, J.F., & Altmann, D. (1998). Spatial reasoning in children with congenital adrenal hyperplasia due to 21-hydroxylase deficiency. *Developmental Neuropsychology, 14*, 299–320.

Harasty, J., Double, K., Halliday, G., Kril, J., & McRitchie, D. (1997). Language-associated cortical regions are proportionally larger in the female brain. *Archives of Neurology, 54*, 171–176.

Hechter, O., Grossman, A., & Chatterton, R.T. (1997). Relationship of dehydroepiandrosterone and cortisol in disease. *Medical Hypotheses, 49*(1), 85–91.

Heister, G., Landis, T., Regard, M., & Schroeder-Heister, P. (1989). Shift of functional cerebral asymmetry during the menstrual cycle. *Neuropsychologia, 27*, 871–880.

Helleday, J., Siwers, B., Ritzen, E., & Hugdahl, K. (1994). Normal lateralization for handedness and ear advantage in a verbal dichotic listening task in women with congenital adrenal hyperplasia (CAH). *Neuropsychologia, 32*, 875–880.

Henderson, V.W., Paganini-Hill, A., Miller, B.L., Elble, R.J., Reyes, P.F., Shoupe, D. et al. (2000). Estrogen for Alzheimer's disease in women: Randomized, double-blind, placebo-controlled trial. *Neurology, 54*(2), 295–301.

Hier, D., & Crowley, W. (1982). Spatial ability in androgen-deficient men. *The New England Journal of Medicine, 302*, 1202–1205.

Hines, M., & Sandberg, E. (1996). Sexual differentiation of cognitive abilities in women exposed to diethylstilbestrol prenatally. *Hormones and Behavior, 30*, 354–363.

Hines, M., & Shipley, C. (1984). Prenatal exposure to diethylstilbestrol (DES) and the development of sexually dimorphic cognitive abilities and cerebral lateralization. *Developmental Psychology, 20*, 81–94.

Imperato-McGinley, J., Pichardo, M., Gautier, T., Voyer, D., & Bryden, M.P. (1991). Cognitive abilities in androgen-insensitive subjects: Comparison with control males and females from the same kindred. *Clinical Endocrinology, 34*, 341–347.

Jacobs, D.M., Tang, M.X., Stern, Y., Sano, M., Marder, K., Bell, K.L. et al. (1998). Cognitive function in nondemented older women who took estrogen after menopause. *Neurology, 50*, 368–373.

Janowsky, J.S., Chavez, B., & Orwoll, E. (2000). Sex steroids modify working memory. *Journal of Cognitive Neuroscience, 12*(3), 407–414.

Janowsky, J., Oviatt, S., & Orwoll, E. (1994). Testosterone influences spatial cognition in older men. *Behavioral Neuroscience, 108*, 325–332.

Juraska, J. (1991). Sex differences in "cognitive" regions of the rat brain. *Psychoneuroendocrinology, 16*(1–3), 105–119.

Kalimi, M., Shafagoj, Y., Loria, R., Padgett, D., & Regelson, W. (1994). Anti-glucocorticoid effects of dehydroepiandrosterone (DHEA). *Molecular and Cellular Biochemistry, 131*(2), 99–104.

Kampen, D.L., & Sherwin, B.B. (1994). Estrogen use and verbal memory in healthy post-menopausal women. *Obstetrics and Gynecology, 83*, 979–983.

Kawas, C., Resnick, S., Morrison, A., Brookmeyer, R., Corrada, M., Zonderman, A. et al. (1997). A prospective study of estrogen replacement therapy and the risk of developing Alzheimer's disease: The Baltimore Longitudinal Study of Aging. *Neurology, 48*(6), 1517–1521.

Kelso, W.M., Nicholls, M.E.R., Warne, G., & Zacharin, M. (2000). Cerebral lateralization and cognitive functioning in patients with congenital adrenal hyperplasia. *Neuropsychology, 14*, 370–378.

Kimura, D. (1999). *Sex and cognition*. Cambridge, MA: MIT Press.

Kimura, D., & Hampson, E. (1994). Cognitive pattern in men and women is influenced by fluctuations in sex hormones. *Current Directions Psychological Science, 3*, 57–61.

Lamberts, S.W., van den Beld, A.W., & van der Lely, A.J. (1997). The endocrinology of aging. *Science, 278*, 419–424.

Linn, M., & Petersen, A. (1985). Emergence and characterization of sex differences in spatial ability: A meta-analysis. *Child Development, 56*, 1479–1498.

Maccoby, E.E., & Jacklin, C.N. (1974). *The psychology of sex differences*. Stanford, CA: Stanford University Press.

MacLusky, N., & Naftolin, F. (1981). Sexual differentiation of the central nervous system. *Science, 211*, 1294–1303.

Maki, P.M., & Resnick, S.M. (2000). Longitudinal effects of estrogen replacement therapy on PET cerebral blood flow and cognition. *Neurobiology of Aging, 21*, 373–383.

Maki, P.M., Zonderman, A.B., & Resnick, S.M. (2000). Enhanced verbal memory in non-demented elderly women receiving hormone-replacement therapy. *American Journal of Psychiatry, 158*, 227–233.

Mazzocco, M.M. (1998). A process approach to describing mathematics difficulties in girls with Turner syndrome. *Pediatrics, 102*, 492–496.

McCauley, E., Kay, T., Ito, J., & Treder, R. (1987). The Turner syndrome: Cognitive deficits, affective discrimination and behavior problems. *Child Development, 58*, 464–473.

McEwen, B. (1981). Neural gonadal steroid actions. *Science, 211*, 1303–1311.

McEwen, B. (1991). Non-genomic and genomic effects of steroids on neural activity. *Trends in Pharmacological Science, 12*, 141–147.

Meriggiola, M.C., Noonan, E.A., Paulsen, C.A., & Bremner, W.J. (1996). Annual patterns of luteinizing hormone, follicle stimulating hormone, testosterone and inhibin in normal men. *Human Reproduction, 11*(2), 248–252.

Migeon, C.J., Berkovitz, G., & Brown, T. (1994). Sexual differentiation and ambiguity. In M.S. Kappy, R.M. Blizzard, & C.J. Migeon (Eds.), *Diagnosis and treatment of endocrine disorders in childhood and adolescence* (4th ed.). Springfield, IL: Charles C. Thomas.

Moffat, S.D., & Hampson, E. (1996). A curvilinear relationship between testosterone and spatial cognition in humans: Possible influence of hand preference. *Psychoneuroendocrinology, 21*(3), 323–337.

Moffat, S.D., Zonderman, A.B., Harman, S.M., Blackman, M.R., Kawas, C., & Resnick, S.M. (2000). The relationship between longitudinal declines in dehydroepiandrosterone sulfate concentrations and cognitive performance in older men. *Archives of Internal Medicine, 160*(14), 2193–2198.

Money, J. (1964). Two cytogenetic syndromes: Psychologic comparisons. I. Intelligence and specific-factor quotients. *Journal of Psychiatric Research, 2*, 223–31.

Money, J. (1973). Turner's syndrome and parietal lobe function. *Cortex, 9*, 387–393.

Money, J., & Alexander, D. (1966). Turner's syndrome: Further demonstration of the presence of specific cognitional deficiencies. *Journal of Medical Genetics, 3*, 47–48.

Mulnard, R.A., Cotman, C.W., Kawas, C., VanDyck, C.H., Sano, M., Doody, R. et al. (2000). Estrogen replacement therapy for treatment of mild to moderate Alzheimer disease: A randomized controlled trial. *Journal of the American Medical Association, 283*, 1007–1015.

Murphy, D., DeCarli, C., Daly, E., Haxby, J., Allen, G., White, B. et al. (1993). X-chromosome effects on female brain: A magnetic resonance imaging study of Turner's syndrome. *Lancet, 342*, 1197–2000.

Murphy, D., Mentis, M., Pietrini, P., Grady, C., Daly, E., Haxby, J. et al. (1997). A PET study of Turner's syndrome: Effects of sex steroids and the X chromosome on brain. *Biological Psychiatry, 41*, 285–298.

Nass, R., Baker, S., Speiser, P., Virdis, R., Balsamo, A., Cacciari, E. et al. (1987). Hormones and handedness: Left-hand bias in female congenital adrenal hyperplasia patients. *Neurology, 37*, 711–715.

Neave, N., Menaged, M., & Weightman, D.R. (1999). Sex differences in cognition: The role of testosterone and sexual orientation. *Brain and Cognition, 41*(3), 245–262.

Nieschlag, E. (1974). Circadian rhythm of plasma testosterone. In J. Aschoff, F. Ceresa, & F. Halberg (Eds.), *Chronobiological aspects of endocrinology*. Stuttgart: Schattaquer Verlag.

Nyborg, H. (1983). Spatial ability in men and women: Review and new theory. *Advances in Behavior Research and Therapy, 5*, 89–140.

Pang, S. (1997). Congenital adrenal hyperplasia. *Endocrinology and Metabolism Clinics of North America, 26*(4), 853–891.

Phillips, S.M., & Sherwin, B.B. (1992). Variations in memory function and sex steroid hormones across the menstrual cycle. *Psychoneuroendocrinology, 17*, 497–506.

Plante, E., Bollek, C., Binkiewicz, A., & Erly, W.K. (1996). Elevated androgen, brain development and language/learning disabilities in children with congenital adrenal hyperplasia. *Developmental Medicine and Child Neurology, 38*, 423–437.

Plomin, R., & Foch, T.T. (1981). Sex differences and individual differences. *Child Development, 52*, 383–385.

Postma, A., Winkel, J., Tuiten, A., & van Honk, J. (1999). Sex differences and menstrual cycle effects in human spatial memory. *Psychoneuroendocrinology, 24*(2), 175–192.

Reiss, A.L., Mazzocco, M.M., Greenlaw, R., Freund, L.S., & Ross, J.L. (1995). Neurodevelopmental effects of X monosomy: A volumetric imaging study. *Annals of Neurology, 38*, 731–738.

Resnick, S.M. (1982). *Psychological functioning in individuals with congenital adrenal hyperplasia: Early hormonal influences on cognition and personality*. Doctoral dissertation, University of Minnesota, Minneapolis.

Resnick, S.M., Berenbaum, S.A., Gottesman, I.I., & Bouchard, T.J. (1986). Early hormonal influences on cognitive functioning in congenital adrenal hyperplasia. *Developmental Psychology, 22*, 191–198.

Resnick, S.M., & Maki, P.M. (1999). Sex differences in regional brain structure and function. In P.W. Kaplan (Ed.), *The neurology of women* (pp. 3–10). New York: Demos Vermande.

Resnick, S.M., Maki, P.M., Golski, S., Kraut, M.A., & Zonderman, A.B. (1998). Estrogen effects on PET cerebral blood flow and neuropsychological performance. *Hormones and Behavior, 34*, 171–184.

Resnick, S.M., Metter, E.J., & Zonderman, A.B. (1997). Estrogen replacement therapy and longitudinal decline in visual memory: A possible effect? *Neurology, 49*, 1491–1497.

Roberts, E., Bologa, L., Flood, J.F., & Smith, G.E. (1987). Effects of dehydroepiandrosterone and its sulfate on brain tissue in culture and on memory in mice. *Brain Research, 406*(1–2), 357–362.

Roberts, J.A., Gilardi, K.V., Lasley, B., & Rapp, P.R. (1997). Reproductive senescence predicts cognitive decline in aged female monkeys. *NeuroReport, 8*(8), 2047–2051.

Robinson, D., Friedman, L., Marcus, R., Tinklenberg, J., & Yesavage, J. (1994). Estrogen replacement therapy and memory in older women. *Journal of the American Geriatrics Society, 42*, 919–922.

Roof, R.L., & Havens, M.D. (1992). Testosterone improves maze performance and induces development of a male hippocampus in females. *Brain Research, 572*, 310–313.

Ross, J.L., Roeltgen, D., Feuillan, P., Kushner, H., & Cutler, G.B. (1998). Effects of estrogen on nonverbal processing speed and motor function in girls with Turner's syndrome. *Journal of Clinical Endocrinology and Metabolism, 83*, 3198–3203.

Ross, J.L., Roeltgen, D., Feuillan, P., Kushner, H., & Cutler, G.B. (2000b). Use of estrogen in young girls with Turner syndrome: Effects on memory. *Neurology, 54*, 164–170.

Ross, J.L., Roeltgen, D., Kushner, H., Wei, F., & Zinn, A.R. (2000a). The Turner syndrome-associated neurocognitive phenotype maps to distal Xp. *American Journal of Human Genetics, 67*, 672–681.

Rovet, J. (1990). The cognitive and neuropsychological characteristics of females with Turner syndrome. In D.B. Berch & G.B. Bender (Eds.), *Sex chromosome abnormalities and human behavior* (pp. 38–77). New York: American Association for the Advancement of Science.

Rovet, J., & Netley, C. (1980). The mental rotation task performance of Turner syndrome subjects. *Behavior Genetics, 10*, 437–443.

Sanders, G., & Wenmoth, D. (1998). Verbal and music dichotic listening tasks reveal variations in functional cerebral asymmetry across the menstrual cycle that are phase and task dependent. *Neuropsychologia, 36*(9), 869–874.

Shaywitz, B.A., Shaywitz, S.E., Pugh, K.R., Constable, R.T., Skudlarski, P., Fulbright, R.K. et al. (1995). Sex differences in the functional organization of the brain for language. *Nature, 373*, 607–609.

Shaywitz, S.E., Shaywitz, B.A., Pugh, K.R., Fulbright, R.K., Skudlarski, P., Mencl, W.E. et al. (1999). Effect of estrogen on brain activation patterns in postmenopausal women during working memory tasks. *Journal of the American Medical Association, 281*(13), 1197–1202.

Sherwin, B.B. (1988). Estrogen and/or androgen replacement therapy and cognitive functioning in surgically menopausal women. *Psychoneuroendocrinology, 13*, 345–357.

Sherwin, B.B. (1997). Estrogen effects on cognition in menopausal women. *Neurology, 48*(suppl. 7), S21–S26.

Shumaker, S.A., Reboussin, B.A., Espeland, M.A., Rapp, S.R., McBee, W.L., Dailey, M. et al. (1998). The Women's Health Initiative Memory Study (WHIMS): A trial of the effect of estrogen therapy in preventing and slowing the progression of dementia. *Controlled Clinical Trials, 19*(6), 604–621.

Sih, R., Morley, J.E., Kaiser, F.E., Perry, H.M., Patrick, P., & Ross, C. (1997). Testosterone replacement in older hypogonadal men: A 12-month randomized controlled trial. *Journal of Clinical Endocrinology and Metabolism, 82*(6), 1661–1667.

Silverman, I., Kastuk, D., Choi, J., & Phillips, K. (1999). Testosterone levels and spatial ability in men. *Psychoneuroendocrinology, 24*(8), 813–822.

Silverman, I., & Phillips, K. (1993). Effects of estrogen changes during the menstrual cycle on spatial performance. *Ethology and Sociobiology, 14*, 257–269.

Skuse, D.H., James, R.S., Bishop, D.V.M., Coppin, B., Dalton, P., Aamodt-Leeper, G. et al. (1997). Evidence from Turner's syndrome of an imprinted X-linked locus affecting cognitive function. *Nature, 387*, 705–708.

Speiser, P. (2001). Congenital adrenal hyperplasia owing to 21-hydroxylase deficiency. *Endocrinology and Metabolism Clinics of North America, 30,* 31–59.

Szklo, M., Cerhan, J., Diez-Roux, A.V., Chambless, L., Cooper, L., Folsom, A.R. et al. (1996). Estrogen replacement therapy and cognitive functioning in the Atherosclerosis Risk in Communities (ARIC) study. *American Journal of Epidemiology, 144*(11), 1048–1057.

Tager-Flusberg, H. (2002). Developmental disorders of genetic origin. In M. de Haan & M.H. Johnson (Eds.), *The cognitive neuroscience of development*. Hove, UK: Psychology Press.

Tang, M.-X., Jacobs, D., Stern, Y., Marder, K., Schofield, P., Gurland, B. et al. (1996). Effect of oestrogen during menopause on risk and age at onset of Alzheimer's disease. *Lancet, 348*, 429–432.

Temple, C.M., & Carney, R.A. (1995). Patterns of spatial functioning in Turner's syndrome. *Cortex, 31*, 109–118.

Tirosh, E., Rod, R., Cohen, A., & Hochberg, Z. (1993). Congenital adrenal hyperplasia and cerebral lateralizations. *Pediatric Neurology, 9*(3), 198–201.

Vandenberg, S.G., & Kuse, A.R. (1978). Mental rotations: A group test of three-dimensional spatial visualization. *Perceptual and Motor Skills, 47*, 599–605.

Verghese, J., Kuslansky, G., Katz, M., Sliwinski, M., Crystal, H., Buschke, H., & Lipton, R. (2000). Cognitive performance in surgically menopausal women on estrogen. *Neurology, 55*, 872–874.

vom Saal, F., Clark, M., Galef, B., Drickamer, L., & Vandenbergh, J. (1998). Intrauterine position phenomenon. In E. Knobill & J. Neill (Eds.), *Encyclopedia of reproduction*. Orlando, FL: Academic Press.

Waber, D.P. (1979). Neuropsychological aspects of Turner syndrome. *Developmental Medicine and Child Neurology, 21*, 58–70.

Wang, P.N., Liao, S.Q., Liu, R.S., Liu, C.Y., Chao, H.T., Lu, S.R. et al. (2000). Effects of estrogen on cognition, mood, and cerebral blood flow in AD: A controlled study. *Neurology, 54*(11), 2061–2066.

Williams, C.L., Barnett, A.M., & Meck, W.H. (1990). Organizational effects of early gonadal secretions on sexual differentiation in spatial memory. *Behavioral Neuroscience, 104*, 84–97.

Williams, C., & Meck, W. (1991). The organizational effects of gonadal steroids on sexually dimorphic spatial ability. *Psychoneuroendocrinology, 16*(1–3), 155–176.

Wisniewski, A.B. (1998). Sexually-dimorphic patterns of cortical asymmetry, and the role for sex steroid hormones in determining cortical patterns of lateralization. *Psychoneuroendocrinology, 23*(5), 519–547.

Witelson, S., Glezer, I., & Kigar, D. (1995). Women have greater density of neurons in posterior temporal cortex. *Journal of Neuroscience, 15*, 3418–3428.

Wolf, O.T., & Kirschbaum, C. (1999). Dehydroepiandrosterone replacement in elderly individuals: Still waiting for the proof of beneficial effects on mood or memory. *Journal of Endocrinological Investigation, 22*(4), 316.

Wolf, O.T., Kudielka, B.M., Hellhammer, D.H., Hellhammer, J., & Kirschbaum, C. (1998b). Opposing effects of DHEA replacement in elderly subjects on declarative memory and attention after exposure to a laboratory stressor. *Psychoneuroendocrinology, 23*(6), 617–629.

Wolf, O.T., Naumann, E., Hellhammer, D.H., & Kirschbaum, C. (1998a). Effects of dehydroepiandrosterone replacement in elderly men on event-related potentials, memory, and well-being. *Journal of Gerontology A Biological Sciences and Medical Sciences, 53*(5), M385–M390.

Wolf, O.T., Neumann, O., Hellhammer, D.H., Geiben, A.C., Strasburger, C.J., Dressendorfer, R.A. et al. (1997). Effects of a two-week physiological dehydroepiandrosterone substitution on cognitive performance and well-being in healthy elderly women and men. *Journal of Clinical Endocrinology and Metabolism, 82*(7), 2363–2367.

Woolley, C.S., Gould, E., Frankfurt, M., & McEwen, B.S. (1990). Naturally occurring fluctuation in dendritic spine density on adult hippocampal pyramidal neurons. *Journal of Neuroscience, 10*(12), 4035–4039.

Woolley, C.S., & McEwen, B.S. (1994). Estradiol regulates hippocampal dendritic spine density via an *N*-methyl-D-aspartate receptor-dependent mechanism. *Journal of Neuroscience, 14*(12), 7680–7687.

Yaffe, K., Sawaya, G., Lieberburg, I., & Grady, D. (1998). Estrogen therapy in postmenopausal women: Effects on cognitive function and dementia. *Journal of the American Medical Association, 279*, 688–695.

Yoo, A., Harris, J., & Dubrovsky, B. (1996). Dose-response study of dehydroepiandrosterone sulfate on dentate gyrus long-term potentiation. *Experimental Neurology, 137*(1), 151–156.

CHAPTER TEN

Developmental disorders of genetic origin

Helen Tager-Flusberg
Boston University, School of Medicine, Boston, USA

INTRODUCTION

The primary goals of the field of developmental disorders are to understand the biological basis of different syndromes and the mappings between the genetic cause, the abnormalities in brain development, and the cognitive and behavioural consequences or outcomes, including mental retardation, that are characteristic of the majority of individuals with specific disorders. This is a field that has made remarkably rapid progress in recent years and, because it is concerned with a theoretical integration of knowledge across all these levels of analysis—genetics, developmental neurobiology, cognitive science, and psychology—it is now taking its place within the broader enterprise of developmental cognitive neuroscience (Tager-Flusberg, 1999).

Ultimately, the objectives of this area of inquiry are to provide a complete description and understanding of a disorder, such as Down's syndrome or autism, from the underlying DNA sequences to the observable behaviours and symptoms, which will entail hierarchical conceptual models at both the biological and cognitive systems levels (Morton & Frith, 1995; Pennington, 1999; Pennington & Welsh, 1995). We are clearly only at the beginning of this important enterprise but at this stage an integrated perspective on developmental disorders is emerging as a result of revolutionary changes that have taken place in recent years in genetics, developmental neuroscience, and the cognitive sciences. This chapter provides an overview of the history of the field of developmental disorders, an outline of the advances that have been made in recent years in the disciplines that contribute to this field, and offers a few examples of developmental disorders that illustrate the framework for understanding disorders within a developmental cognitive neuroscience framework.

HISTORICAL BACKGROUND

In the 1960s, an interdisciplinary synthesis for understanding developmental disorders would have been inconceivable. Concepts in the genetics of developmental disorders were still in their infancy and knowledge was limited to those genetic abnormalities that could be observed using cytogenetic methods, such as the absence of a second X chromosome in girls with Turner's syndrome, or the additional chromosome 21 in Down's syndrome.

At the same time, psychologists focused on mental retardation or learning disabilities without regard to differences in aetiology associated with developmental disorders. Initially influenced by behaviourism, investigators pooled together in their studies children and adults with different aetiologies, and restricted their research to observable behaviours, response repertoires, and rewards and punishments. By the 1960s, developmental and cognitive approaches were incorporated into the study of developmental disorders (Hodapp, Burack, & Zigler, 1998). Researchers under the influence of Piagetian theory began to recognize the importance of considering differences in aetiology, but emphasized the role of general cognitive processes that cut across groups of individuals with mental retardation (Zigler, 1969). An alternative approach grew out of the behaviourist perspective and argued that, regardless of aetiology, mental retardation was the result of a specific deficit in stimulus traces (Ellis, 1963), attention (Zeaman & House, 1963), executive processes (Belmont & Butterfield, 1971) or other cognitive processes.

There were problems with both these approaches (Crnic & Pennington, 2000). The specific deficit approach continued to ignore the role of aetiology, assuming that the same cognitive deficit explained mental retardation across all disorders. The developmental approach emphasized general cognitive processes, which accounts for the important role of mental age in predicting performance across many areas of functioning (Detterman & Daniel, 1989; Mervis, Morris, Bertrand, & Robinson, 1999), and the finding that people with developmental disorders generally follow the normal sequence of development (Hodapp et al., 1998). However, this approach did not explain the data showing that there are clear differences across disorders in cognitive and behavioural profiles, and that certain domains can be identified as areas of specific deficit associated with particular disorders. For example, people with Williams syndrome are strikingly impaired in visual–spatial cognition, which contrasts with their relatively good language skills (Bellugi, Wang, & Jernigan, 1994). The opposite pattern is found in Down's syndrome, where language skills are almost always significantly impaired, and visual–spatial ability is relatively spared (Crnic & Pennington, 2000). These kinds of findings paved the way for a new approach within psychology: to explore syndrome-specific profiles of cognitive sparing and deficit, using established paradigms and methods from psychometrics and cognitive psychology.

GENETICS OF DEVELOPMENTAL DISORDERS

There has been an explosion of knowledge and technical advances in the field of molecular genetics, resulting in the recent publication of the human genome project that has mapped the complete genetic code for humans. The significance of these new advances is that they allow researchers to locate and sequence genes, including those that cause developmental disorders, without regard for knowing in advance how they work or where they are expressed.

The foundation of the field of genetics is the understanding of genomic structure. The genome is the term applied to the total complement of DNA—deoxyribonucleic acid—which consists of two chains of four different nucleotide bases (adenine, A; guanine, G; cytosine, C; and thymidine, T) that are wrapped around each other to form a double helix. In humans, DNA molecules are organized into approximately 30,000 functional units, called genes. Genes themselves have quite a complex structure. Part of the DNA, in the central or coding region of the gene, codes for structural information that, for example, leads to the production of relevant proteins, through a complex process known as transcription. Other DNA surrounding the coding region exists to regulate the expression of the coding region. One important regulating component is the promoter region of the gene, which is needed for activating gene transcription. As we will see, some developmental disorders are related to mutations in the promoter region of specific genes.

In cells, genes are packaged into units called chromosomes. Each cell (except for sperm and egg cells) contains 23 pairs of chromosomes, with one member of the pair coming from the father and one from the mother. One of the chromosome pairs is designated as the sex chromosomes, consisting of two Xs in females and an X and Y in males. The remaining 22 pairs are called autosomes. Chromosomes have a characteristic structure with a central constriction, called the centomere, and "arms" leading from the centomere that show characteristic stripes or "bands". There is a conventional system for numbering the bands from the centomere out to the telomeres, or the ends of the chromosomes. The shorter arm on each chromosome is labelled p and the longer arm is q.

Genetically based developmental disorders can be classified into several main groups. In this chapter we will limit our survey of developmental disorders to:

1. *Single gene disorders*: these are disorders that are caused by a mutation (altered DNA structure) in a single gene, or pair of genes. These disorders follow Mendelian patterns of inheritance and can be divided into autosomal dominant (e.g. neurofibromatosis type 1, NF1; Cawthon et al., 1990) recessive (e.g. phenylketonuria, PKU; Lidsky et al., 1984), or X-linked (e.g. fragile X syndrome, FMR1; Verkerk et al., 1991).
2. *Polygenic disorders*: also known as multifactorial or complex, these disorders are caused by multiple inherited genes. The disorders typically involve quantitative traits, such as intelligence or personality features, that do not conform to simple Mendelian patterns. Examples of polygenic disorders include autism (Santangelo & Folstein, 1999) and dyslexia (Grigorenko, et al., 1997; Pennington, 1999).
3. *Chromosome disorders*: in these conditions either an entire chromosome (e.g. Down's syndrome or Turner's syndrome) or segments of a chromosome

(e.g. Williams syndrome or Prader–Willi syndrome) are missing or duplicated. These disorders almost always occur spontaneously as a result of errors during meiosis, when sperm and egg cells are formed.

Recently, a number of interesting and non-traditional patterns of inheritance have been identified in the molecular analysis of some developmental disorders:

1. *Mosaicism*: in some cases of genetic disorders, not all cells display the genetic or chromosomal abnormality. This is known as mosaicism and it is often associated with a less severe manifestation of the disorder (e.g. in Down's syndrome; Cody & Kamphaus, 1999).
2. *Anticipation*: single gene disorders, such as fragile X syndrome, show an interesting pattern of inheritance, known as anticipation, in which later generations in a family tree exhibit an earlier age of onset and more severe phenotypic expression of the disorder. The normal FMR1 gene (associated with fragile X syndrome) has a section in the promoter region consisting of repeat sequences of DNA nucleotides (CGG), ranging from about 6 to 52 repeats in length. Carriers of the FMR1 mutation that causes fragile X syndrome have longer than usual repeat patterns (between 53 and 200), but not long enough to disrupt the function of the gene. As this expanded repeat mutation gets passed on from one generation to the next the number of repeats increases, often to more than 1000 and, with each increase, gene function is more severely affected as the transcription process is interrupted (Fu et al., 1991).
3. *Genetic imprinting*: this refers to differential expression of genetic information, which depends on the parent of origin. Some, but not all, regions of the human genome show imprinting effects. The best-known example is a region close to the centromere on the long arm of chromosome 15. A deletion in this region on the paternally donated chromosome results in a developmental disorder called Prader–Willi syndrome. A deletion in this region on the maternally donated chromosome results in a completely different developmental disorder: Angelman syndrome (Butler & Palmer, 1983).
4. *Uniparental disomy*: in some cases of Prader–Willi syndrome there is no deletion on chromosome 15; instead the genome includes two copies of the chromosome inherited from the mother and none from the father (Nicholls, Knoll, Butler, Karam, & Lalande, 1989). The loss of the paternally donated genes on this chromosome results in the same disorder, although there can be subtle phenotypic differences between deletion and uniparental disomy cases of Prader–Willi syndrome (Roof et al., 2000).

This brief overview of genetic factors associated with different developmental disorders demonstrates the complexity and variety of genetic aetiologies that have been discovered thus far. Much more is known about the genetics of single gene and chromosomal disorders. Among polygenic disorders we have yet to identify and map a single specific gene associated with one of these disorders, although some progress has been made in locating regions of interest in autism and dyslexia, for example, using a number of different methods.

Identifying genes associated with polygenic disorders involves a combination of methods from behavioural and molecular genetics. First, researchers must establish whether a disorder is inherited, using a combination of family studies and twin studies. A comparison of the presence of the disorder in one or both members of pairs of monozygotic (MZ, who have identical genes) and dizygotic (DZ, who share the same percentage of genes as siblings) twins establishes the heritability rate of a disorder. For example, twin studies of autism show that both members of MZ pairs are much more likely to have autism than both members of DZ pairs, leading researchers to conclude that this is a highly heritable disorder (Santangelo & Folstein, 1999). The next stage uses family data, segregation analysis or pedigree analysis, to follow patterns of inheritance across generations, to determine the genetic model that best explains the pattern of inheritance, and the number of likely genes that are involved. The final stages involve linkage studies or population-based association analysis to locate sites for candidate genes. These methods are quite complex, involving an interdisciplinary effort among behavioural geneticists, molecular biologists, epidemiologists, and statisticians (see Harris, 1998, for a more detailed discussion).

Many factors complicate the process of identifying genes associated with polygenic disorders (Lander & Schork, 1994). Perhaps the most significant is the possibility of genetic heterogeneity: Several different mutations on different genes might contribute to a disorder, and these might differ across individuals with the same syndrome. Thus one set of genetic mutations could lead to autism, for example, in one individual, and a different, although overlapping set, could be responsible for autism in another individual. Another factor is the possibility that several genes are involved, each causing a small effect in isolation that cannot easily be picked up in traditional linkage studies (Lombroso, Pauls, & Leckman, 1994).

Finally, we should consider how genetic abnormalities lead to the resulting observable characteristics of a disorder. In most cases, the relationship between genes and behaviour is quite indirect. Genes contribute to variation in behaviour through interactions with a network of other similar genes, so that the specific effects might be the result of a disturbance in the balance of the network, rather than in a particular gene. Moreover, genes might participate in a number of different such networks (Flint, 1996). On this view, the relationship between genes and behaviour associated with a particular disorder involves a network of interacting factors, rather than a linear link between a mutant gene to a specific, yet distant, phenotype. These complexities in how we might understand the genetic basis of developmental disorders suggest that we must be cautious in the way we describe achievements in finding genes or genetic markers associated with particular disorders.

NEUROBIOLOGY OF DEVELOPMENTAL DISORDERS

Genetic abnormalities lead to cognitive and behavioural deficits in developmental disorders by disrupting the normal development and functioning of the brain. Brain development is the result of a complex interaction of genetic and environmental factors that depend on the exquisite timing and sequencing of a cascade of events. The process begins early in embryological development with the formation of the neural tube and does not end until late in adolescence (see Chapter 3). The environment plays a significant role at all stages of brain development, and the notion of plasticity is crucial in considering brain development in both normal children and children with developmental disorders.

Disruption in the normal process of brain development as a result of genetic factors can occur at all stages. A group of regulatory genes critical to the very early stages in the development of the nervous system are expressed only during this transitory period. Certain neurons also exist briefly to help migrating neurons find their targets in the different layers of the cortex (Ciaranello et al., 1995). Defects in these regulatory genes or neurons can lead to subtle neuropathology in developmental disorders, but they cannot be easily detected. The hallmark of neurological impairment in developmental disorders, which might also not be directly visible, are anomalies in synaptic connections, cell migration, pruning of axons, or growth of dendritic trees. Some genetically based migration disorders result in widespread disruption of normal brain architecture. Others can lead to abnormalities that are distributed sporadically, or limited to a single region of the brain (Goodman, 1994). Abnormalities in the selective pruning of synaptic connections can have consequences at the level of functional deficit. Diffuse overconnection can result in poor signal-to-noise ratio, and result in impairments in attention, learning, or coordination (Muller & Courchesne, 2000).

In recent years, studies of brain structure using magnetic resonance imaging (MRI) in children and adults with developmental disorders have proliferated (Lyon & Rumsey, 1996; Thatcher, Lyon, Rumsey, & Krasnegor, 1996). These studies have been concerned primarily with investigations of differences in overall and regional changes in brain size and volume, with only limited analyses of morphological differences that might be associated with developmental disorders. Courchesne and colleagues (Courchesne, Townsend, & Chase, 1995) remind us that an image from the brain of a child with a developmental disorder offers a view only of the end product of abnormal brain development; longitudinal studies following brain growth and change from infancy through adolescence have not yet been conducted.

The studies that have been carried out thus far on many disorders have not provided a clear picture of brain abnormalities associated with different specific developmental disorders. To some extent this is because of methodological problems (Courchesne & Plante, 1996; Filipek, 1996). Genetically based developmental disorders do not lead to areas of focal damage, as is found in acquired disorders. Instead, there are often changes in brain size (e.g. microcephaly in Down's syndrome and Williams syndrome and macrocephaly in autism and fragile X syndrome), and evidence of diffuse cortical damage. These kinds of finding suggest that developmental disorders are associated with more widespread deficits that affect complex neural (and cognitive) systems, rather than simple localized regions. Furthermore, across many developmental disorders not only are cortical systems affected but specific subcortical structures are also involved. These subcortical areas (such as parts of the limbic system in autism or the hypothalamus in Prader–Willi syndrome) might be more critical for interpreting the cognitive and behavioural features of such disorders (Tager-Flusberg, 2000).

Functional brain imaging techniques have only recently been applied to research with developmentally disordered populations (Ernst & Rumsey, 2000). There are formidable methodological and ethical challenges that need to be considered, especially when children with developmental disorders are included in such studies (Arnold, Zametikin, Caravella, & Korbly, 2000). At the same time, researchers recognize that these methods provide unique opportunities to discover how the brains of children with disorders function under different conditions. The full array of functional imaging methods, such as positron emission tomography (PET) or event-related potentials (ERPs) can be applied to exploring questions about brain functioning in people with developmental disorders. However, there is a growing bias toward relying more on non-invasive approaches, such as functional magnetic resonance imaging (fMRI), or magnetic resonance spectroscopy (MRS; see Chapter 2). Research has also started out by including adults with these disorders as participants, particularly those who are relatively high functioning without significant mental retardation, in order to avoid some of the difficulties of working with more impaired children in these challenging environments.

Functional brain imaging studies in developmentally disordered populations have begun to investigate a number of different factors that might signal abnormalities, including brain metabolites, neurotransmitter systems, and regional localization of cognitive processing. Some provocative initial findings have been reported in the literature. For example, one study comparing adolescents with autism with normal controls, using PET, found decreased dopaminergic function in prefrontal cortex of the adolescents with autism (Ernst, Zametkin, Matochik, Pascualvaca, & Cohen, 1997); a finding that supports cognitive studies on executive deficits in this population (Joseph, 1999). Chugani and her colleagues used MRS to investigate brain metabolites, comparing young children with autism to their unimpaired siblings (Chugani, Sundram, Behan, Lee, & Moore, 1999). They found reduced levels of *N*-acetylaspartate (NAA), a putative marker for neuronal function and viability, particularly in the cerebellums of the children with autism. Again, these findings are consistent with, and complement, neuropathological reports of reductions in groups of cells in the cerebellar cortex in autism (Bauman & Kemper, 1994). Finally, studies using fMRI have demonstrated that there are regional differences in brain activation patterns associated with particular cognitive tasks in individuals with developmental disorders such as dyslexia, attention deficit or autism (e.g. Eden & Zeffiro, 2000).

NEUROPSYCHOLOGY AND COGNITIVE SCIENCE OF DEVELOPMENTAL DISORDERS

From the psychological perspective, children with developmental disorders are assessed on a battery of psychometric tests, and their behaviour and symptoms are observed and recorded. In this way, a profile of the phenotype associated with a particular disorder can be assembled, although this goal is made more difficult because there is considerable variability within each disorder, and overlap across different disorders (Dykens, 1995; Flint, 1996). Standardized neuropsychological measures allow one to compare the performance of individuals with a disorder to population norms and patterns of performance across a range of tests are used to identity areas of deficit and sparing across cognitive domains. In the case of Williams syndrome, for example, a unique cognitive profile has been identified and operationalized (Mervis et al., 1999). In contrast, no unique or specific profile is associated with other disorders, such as Prader–Willi syndrome (Dykens, 1999) or Down's syndrome (Crnic & Pennington, 2000).

Patterns of performance on neuropsychological tests are often used to make inferences about areas of brain dysfunction in developmental disorders (Reynolds & Mayfield, 1999). However, the models of brain function that are based on neuropsychological test batteries are typically derived from the adult brain lesion literature (Bishop, 1997). Tests that capture the parameters of a static focal injury might not map onto the same brain/behaviour relations in children. Conceptually, then, this approach is not sensitive to the distinct characteristics of developmental disorders that involve dynamic alterations to brain organization that begin at the earliest embryological stages (Karmiloff-Smith, 1998; Tager-Flusberg, 1999).

The cognitive science perspective, which is concerned with cognitive processes or operations, and the representations that underlie such operations, holds particular advantages for identifying cognitive aspects of dysfunction in developmental disorders. One advantage is the focus on dissecting cognitive domains into subcomponents and underlying computations, which can lead to a more unified interpretation of seemingly unrelated symptoms. A striking example of this approach comes from the study of autism in which the primary social, language, and repetitive behaviour symptoms can be explained in terms of an underlying deficit in theory of mind (Baron-Cohen, 1995; Baron-Cohen, Tager-Flusberg & Cohen, 2000). A second advantage is that it is especially well suited to a developmental approach because of its concern with representational change and processing aspects of cognition.

Our understanding of the complex design of cognitive systems is enriched by the study of children with developmental disorders whose deficits can be defined with greater precision with a cognitive science framework. In developmental disorders, impairments do not occur across broadly defined functional systems. Instead, we see fractionations and dissociations within major domains. For example, in Williams syndrome there are striking impairments in visual–spatial cognition, although face perception and recognition remain relatively intact (Bellugi, Mills, Jernigan, Hickok, & Galaburda, 1999). At the same time, defining the cognitive deficits in developmental syndromes remains a challenge for researchers because patterns of impairment and cognitive dissociations can change over time. Cognitive systems are defined by their plasticity in development, which means that some early deficits can be resolved through developmental change or compensation, whereas others are not (Bates, Vicari, & Trauner, 1999).

We turn now to a discussion of a number of different developmental disorders that have been chosen to illustrate some of the principles that have been introduced in this chapter.

PHENYLKETONURIA

Phenylketonuria (PKU) is often considered the most significant success story among developmental disorders. It is caused by a family of mutations on a single recessive gene, the PAH gene, located on the long arm of chromosome 12 (DiLella, Marvit, Lidsky, Guttler, & Woo, 1986). This gene is responsible for producing an enzyme that metabolizes phenylalanine, which is found largely in proteins and thus is present in all normal diets. If it is not properly metabolized, phenylalanine builds up in the bloodstream, eventually leading to brain damage and mental retardation. Beginning in the 1950s, it was shown that significant brain damage could be prevented by keeping children born with PKU on diets that severely limit the intake of proteins, including, milk, fish, and meat (Bickel, Gerrard, & Hickmans, 1954). Soon a screening programme was introduced to test all newborns for PKU at birth (Guthrie & Susi, 1963); those identified with the disorder are now routinely placed on a low phenylalanine diet. Thus, PKU came to be viewed as a model example of how a developmental disorder can be prevented by implementing an environmental programme of identification and treatment to combat a genetic disease. It highlights the significance of considering gene/environment interactions in contributing to the development of developmental disorders.

In recent years, however, the PKU story has become somewhat more complicated (Waisbren, 1999). When the PAH gene is working normally, it produces enzymes that convert phenylalanine into tyrosine, which is a precursor for the neurotransmitter, dopamine. It was originally thought that brain damage in PKU was caused by elevated phenylalanine levels, and the focus of treatments was on their reduction. But another consequence of PKU is that tyrosine levels are lower than normal. According to recent studies, sometimes even in treated PKU there is still an imbalance between phenylalanine and tyrosine. Phenylalanines cannot be completely removed from the diet of children with PKU, so that even when a fairly strict diet is followed, neither phenylalanine nor tyrosine levels are completely normal and this appears to lead to subtle deficits (Smith & Beasley, 1989).

Diamond and colleagues (Diamond, Prevor, Callender, & Druin, 1997) have argued that the most significant effects of even a mild imbalance between phenylalanine and tyrosine are on areas of the brain that are most sensitive to changes in dopamine levels, specifically, prefrontal cortex. The frontal lobes are the primary site for projections of dopaminergic neurons, and prefrontal cortex has one of the highest levels of dopamine turnover in the brain. Deficits in executive functions that are dependent on prefrontal cortex, including inhibitory control and working memory, are most affected in children with early treated PKU (Welsh, Pennington, Ozonoff, Rouse, & McCabe, 1990). In a longitudinal study, Diamond et al. (1997) found a direct correlation between concurrent phenylalanine levels and performance on tasks that are dependent on prefrontal cortex, in infants as well as preschoolage children, supporting the hypothesis that an imbalance between phenylalanine and tyrosine does have effects on the dopamine system even in very young children with treated PKU.

These new findings provide a richer understanding of the biological mechanisms that underlie PKU. They illustrate the complex interaction between genetic, metabolic, neurochemical, and neuropsychological contributions to a developmental disorder. With these recent advances, researchers can explore new options for using dietary restrictions or other pharmacological treatments to minimize the adverse effects of low tyrosine levels and their effects on regions of the prefrontal cortex that are critical for intact neuropsychological functioning in people with PKU.

FRAGILE X SYNDROME

Fragile X syndrome is the most common inherited form of mental retardation. We have already reviewed what is known about the interesting genetic mechanisms that cause fragile X: the expanded CGG repeat in the promoter region of the FRX1 gene, which affects the production of the protein produced by this gene, called FMRP. Because it is an X-linked disorder, the expansion occurs at a full mutation level when the gene is passed on from the premutation level through the female line in a family, in accordance with the mechanism known as anticipation.

The consequences of having the full-blown effects of fragile X syndrome, presumably the result of diminished levels of FMRP in the brain and elsewhere, are somewhat different in males and females. In males there is the array of physical, behavioural, and neuropsychological features characterizing the phenotype that are quite variable in expression across individuals. Typical physical features include long prominent ears, a long face and large head, flat feet, a cardiac murmur or click, unusual finger and thumb joints, a high palate, and, by adolescence, enlarged testicles (Hagerman, 1999). These features suggest FMRP is a significant protein from the earliest stages of embryological development. Psychological features include mental retardation, with IQ declining in adolescence; hyperactivity and attentional problems; repetitive motor behaviours and stereotypies; language delays and deficits, especially in discourse; perseveration; hyperarousal; social anxiety and poor eye contact; tantrums and mood disorders. There is some overlap with features that are used in the diagnosis of autism, and about 15 per cent of males with fragile X syndrome meet criteria for autism (Reiss & Freund, 1991).

The phenotype found in females with the full mutation is even more variable than in males (Mazzocco & Reiss, 1999). For example, only about half of all females with the full mutation fall into the mental retardation range on IQ tests. On neuropsychological assessments, girls and women with fragile X syndrome generally show specific weaknesses in performance on tests of visual–spatial ability, mathematics, and problem solving, and relative strengths on verbal performance, memory, and social cognition (Mazzocco, Hagerman, Cronister, & Pennington, 1992). Girls also have attentional problems and hyperactivity, as well as higher levels of mood disorders and anxiety, and social difficulties compared with normal or IQ-matched controls (Freund, Reiss & Abrams, 1993; Lachiewicz, 1992). These findings also hold for girls with higher overall IQ levels, suggesting that the profile that has been identified is relatively specific and not related to mental retardation (Mazzocco et al., 1992).

The greater variability in phenotypic expression, and the overall milder effects found in girls, are thought to be because they have inherited the mutated gene on only one of their two X chromosomes (Hagerman, 1999). It is hypothesized that, in females, the genes on one X chromosome are activated but the genes on the other X are inactivated. So the affected X will be activated in some cells but not in others, thus leading to the production of varying amounts of FMRP. Researchers have quantified this activation ratio, which represents the proportion of cells that have an active unaffected X chromosome versus cells with an active mutated X chromosome (Abrams et al., 1994).

Although questions remain over whether the way that activation ratios are measured actually reflects the ratio of FMRP present in brain tissue, there have been some interesting studies exploring the relationship between the activation ratio and phenotypic expression of fragile X syndrome. For example, Abrams et al. (1994) found a significant correlation between activation ratio and degree of intellectual impairment in a group of girls with the fragile X full mutation. Other studies have found a significant relationship between activation ratio and executive functions (Sobesky, Taylor, Pennington, Riddle, & Hagerman, 1996) and performance IQ measures (Riddle et al., 1998).

Among males with fragile X, a different approach has been taken to explore relationships between molecular and clinical expressions of the disorder. Studies have compared males with the full mutation to those with a mosaic pattern, in whom there is some production of FMRP depending on the degree of mosaicism—defined as the proportion of cells containing a normal or mutated FMR1 gene. Merenstein and colleagues found that male mosaic adolescents had significantly higher IQ levels than non-mosaic full mutation males (Merenstein et al., 1996), and Cohen and colleagues found that mosaics had more advanced adaptive skills (Cohen et al., 1996). These studies of both males and females with fragile X syndrome suggest that it is possible to identify close links between variability in the genotype and variability in the expression of the phenotype, although more research in this area is needed to understand the mechanisms that mediate these relationships.

Considerable progress has been made in identifying patterns of neuroanatomical abnormalities associated with fragile X syndrome, based on investigations using MRI. Research has shown that both males and females with fragile X have smaller posterior cerebellar volumes than both normal and other developmentally delayed subjects (Reiss, Freund, Tseng, & Joshi, 1991) and larger volumes for other regions, including the caudate nucleus, hippocampus, and lateral ventricles (Reiss, Lee, & Freund, 1994). How does this pattern of neuroanatomical findings fit with what is known about the fragile X phenotype? Mazzocco and Reiss (1999) suggest that links between brain and cognitive or behaviour patterns can be found. For example, the cerebellar vermis is thought to play a role in mediating sensory stimulation and arousal, so the abnormalities in this region might be related to the arousal, attention problems, and tactile defensiveness features. Also, the caudate is important for mood regulation and control of higher-order cognitive processes, including inhibition, all areas of difficulty for people with fragile X.

Investigators have also begun to explore the relationship between these neuroanatomical findings and cognitive and genetic variability. Mostofsky et al. (1996) found that the size of the posterior cerebellar vermis is positively correlated with performance on IQ and visual–spatial measures in girls with fragile X syndrome, and Mazzocco et al. (1997) found that it is negatively correlated with abnormalities in communication and behaviour. Reiss and colleagues (Reiss, Abrams, Greenlaw, Freud, & Denckla, 1995) found that the activation ratio in girls predicts the degree to which the caudate and ventricular volumes are increased in size, relative to controls. Although we still do not understand the role that FMRP plays in brain development and function, fragile X syndrome offers an interesting model of associations between gene expression, brain pathology, and phenotypic variability.

TURNER'S SYNDROME

Turner's syndrome is another disorder related to the X chromosome. It is typically associated with the absence of one of the X chromosomes in females, although there are quite a number of genetic variants, including mosaicism and partial deletions (Ross & Zinn, 1999). The syndrome has a number of physical characteristics, the most common being short stature, short webbed neck, broad chest, and other physical stigmata (Powell & Schulte, 1999). In addition, the ovaries fail to develop normally, which leads to a lack of ovarian oestrogen production, infertility, and failure to undergo the normal changes associated with puberty (see Chapter 9 for further discussion on hormonal influences on cognition in Turner's syndrome).

Girls with Turner's syndrome are generally not mentally retarded, although they have a striking cognitive profile. Their verbal IQ scores are typically well within the normal range but performance on non-verbal IQ subtests, especially those tapping visual–spatial tasks, is significantly depressed (Rovet & Buchanan, 1999). Shaffer (1962), for example, found that performance IQ was almost 20 points lower than verbal IQ in Turner's syndrome. Girls with Turner's syndrome have difficulty with tasks tapping visual–spatial analysis, visual memory, visual–motor skills, arithmetic, and working memory—a pattern that some researchers suggest could be related to differences in lateralization (Rovet, 1995).

There are also a number of social and psychological features associated with Turner's syndrome. Girls with Turner's syndrome often have low self-esteem, which can be related to teasing by others because of their short stature and unusual appearance (McCauley, Ito, & Kay, 1986; Skuse, 1987). They also have more behaviour problems, are socially immature, have poor peer relationships, and have difficulties with attention and impulsivity, compared with girls of the same height but without Turner's syndrome (McCauley et al., 1986; Rovet & Ireland, 1994).

As in all developmental disorders, there is considerable variability in the expression of the cognitive and psychosocial characteristics associated with Turner's syndrome. There have been several interesting approaches to investigating the role of underlying biological and genetic factors in understanding some of this variability. One line of work has been to study the role of oestrogen, which is known to be important in brain development. Girls with Turner's syndrome have diminished oestrogen production and it has been hypothesized that this might, at least partially, explain some of the deficits that have been reported (Nielson & Nyborg, 1981).

The most comprehensive investigation of the effects of oestrogen in Turner's syndrome has been conducted by Ross and colleagues (Ross & Zinn, 1999). In one study, a group of girls aged 12 were all put on low-dosage oestrogen replacement therapy, and then followed during adolescence. Self-esteem, behaviour, and social difficulties showed significant improvement over a 3-year period, which was related to the oestrogen treatment. Another study, which involved a randomized, double-blind design comparing matched groups of girls aged 7–9 years old, receiving either oestrogen or placebo, explored the effects of oestrogen on memory (Ross, Roeltgen, Feuillan, Kushner, & Cutler, 2000). The group receiving oestrogen treatment performed significantly better than the placebo controls on verbal memory and working memory tasks, suggesting that this hormone plays an important role in the development of these cognitive abilities.

Genetic contributions to the phenotypic expression of Turner's syndrome have also been found. It is hypothesized that the cognitive phenotype in Turner's syndrome is due to reduced dosage of X-linked genes. Evidence for this comes from several studies that found that mosaic Turner's syndrome girls are less severely affected than non-mosaics, especially on tasks tapping visual–spatial skills (Murphy et al., 1994; Ross & Zinn, 1999; Rovet, 1991; Temple & Carney, 1995).

A different way of looking at genetic contributions to the Turner's syndrome phenotype is to consider whether some of the genes on the X chromosome are imprinted. On this view, the parental origin of the single X chromosome should have a significant effect on phenotypic expression. Typically, about 70 per cent of girls with Turner's syndrome derive their X from their mothers, and 30 per cent from their fathers. Although global measures of verbal and performance IQ do not reveal any imprinting effects (Ross & Zinn, 1999), a recent study by Bishop and colleagues did find that girls with a single paternally derived X had significantly lower non-verbal memory scores compared to controls, whereas girls with a single maternally derived X had significantly lower verbal memory scores (Bishop et al., 2000). Skuse et al. (1997) also reported interesting imprinting effects. In their study, girls with a paternally derived X had higher verbal skills, higher scores on a parent interview measure of social cognition, and performed better on measures of behavioural inhibition.

Taken together, these studies of Turner's syndrome illustrate a number of interesting and important ways in which hormones and genes contribute to neurocognitive development. Turner's syndrome offers a unique model for investigating the specific role of genes on the X chromosome, and the putative effects of genetic imprinting in the human genome on phenotypic expression. The studies of oestrogen replacement therapy also point to new ways of treating Turner's syndrome, which, if administered early enough in development, could alter the course of brain development and eliminate the cognitive and psychosocial deficits associated with the disorder.

WILLIAMS SYNDROME

In recent years, Williams syndrome has captured the interest and imagination of cognitive and developmental neuroscientists in the expectation that investigations of people with this disorder can inform our understanding of the genetic, neural, and computational mechanisms that underlie our cognitive systems. It is caused by a microdeletion on the long arm of chromosome 7, a region that includes at least 19 genes (Morris & Mervis, 1999). Many of the genes have been mapped, although for most we still do not know how they might be related to the Williams syndrome phenotype (Korenberg et al., 2000).

Williams syndrome is characterized by a phenotype that typically includes cardiovascular disease, especially supravalvular aortic stenosis (SVAS), connective tissue abnormalities, craniofacial dysmorphology (referred to as elfin facies), and an unusual combination of cognitive and behavioural features (Morris & Mervis, 2000). The majority of people with Williams syndrome have mild to moderate levels of mental retardation but their performance on standard IQ tests shows striking unevenness across subtests measuring different cognitive abilities (Bellugi et al., 1999). The cognitive profile of Williams syndrome is characterized by strengths in a number of domains, including language, especially vocabulary, auditory rote memory, face recognition skills, and good expressive language. At the same time, other cognitive domains are extremely impaired, especially visual–spatial construction, as measured, for example, on block design or drawing tasks (Bellugi et al., 1994; Mervis et al., 1999). There are also a number of other behavioural features that are found in many children with Williams syndrome, including anxiety, poor attention, and responding in an overly friendly manner, especially towards strangers (Gosch & Pankau, 1997; Mervis & Klein-Tasman, 2000). People with Williams syndrome are extremely sociable, extroverted, and empathic in their responses to other people (Gosch & Pankau, 1994). However, this sociability does not translate into more advanced social cognitive abilities, such as performance on standard theory-of-mind tasks (Tager-Flusberg & Sullivan, 2000).

One of the most interesting directions taken in current research on Williams syndrome has been to begin mapping specific components of the phenotype onto specific genes that are in the deleted region associated with this disorder. Almost everyone with Williams syndrome has a deletion that is the same length, although there are a small number of individuals, representing less than 5 per cent of the population meeting most clinical criteria for the disorder, who either have slightly longer deletions or slightly shorter ones. There are also a small number of people who do not have Williams syndrome but who share one or more of the features that are part of the phenotype. By investigating these exceptional cases, researchers have made progress relating at least two components of the phenotype to specific genes.

The genetic cause of Williams syndrome was initially discovered by pursuing leads provided by some of these exceptional cases. Many people with Williams syndrome have the heart malformation known as SVAS. It was known that SVAS not only occurred in association with a developmental disorder but, in quite different individuals, was also an inherited form of heart disease, transmitted in an autosomal dominant fashion. By finding the gene associated with this inherited heart disease, Morris and colleagues hypothesized that this path would lead to the genetic basis for Williams syndrome. Using linkage analysis on a number of pedigrees, Ewart et al. (1993) found that the patients with SVAS had a mutation on the elastin gene (ELN). They followed-up these findings by demonstrating that people with Williams syndrome were missing one copy of this gene, a finding that led also to the development of a simple genetic test for the disorder. The ELN mutation is responsible for the cardiovascular problems in Williams syndrome, as well as other physical features such as the connective tissue abnormalities (Mervis et al., 1999).

Morris and colleagues followed-up this initial success by turning their attention to the relationship between some of the genes adjacent to ELN, and other aspects of the Williams syndrome phenotype. Three of the SVAS pedigrees that led to the discovery of ELN included members with SVAS who had also been reported as having academic problems; other pedigrees did not. The members of these families were administered an extensive cognitive battery that had been used to define and operationalize the Williams syndrome cognitive profile (Mervis et al., 2000). Those meeting the profile, which is especially sensitive to the visual–spatial deficits, came from two pedigrees and were found to have a very small deleted region on chromosome 7 that included the ELN gene. Eventually, Frangiskakis et al. (1996) were able to show that the people in those families who met the cognitive profile were also missing a gene adjacent to ELN, called lim-kinase 1 (LIMK1). In this way, the researchers demonstrated that this gene, which we know is expressed in the brain, is associated with a specific cognitive function, namely visual–spatial constructive ability.

This is only one part of the Williams syndrome story, showing how systematic investigations of a developmental disorder might lead us to map genes associated with cognitive functions. Ongoing work is continuing this approach to map the genes in the critical Williams region to other features of the disorder, including key behavioural characteristics. In addition, there are exciting preliminary findings linking the cognitive and behavioural features to aspects of brain structure and function, thus confirming the expectation that interdisciplinary investigations of people with developmental disorders that involve known genetic mechanisms will advance our understanding of gene, brain, and behaviour connections (Bellugi & St. George, 2000).

AUTISM

Autism is a complex behavioural syndrome that was first identified by Leo Kanner (1943). Unlike the other disorders considered thus far, we still do not know the genes that cause autism. On the basis of evidence from several twin studies, we know that it is a highly heritable disorder and it is believed to be a complex genetic disorder caused by mutations on several interacting genes (Santangelo & Folstein, 1999).

Autism is defined on the basis of three cardinal features: impairments in social functioning, impairments in language and communication, and a restricted repertoire of activity and interests (American Psychiatric Association, 1994). It is generally diagnosed between the ages of two and five, although symptoms are almost always present before children reach their third birthday. There are a number of additional features associated with the disorder that are not included in the diagnostic criteria. These include mental retardation, abnormal responses to sensory stimuli, savant abilities, atypical sleeping and eating patterns, and behavioural problems such as tantrums, aggression, attentional difficulties, anxiety, and depression. Because the symptoms vary in their severity, autism is now viewed as a spectrum of conditions ranging from severely retarded non-verbal children, to high-functioning individuals with excellent language, milder forms of social and communicative difficulties, and circumscribed interests (Tager-Flusberg, Joseph, & Folstein, 2001).

Advances have been made in our understanding of the cognitive deficits that underlie the social and communicative aspects of autism. Based on the seminal work of Baron-Cohen and colleagues, autism is viewed as involving core difficulties in understanding other minds: known as the theory-of-mind hypothesis of autism (Baron-Cohen, Tager-Flusberg, & Cohen, 1993, 2000). Impaired theory-of-mind abilities can explain the social difficulties, as well as the problems in communication, both of which entail an appreciation of mental states in people. More broadly, people with autism show significant differences in the way they process social stimuli, including faces and language (Klin, Schultz, & Cohen, 2000; Tager-Flusberg, 2001).

Functional brain imaging studies are beginning to delineate the brain areas that are involved in social and theory-of-mind processing, which include parts of the medial–temporal cortex including the limbic system, prefrontal cortical regions, including the orbitofrontal and medial areas, and related regions. However, some interesting recent studies suggest that people with autism spectrum disorders do not activate these same regions when they engage in social information processing. For example, Schultz and colleagues (Schultz et al., 2000) found that, unlike matched normal controls, adults with autism did not activate the so-called "face" area in the fusiform gyrus when they were shown a series of faces and objects. Instead, they activate the inferior temporal gyri, which was activated in controls when they processed objects. In another study, Baron-Cohen et al. (1999) asked adults with autism and normal controls to judge the mental state expressed in the eye region of the face. Unlike the controls, adults with autism did not activate the amygdala when making these judgements; instead they only activated cortical regions in the prefrontal cortex and superior temporal gyrus, which are usually involved in processing this mental state information.

Fletcher and colleagues (1995) conducted a PET study comparing activation patterns in healthy adults to stories requiring physical causal reasoning versus mental state reasoning. The mental state, or theory-of-mind, stories were associated with unique activation in regions of the left medial frontal cortex (Brodmann's areas 8 and 9). By contrast, Happé and colleagues (1996), using the same paradigm with five adults with Asperger's syndrome, found significantly less activation in this region for the mental state stories. Instead, the adults with Asperger's syndrome activated brain regions that are associated with more general-purpose reasoning, rather than with social or mental state reasoning. Several other studies (cited in Frith & Frith, 2000), have also found that adults with autism or Asperger's syndrome fail to activate the same regions as non-autistic adults when given tasks that involve theory-of-mind-related abilities. These studies suggest that, in non-autistic people, specialized brain regions, including areas of the medial frontal cortex and medial temporal cortex, are involved in making mental state or related social attributions. By contrast, when people with autism are presented with these kinds of tasks they tend to rely on more general-association areas of the brain for processing social stimuli. Taken together, these studies of functional brain imaging provide an interesting and significant bridge between the studies of cognitive of impairments in autism and studies of brain pathology.

CONCLUSIONS

The past two decades have witnessed very rapid growth in our understanding of developmental disorders, especially new research in the foundational disciplines. In this chapter we have highlighted:

1. Research demonstrating the wide range of genetic mechanisms known to cause developmental disorders. Rapid advances in the human genome project will open up new knowledge in the next decades.
2. How genetic defects cause disruptions in brain development. New techniques for imaging brains, to detect both structural and functional abnormalities, provide us with a perspective on the underlying neurobiology for many different disorders.
3. The growth in neuropsychological and cognitive science research, which offers detailed descriptions of the phenotypic expression and variability found in different disorders.
4. The close relationship between genetic variation and phenotypic expression as illustrated in fragile X syndrome and Williams syndrome.
5. The interactions between genes and environment, as illustrated by research on PKU.
6. The role of hormones and imprinting mechanisms in the expression of social and cognitive impairments in Turner's syndrome.
7. How the study of autism can help to delineate the brain regions involved in social information processing.

We are still at the exploratory stage of integrating the components that make up a cognitive neuroscience of developmental disorders in a meaningful and mechanistic way. The examples presented here demonstrate that progress has been made in creating the science that links genetics and neuroscience to cognition within a developmental framework. Through multidisciplinary research on developmental disorders that includes genetic mechanisms, developmental neurobiology, and cognitive science we will formulate the theoretical models of how basic genetic and environmental building blocks build a brain and mind.

ACKNOWLEDGEMENTS

Preparation of this chapter was supported by grants from NIDCD (PO1 DC 03610), NICHD (RO1 HD 33470) and NINDS/NIMH (RO1 NS 38668).

REFERENCES

Abrams, M., Reiss, A., Freund, L., Baumgardner, T., Chase, G., & Denckla, M. (1994). Molecular–neurobehavioural associations in females with the fragile X full mutation. *American Journal of Medical Genetics, 51*, 317–327.

American Psychiatric Association (1994). *Diagnostic and statistical manual of mental disorders (DSM-IV)* (4th ed.). Washington DC: APA.

Arnold, L.E., Zametkin, A.J., Caravella, L., & Korbly, N. (2000). Ethical issues in neuroimaging research with children. In M. Ernst & J.M. Rumsey (Eds.), *Functional neuroimaging in child psychiatry* (pp. 99–109). Cambridge: Cambridge University Press.

Baron-Cohen, S. (1995). *Mindblindness: An essay on autism and theory of mind.* Cambridge, MA: MIT Press.

Baron-Cohen, S., Tager-Flusberg, H., & Cohen, D.J. (Eds.). (1993). *Understanding other minds: Perspectives from autism.* Oxford: Oxford University Press.

Baron-Cohen, S., Tager-Flusberg, H., & Cohen, D.J. (Eds.). (2000). *Understanding other minds: Perspectives from developmental cognitive neuroscience* (2nd ed.). Oxford: Oxford University Press.

Baron-Cohen, S., Ring, H., Wheelwright, S., Bullmore, E., Brammer, M.J., Simmons, A. et al. (1999). Social intelligence in the normal and autistic brain: An fMRI study. *European Journal of Neuroscience, 11*, 1891–1898.

Bates, E., Vicari, S., & Trauner, D. (1999). Neural mediation of language development: Perspectives from lesion studies of infants and children. In H. Tager-Flusberg (Ed.), *Neurodevelopmental disorders* (pp. 533–581). Cambridge, MA: MIT Press.

Bauman, M., & Kemper, T. (1994). Neuroanatomic observations of the brain in autism. In M. Bauman & T. Kemper (Eds.), *The neurobiology of autism* (pp. 119–141). Baltimore, MD: Johns Hopkins University Press.

Bellugi, U., & St George, M. (Eds.) (2000). Linking cognitive neuroscience and molecular genetics: New perspectives from Williams syndrome. *Journal of Cognitive Neuroscience, 12*, (suppl. 1). Special Issue.

Bellugi, U., Mills, D., Jernigan, T., Hickok, G., & Galaburda, A. (1999). Linking cognition, brain structure, and brain function in Williams syndrome. In H. Tager-Flusberg (Ed.), *Neurodevelopmental disorders* (pp. 111–136). Cambridge, MA: MIT Press.

Bellugi, U., Wang, P.P., & Jernigan, T.L. (1994). Williams syndrome: An unusual neuropsychological profile. In S.H. Broman & J. Grafman (Eds.), *Atypical cognitive deficits in developmental disorders: Implications for brain function* (pp. 23–56). Hillsdale, NJ: Lawrence Erlbaum Associates Inc.

Belmont, J., & Butterfield, E. (1971). Learning strategies as determinants of memory deficiencies. *Cognitive Psychology, 2*, 411–420.

Bickel, H., Gerrard, J., & Hickmans, E.M. (1954). The influence of phenylalanine intake on the chemistry and behaviour of a phenylketonuric child. *Acta Paediatrica, 43*, 64–77.

Bishop, D.V.M. (1997). *Uncommon understanding: Development and disorders of language comprehension in children*. London: Psychology Press.

Bishop, D.V.M., Canning, E., Elgar, K., Morris, E., Jacobs, P., & Skuse, D. (2000). Distinctive patterns of memory function in subgroups of females with Turner syndrome: Evidence for imprinted loci on the X-chromosome affecting neurodevelopment. *Neuropsychologica, 38*, 712–721.

Butler, M., & Palmer, C.G. (1983). Parental origin of chromosome 15 deletion in Prader–Willi syndrome. *Lancet, 1 (8336)*, 1285–1286.

Cawthon, R., Weiss, R., Xu, G.F., Viskochil, D., Culver, M., Stevens, J. et al. (1990). A major segment of the neurofibromatosis type 1 gene: cDNA sequence, genomic structure, and point mutations. *Cell, 62*, 193–201.

Chugani, D.C., Sundram, B.S., Behen, M., Lee, M.-L., & Moore, G. (1999). Evidence of altered energy metabolism in autistic children. *Progress in Neuropharmacology and Biological Psychiatry, 23*, 635–641.

Ciaranello, R., Aimi, J., Dean, R.R., Morilak, D., Porteus, M.H., & Cicchetti, D. (1995). Fundamentals of molecular neurobiology. In D. Cicchetti & D.J. Cohen (Eds.), *Developmental psychopathology. Volume I: Theory and methods* (pp. 109–160). New York: Wiley.

Cody, H., & Kamphaus, R.W. (1999). Down syndrome. In S. Goldstein & C.R. Reynolds (Eds.), *Handbook of neurodevelopmental and genetic disorders in children* (pp. 385–405). New York: Guilford Press.

Cohen, I., Nolin, S., Sudhalter, V., Ding, X.-H., Dobkin, C., & Brown, W. (1996). Mosaicism for the FMR1 gene influences adpative skills development in fragile-X affected males. *American Journal of Medical Genetics, 64*, 365–369.

Courchesne, E., & Plante, E. (1996). Measurement and analysis issues in neurodevelopmental magnetic resonance imaging. In R.W. Thatcher, G.R. Lyon, J. Rumsey, & N. Krasnegor (Eds.), *Developmental neuroimaging: Mapping the development of brain and behaviour* (pp. 43–65). New York: Academic Press.

Courchesne, E., Townsend, J., & Chase, C. (1995). Neurodevelopmental principles guide research on developmental psychopathologies. In D. Cicchetti & D.J. Cohen (Eds.), *Developmental psychopathology. Volume I: Theory and methods* (pp. 195–226). New York: Wiley.

Crnic, L., & Pennington, B. (2000). Down syndrome: Neuropsychology and animal models. In C. Rovee-Collier, L.P. Lipsitt, & H. Hayne (Eds.), *Progress in infancy research, Volume 1*. Mahwah, NJ: Lawrence Erlbaum Associates Inc.

Detterman, D., & Daniel, M. (1989). Correlations of mental tests with each other and with cognitive variables are highest for low IQ groups. *Intelligence, 13*, 349–359.

Diamond, A., Prevor, M.B., Callender, G., & Druin, D.P. (1997). Prefrontal cortex cognitive deficits in children treated early and continuously for PKU. *Monographs of the Society for Research in Child Development, 62*. Serial No. 252.

DiLella, A.G., Marvit, J., Lidsky, A.S., Guttler, F., & Woo, S. (1986). Tight linkage between a splicing mutation and a specific DNA haplotype in phenylketonuria. *Nature, 322*, 799–803.

Dykens, E. (1995). Measuring behavioural phenotypes: Provocations from the "new genetics". *American Journal on Mental Retardation, 99*, 522–532.

Dykens, E. (1999). Prader–Willi syndrome: Toward a behavioural phenotype. In H. Tager-Flusberg (Ed.), *Neurodevelopmental disorders* (pp. 137–154). Cambridge, MA: MIT Press.

Eden, G., & Zeffiro, T. (2000). Functional magnetic resonance imaging. In M. Ernst & J.M. Rumsy (Eds.), *Functional neuroimaging in child psychiatry* (pp. 45–58). Cambridge: Cambridge University Press.

Ellis, N.R. (1963). The stimulus trace and behavioural inadequacy. In N.R. Ellis (Ed.), *Handbook of mental deficiency, psychological theory, and research* (pp. 134–158). New York: McGraw-Hill.

Ernst, M., & Rumsey, J. (Eds.). (2000). *Functional neuroimaging in child psychiatry*. Cambridge: Cambridge University Press.

Ernst, M., Zametkin, A., Marochik, J., Pascualvaca, D., & Cohen, R. (1997). Low medial prefrontal dopaminergic activity in autistic children. *Lancet, 350*, 638.

Ewart, A.K., Morris, C.A., Atkinson, D., Jin, W., Sternes, K., Spallone, P. et al. (1993). Hemizygosity at the elastin locus in a developmental disorder, Williams syndrome. *Nature Genetics, 5*, 11–16.

Filipek, P. (1996). Structural variations in measures in the developmental disorders. In R.W. Thatcher, G.R. Lyon, J. Rumsey, & N. Krasnegor (Eds.), *Developmental neuroimaging: Mapping the development of brain and behaviour* (pp. 169–186). New York: Academic Press.

Fletcher, P.C., Happé, F., Frith, U., Baker, S.C., Dolan, R.J., Frackowiak, R.S.J. et al. (1995). Other minds in the brain: A functional imaging study of "theory of mind" in story comprehension. *Cognition, 57*, 109–128.

Flint, J. (1996). Annotation: Behavioural phenotypes: A window onto the biology of behaviour. *Journal of Child Psychology and Psychiatry, 37*, 355–367.

Frangiskakis, J.M., Ewart, A.K., Morris, C.A., Mervis, C.B., Bertrand, J., Robinson, B. et al. (1996). LIM-kinase 1 hemizygosity implicated in impaired visuospatial constructive cognition. *Cell, 86*, 59–69.

Freund, L., Reiss, A.L., & Abrams, M. (1993). Psychiatric disorders associated with fragile X in the young female. *Pediatrics, 91*, 321–329.

Frith, C., & Frith, U. (2000). The physiological basis of theory of mind: Functional neuroimaging studies. In S. Baron-Cohen, H. Tager-Flusberg, & D. Cohen (Eds.), *Understanding other minds: Perspectives from autism and developmental cognitive neuroscience* (2nd ed., pp. 334–356). Oxford: Oxford University Press.

Fu, Y-H., Kuhl, D.P., Pizzuti, A., Pieretti, M., Sutcliffe, J., Richards, S. et al. (1991). Variation of the CGG repeat at the fragile X site results in genetic instability: Resolution of the Sherman paradox. *Cell, 67*, 1047–1058.

Goodman, R. (1994). Brain development. In M. Rutter & D. Hay (Eds.), *Development through life: A handbook for clinicians* (pp. 49–78). Oxford: Blackwell.

Gosch, A., & Pankau, R. (1994). Social–emotional and behavioural adjustment in children with Williams–Beuren syndrome. *American Journal of Medical Genetics, 53*, 335–339.

Gosch, A., & Pankau, R. (1997). Personality characteristics and behaviour problems in individuals of different ages with Williams syndrome. *Developmental Medicine and Child Neurology, 39*, 327–533.

Grigorenko, E., Wood, F., Meyer, M., Hart, L., Speed, W., Shuster, A., et al. (1997). Susceptibility loci for distinct components of developmental dyslexia on chromosome 6 and 15. *American Journal of Human Genetics, 60*, 27–39.

Guthrie, R., & Susi, A. (1963). A simple phenylalanine method for detecting phenylketonuria in large populations of newborn infants. *Pediatrics, 32*, 338–343.

Hagerman, R.J. (1999). Clinical and molecular aspects of fragile X syndrome. In H. Tager-Flusberg (Ed.), *Neurodevelopmental disorders* (pp. 27–42). Cambridge, MA: MIT Press.

Happé, F., Ehlers, S., Fletcher, P., Frith, U., Johansson, M., Gillberg, C. et al. (1996). "Theory of mind" in the brain. Evidence from a PET scan study of Asperger syndrome. *NeuroReport, 8*, 197–201.

Harris, J.C. (1998). *Developmental neuropsychiatry. Volume I: Fundamentals*. New York: Oxford University Press.

Hodapp, R., Burack, J., & Zigler, E. (1998). Developmental approaches to mental retardation: A short introduction. In J. Burack, R.M. Hodapp, & E. Zigler (Eds.), *Handbook of mental retardation and development* (pp. 3–19). New York: Cambridge University Press.

Joseph, R. (1999). Neuropsychological frameworks for understanding autism. *International Review of Psychiatry, 11*, 309–325.

Kanner, L. (1943). Autistic disturbances of affective contact. *Nervous Child, 2*, 217–250.

Karmiloff-Smith, A. (1998). Is atypical development necessarily a window on the normal mind/brain?: The case of Williams syndrome. *Developmental Science, 1*, 273–277.

Klin, A., Schultz, R., & Cohen, D.J. (2000). Theory of mind in action: Developmental perspectives on social neuroscience. In S. Baron-Cohen, H. Tager-Flusberg, & D.J. Cohen (Eds.), *Understanding other minds: Perspectives from developmental cognitive neuroscience* (2nd ed., pp. 357–388). Oxford: Oxford University Press.

Korenberg, J., Chen, X.-N., Hirota, H., Lai, Z., Bellugi, U., Burian, D. et al. (2000). Genome structure and cognitive map of Williams syndrome. *Journal of Cognitive Neuroscience, 12 (suppl.)*, 89–107.

Lachiewicz, A.M. (1992). Abnormal behaviours of young girls with fragile X syndrome. *American Journal of Medical Genetics, 43*, 72–77.

Lander, E., & Schork, N.J. (1994). Genetic dissection of complex traits. *Science, 265*, 2037–2048.

Lidsky, A.S., Robson, K.J.H., Thirumalachary, C., Baker, P.E., Ruddle, F.H., & Woo, F.H.C. (1984). The PKU locus in man is on chromosome 12. *American Journal of Human Genetics, 36*, 527–535.

Lombroso, P.J., Pauls, D., & Leckman, J. (1994). Genetic mechanisms in childhood psychiatric disorders. *Journal of the American Academy of Child and Adolescent Psychiatry, 33*, 921–938.

Lyon, R., & Rumsey, J. (Eds.) (1996). *Neuroimaging: A window to the neurological foundations of learning and behaviour in children.* Baltimore, MD: Paul Brookes.

Mazzocco, M.M., Hagerman, R., Cronister, S., & Pennington, B. (1992). Specific frontal lobe deficits among women with the fragile X gene. *Journal of the American Academy of Child and Adolescent Psychiatry, 31*, 1141–1148.

Mazzocco, M.M., Kates, W., Freund, L., Baumgardner, T. & Reiss, A.L. (1997). Autistic behaviour among girls with fragile X syndrome, *Journal of Autism and Developmental Disorders, 27*, 415–435.

Mazzocco, M.M. & Reiss, A.L. (1999). A behavioural neurogenetics approach to understanding the fragile X syndrome. In H. Tager-Flusberg (Ed.), *Neurodevelopmental disorders* (pp. 43–63). Cambridge, MA: MIT Press.

McCauley, E., Ito, J., & Kay, T. (1986). Psychosocial functioning in girls with the Turner syndrome and short stature. *Journal of the American Academy of Child Psychiatry, 25*, 105–112.

Merenstein, S., Sobesky, W., Taylor, A., Riddle, J., Tran, H., & Hagerman, R. (1996). Molecular–clinical correlations in males with an expanded FMR1 mutation. *American Journal of Medical Genetics, 64*, 388–394.

Mervis, C.B., & Klein-Tasman, B.P. (2000). Williams syndrome: Cognition, personality, and adaptive behaviour. *Mental Retardation and Developmental Disabilities Research Reviews, 6(2)*, 148–158.

Mervis, C.B., Morris, C.A., Bertrand, J., & Robinson, B.F. (1999). Williams syndrome: Findings from an integrated program of research. In H. Tager-Flusberg (Ed.), *Neurodevelopmental disorders* (pp. 65–110). Cambridge, MA: MIT Press.

Mervis, C.B., Robinson, B.F., Bertrand, J., Morris, C., Klein-Tasman, B.P., & Amstrong, S.C. (2000). The Williams syndrome cognitive profile. *Brain and Cognition, 44*, 604–628.

Morris, C.A., & Mervis, C. (1999). Williams syndrome. In S. Goldstein & C. Reynolds (Eds.), *Handbook of neurodevelopmental and genetic disorders in children.* (pp. 555–590). New York: Guilford Press.

Morton, J., & Frith, U. (1995). Causal modeling: A structural approach to developmental psychopathology. In D. Cicchetti & D.J. Cohen (Eds.), *Developmental psychopathology. Volume I: Theory and methods* (pp. 357–390). New York: Wiley.

Mostofsky, S.H., Mazzocco, M.M., Aakalu, G., Warsofsky, I., Denckla, M., & Reiss, A. (1996). Decreased posterior cerebellar vermis size in fragile X syndrome. *Neurology, 50*, 121–130.

Muller, R.-A., & Courchesne, E. (2000). The duplicity of plasticity: A conceptual approach to the study of early lesions and developmental disorders. In M. Ernst & J. Rumsey (Eds.), *Functional neuroimaging in child psychiatry* (pp. 335–365). Cambridge: Cambridge University Press.

Murphy, D., Allen, G., Haxby, J., Largay, K., Daly, E., White, B. et al. (1994). The effects of sex steroids and the X chromosome on female brain function: A study of the neuropsychology of adult Turner syndrome. *Neuropsychologia, 32*, 1309–1323.

Nicholls, R.D., Knoll, J.H., Butler, M.G., Karam, S., & Lalande, M. (1989). Genetic imprinting suggested by maternal heterodisomy in nondeletion Prader–Willi syndrome. *Nature, 342*, 281–285.

Nielson, J., & Nyborg, H. (1981). Sex hormone treatment and spatial ability in women with Turner's syndrome. In W. Schmid & J. Nielson (Eds.), *Human behaviour and genetics* (pp. 167–181). Amsterdam: Elsevier.

Pennington, B. (1999). Dyslexia as a neurodevelopmental disorder. In H. Tager-Flusberg (Ed.), *Neurodevelopmental disorders* (pp. 307–330). Cambridge, MA: MIT Press/ Bradford Books.

Pennington B., & Welsh, M. (1995). Neuropsychology and developmental psychopathology. In D. Cicchetti & D.J. Cohen (Eds.), *Developmental psychopathology. Volume I: Theory and methods* (pp. 254–290). New York: Wiley.

Powell, M.P., & Schulte, T. (1999). Turner syndrome. In S. Goldstein & C.R. Reynolds (Eds.), *Handbook of neurodevelopmental and genetic disorders in children* (pp. 277–297). New York: Guilford Press.

Reiss, A.L., Abrams, M., Greenlaw, R., Freund, L., & Denckla, M. (1995). Neurodevelopmental effects of the FMR-1 full mutation in humans. *Nature Medicine, 1*, 159–167.

Reiss, A.L., & Freund, L. (1991). Behavioural phenotype of fragile X syndrome: DSM-III-R autistic behaviour in male children. *American Journal of Medical Genetics, 43*, 35–46.

Reiss, A.L., Freund, L., Tseng, J., & Joshi, P. (1991). Neuroanatomy in fragile X females: The posterior fossa. *American Journal of Human Genetics, 49*, 279–288.

Reiss, A.L., Lee, J., & Freund, L. (1994). Neuroanatomy of fragile X syndrome: The temporal lobe. *Neurology, 44*, 1317–1324.

Reynolds, C.R., & Mayfield, J.W. (1999). Neuropsychological assessment in genetically linked neurodevelopmental disorders. In S. Goldstein & C.R. Reynolds (Eds.), *Handbook of neurodevelopmental and genetic disorders in children* (pp. 9–37). New York: Guilford Press.

Riddle, J., Cheema, A., Sobesky, W., Gardner, S., Taylor, A., Pennington, B., & Hagerman, R. (1998). Phenotype in females with the FMR1 gene mutation. *American Journal of Mental Retardation, 102*, 590–601.

Roof, E., Stone, W., MacLean, W., Feurer, I.D., Thompson, T., & Butler, M.G. (2000). Intellectual characteristics of Prader–Willi syndrome: Comparison of genetic subtypes. *Journal of Intellectual Disability Research, 44*, 25–30.

Ross, J.L., Roeltgen, D., Feuillan, P., Kushner, H., & Cutler, G. (2000). Use of estrogen in young girls with Turner syndrome: Effects on memory. *Neurology, 54*, 164–170.

Ross, J.L., & Zinn, A. (1999). Turner syndrome: Potential hormonal and genetic influences on the neurocognitive profile. In H. Tager-Flusberg (Ed.), *Neurodevelopmental disorders* (pp. 251–268). Cambridge, MA: MIT Press/Bradford Books.

Rovet, J. (1991). The cognitive and neuropsychological characteristics of females with Turner syndrome. In B. Bender & D. Berch (Eds.), *Sex chromosome abnormalities and behaviour: Psychological studies* (pp. 39–77). Boulder, CO: Westview Press.

Rovet, J. (1995). Behavioural manifestations of Turner syndrome in children: A unique phenotype. In K. Albertsson-Wikland & M.B. Ranke (Eds.), *Turner syndrome in a life span perspective: Research and clinical aspects* (pp. 297–308). Amsterdam: Elsevier.

Rovet, J., & Buchanan, L. (1999). Turner syndrome: A cognitive neuroscience perspective. In H. Tager-Flusberg (Ed.), *Neurodevelopmental disorders* (pp. 221–249). Cambridge, MA: MIT Press/Bradford Books.

Rovet, J., & Ireland, L. (1994). The behavioural phenotype of children with Turner syndrome. *Journal of Pediatric Psychology, 19*, 779–790.

Santangelo, S., & Folstein, S.E. (1999). Autism: A genetic perspective. In H. Tager-Flusberg (Ed.), *Neurodevelopmental disorders* (pp. 431–447). Cambridge, MA: MIT Press/Bradford Books.

Schultz, R.T., Gauthier, I., Klin, A., Fulbright, R.K., Anderson, A.W., Volkmar, F. et al. (2000). Abnormal ventral temporal cortical activity during face discrimination among individuals with autism and Asperger syndrome. *Archives of General Psychiatry, 57*, 331–340.

Shaffer, J. (1962). A specific cognitive deficit observed in gonadal aplasia (Turner's syndrome). *Journal of Clinical Psychology, 18*, 403–406.

Skuse, D. (1987). Annotation: The psychological consequences of being small. *Journal of Child Psychology and Psychiatry, 28*, 641–650.

Skuse, D., James, R., Bishop, D.V.M., Coppin, B., Dalton, P., Aamodlt-Leeper, G. et al. (1997). Evidence from Turner's syndrome of an imprinted X-linked locus affecting cognitive function. *Nature, 387*, 705–708.

Smith, I., & Beasley, M. (1989). Intelligence and behaviour in children with early treated phenylketonuria. *European Journal of Clinical Nutrition, 43*, 1–5.

Sobesky, W., Taylor, A., Pennington, B., Riddle, J., & Hagerman, R. (1996). Molecular/clinical correlations in females with fragile X. *American Journal of Medical Genetics, 64*, 340–345.

Tager-Flusberg, H. (1999). Introduction to research on neurodevelopmental disorders from a cognitive neuroscience perspective. In H. Tager-Flusberg (Ed.), *Neurodevelopmental disorders* (pp. 3–24). Cambridge, MA: MIT Press/Bradford Books.

Tager-Flusberg, H. (2000). Differences between neurodevelopmental disorders and acquired lesions. *Developmental Science, 3*, 33–34.

Tager-Flusberg, H. (2001). A re-examination of the theory of mind hypothesis of autism. In J. Burack, T. Charman, N. Yirmiya, & P. Zelazo (Eds.), *The development of autism: Perspectives from theory and research*. Mahwah, NJ: Lawrence Erlbaum Associates Inc.

Tager-Flusberg, H., Joseph, R., & Folstein, S. (2001). Current directions in research on autism. *Mental Retardation and Developmental Disabilities Research Reviews, 7*, 21–29.

Tager-Flusberg, H., & Sullivan, K. (2000). A componential view of theory of mind: Evidence from Williams syndrome. *Cognition, 76*, 59–89.

Temple, C.M., & Carney, R.A. (1995). Patterns of spatial functioning in Turner's syndrome. *Cortex, 31*, 109–118.

Thatcher, R.W., Lyon, G.R., Rumsey, J., & Krasnegor, N. (Eds.) (1996). *Developmental neuroimaging: Mapping the development of brain and behavior*. New York: Academic Press.

Verkerk, A.J., Pieretti, M., Sutcliffe, J., Fu, Y., Kuhl, D.P., & Warren, S.T. (1991). Identification of a gene containing a CGG repeat coincident with a breakpoint cluster region exhibiting length variation in fragile X syndrome. *Cell, 65*, 905–914.

Waisbren, S.E. (1999). Phenylketonuria. In S. Goldstein & C.R. Reynolds (Eds.), *Handbook of neurodevelopmental and genetic disorders in children* (pp. 433–458). New York: Guilford Press.

Welsh, M.C., Pennington, B., Ozonoff, S., Rouse, B., & McCabe, E. (1990). Neuropsychology of early treated phenylketonuria: Specific executive function deficits. *Child Development, 61*, 1697–1713.

Zeaman, D., & House, B. (1963). The role of attention in retardate discriminant learning. In N.R. Ellis (Ed.), *Handbook of mental deficiency, psychological theory, and research* (pp. 159–223). New York: McGraw-Hill.

Zigler, E. (1969). Developmental versus difference theories of mental retardation and the problem of motivation. *American Journal of Mental Deficiency, 73*, 536–556.

Glossary

Action potential: An electrochemical impulse that travels through the neuron from the *dendrites* down to the end of the *axon*.

Aphasia: A disturbance in producing language or in comprehending written or spoken language, often as a result of a stroke.

Aromatization: The process by which androgens are converted to oestrogens.

Axon: The thread-like part of the neuron that sends information to target cells.

Basal ganglia: Clusters of grey matter (neuron cell bodies), located deep in the brain, including the caudate nucleus, putamen, globus pallidius, claustrum, and substantia nigra. They play an important role in movement.

Chromosomes: Found within the cell nucleus. They contain the DNA that transmits genetic information. The normal number of chromosomes for humans is 46.

Congenital adrenal hyperplasia (CAH): A genetic disorder in which there is a deficiency in the enzyme that produces two important hormones, cortisol and aldosterone. Because cortisol is deficient, the adrenal gland overproduces androgens (male steroid hormones). The incidence is 1 in 10,000.

Corticotrophin-releasing hormone (CRH): A chemical messenger, produced in the brain, that controls the secretion of stress-related hormones by the pituitary gland.

Dehydroepiandrosterone (DHEA): The androgen hormone secreted, in greatest quantities, by the adrenal glands.

Dendrite: A tree-like extension of the neuron cell body. Along with the cell body, it receives information from other neurons.

Dipole: Consists of two equal and opposite electrical charges separated by a distance. In attempts to model the location of the neural sources of brain activity recorded from the scalp, the sources are often modelled as dipoles.

Depolarization: A change in the resting potential of the nerve cell membrane; the inside of the membrane becomes more positive. See also *action potential*.

Electroencephalogram (EEG): A recording of brain electrical activity measured by electrodes placed on the scalp.

Event-related potential (ERP): A recording of brain electrical activity measured by electrodes placed on the scalp. An ERP reflects the activity evoked by a particular stimulus. The term is sometimes used to refer specifically to activity related to sensory processing (e.g. the visual evoked potential).

Frequency: The number of cycles or repetitions of any periodic wave or process per unit time. It is often expressed in units of hertz (Hz), where 1Hz = 1 cycle per second.

Functional magnetic resonance imaging (fMRI): A non-invasive technique that uses powerful magnets and radio waves to measures changes in brain activity. It relies on the assumption that changes in brain activity are associated with changes in blood flow and oxygenation.

Gamma-amino butyric acid (GABA): An amino acid transmitter in the brain whose primary function is to inhibit the firing of neurons.

Glia: Glia are non-neuronal "support cells" in the central nervous system. They are much more numerous than neurons.

Glucocorticoids: Hormones manufactured by the outer cortex of the adrenal gland. Cortisol is the main glucorticoid in humans; corticosterone is the main one in rats. The general metabolic effects of glucocorticoids are to prepare the body for action.

Glutamate: An amino acid neurotransmitter in the brain that excites neurons (including receptors involved in learning and memory, the *NMDA receptors*).

Haemoglobin: The oxygen-carrying pigment of red blood cells.

Homeobox gene: Gene with a DNA sequence that codes the homeodomain (a DNA binding area). Homeobox genes are usually involved in developmental processes, such as embryonic patterning, organogenesis, and/or cell differentiation.

Lateral geniculate nucleus (LGN): The lateral geniculate nucleus is located deep in the brain in the thalamus, and is part of the visual pathway from the retina to the cortex.

Long-term potentiation (LTP): A long-lasting increase in synaptic effectiveness, which occurs after high frequency stimulation of the input fibres. This might be one mechanism whereby memories are formed in the brain.

Magnetic resonance imaging (MRI): A non-invasive technique that uses powerful magnets and radio waves to construct images of organs inside the body. It is based on the electromagnetic properties of different atomic particles.

Magnocellular pathway: One of two major cell types and pathways involved in early visual processing. Thought to be involved primarily in transmission of information about visual motion and some information about three-dimensional vision.

N-methyl-D-aspartate (NMDA) receptor: A receptor for the neurotransmittor *glutamate*. When activated it allows calcium into the cell. It is implicated in synaptic plasticity, stroke damage, and seizure disorders.

Nuclear magnetic resonance (NMR): A property of certain molecules whereby their orientation can be altered by a combination of magnetic fields and radio waves. This characteristic provides the basis of magnetic resonance imaging.

Optokinetic nystagmus: A type of eye movement that occurs with uniform movement of a large part of the visual field (e.g. when looking out the window of a moving train): the eyes slowly follow the object and then quickly jerk back to start over again.

Paramagnetic substance: A substance with weak magnetic properties.

Parvocellular pathway: One of two major cell types and pathways involved in early visual processing. Thought to be involved primarily in transmission of information for form and colour vision.

Phenylketonuria (PKU): A hereditary disease caused by the lack of a liver enzyme required to digest the amino acid phenylalanine, which is most commonly found in protein-containing foods such as meat, cow's milk, and breast milk. Signs also include skeletal changes such as a small head, short stature, and flat feet.

Positron emission tomography (PET): This technique creates an image of internal organs, such as the brain, or other metabolically active sites, after the injection of a very low dose of a radioactive form of a substance such as glucose (sugar).

Proton: A positively charged particle located in the nucleus of an atom. The chemical properties of an element are governed by the number of protons in its nucleus.

Radio frequency (RF): An electromagnetic wave with a frequency that is in the same general range as that used for the transmission of radio and television signals. The RF pulses used in MRI are commonly in the 1–100 megaHertz range.

Relaxation time: In MRI, after excitation the spins will tend to return to their equilibrium distribution in which there is no transverse magnetization and the longitudinal magnetization is at its maximum value and oriented in the direction of the static magnetic field. After excitation, the transverse magnetization decays towards zero with a characteristic time-constant T2, and the longitudinal magnetization returns towards equilibrium with a characteristic time-constant T1.

Saccade: A rapid, jerky, or quick eye movement.

Signal-to-noise ratio: The ratio between the amplitude of the received signal and background noise, which tends to obscure that signal.

Spatial resolution: The ability to define minute adjacent objects/points in an image.

Spin: The spinning of a proton within a nucleus around its axis, which creates a magnetic field.

Striatum: Part of the basal ganglia, the striatum consists of the caudate nucleus and the putamen. The neurons of the striatum require dopamine to function.

T1-weighted image: An MRI image generated using a single 90-degree *radio frequency* pulse. T1 images show anatomical detail and differentiation between solid and fluid-filled structures (e.g. between grey matter in ventricles in the brain).

T2-weighted image: An MRI image generated using a 90-degree *radio frequency* pulse followed by a 180-degree pulse. T2 images show local pathology more clearly than *T1-weighted images* and have high signal intensity from water, haematoma, tumours, inflammation, etc.

T2* ("T-two-star") relaxation: Refers to the gradual loss of transverse magnetization as the system returns to its equilibrium state. This signal loss is due to both macroscopic and microscopic magnetic factors. The relaxation process is typically described by an exponential decay with a characteristic time given by T2*.

Turner's syndrome: A rare chromosomal disorder of females (1:2500) characterized by short stature and the lack of sexual development at puberty. Normally, females have two X chromosomes but in some cases of Turner's syndrome one X chromosome is missing, sometimes with some Y chromosomal material present.

Specific absorption rate: A radio frequency exposure concern that describes the potential for heating of the patient's tissue due to the application of the *radio frequency* energy necessary to produce the *NMR* signal.

Visual evoked potential (VEP): See *event-related potential.*

Williams syndrome: A developmental disorder of genetic origin (chrom.#: 7q11.23) classically characterized by three signs: facial features, infantile hypercalcemia, and supravalvular aortic stenosis. The incidence is 1/10,000 to 1/50,000.

Author Index

Subject index